Education Studies in Aotearoa:
Key disciplines and emerging directions

Education Studies in Aotearoa:
Key disciplines and emerging directions

Edited by Annelies Kamp

2019

NZCER PRESS

NZCER PRESS
New Zealand Council for Educational Research
PO Box 3237
Wellington
New Zealand

www.nzcer.org.nz

© Authors, 2019

ISBN: 978-1-98-854279-9

No part of the publication may be copied, stored, or communicated in any form by any means (paper or digital), including recording or storing in an electronic retrieval system without the written permission of the publisher. Education institutions that hold a current licence with Copyright Licensing New Zealand may copy from this book in strict accordance with the terms of the CLNZ Licence.

A catalogue record for this book is available from the National Library of New Zealand.

Designed by Smartwork Creative Ltd

Contents

Acknowledgements   vii
About the authors   ix

Introduction   Thinking about education   1
John Freeman-Moir

Part One: Key disciplines

Chapter 1   Indigenous and sociocultural imperatives for educational practice   9
Sonja Macfarlane and Angus Macfarlane

Chapter 2   Philosophy of education   25
Peter Roberts

Chapter 3   Education and history   47
David Small

Chapter 4   Sociology of education   68
Annelies Kamp

Chapter 5   Psychology of education   88
Valerie Sotardi and Myron Friesen

Chapter 6   Curriculum studies   112
Jane Abbiss

Part Two: Emerging directions

Chapter 7   Student engagement in flexible and distance learning in Aotearoa New Zealand   133
Cheryl Brown, Niki Davis, and William Eulatth-Vidal

Chapter 8   Diversity, education, and inclusion in Aotearoa New Zealand   151
Christoph Teschers and Trish McMenamin

Chapter 9   Community engagement as a particularly appropriate pedagogy for Aotearoa New Zealand   166
Billy O'Steen

Chapter 10   The role of emotions in education in Aotearoa   179
Veronica O'Toole and Rachel Martin

Chapter 11   Media literacy and digital citizenship in Aotearoa New Zealand   201
Christoph Teschers and Cheryl Brown

Chapter 12   What's in a name? Finding ways to articulate leadership by teachers   216
Susan Lovett

Chapter 13   The complex epistemological terrain of teacher education   234
Mistilina Sato

Chapter 14   The changing spaces of education in Aotearoa New Zealand   254
Letitia Fickel, Julie Mackey, and Jo Fletcher

Index   270

Acknowledgements

The inspiration for this edited collection was not my own. Rather, it travelled with me from the Republic of Ireland to Aotearoa New Zealand. From 2011 to 2015 I had the pleasure of working in the School of Educational Studies at Dublin City University, Ireland. As I began my tenure, my then colleague, Dr Brendan Walsh, had just published an edited collection titled *Education Studies in Ireland: The Key Disciplines*. Five years later, as I prepared to head home to take up a new role at the University of Canterbury, Brendan and I agreed that it would be a fine idea indeed to repeat the book concept in Aotearoa. It is such a pleasure, in my current role as Head of School for Educational Studies and Leadership at the University of Canterbury, to bring that fine idea to fruition. Accordingly, thank you Brendan for the inspiration for this collection.

My thanks also go to present and former whānau in the College of Education, Health and Human Development at the University of Canterbury, some of whom have authored contributions to this collection. As a College, and as a University, our commitment to kotahitanga—unity and collective action—is made manifest in endeavours such as this collection. While some are named as authors, everyone contributes in one way or another to the realisation of our diverse academic projects. I am privileged to serve as one of three Heads of School in this College. I value the whanaungatanga—the sense of positive relationship—which frames our daily work. In this, I acknowledge our Acting PVC, Professor Letitia Fickel, and our School Administrator, Tina Frayle.

For the cover of the collection, I am indebted to my colleague, Kay-Lee Jones, Te Aitanga-a-Māhaki, who introduced me to Petrus King-Blokker, Ngāti Ruahine. From his perspective as a secondary student in Aotearoa, Petrus has portrayed rauru—the internal spiral design—as a representation of knowledge coming to humankind through the separation of Ranginui and Papatūānuku. The koru on the outside of the image represents that knowledge spreading out into the world. Such a representation is completely in keeping with our kaupapa for this collection and we are indebted to Kay-Lee and Petrus for their assistance, and to David Ellis at NZCER for his support of the cover concept.

Finally, my immense and enduring gratitude to my own whānau whose love and belief sustains me in my every endeavour. This book is dedicated to my grandchildren, Poppy and Oliver, as they now journey through education, and into the future, in Aotearoa New Zealand.

About the authors

Associate Professor Jane Abbiss
School of Teacher Education, University of Canterbury
Dr Abbiss's research interests include curriculum studies and curriculum issues, with special interest in social sciences education, gender relations and ICT, knowledge and learning, learner experiences, and teacher learning and identity. Her recent research was titled *Shifting the Conceptualisation of Knowledge and Learning in the Integration of the new New Zealand Curriculum in Initial and Continuing Teacher Education.*

Associate Professor Cheryl Brown
School of Educational Studies and Leadership, University of Canterbury
Cheryl is Associate Professor of e-Learning and co-Director of the e-Learning Research Lab. She has worked in the higher education sector for the past 20 years in South Africa, Australia, and now New Zealand. She is involved in a global Commonwealth of Learning project on *Digital Education Leadership* and is passionate about developing a healthy and critical awareness of both the opportunities and challenges of living and learning in a digital world.

Distinguished Professor Niki Davis
School of Educational Studies and Leadership, University of Canterbury
Niki Davis is a Distinguished Professor of e-Learning and founding Director of UC e-Learning Research Lab. Recognised internationally as a leading expert in ICT in teacher education, her recent research collaborations include culturally sensitive e-learning with a focus on Indigenous peoples, including *Emergent Bilinguals in a Digital World* which lies within the E Tipu e Rea / A Better Start, National Science Challenge research programme.

Mr William Eulatth Vidal
School of Educational Studies and Leadership, University of Canterbury
William Eulatth Vidal is a doctoral candidate in the School of Educational Studies and Leadership, University of Canterbury. He has over 10 years' experience as a teacher, researcher, and project manager across four continents. His doctoral research explores success at university from the perspective of international students in one university in Aotearoa New Zealand.

Professor Letitia Hochstrasser Fickel
University of Canterbury
Letitia Fickel is Professor of Teacher Education and Acting Pro-Vice Chancellor of the College of Education, Health and Human Development. She is an experienced academic, researcher, and programme evaluator whose work focuses on high-quality initial teacher education and teacher professional learning and development that supports culturally and linguistically responsive practice and enhanced student learning.

Associate Professor Jo Fletcher
School of Teacher Education, University of Canterbury
Jo Fletcher is Associate Professor in Literacy Education and Associate Deputy Head of School in the School of Teacher Education. Jo started her career as a primary teacher. Her research interests include effective pedagogical practices in primary teaching. Recently, she has been part of a collaborative team exploring what is happening in innovative learning environments.

Associate Professor John Freeman-Moir
School of Educational Studies and Leadership, University of Canterbury
John Freeman-Moir taught in the Faculties of Arts and Education at Canterbury University and served as the inaugural Dean of Education. He is now Adjunct Associate Professor in the College of Education, Health and Human Development. His interests in education lie at the intersection of philosophy, psychology, and sociology.

Dr Myron Friesen
School of Educational Studies and Leadership, University of Canterbury
Myron is a Senior Lecturer in the College of Education, Health, and Human Development at the University of Canterbury. He teaches into the Bachelor of Arts in Education and the graduate programme in Child and Family Psychology. Myron's primary research interests include predictors of parenting, parental development, and parenting programme evaluation and positive youth development.

Associate Professor Annelies Kamp
School of Educational Studies and Leadership, University of Canterbury
Annelies is Associate Professor of Leadership and Head of School, Educational Studies and Leadership; she is also Deputy Pro-Vice Chancellor for the College

of Education, Health and Human Development. Her research interests focus on system leadership, critical youth studies, contemporary theory, and new materialism. Her most recent co-edited book is available fully open source: *Re/Assembling the Pregnant and Parenting Teenager* (2017).

Associate Professor Susan Lovett
School of Educational Studies and Leadership, University of Canterbury
Susan Lovett is an Associate Professor in Educational Leadership in the College of Education, Health and Human Development. Her research and teaching interests include leadership learning and development, with a particular focus on teacher leadership and early career teachers' emerging leadership influence.

Professor Angus Macfarlane
School of Teacher Education, University of Canterbury
Dr Angus Hikairo Macfarlane is Professor of Māori Research at the University of Canterbury. His research and teaching focus on Indigenous and sociocultural imperatives that influence education and psychology, pioneering several theoretical frameworks to guide culturally-responsive professional practice. Professor Macfarlane's prolific publication portfolio has earned him national and international recognition.

Dr Sonja Macfarlane
Practice and Implementation Adviser—Māori Focus, Ministry of Education
Until mid-2019, Dr Macfarlane was an Associate Professor at the University of Canterbury. Her research focuses on culturally responsive evidence-based approaches in education and psychology. Her research has been acknowledged and widely published in leading research journals, both nationally and internationally.

Associate Professor Julie Mackey
University of Canterbury
Julie Mackey is an Associate Professor and Dean to the Assistant Vice Chancellor (Academic) at the University of Canterbury. She has held roles as Head of School, Dean of Education and Health Sciences, and deputy to the Pro-Vice Chancellor in the College of Education, Health and Human Development. Her research interests include e-learning and digital technologies, teacher professional development and innovative learning environments.

Dr Trish McMenamin
School of Educational Studies and Leadership, University of Canterbury
Trish McMenamin is a Senior Lecturer at the University of Canterbury. Her research interests include inclusive education, diversity, philosophy of education, and education policy. Trish has published books and articles in these areas including most recently the sole authored book *Special Schools, Inclusion, and Justice* (2018) and a co-edited volume *Belonging: Rethinking Inclusive Practices to Support Well-Being and Identity* (2018).

Dr Rachel Martin
College of Education, University of Otago
Rachel Martin, who affiliates to the Waitaha, Kāti Mamoe and Ngāi Tahu tribe in the South Island from Kaikōura to Rākiura, works on culturally and linguistically sustaining Te Tiriti-based frameworks for research. She has extensive experience in bilingual education, Māori education, intergenerational transmission of te reo Māori, intergenerational and historical trauma, kaupapa Māori research, primary teacher education, te reo Māori online learning, and indigenous education.

Associate Professor Billy O'Steen
School of Educational Studies and Leadership, University of Canterbury
Throughout his 25-year career in education, Dr O'Steen has researched and taught with immersive experiential education, which has led to significant external funding, numerous presentations and publications, and his appointment as the inaugural Associate Professor of Community Engagement and Director of the University of Canterbury Community Engagement Hub.

Dr Veronica O'Toole
School of Educational Studies and Leadership, University of Canterbury
Dr O'Toole is a Senior Lecturer in the College of Education, Health and Human Development. Her current research interest focuses on teachers' emotions, social emotional learning, emotional intelligence, and emotional wellbeing. Dr O'Toole's research on the emotional impacts of the Christchurch earthquakes on teachers has been published in highly ranked journals, including *Teaching and Teacher Education*, and *Social Psychology of Education*.

Professor Peter Roberts
School of Educational Studies and Leadership, University of Canterbury
Peter Roberts is Professor of Education and Director of the Educational Theory,

Policy and Practice Research Hub at the University of Canterbury. His primary areas of scholarship are philosophy of education and educational policy studies.

Associate Professor Mistilina Sato
School of Teacher Education, University of Canterbury
Mistilina Sato is Associate Professor and Head of School for the School of Teacher Education at the University of Canterbury. Her research addresses teaching across the career continuum, including teacher preparation, performance assessment, policies that support teaching practice, and teacher leadership. She began her career as a science teacher in the United States and received her PhD from Stanford University.

Dr David Small
School of Educational Studies and Leadership, University of Canterbury
David is Acting Dean of Education and Health at the University of Canterbury. He is also a Barrister of the High Court of New Zealand. His academic and legal work is shaped by a history of social activism. His current research interests include understanding ways that racism and social inequality are shaped by education policy, and analysing higher education, particularly how the neoliberal university is transforming students, staff, and society.

Dr Valerie Sotardi
School of Educational Studies and Leadership, University of Canterbury
Valerie Sotardi is a Lecturer of educational psychology in the College of Education, Health and Human Development. She teaches into the Bachelor of Teaching and Learning, Bachelor of Arts in Education, and the post-graduate programmes in ECE, Primary, and Secondary Teaching. Valerie's primary research interests include the study of motivation and its impact on learning and achievement during schooling transitions.

Dr Christoph Teschers
School of Educational Studies and Leadership, University of Canterbury
Christoph Teschers is a Senior Lecturer at the College of Education, Health and Human Development. He has published several articles and book chapters and is author of *Education and Schmid's Art of Living* (2018). His work is interdisciplinary, focusing on the relationship between wellbeing, the philosophical notion of the art of living, and educational theory and practice. He has interests in social justice, democratic citizenship, and digital media literacy.

Introduction
Thinking about education
John Freeman-Moir

This book has two aims. The first is to introduce the core disciplines and principal areas of educational study to students in teacher education programmes, as well as to students studying education in other degrees. The second is to provide a resource for professionals, teachers, and administrators interested in updating their knowledge of educational research in Aotearoa New Zealand. This introduction provides an overall framework for the 14 essays that follow. The core of this framework is the idea that educational theory and practice can only properly be understood when located in relation to both wider social structures and more intimate settings.

When we think about education in the course of everyday life it seems, perhaps, a rather straightforward affair, prosaic and easily described. This sense of familiarity results from our own extensive educational experiences, formal and informal, over many years—variously, in communities, childcare facilities, preschools, primary and secondary schools, polytechnics, and universities. We all know that educational activity is central to society. This is evidenced, for example, by the size of Vote Education which accounts for vast financial expenditures year-on-year. Education, then, represents a set of well-defined experiences that are, with variations in content and duration, broadly shared by members of our society. We are knowledgeable about education, and we talk easily about kinds of schools, regimes of discipline, curriculum schemes, aims, teachers, and teaching, and we remember memorable teachers who once taught us. Several names come spontaneously to my mind, remembered perhaps because they exemplify much of what I take education properly to be about, both in principle and method. Nothing much in education seems, then, to be beyond our understanding, even when we are adapting to the latest innovations. I have spent a career in the area of educational studies and yet, usually, I feel no more especially expert than my neighbours and friends in conversations about educational matters, as they occur at social gatherings on the street and across the fence.

All this is a good thing for communities because education and schooling in a democracy is a social virtue that is, or should be, a substantially common experience. It is this broad and motivated experience that provides an important foundation for both educational conversation and scholarly thinking about research, theory, and practice. A famous illustration of this point is to be found in the conversation recorded in Plato's dialogue, *The Republic*. Following a religious celebration in honour of a Greek goddess about 2,400 years ago, a group of friends gathered together on a balmy evening in Piraeus, the port town of Athens, to drink wine, socialise, and, most importantly for our purposes, to debate the meanings and methods of education and justice. In various ways, this same debate has continued as a many-braided stream of thought and research to this day. Let me give another well-known example of what I am pointing to. In the 18th century, in *Thoughts on Education*, the brilliant Immanuel Kant matter-of-factly concluded that, "insight depends on education, and education in turns depends on insight". I invite you to play with this idea a little. You will likely discover that it very quickly widens out in myriad directions. Considered from a range of perspectives—developmental, philosophical, political, psychological, and sociological—we can ask good questions about what facilitates the interplay of insight and education, and what stifles and stops it dead. It is to the disciplines and areas of educational research that we turn in order to find deeper and more precise understandings of the fundamental interactions between insight and education. For this reason, Kant concluded that education is the greatest and most important question that we can devote ourselves to.

Now, if thinking systematically about education interests you, if it catches your attention, then, certainly, you have found a line of work that will last a lifetime. Suppose, indeed, that education turns out to be your vocation. I hazard the guess that when you finally come to look back across your career in education you will find that you have returned to the beginning, and come to know it as if for the first time. Put more simply, your quest in the area of educational studies will not, and never can be, finished.

I want to turn now and say something about how the disciplines and areas of educational study can open you to insight and understanding. Not infrequently, it comes as something of a surprise to many undergraduate students, enrolled in their first education courses, that the area of educational studies at university is both broad and variegated. Let me recall a sliver of my own experience to make this point.

Not surprisingly, I remember almost nothing of the detail of the first university lecture in education I attended, but a fragment of memory does remain. By the end of that class a completely new and radical thought was knocking around in my head: specifically, the thought that the study of education would connect me to problems and puzzles across widespread areas of life. This idea seemed fantastically exciting to me, out of control, apparently boundless. On the first hearing it felt like a good idea, it still does. In a nutshell, education means making worlds and exploring them, as children do, as we all do, across our lives and our societies. After just 50 minutes, 55 years ago, I was on the edge of discovering, and then grasping the notion that education is a field of study, an intricately interwoven tapestry, replete with knots and entanglements, successes and failures; a record of our endlessly creative efforts to understand such matters as teaching and learning, and much more.

Another way of putting this insight is to say that educational study is interdisciplinary because it requires attention, for example, to historical political, psychological, sociological, and philosophical perspectives in fields of interest such as curriculum, the role of emotions in learning, citizenship, democracy, diversity, media, and leadership. Taking note of just the Western intellectual tradition, this broad perspective first came into focus in ancient Greece, in the speculations of Socrates, Plato, and Aristotle, among others. And in many societies and periods of history since, and in traditions other than European, these same kinds of discussions have given birth to new kinds of ideas about education, both in theory and practice. Different societies mean different traditions, different histories, and different perspectives on education. This is a useful maxim to hold in mind as you begin your study of education.

You, the reader, may already be thinking that no one could possibly achieve the wide range of thinking to which I have just referred. After all, what scholar or educational practitioner could be knowledgeable in all the areas of educational study? The honest answer is, probably none. But this fact about our human limitations, in what we can each know and do, is not as fatal as it might seem at first sight. Our individual limits do not matter too much, and they are not fatal. What is important is being aware of the broad traditions of educational analysis and, further, that these traditions are available to any educationist, you and me included. We can all draw on these traditions of theory, regardless of whether we are undergraduates, practitioners, or academics. Being well versed in some parts of education and having a sense of the range of educational theory is necessary for sure. From this position we can navigate to other parts of education that are, as yet, unknown to us or poorly understood, but which, for one reason or another, we need to find out more about.

The disciplines of education, I suggest, are best thought of as perspectives, as windows looking out on to a centrally important part of the world. To change the metaphor, the well-known philosopher of science, Karl Popper, pointed out that theories are like nets with which we can catch what we call 'the world'. In other words, theories are tools to bring the world of interest within reach so that we can inspect it systematically—by asking questions, probing, reaching beyond what we currently know, speculating with new ideas, as yet provisional, which may lead to further research, and so on. Looked at from this point of view the disciplines of education and their areas of interest interact with each other. Changing interests pose new questions for research, while carefully disciplined research and thinking leads to new understandings, and to overly familiar things being seen afresh, perhaps in surprising ways. The chapters in the book will be suggestive to you if read from an inquiring research perspective.

Having noted the interdisciplinary nature of education I would like to suggest an orientation that might be taken up by any reader of this book. It is important not to get overwhelmed by too many perspectives all at once, but to find ways to explore different and even contradictory perspectives. Start with what interests you most, what seems the most exciting. And do not expect to find the picture of the educational landscape to be as neat and as fully resolved as a jigsaw puzzle.

The plain statement "the wide scope of educational studies" should alert the reader to an important fact. Education, like life itself, is a messy business. Boundaries are never firm and categorical, and historical developments lead to changes of educational emphasis and direction. One immediate effect of this might be to render irrelevant some previously fixed, unquestioned opinion. Another possible effect is to shed new light on long-held views and, as a consequence, force a rethink. And both these possibilities can occur more or less simultaneously.

Consider the following example of educational thinking—one of the most significant statements in our history. It illustrates the centrality of systematic disciplinary thinking in education, and what needs to be attended to in translating theory into practice. In 1939, an Assistant Director of Education (soon to be Director), Clarence Beeby, penned a view of education in a democracy for the then incoming Labour Government:

> The Government's objective, broadly expressed, is that every person, whatever his level of academic ability, whether he be rich or poor, whether he live in town or country has a right as a citizen, to a free education of the kind for which he is best fitted, and to the fullest extent of his powers. So far is this from being a mere pious platitude that the full acceptance of the principle will involve the reorientation of the education system. Continued education is no longer a special privilege of the well-to-do or the academically able, but a right to be claimed by all to the fullest extent that the State can provide. (quoted in Beeby, 1992, p. 124)

Important consequences follow from the acceptance of this principle. Beeby and the Government wanted to reorient education at the level of society, the community, and the individual. The longer-term effects of this picture of education continue to be felt to the present day. Beeby thought that the place of education in society should be understood from a democratic point of view, as he made clear. This introduction is not the place to provide a detailed account or assessment of this significant moment in our educational history. But the reader should be able to sense that unpacking Beeby's statement will require the methods of several academic disciplines, and attention to a wide range of educational concerns. In the process, the analysis will show that the reach of education is extensive indeed. In fact, it takes in the whole of society. At the very least, our educational understanding will entail questions of economic cost, curriculum, the relevance of teaching methods to the development of abilities and interests among learners, and the necessity of all this for a richly democratic form of society.

It is of more than passing interest that Beeby, many years later, in 1992, regretted having used male pronouns in his, by then, influential statement. In the interim, the great social and political movements of the 1960s and 1970s, and especially the feminist movement, had substantially transformed how education and its scope were to be thought about. A whole new area of research—feminist theory and pedagogy—had opened up an expanded understanding and expectation of what counts as education relevant to the fullest extent of a learner's powers. This illustrative anecdote is of interest in here because it points towards the permanent interaction between the disciplines of educational research on the one hand and emerging areas of social and educational interest on the other.

Any theoretical account of education and any educational method necessarily give answers to two intimately linked questions, as follows:

1. How shall we live?
2. What are people (and what is each person) actually able to do and be?

These are the two most fundamental educational questions it is possible to ask, though you will notice that, as stated, they say nothing at all about teaching or learning or socialisation. But now, try answering these questions by filling in some possible detail. Immediately, you will find that educational matters come to the fore. The first question points us in the direction of what will need to be taught and learnt so that human development may proceed in an appropriate direction. And the more detailed is the answer, the more detailed will the educational programme have to be. The second question asks about the capabilities of people, and, more specifically, it requires that we find out how to develop these in ways that are relevant to our society. Together, these questions, as asked and answered, define the educational imagination of a society.

For example, consider two possible answers to the question, "How shall we live?" One answer supposes that life will be lived in a republican dictatorship administered by just rulers, the other, that it will be lived in a social democracy. You and I will almost certainly favour the latter answer, Socrates and Plato favoured the former. Though it would take a good deal of work to figure out answers appropriate to the two alternatives, it is easy to see that, in the two kinds of society, children and citizens will be learning radically different things, accepting different moralities, being initiated into different customs, beliefs, and ideals. Observing our own society we can see that the answers given over time change. For example, it is integral to contemporary Aotearoa New Zealand and its future that biculturalism lies at the centre of social and educational organisation. Insofar as we take this seriously, education will be imbued with this perspective.

From the moment of birth the actions and understandings of educators are crucial influences on children. The kinds of roles that, more or less, fall broadly under the title of 'educator', include the following: mātua, parent; koroua, grandparent; kaiako, teacher, coach, counsellor, adviser; kaitohutohu, demonstrator; kaiwhakaako, tutor, friend, confidant; kaitautoko, mentor; rangatira, leader, supervisor, trainer, therapist, and instructor. Implicitly and explicitly, people in these roles are offering answers, or partial answers, to the two fundamental educational questions.

In the first chapter, for example, the authors consider Te Tiriti o Waitangi and biculturalism as a central perspective from which to understand educational development. As answers to the question how we should live change, so too will our national practices, and, as these change, so will the ways of asking and answering the original question change.

All the chapters implicitly invite readers to examine their own educational and social beliefs, intuitions, hopes, and ideals. The answers given—no matter how familiar, or comfortable, or taken for granted—can, and should be, subjected to critical scrutiny. If this is so, then we must ask further: "How good are our answers (yours and mine)?", "Are we satisfied with them?", "How far do we even understand them?"

Asking and answering questions like these, and doing something about the answers, is the work of educational theory and practice. As a result, individual and collective versions of the educational imagination will be expressed. This is how we develop our theories and methods of education, and come to see them within an overall explanatory context.

Above, I spoke of educational research and professional pedagogy as the making and exploring of worlds, suggesting, in passing, that this is also what children do. John Dewey elegantly observed that "children simply like to do things, and watch to see what will happen" (Dewey, 1915, p. 60). With this comparison in mind, the activities of educationists at whatever level, can be pictured as "hovering on the borders of the unknown, conducted, even in the realm of the already ascertained, in a spirit of doubt and enquiry ... [In this way] teaching and research are complementary parts of a single activity" (Allan et al., 1945, p. 1)

The disciplines and interests of education are the entries though which the reader can walk towards questions to be asked. More particularly, disciplines are the cognitive and knowledge structures in terms of which systematic speculation, inquiry, and research goes on. This book will, then, assist you to see educational theory and practice as intimately related, and, at the same time, to gain insight into the methods for understanding the meaning of education.

To end on a practical note, I invite the reader to use this book as a toolbox of resources. The chapters will help deepen your understanding and lead you to further questions and puzzles about education.

References

Allan, R. S. et al. (1945). *Research and the university: A statement by a group of teachers in the University of New Zealand*. Christchurch: Caxton Press.

Beeby, C.E. (1992). *The biography of an idea: Beeby on education*. Wellington: New Zealand Council for Educational Research.

Dewey, J. (1915). *The school and society*. Chicago, IL: The University of Chicago Press.

Chapter 1
Indigenous and sociocultural imperatives for educational practice

Sonja Macfarlane and Angus Macfarlane

Introduction

It seems timely that the first chapter of this collection—a collection focused on education studies in the context of Aotearoa—offers a reflection on the potential for culturally competent educational practice and how it might be attained. Developing educational practitioner cultural competence involves growing awareness, knowledge, and understanding of the cultural values, beliefs, traditions, and customs of those with whom we work—in this case, Māori, the tangata whenua (Indigenous people) of Aotearoa New Zealand. For educational practitioners, this competence involves interactions with colleagues in their workspace, tamariki (children, young learners), and their whānau (family, extended family, caregivers). Key to the development of practitioner cultural competence is the realisation on the part of practitioners of their cultural self, including their cultural privilege and positionality. Most educational practitioners want the best for Māori learners—and indeed all learners—but many will concede that, while they have the will, they would benefit immensely if tools and resources were created and made available to them so as to help them provide more and better inroads into culturally responsive education practice. This aspect is significant also in terms of how Initial Teacher Education (ITE) is shaped in Aotearoa. By including culturally congruent tools and resources in ITE and in-service professional development for teachers, then benefits will surely accrue for them, for tamariki, and for whānau.

Noting the significant need for culturally relevant resources, a team of researchers assembled in early 2019 with the aim of developing a tool that might contribute to the development of culturally relevant resources while simultaneously ensuring the benefits of such resources ripple out to tamariki and whānau. An existing tribally located programme was considered by the research team to be a step in the right direction at the embryonic stage of the project.

While so many important aspects related to cultural competence are covered across the education and health sectors, resources showing practitioners' techniques for implementation were not so plentiful. On that basis, and after consultation with cohorts of professional practitioners, the research team made the decision to draw from existing theoretical underpinnings as a platform on which to build the resource, but to not allow theory to dominate. The appetite clearly was for a move toward concrete strategies, which could be applied in the busy environments that characterise early childhood centres and schools. Our own experiences in ITE and in-service professional development for teachers continually highlighted the reality that teachers were regularly searching for tools and strategies that would support them to work in culturally responsive ways with tamariki and whānau. They would reflect on their obligations as teachers specific to upholding the three Treaty of Waitangi principles (partnership, protection, participation), as espoused in a wide range of key educational policies and strategy documents. In essence, teachers would state that they understood *why* they needed to be culturally responsive, but did not know *what* they needed to do or *how* to instantiate particular strategies and approaches into their practice.

The early thinkers
The early years of educational theory were marked by a succession of different schools of thought, which included the work of John Dewey (1916), Edward Thorndike (1921), and Ralph Tyler (1950). Dewey believed that much of what was being taught in traditional education settings paid little

attention to the needs and experiences of the growing child. He saw the child as being too passive: the child receiving the information from the teacher was like the big jug pouring water into the little mug. The result, Dewey believed, was temporary learning that never became a part of the child's motivational repertoire. For growth to occur, the child needs a stake in the learning activity. Dewey contended that the teacher's task was to create conditions that would generate in the child a sense of inquiry. Tyler's thinking, not unlike that of Dewey and Thorndike, had a profound effect on curriculum at that time, and continues to influence contemporary theory and practice. Thorndike's method was systematic and offered a kind of technology of practice that would take chance out of learning and teaching. A psychologist, he connected observable behaviour as evidence of learning. His work made it possible to hope that there would eventually be a science of teaching, something that would be both efficient and effective, albeit somewhat linear. Tyler posed challenging questions, asking what educational purposes are being sought, what educational experiences are provided for these purposes to be attained, and how it can be determined whether the purposes are being attained.

In more recent times, these iconic figures have been joined by Linda Darling-Hammond (2010), while several others have added to the thinking pool by boldly introducing "culture" into the mix. Eisner's (1994) work on the design and evaluation of school programmes has had a profound influence on curriculum theory and teacher practice, while Darling-Hammond's work has focused on school restructuring and educational equity. Gloria Ladson-Billings (1995), Geneva Gay (2002), and Lisa Delpit (2003) argue for a change in attitudes and actions on the part of educators working with learners from diverse backgrounds. Paris (2012) encourages advancing from culturally responsive pedagogies to those that are culturally sustaining. Each of these eminent scholars encourage educators to step away from looking through the Eurocentric lens, and in a bid to enable better teacher–learner interaction, to employ a more culturally inclusive lens.

Aotearoa New Zealand, too, has had a succession of educational dream-makers through the years. Following World War Two, Āpirana Ngata inspired the nation with the following axiom, *E tipu e rea*, a culturally inclusive statement, which he wrote in the autograph book of a student encouraging her to remember the treasures of ancestors, and to acknowledge educational success as the pathway for reaching goals and destinations:

E tipu e rea, mō ngā rā o tōu ao, ko to ringa ki ngā rākau a te Pākehā hei ora mō te tinana, kō tō ngākau ki ngā taonga a ō tīpuna Māori hei tikitiki mō to mahuna, a kō tō wairua ki tō Atua, nāna nei ngā mea katoa.

Thrive in the days destined for you, your hand to the tools of the Pākehā to provide physical sustenance, your heart to the treasures of your ancestors to adorn your head, your soul to God to whom all things belong.

According to Macfarlane (2019), renowned leaders such as Te Rangi Hīroa, Maharaia Winiata, Meremere Penfold, Kāterina Mataira, and Ranginui Walker followed, paving the way for other noted educational contributors such as Rose Pere, Iritana Tāwhiwhirangi, Patu Hohepa, Hirini Moko Mead, Naida Glavish, Toby Curtis, Kuni Jenkins, and Pita Sharples. Each has put a stake in the educational terrain and they, like those before them, provided the passage for contemporary educators to operationalise their prowess within their respective spheres of influence.[1]

The challenges of diversity

Life in the educational professions has always been fraught with intrigue, and often with ambiguity. As our communities continue to become more ethnically diverse due to the impact of globalisation, increased mobility, and changing family structures, so does the learner population. It is clear that diversity within our society has broadened human understanding, facilitated positive interactions, tolerance, and understanding, and kindled our creativity. It has also challenged ITE to consider how education settings can effectively embrace and engage all learners as diversity continues to become the established 'norm'. How are we to understand the worldviews and learning styles of the diverse cultures that populate today's early childhood centres and schools? What are the origins of these orientations, and what are the most appropriate responses that education professionals can offer? How can we assess the effects of our teaching, and what are the implications for learners' outcomes? These questions have stimulated lively and sometimes irascible discussion.

---

1   Contemporary educators: Macfarlane (2015) refers to a cohort of leading thinkers and writers in a special (anniversary) publication of the *New Zealand Journal of Educational Studies*.

Teacher education programmes are charged with the daunting task of preparing the next generation of teachers. However, the literature has documented that the majority of teacher education programmes have struggled to effectively prepare teacher candidates with adequate cultural competence to meet the needs of our increasingly diverse population (Education Review Office, 2016). Culturally relevant pedagogy is a social justice framework posited to support academic achievement of learners, as well as the cultural competence and critical consciousness of teachers (Allen, Hancock, Lewis, & Starker-Glass, 2017). And while ITE is attempting to 'get in early', and prepare teachers pedagogically for the reality of diversity, there are literally tens of thousands of experienced teachers and paraprofessionals who are sounding a clarion call for resources to be made available to the profession. They are calling for functional resources that would take them closer to a set of new agenda—particularly those that are concerned with better outcomes for Māori learners. To this end, this chapter examines the feasibility of the integration of culturally responsive pedagogies into ITE while simultaneously responding to the needs of the numerous practising teachers who constantly express a desire for access to resources that would assist them to be more culturally adept at their craft.

The thinking that led to a decision to do something about this predicament arose out of the relatively constant mismatch between the fixed—sometimes linear—scientific approaches that the evidence-based movement seems to claim, and the pragmatic, workable approach proposed by the world of practice. This chapter advances the notion that drawing from both approaches would be more robust than either approach would be on its own, and more effective than one approach dominating over the other. As a means of promoting the position of merging of the approaches, the research team turned its attention to the possibility of galvanising an existing resource that has been trialled on several educational sites. The resource, the Hikairo Schema, will be introduced in later sections of this chapter. Before then, however, we present a brief discussion on evidence-based practice, culturally-based evidence, and culturally-based practice.

Evidence-based practice vs. culturally-based evidence?

Evidence-based practice has its genesis in the health professions but is now a commonly used term across the allied health and education professions. All Aotearoa New Zealand professional ITE training programmes purport to be grounded in empirical research in terms of the courses they offer. Evans and Fitzgerald (2007) outline three ways in which professionals are able to use evidence to facilitate change. The first and most frequent is to derive one's practice from well-established principles of pedagogy to provide indications of learners' motivation (Ames, 1992). The second is to systematically gather data to record learner progress and objectively determine the nature of planning for proximal and distal planning. The third is to draw from processes and procedures that have been shown to be effective in other settings by other professionals. In recent years, there has been increasing emphasis placed on the third way, with the implementation of procedures that are validated by Indigenous epistemologies (Clarke, Macfarlane, & Macfarlane, 2017).

Few dispute the principle that practice should be based on the best available evidence, or that the basic tenets of evidence-based practice are potentially beneficial to practice for learners' outcomes. However, Dopson and Fitzgerald (as cited in Gabbay & Le May, 2011) contend that there have been many barriers to overcome, not least the defiance of some professionals who argue that the evidence is often impracticable, irrelevant, or absent, and takes time to obtain. Gabbay and Le May add that, even with a willingness to adopt evidence to change practice, organisational barriers—such as inadequate resources or inappropriate systems—have provided further obstacles. Additional concerns have included the noticeable gaps between research and practice, particularly scant regard for evidence from the reality of what occurs within the hurly-burly of classrooms and centres, and models of good practice derived from culturally responsive pedagogies. With this concern in mind, the need to consider culturally-based evidence to inform practice is paramount.

Culturally-based evidence drives the contention that solutions and understandings for Indigenous peoples do not necessarily reside within the culture that has traditionally been responsible for their marginalisation; rather, the solutions and understandings for resolving the range of issues that Indigenous peoples face are located within the Indigenous culture itself (Peterson & Ishii-Jordan, 1994). For example, a programme titled the Hikairo Schema (Macfarlane et al., 2019) is a tool for teachers in Aotearoa New Zealand that draws from culturally-based evidence. The Schema, which first appeared on the scene some 25 years ago, emanates from a tribal event, discussed further on in this chapter. Over that time, the Schema has been sanctioned by the tribe holding the mana of an historical narrative, enriched by cultural ideology, espoused by educational leaders as a worthy resource, introduced to postgraduate students and ITE programmes, used by teachers and psychologists, reviewed by specialists in the field, and revised and galvanised by its creators and co-creators in more recent times.

The Hikairo Schema: A culturally-based approach

Fundamentally, the Hikairo Schema is a resource that has been developed to support teachers' practice in early childhood centres and schools in Aotearoa New Zealand. It assists teachers in reflecting on the ways in which they engage with tamariki in the curriculum and in the learning environments, and encourages teachers' increased adeptness toward connectedness to learners and their whānau. The Hikairo Schema acknowledges the official place and contribution of the national Māori Strategy *Ka Hikitia* (Ministry of Education, 2013), and the early childhood curriculum *Te Whāriki* (Ministry of Education, 2017), as providing the 'what' in terms of the sectors' responsibilities. It is proposed that the Hikairo Schema provides the 'how', and with that comes a number of questions.

The resource derives its name from the Ngāti Rangiwewehi chief, Hikairo, who used an assertive and simultaneously warm approach to resolve a series of inter-tribal encounters on Mokoia Island (Te Motu Tapu ā Tinirau) in 1823. Not unlike a good teacher in contemporary times, Hikairo exemplified qualities of mana and goodwill—showing that calm conveys strength. Hikairo's sincere approach brought about change, both in attitude and behaviour. The Schema is a resource that honours the way in which Hikairo (as a leader) was able to model inclusion, inspire others to work together respectfully, and create a positive environment where everyone felt a sense of belonging. The demeanour that Hikairo modelled during these encounters is reflective of the style that culturally responsive teachers exhibit on a day-to-day basis. It is a classic example of culture growing out of the past, and functioning in the present.

There are seven dimensions, and each is represented by one of the seven letters in the name 'HIKAIRO'. Figure 1.1 below is a visual representation of what these seven dimensions encapsulate.

Figure 1.1. **Key dimensions of the Hikairo Schema**

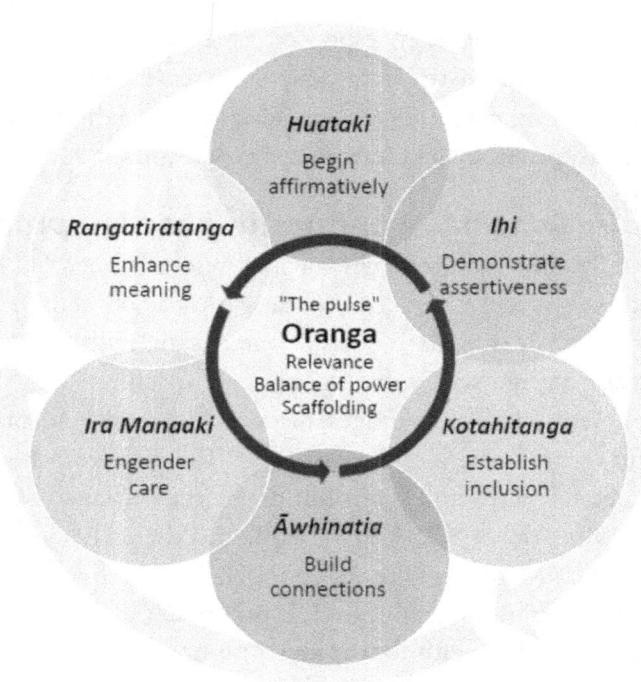

Although each of the dimensions represents a particular aspect of culturally responsive teaching practice, they should not be viewed in isolation, as they naturally interconnect and merge during teaching and learning activities. At this juncture, each of these dimensions will be succinctly explained:

Huataki: *Begin affirmatively.* In 1823, Hikairo demonstrated the process of 'getting in early'. *Huataki* is about teachers avoiding potential challenges by starting lessons with purpose and confidence. *Huataki* it is about opening doorways to learning—for tamariki and whānau.

Ihi: *Demonstrate assertiveness.* In 1823, Hikairo was assertive in his approach to achieving a meaningful resolution. *Ihi* requires teachers to adopt a structured and systematic style. *Ihi* is a no-nonsense, power-sharing approach that is simultaneously warm.

Kotahitanga: *Establishing inclusion.* In 1823, Hikairo adopted an approach that was collaborative. *Kotahitanga* refers to teachers using strategies that create an environment where tamariki and kaiako (teachers) feel a sense of belonging and connectedness. *Kotahitanga* creates a sense of unity where people interact as kin. In this environment, kinship is 'felt' between kaiako and tamariki. The adage "Ko au ko koe, ko koe ko au" ("I am you, you are me") is fitting within the *Kotahitanga* nomenclature.

Awhinatia: *Build connections.* In 1823, Hikairo likely preferred a smooth momentum in the interactions with tribal counterparts. *Awhinatia* requires teachers to reduce or eliminate disjointedness, and to "stay on track". *Awhinatia* creates an environment that fosters cohesion and continuity for tamariki in their learning activities.

Ira Manaaki: *Engender care.* In 1823, Hikairo displayed courtesy and respect for the dignity of others. *Ira Manaaki* refers to teachers adopting a positive attitude based on mutual respect and care. *Ira Manaaki* contributes to a favourable environment that supports learning because kaiako demonstrate that they care by knowing the background and the learning styles of tamariki. An atmosphere of trust reigns when *Ira Manaaki* is present.

Rangatiratanga: *Enhance meaning.* In 1823, Hikairo used critical thinking to achieve resolution. *Rangatiratanga* requires teachers to promote challenging and engaging learning opportunities. *Rangatiratanga* enables tamariki to expand on and strengthen their cognitive and social development.

Oranga: *Maintain the pulse.* In 1823, Hikairo was able to highlight the significance of his thinking, model an equity-based approach, and enable connections to be made between his ideas and those of others. *Oranga* is at the core of the Hikairo Schema; it is a pulsating organism that draws sustenance from the six outer dimensions. *Oranga* requires teachers to take into account three core principles as they work through the other six dimensions. The three core principles of the Schema are *relevance, balance of power*, and *scaffolding*. As kaiako work through each of the outer six components, their teaching practice and the learning environment should reflect these three key principles, outlined in more detail below.

The principle of relevance encourages the alignment of learning with school values, as well as the cultural and personal identities of tamariki. Achieving cultural relevance is a driving factor in motivating tamariki from cultures that are a numerical minority. *Relevance* is encouraging the creation of culturally safe environments wherein the cultural capacity of learner and teacher is extended, thus increasing the viability of the learning context, and alleviating or eliminating states of 'cultural lag'.[2] Strategies include developing a sense of community, organising the programme and the physical setting so that the culture of each learner is visible, and forming experiences that help tamariki to understand their physical and social environments—while enhancing cognitive understandings of te taiao and mana tangata (respect and care for the world and its people).

The balance of power principle encourages enhancing ako (reciprocal teaching and learning) through co-constructing learning contexts (Glasser, 1993; Pere, 1982). The notion of co-constructing is evident when opportunities are provided for tamariki to lead their own learning experiences, to provide feedback to their peers and kaiako, and to adopt mindful behaviours that strengthen interpersonal relationships and the setting culture. Through co-construction, tamariki are able to take part in experiences grounded in mutual care, trust, and respect. Tamariki are also urged to build competence and confidence for leadership, for autonomy, and for engaging others in meaningful relationships. Experiences are collaborative undertakings, co-led by kaiako, tamariki, and, where appropriate, whānau. Learning environments foster productive and supportive relationships when cultures are seen, felt, and valued. Strategies for balancing power include: establishing co-operative working teams; discussing, negotiating, and agreeing on appropriate behaviours; and engaging in open-ended dialogue between and amongst kaiako, tamariki, and—where appropriate—whānau.

Finally, the scaffolding principle encourages the pursuit of educational outcomes that are within the grasp and capability of tamariki, while providing any necessary resources and support that increase the likelihood of success. Modern teaching pedagogies promote learning experiences that are specific, child-centred, credit-based, and at an appropriate level of challenge. Scaffolding supports tamariki by engaging them in learning activities that are mana enhancing. Strategies for scaffolding include providing clear feedback that promotes confidence and self-efficacy, and designing tasks that offer opportunities for tamariki to taste success while simultaneously extending their capacity to complete tasks to the best of their respective capacities.

The core of the nested educational system (the centre or classroom) is a busy and multifaceted paradigm where learning interactions are oftentimes

---

2   Cultural lag in this instance describes what happens in the social system when certain ideals that regulate life do not keep pace with other changes.

challenging, both emotionally and physically. The soundness and strength of the *oranga* is, therefore, critical. The Hikairo Schema proclaims that many benefits accrue when the *oranga* is in a state of firmness.

Resource or ideology?

Getzels (1974) has described how models of the learner can potentially influence images of the learning environment. When learners are regarded as passive receptacles to be filled rather than active, stimulus-seeking beings, bolting down desks in orderly rows makes sense. If they are thought of as stimulus-seeking beings, then the environment is likely to have a very different look. In this age where diversity is ubiquitous and the learners themselves look different, the demand on teacher competency escalates to another level. They are bound to encourage stimulus-seeking tamariki while demonstrating a connectedness to the culture of the tamariki. The clarion call for resources that are low on intricacy, high on understandability, and reasonably readily implementable, raises its pitch and widens its scope.

The Hikairo Schema is a humble resource created to help educational professionals to address some of the important facets of cultural influence while seeking to avoid standardising the content therein. The resource, however, grew out of an ideology. Summed up neatly by Eisner (1994), ideologies are belief systems that provide the value premises from which the decisions about practical educational matters are made. In some ways, ideologies derive from *he tirohanga*—a worldview, in this case, a Māori worldview, *mai i he tirohanga* Māori. Ideologies in education have the potential to influence what is considered challenging in the curriculum—and positively connecting to things cultural has presented as a challenging reality for decade, after decade, after decade. The Hikairo Schema is an example of the conception of some of the foundations of culturally responsive pedagogy rooted in the desire by teachers to better connect with tamariki and whānau as they go about their daily and weekly professional tasks.

The Hikairo Schema is an adaptable and self-paced guide that can support teachers to rethink their approaches to engaging tamariki, to revise teaching strategies, and, where necessary, to modify their approaches to teaching and learning. It also enables teachers to work collaboratively with whānau and tamariki in terms of co-constructing goals and outcomes that are relevant to their learning contexts and community. There are several ways that the Hikairo Schema can be employed. One such way is to allocate a time frame of several weeks for working on each dimension one at a time, so as to take small steps and try new approaches. An alternative way is to try something for each dimension concurrently over a period of several weeks. The main intention is to ensure that the approach is at a pace that is manageable, comfortable, and enables everyone to adjust and respond to challenges and opportunities in the learning environments. As each dimension is introduced, teachers and teaching teams have the jurisdiction to explore how the Schema could be adapted and applied in their particular context. It is important that they become familiar with cultural meanings behind the Schema's dimensions, and that the Schema's cultural narrative is shared with the tamariki.

It is critical to retain a focus on the three core principles as they relate to the learning environment, and that set goals are constantly on the agenda. The Hikairo Schema is generous in terms of offering examples that support the planning and goal-setting process. Goals and plans need to be revisited periodically, and revised as cultural responsivity of both kaiako and tamariki attains higher levels. The Schema also provides a measuring apparatus by way of a poutama (stepped pattern) which allows teachers to scaffold their competency development and gauge their learning and progress. The poutama encapsulates five stages of competency, starting at Level One (envisioning a learning journey), through to Level Five (providing cultural leadership). As teachers are working on each of the Hikairo dimensions, they are able to take an aspirational approach to adopting particular strategies that will support them in moving from one level up to the next. For ITE, the impact of this is significant, as it provides scope and opportunity for targeted teaching and assessment specific to culturally responsive pedagogy.

The guiding values and metaphors of the Hikairo Schema come from within a Māori worldview, which means that it is effective for use with *all* tamariki and teachers—Māori and non-Māori. However, one cannot assume that the Schema is for all settings and for all teachers. In the public domain of education, ideas about priorities, goals, and the selection of resources on offer must survive a tough array of competing proposals from those who feel equally convinced of the correctness of their views. Teachers still close the early childhood centre or classroom door, doing what they know how to do, believing that what they do is best for the tamariki they teach. In this sense, changes in teachers' ideology may be among the most important transformations that can be made in the field of education.

Linking the cultures of past and present

The formulation and introduction of a resource for the education sector is not a new phenomenon. Many have come and gone, while others have stood the test of time. It would not be a healthy sign if an important social arena like education did not present some challenges, both theoretical and practical. One of the chief changing roles of teachers is in educating the diversity of learners in our present society. This has implications for ITE and the multitude of teachers operating in early childhood centres and schools across the nation. Educators must be able to conceptualise what culture is, and how learners' cultural nuances influence their cognitive and social success. Understanding the acquisition and manifestation of those nuances can help educators realise the effects of certain methodologies and teaching techniques on learners. In the context of an education studies programme uniquely suited to Aotearoa New Zealand, knowledge of cultural diversity is one aspect of teacher effectiveness—having the appropriate tools to instantiate culturally responsive pedagogies is another. The Hikairo Schema is merely one of many resources available that move beyond the conceptualisation phase and into the conundrum of the practice space.

As noted earlier in the chapter, the Schema does not stand apart. It has resonance with early educational thinkers' contentions. For instance, Dewey (1916) asserted that the child needed to have a stake in the learning activity, and that the teacher's task was to create conditions that would generate in the child a sense of inquiry; this echoes Rose Pere's notions of the *Ako* construct. Thorndike (1921) introduced the term 'connectionism', and this aligns with Durie's (2006) predilection for a convergence of knowledge streams. Tyler (1950) put forward questions that were concerned with educational purposes sought, educational experiences tasted, and knowledge attained and measured. Penetito (2010) asked similar questions of educational practitioners but with an added emphasis on compatibility with the culture of Māori learners. It is argued here that all of the early thinkers discussed in the opening section of this chapter believed in the unity of theory and practice—and, indeed, most orientated their writings accordingly. It is also contended here that the Hikairo Schema is structured around the unity of theory and practice, and thus resonates with the lines that the early thinkers offered. And, finally, it borrows from the past to inform the present. Eisner (1994) issued a reminder that those familiar with the history of education know that the aspiration to standardise educational practice is not a newcomer to the educational scene. He refers to the age-old adage that those who are ignorant of the past are condemned to repeat it.

Concluding thoughts: The promises of diversity

Pursuing cultural competence in educational planning, activities, and monitoring is more important than ever before, given the projected increases in the presence of diversity across a shrinking, global world. This pursuit also has local importance because in Aotearoa New Zealand the growing prominence of Māori phenomena in the many and varied opportunities in early childhood settings and classrooms, is manifest. While the goal of educators to increase their cultural competence in all aspects of their work may be seen by some as too great a challenge to overcome, commitment to the goal—by way of aspirational tenets of mana mātauranga (Māori knowledge having an integrity of its own)—must never waver. The inclusive camber of this chapter, and the background and descriptions of a single culturally imbued educational resource offered here, had three aims in mind. The first aim was to embolden practitioners to become more confident in enhancing their awareness and knowledge bases of things Māori. The second aim was to support practitioners to prepare themselves to adopt and adapt resources that have relevance for Māori learners. The third aim was to encourage practitioners to acknowledge that power-sharing and scaffolding play an important part in their work because, as key concepts, power-sharing promotes equity, and scaffolding ensures that support is at hand. While this paper espoused one resource that is on offer to early childhood centres and schools, it acknowledges that there is a generous selection of programmes designed to lift the performance of tamariki and kaiako, and inspire whānau to take their rightful place in the educational communities across Aotearoa New Zealand. The sector is ready.

Recommendations for further reading

Gay, G. (2010). *Culturally responsive teaching: Theory, research and practice* (2nd ed.). New York, NY & London, UK: Teachers College Press.

Macfarlane, A., Macfarlane, S., Graham, J., & Clarke, T. (2017). Social and emotional learning and Indigenous ideologies in Aotearoa New Zealand: A biaxial blend. In E. Frydenberg, A. Martin, & R. Collie (Eds.), *Social and emotional learning in Australia and the Asia Pacific* (pp. 273–289). Sydney, NSW: Springer.

Turner, H., Rubie-Davies, C. M., & Webber, M. (2015). Teacher expectations, ethnicity and the achievement gap. *New Zealand Journal of Educational Studies, 50*(1), 55–69. 10.1007/s40841-015-0004-1 URL: http://hdl.handle.net/2292/30802

References

Allen, A., Hancock, S., Lewis, C., & Starker-Glass, T. (2017). Mapping culturally relevant pedagogy into teacher education programs: A critical framework. *Teachers College Record, 119*(1), 1–26.

Ames, C. (1992). Classrooms: Goals, structures, and student motivation. *Journal of Educational Psychology, 84*(3), 261–271.

Clarke, T., Macfarlane, S., & Macfarlane, A. (2017). Indigenous frameworks to ignite understandings within initial teacher education—and beyond. In P. Whitinui, C. Rodriguez de France, & O. McIvor (Eds.), *Promising practices in Indigenous teacher education* (pp. 71–86). Victoria, CA: Springer Education.

Darling-Hammond, L. (2010). *The flat world and education: How America's commitment to equity will determine our future.* New York, NY: Teachers College Press.

Delpit, L. (2003). Language diversity and learning. In A. Darder, M. Baltodano, & R. Torres (Eds.), *The critical pedagogy reader* (pp. 388–403). New York, NY: Routledge.

Dewey, J. (1916). *Democracy in education.* New York, NY: Macmillan.

Durie, M. (2006). *The Treaty of Waitangi: Domestic relations, global impacts and a New Zealand agenda.* Seminar delivered at the Treaty Debate Series 2010. Te Papa Tongarewa, Wellington, New Zealand.

Education Review Office. (2016). *Ethnic diversity in New Zealand state schools.* Retrieved from: https://www.ero.govt.nz/footer-upper/news/ero-insights-term-1/ethnic-diversity-in-new-zealand-state-schools/

Eisner, E. (1994). *The educational imagination: On the design and evaluation of school programs* (3rd ed.). New York, NY: Macmillan.

Evans, I. M., & Fitzgerald, J. (2007). Integrating research and practice in professional psychology: Models and paradigms. In I. M. Fitzgerald, J. J. Rucklidge, & M. O'Driscoll (Eds.), *Professional practice of psychology in Aotearoa New Zealand* (pp. 283–300). Wellington: The New Zealand Psychological Society.

Gabbay, J., & Le May, A. (2011). *Practice-based evidence for healthcare.* Oxford, UK: Routledge.

Gay, G. (2002). Preparing for culturally responsive teaching. *Journal of Teacher Education, 53*(2), 106–116.

Getzels, J. (1974). Images of the classroom and visions of the learner. *School Review, 82*(4), 527–540.

Glasser, W. (1993). *The quality school teacher.* New York, NY: Harper Perennial.

Ladson-Billings, G. (1995). Toward a theory of culturally relevant pedagogy. *American Educational Research Journal, 32*(3), 465–491.

Macfarlane, A. (2015). Restlessness, resoluteness and reason: Looking back at 50 years of Māori education. *New Zealand Journal of Education Studies, 50*(2), 177–193.

Macfarlane, A. (2019, May). *Ngā Pae o te Māramatanga: Practices of sustenance.* Keynote presentation at Platform Project Wānanga, University of Canterbury, Christchurch, New Zealand.

Macfarlane, A., Macfarlane, S., Tierney, S., Kuntz, J., Rarere-Briggs, B., Currie, M., Gibson, M., & Macfarlane, R. (2019). *The Hikairo Schema: Culturally responsive teaching and learning in early childhood settings.* Wellington: NZCER Press.

Ministry of Education. (2013). *Ka hikitia Māori education strategy: Accelerating success 2013–2017.* Wellington: Author.

Ministry of Education. (2017). *Te whāriki: He whāriki mātauranga mō ngā mokopuna o Aotearoa. Early childhood curriculum.* Wellington: Author.

Paris, D. (2012). Culturally sustaining pedagogy: A needed change in stance, terminology, and practice. *Educational Researcher, 41*(3), 93–97.

Penetito, W. (2010). *What's Māori about Māori education?* Wellington: Victoria University Press.

Pere, R. (1982). *Ako: Concepts and learning in the Māori tradition.* Working paper, University of Waikato, Hamilton, New Zealand.

Peterson, R., & Ishii-Jordan, S. (Eds.). (1994). *Multicultural issues in the education of students with behavioural disorders.* Cambridge, MA: Brookline Books.

Thorndike, E. (1921). *Educational psychology.* New York, NY: Teachers College.

Tyler, R. (1950). *Basic principles of curriculum and instruction.* Chicago, IL: University of Chicago Press.

Chapter 2
Philosophy of education

Peter Roberts

Introduction

The emergence of philosophy of education as a recognised field of inquiry is often traced back to the 1960s and 1970s. During that period, a body of work now known as "analytic philosophy of education" came into prominence. Courses in philosophy of education became a well-established part of the curriculum in colleges and faculties of education, complementing contributions made by scholars in the other three main 'disciplinary' areas of educational study: sociology, history, and psychology. The analytic approach was, however, only *one* way of addressing educational questions from a philosophical point of view. Other approaches were evident during the 1960s and 1970s, and the roots of philosophy of education go much deeper than this. In the West, philosophers have addressed educational questions since the time of the ancient Greeks. In the work of Plato and Aristotle, for example, educational themes emerge as part of a broader investigation of ethical and political matters. In subsequent centuries, thinkers such as Quintilian, Augustine, Aquinas, Loyola, Comenius, Locke, Rousseau, Kant, Wollstonecraft, Pestalozzi, Herbart, Froebel, Montessori, and Dewey, among others, have all added to this ongoing educational conversation. There is a similarly lengthy history of inquiry in the East, with pedagogical questions arising, for instance, in the writings and teachings associated with

Taoist, Confucian, and Buddhist traditions of thought. Philosophy of education in this broader sense is thus more than 2000 years old.[1]

What, then, is philosophy of education 'about' and what do philosophers of education 'do'?[2] We might also ask: Why does work in this field matter? Education is almost always in the news. It is a frequent topic of discussion and debate among politicians, journalists, and parents. Most New Zealanders are schooled for at least a decade of their lives, and hundreds of millions of dollars are devoted to education every year. Yet, we seldom pause to reflect, carefully and rigorously, on fundamental questions: What *is* education? How is it different, if at all, from 'learning' or 'socialisation' or 'indoctrination'? What does it mean to be an educated person? *Why* should we educate? How might education contribute to human fulfilment and the building of better social worlds? What are some of the impediments to the pursuit of our ideals? Philosophy of education, this chapter suggests, has something important to offer in addressing these questions. Philosophers of education focus on argument, analysis, and critique. They explore, clarify, and deconstruct educational concepts. They probe the assumptions that underpin claims about education, place pedagogical problems in their broader contexts, and consider educational alternatives. The first part of the chapter provides a philosophical perspective on learning, education, and the educated person. The second section considers the value of philosophical work for teachers and makes a case for continuing critical engagement with policy.

Learning, education, and the educated person

We hear a great deal about 'learning' these days. In some respects, this is hardly surprising. Learning, we can readily appreciate, is necessary to succeed in school, progress to tertiary education, and do well in the world of work. We are all learners of one kind or another. Indeed, many people profess to having a 'love of learning' and commit themselves to it throughout their

---

1   See Aristotle (1976, 1981); Boyd and King (1964); Confucius (1979); Curtis and Boultwood (1965); Freeman Butts (1955); Glanz (1997); Johnson (2002); Lao Tzu (1963); Mackinnon (1996); Plato (1974, 1975); Rusk (1956); Shim (2007); Tan (2013); Wong (2004).

2   Over the years, these questions have been the subject of much debate. For a range of views on the nature, scope, and purpose of philosophy of education, see Carr (2004); Clark (2006); Feinberg (2006); Howe (2014); Laverty (2014); Noddings (2012); Pring (2000); Quay, Bleazby, Stolz, Toscano, and Webster (2018); Roberts (2015, 2018); Siegel (2009); Standish (2007); Vokey (2006); J. White (2013); Wilson (2003).

lives. At times, however, discourses on learning appear to lack a strong sense of history. From the language employed and the statements made in many policy documents, institutional marketing materials, and press releases on education, it sometimes seems as if anything worth knowing about learning is relatively new. Where there is money to be made, claims about newness are often particularly conspicuous. Whether it is 'brain-based learning', 'e-learning', or 'innovative learning environments', the emphasis appears to be on the latest developments, frequently promoted on the basis that they offer something more exciting, effective, relevant, or scientific than what has gone before. Yet there is a long history of philosophical thought on learning, and the ideas of thinkers from the past provide a helpful sense of perspective when examining more contemporary initiatives. In this section, brief summaries of three classic accounts from Plato, Locke, and Dewey will be offered before turning to debates over education and the educated person in the second half of the 20th century and first two decades of the 21st century.

Perhaps the most famous philosopher in the Western tradition, Plato (427–347BC) had much to say about education, knowledge, and learning. Education is a key theme in his best known work, *The Republic* (Plato, 1974), where he outlines a 50-year programme for the preparation of philosopher rulers in his ideal society. But Plato also addresses educational questions in other dialogues such as *The Laws* (Plato, 1975) and *The Meno* (Plato, 1949). In *The Meno* Plato poses a key problem in thinking about learning: "How is it that a learner is able to understand anything new?" (Phillips & Soltis, 2009, p. 9). He seems to suggest that we cannot inquire about either that which is known to us or that which is unknown to us. If we know, inquiry is not necessary; yet if we do not know, we will not know what to inquire about. One answer to this problem is to see learning as something that is based on, and builds upon, prior knowledge. But this, as Phillips and Soltis (2009) point out, raises the further question of where that knowledge originated: "Learning is possible only if some prior things are known, and these prior things could have been learned only if something prior to them had been learned, and so on!" (p. 10). Plato's solution to this difficulty is to see knowledge as innate, as something that is within us at birth. In *The Republic*, he argues that the soul is immortal; it exists forever and nothing, not even the most abominable wickedness, can destroy it (Plato, 1974, pp. 441–443). In *The Meno*, he maintains that the soul, "having been often born", will hitherto have "known all things" (Plato, 1949, pp. 100–101). Learning is a process of inquiry that involves recalling or recovering this "ancient knowledge" (p. 101). Plato demonstrates his theory by having Socrates ask Meno, a servant boy, a series of questions relating to a geometrical problem. Meno might think he knows nothing about geometry, but if the right questions are asked, it can be shown that the knowledge was there all along; it simply had to be drawn out.

Plato's recollectionist account of learning is open to interrogation from a number of different angles. Much depends on how convincing we find his concept of an immortal soul. The epistemology that underpins his account can be challenged by those who see knowledge not as something innate but as socially constructed. Moreover, while it is possible to see the process described by Plato as a form of "learning without teaching" (Weiss, 2006), it can also be argued that Socrates' questions, prompts, and interactions with Meno are precisely those of a teacher. Meno is guided and shaped rather more by Socrates than Plato seems to suggest. Many centuries later, the British philosopher John Locke (1632–1704) offered an alternative account of learning. Rejecting Plato's position that knowledge is innate, Locke argues instead that we come into the world with a mind "completely devoid of content"—a *tabula rasa* or blank tablet (Phillips & Soltis, 2009, p. 13). If the 'tablet' is blank, how does a child learn? Locke's position relies on the idea of a child having preformed abilities that lie dormant, waiting to be applied. As we experience the environment via our senses, we learn. Our memory allows us to retain and build ideas. Locke's approach prompts us to consider the question of prerequisites for learning: "What experiences or simple ideas must a child have had in order to be able to go ahead and learn some new material?" (p. 15). This question is one we continue to ask today; not only in working with young children but at all levels in the education system.

Locke's position, too, is open to critique. A key problem is that of passivity: experience seems to simply 'happen' to the learner, and the blank tablet is filled. Other thinkers stress more active engagement and interaction between the learner and his or her surroundings. Locke's 'atomism' is too simplistic: ideas and experience cannot simply be bundled together to create meaningful, complex knowledge (see Phillips & Soltis, 2009, pp. 17–18). Closer to our present day, John Dewey (1859–1952) offered a pragmatic approach that contrasts in some significant ways with both Plato and Locke. Dewey argues that we learn by *doing* things, with others (Biesta, 2009, p. 70). For Dewey (1966, 1997), learning is closely connected with *experience*. According to Dewey, experience has both active and passive elements:

> On the active hand, experience is *trying*—a meaning which is made explicit in the connected term experiment. On the passive, it is *undergoing*. When we experience something we act upon it, we do something with it; then we suffer or undergo the consequences. (1966, p. 139, emphasis in original).

Dewey adds: "When the change made by action is reflected back into a change made in us ... [w]e learn something" (p. 139). Learning integrates 'theory' with 'practice'. We learn through trial and error, but if this is to be intelligent action, *thinking* is important (Biesta, 2009, pp. 64–65). Learning is a never-ending process, a form of *growth* that continues across the lifespan. For Dewey, "learning has no natural end point where we arrive at 'The Truth'"; rather, "[i]t is an ongoing creative exploration of possibilities in a process where learning feeds into action and action feeds back into learning" (p. 68). We learn not in isolation but through communication and participation. Learning within the school, Dewey says, should be continuous with learning out of school. The school can be seen as a community, in close and constant interaction with "other modes of associated experience beyond school walls" (Dewey, 1966, p. 360). Learning from "all the contacts of life" is not simply a matter of accumulating facts; it is also a process of *moral formation* (p. 360).

The ideas of Plato, Locke, and Dewey form but a small part of a larger picture of philosophical investigation into learning over the ages. But 'learning' is not the same as 'education'. Indeed, some forms of learning—for example, learning through indoctrination—are arguably *anti*-educational. What, then, might we mean by 'education'? And, what are some of the distinguishing features of an 'educated person'? Analytic philosophy of education can help in answering those questions. Led by scholars such as R. S. Peters, Paul Hirst, and Robert Dearden (the 'London School') in the United Kingdom and Israel Scheffler in the United States, analytic philosophers of education concentrated on the detailed examination of key concepts such as 'education', 'teaching', and 'indoctrination'. Peters' account of education and the ideal of the 'educated man' has been particularly influential. For Peters, 'education', like 'reform', implies a change for the better. 'Education' signals the transmission of something worthwhile "to those who become committed to it"; it involves the development of knowledge, understanding, and cognitive perspective;

and it requires a certain "wittingness and voluntariness" on the part of learners (R. S. Peters, 1970, p. 45). Peters observes:

> People ... think that education must be for the sake of something extrinsic that is worthwhile, whereas the truth is that being worthwhile is part of what is meant by calling it 'education'. (R. S. Peters, 1973, p. 87)

Education, as Peters conceives of it, is a process of initiation into disciplines and activities through which a desirable state of mind develops. For Peters, as for Hirst and Dearden, reason is central to the educational process. An educated person is a *rational* person. Scheffler, too, places considerable emphasis on reason, arguing that rationality is the basis for democratic, pedagogical, and moral life. He sees reason as a potentially unifying force in education, capable of bridging different humanistic and progressive traditions. For Scheffler, the pursuit of rationality is not an abstract ideal but a practical, principled endeavour; it is embodied not in a single subject area but in multiple, dynamic, ever evolving traditions (Scheffler, 1973).[3]

One way of sharpening our sense of what 'education' is or might be is to contrast it with something else: for example, indoctrination, training, or schooling. This was a common focus for philosophers of education in the 1960s and 1970s, with the notion of indoctrination attracting particular scrutiny (Snook, 1972a, 1972b). A number of possible criteria for indoctrination can be considered. We can, for instance, focus on the content of a lesson or a book or a curriculum—that is, on *what* is taught. In such cases, questions might be asked about the accuracy, balance, and relative narrowness or breadth of the material under examination. Attention can also be paid to *how* content is conveyed. If, for example, students are taught in a manner that encourages them to believe something regardless of compelling evidence to the contrary, this might be interpreted as indoctrinatory. Or, if a teacher actively discourages the asking of questions or the posing of problems, impeding the development of critical thought, this likewise could be seen as a case of indoctrination. Another line of inquiry centres on the consequences for learners—on how they end up thinking and acting following a period of instruction. If learners emerge from a course or programme as dogmatic zealots, fixed in their worldviews and unable to consider competing perspectives, indoctrination might be suspected. Yet another

---

3   See further, K. S. Beckett (2011); Dearden, Hirst, and Peters (1972); Hirst (1974); Hirst and Peters (1970); Roberts and Saeverot (2018); Scheffler (1960, 1991); Siegel (1997a).

approach is to concentrate on the intentions of the teacher: what is it that he or she wants to achieve in working with students? Philosophical investigation in such cases might focus on whether the intention is to foster open-mindedness and an investigative spirit or to inhibit the development of these qualities.

Even while analytic philosophy of education was in its 'heyday', it had its share of critics, and by the late 1970s several key concerns had arisen. One of the major shortcomings of the analytic approach, some theorists argued, was that it largely ignored questions relating to the politics of education. The predominant concern with concepts created a decontextualised picture of education. There was insufficient attention to social and economic structures and little engagement with policy or practice. Conceptual analysis operated in a kind of vacuum. Members of the London School may have expressed an interest in the way we use concepts in our 'ordinary language', but their sense of what counted as everyday discourse was shaped—and restricted—by their own class and culture. For Marxist philosophers such as Kevin Harris (1979, 1982), the work of the London School was hobbled by a blindness to the way ideology works in a capitalist society. From a Marxist perspective, there is in any epoch a close connection between the dominant material force and the ruling ideas. As Marx (1970, p. 21) puts it, "[i]t is not the consciousness of men that determines their existence, but their social existence that determines their consciousness". In a capitalist society, educational arrangements will tend to favour the interests of the capitalist class (Freeman-Moir & Scott, 2003). Perceptions of reality are shaped by the experiences people have in the education system. Through schooling, students learn to comply with authority, accept hierarchies, and see themselves as individuals rather than members of a collective (Bowles & Gintis, 1976). Schools foster the development of a false consciousness: a worldview that is not 'innocent' but structured by the unequal and inequitable class relationships that are at the heart of capitalism as a mode of production. What comes to count as worthwhile in education is a matter not of simple agreement, based on a shared understanding of what is true and valuable, but of contestation. Education is, in part, a process of *struggle* over whose views will come to prevail. Identifying, analysing, and resisting dominant constructions of reality should, Harris (1982) argues, be one of the functions of philosophy of education.

Peters' account has also been found wanting by feminist scholars. Jane Roland Martin (1981, 1985, 1986), for example, offers a trenchant critique of Peters' notion of the 'educated man'. It is not just the use of the term 'man' that is problematic (this was not uncommon at the time) but also what is valued and devalued in Peters' ideal. Emotion, empathy, intuition, and interpersonal relationships are all downplayed in favour of rational, intellectual pursuits. The significance of nurturing roles in educational development is ignored. Martin sees Peters' concept of education as an initiation into male cognitive perspectives. Women are just as capable of men of developing and displaying the rational attributes idealised by Peters but this does not mean the other qualities they bring to the educational process should be denied. Women, if they are to become educated in Peters' sense, must become more like men, but when they succeed in doing so, they will often be cast in a critical light for doing so. They will not be accorded the same respect for their rational abilities as their male counterparts and will be criticised for failing to be sufficiently feminine. Martin argues for a more well-rounded educational ideal. We should, she says, be concerned with developing not just the rational mind but the whole person. Due attention needs to be given to the creation of a rich inner life of feeling as well as thought, to action as well as theory, and to child rearing as well as academic endeavours. Reason continues to be highly valued by educational philosophers but Martin's call to recognise the significance of emotion and care in our educational formation has also been widely shared.[4]

Other concerns can also be raised. Peters' account rests on an understanding of the human being as a rational, autonomous, individual subject—an ontological starting point that has been rendered problematic by postmodern and poststructuralist thinkers. Postmodernists question universalist approaches to philosophy, adopting an attitude of incredulity toward metanarratives (Lyotard, 1984; M. Peters, 1995). Trying to provide an overarching philosophical framework, within which everything can be explained, is, for a postmodernist, an enterprise fraught with difficulties. Postmodernists focus instead on the little, the local, and the particular. Appeals to universal propositions have, some educationists believe, been oppressive to those who are not "European, White, male, middle class, Christian, able-bodied, thin, and heterosexual" (Ellsworth, 1989, p. 304). Philosophy has frequently been premised on the assumption that reason is the same for all people, everywhere, at all times. Science has often been seen in a similar light. Postmodernists and poststructuralists challenge these views, stressing the heterogeneity of worldviews, modes of understanding,

---

4 Compare, Boler (1999); Burbules (1991); Dewhurst (1997); Gaon (2002); Liston and Garrison (2004); Loreman (2011); Moshman (2009); Noddings (1992, 2003); Papastephanou (2001); Robertson (1999); Siegel (1988, 1992, 1997b); Zembylas (2002, 2007).

and forms of life; the emphasis is not on establishing an ideal that will apply to all but rather on acknowledging, engaging, and celebrating differences among human beings (Boler, 2000). We tend to think of ourselves as 'self-contained' individuals but this view does not deal adequately with the complexities we negotiate in our everyday lives. Other accounts of the self and the formation of subjectivities need to be considered (see Besley & Peters, 2008). Postmodernists and poststructuralists show how we are shaped by the multiple discourses in which we participate. We adopt different subject positions in different contexts, and tensions often arise when our identities as part of one group come into conflict with those we forge and inhabit as members of other discourse communities (see Weiler, 1991). This does not mean we must give up on the idea of working effectively with others: dialogue across differences, as some theorists see it, is not only possible but highly desirable (Burbules & Rice, 1992).

From concepts to contexts: Pedagogy, policy, and practice

In the previous section, the focus was principally on learners and those being educated. But what of teachers and the task of educating others? When we talk about teaching or pedagogy, we often spend much of our time considering *methods*. There are endless debates over which methods of instruction should be employed in school classrooms. New fads arise on a regular basis, often accompanied by a kind of educational amnesia. We forget, or ignore, similar ideas from the past—their successes and failures—and keep searching for a methodological holy grail that will solve our educational problems. In colloquial terms, we obsess over 'how to do it', neglecting questions relating to *'why* we do it'. Philosophy of education shifts the emphasis of our investigation. It is not that methods are unimportant; it is just that they only make sense when considered in relation to other elements of the educational process. Philosophers of education recognise that all educational policies and practices have a normative dimension: they imply a view of what we value and what we *ought* to do. At an even more fundamental level, we might say that every educational decision relies on a conception of what it means to be a human being and of how we come to know. For a philosopher of education, then, questions relating to ontology (the study of existence or being), epistemology (the study of knowledge), and ethics (the study of morality, values, and ideals) are vital to educational inquiry. One educational theorist who is especially helpful in exploring these ideas further is Paulo Freire (1921–1997).

Freire was one of the most important educationists of the 20th century (Kirylo, 2011; Mayo, 1999; Schugurensky, 2011). His educational philosophy grew out of his work with impoverished adults in Brazil in the 1950s and 1960s. Freire developed an approach to adult literacy education built on the lived experiences of learners, encouraging participants to read both the 'word' and the 'world' (Freire & Macedo, 1987; Roberts, 1996a). Forced into exile by the military coup in 1964, he went on to work in a number of other countries in South America, Europe, and Africa before returning to Brazil in 1980. One of his early books, *Pedagogy of the Oppressed* (Freire, 1972), has been particularly influential, but he also published prolifically during the last decade of his life. Freire builds his educational theory on an ideal of humanisation. Humanisation is, he argues, an ontological and historical vocation. As beings of praxis, we have the capacity to reflect and act to transform the world. Aware of our location in time and space, we can place the problems of today in broader historical perspective and imagine alternative futures (Freire, 1976, 2004, 2007). We do not, however, do this alone. Freire stresses the importance of communication and dialogue with others in our pursuit of humanisation. Freire's epistemology is consistent with this principle: we come to know, he maintains, through interacting with others and the world. While humanisation is the ideal, *de*humanisation is a reality that must be acknowledged. Denuding others of their dignity as human beings through oppressive social structures, policies, and practices, and impeding their ability to engage in praxis, dehumanises both those subject to such oppression and those responsible for it. Liberation entails both a process of struggle against oppression and the development of key virtues such as love, trust, and hope (Darder, 2002; Freire, 1994, 1996, 1997; Roberts, 2016; Roberts & Freeman-Moir, 2013).

Teaching can, from a Freirean point of view, be a humanising activity. Good teachers, Freire argues, care deeply for the students with whom they work. They display humility and openness in their attitudes, words, and actions. They are curious, probing, and investigative in seeking to know. They are willing to listen and learn. Most of all, they are rigorous, expecting high standards of themselves and their students. Teaching is demanding; it can be both exhilarating and exhausting. To teach takes *courage* (Freire, 1998a). Teaching is a serious undertaking, and with this should come a strong sense of responsibility. This does not mean classrooms have to be sombre spaces. On the contrary: the passion teachers have for their subjects should come through strongly in the way they act in a classroom, and humour can be helpful in fostering a similarly enthusiastic approach to learning among students. Teaching from a Freirean perspective is, however, not just 'fun and games'; it should actively encourage the development of a critical orientation to the world (Freire, 1985, 1998b). The culture created in an educational setting should be such that students will want to ask difficult questions, want to seek evidence for claims made, and want to test their ideas in the company of others. Inculcating and exhibiting a critical consciousness, as Freire understands this term, is not just a matter of possessing skills in argument; it also implies an effort to understand and critique the society in which one lives.

A Freirean approach to teaching emphasises the posing of problems rather than the giving of answers. Freire argues against 'banking' education, where students are expected to sit passively, waiting to receive the content of a lesson from an all-knowing teacher. Under such a model, students are regarded as largely ignorant, with little or nothing to contribute to the educational process (Freire, 1972). For Freire, it is important to build upon, but also to go beyond, the students' previous experience and existing knowledge. Dialogue is essential to this process, but this is not mere idle chatter or casual conversation. Dialogue in Freirean education must have a purpose; it should be well-informed and have a definite sense of structure and direction (Freire & Shor, 1987). Teaching for Freire should be neither authoritarian nor 'anything goes'. Teachers can exercise authority, and be authorities in their subject areas, without being authoritarian. To be authoritarian is to say, in effect, "Do it this way, or else!" Authoritarianism suppresses questioning and dissent. But if there are no rules—no aims or plans, no boundaries or limits—the freedom that is essential to educational life becomes mere licence. This is, in part, why Freire made it clear that he saw himself as a teacher and not merely a 'facilitator' (Freire & Macedo, 1995). We may want to encourage scholarly independence, but this requires guidance. Teaching is not a 'hands off' activity; it is a necessarily *interventionist* process (Roberts, 1996b, 1999, 2003). Intervention, Freire shows, is not the same as *imposition*. Teachers do not have a right to force their views on students; equally, they do not need to shy away from the fact that their actions and decisions may exert a powerful influence over other lives (see Hansen, 1997). From a Freirean perspective, teaching is an ethical and political process, always favouring some ideas, interests, and ideals over others (see Benade, 2012). Teachers cannot be 'neutral'; they must think deeply about what they stand for and why, and structure their pedagogical lives accordingly. This does not mean that a rigid adherence to exactly the same values and ideas throughout a career is necessary or appropriate; a readiness to change, where evidence, argument, and dialogue with others suggests we should do so, is one of the marks of maturity in a teacher.

Freire's work is helpful in reorienting our thinking about teaching methods. Freire, like all teachers, employed certain methods in his work with adult learners. In his literacy initiatives, he would start with a tri-syllabic word (for example, 'tijolo', the Portuguese word for 'brick'), combine the first letter of each syllable with the five vowels (ta, te, ti, to, tu / ja, je, ji, jo, ju / la, le, li, lo, lu), and show how different parts could be recombined to create new whole words: 'tatu' (armadillo), 'loja' (store), 'juta' (jute), 'luta' (struggle), and so on (Freire, 1976). He also preferred to have students sitting in a manner where they could engage in discussion with the teacher and with each other. He used visual representations of aspects of daily life as a prompt for reflection and discussion. But Freire did not regard these methods as fixed or universally applicable for all educationists. Methods, he could see, needed to be appropriate to *contexts* (Roberts, 1996c). We may, from a Freirean point of view, speak of certain principles and ideals that underpin our activities as teachers (for example, a commitment to integrity, a sense of care and responsibility, a valuing of dialogue and critical thought), but in determining what methods might be appropriate, we must pay attention to the distinctive features of the educational situation with which we are dealing. We need to consider what the students bring with them to the educational setting; what they have encountered previously and what they seek to gain from this new experience. We will want to pay close attention to the physical layout of the space in which we are working and assess its constraints and possibilities. We need to think about the subject area with which we are dealing. We will also want to reflect honestly on our own strengths and limitations. In teaching, every context is different, demanding its own methods and judgements about what seems best at a given moment, with a particular group of students, for a specific purpose (see D. Beckett, 2008; Saevi, 2011).

Making questions of context more central to our thinking suggests another important task for philosophers of education, and for teachers: critical engagement with policy. This is by no means straightforward or easy (McLaughlin, 2000). In New Zealand, education has, over the past three decades, been shaped significantly by neoliberal ideas, policies, practices, and structures. Neoliberalism construes human beings as self-interested, rational, autonomous individual consumers. For neoliberals, the market provides the ideal model for human activity, and education is expected to operate, as far as possible, in accordance with market principles. This way of thinking has been particularly evident at the tertiary level. Under neoliberalism, tertiary education is conceived as a form of private benefit, not as a public good. Knowledge becomes a commodity, with an exchange value, and is, in theory, treated in the same manner as other goods and services traded in a capitalist society. Competition within and between institutions is encouraged. Universities are expected to operate like businesses, with authority structures and reporting procedures adopted from the corporate world. There is a heavy emphasis on performance and efficiency. Punitive accountability and auditing measures replace cultures based on the principles of trust and responsibility. Aggressive advertising is undertaken in an effort to sell educational 'products' (courses and programmes) to potential 'consumers' (students), with each institution working hard to carve out a distinctive 'brand' for itself in a crowded tertiary marketplace.

Philosophers of education from New Zealand have responded regularly and at length to these changes, tracing neoliberal policy ideas back to their theoretical roots, critically evaluating policy documents, and arguing for alternative approaches to social and economic life.[5] This is one way of upholding the legal requirement in New Zealand for universities to accept a role as "critic and conscience of society" (Openshaw & Clark, 2012). The idea of serving as someone else's 'conscience' is arguably problematic but this statutory obligation does suggest something important about the ethics of educational existence: to serve in a university, it is not unreasonable to expect that we will be beings of 'good conscience' (Roberts, 2007). The role of 'critic' is more readily accessible as a concept and does not mean simply finding fault; it implies a fair-minded effort to identify strengths and weaknesses, to contextualise, and to probe beneath surface appearances. In this respect, there is always more work to do, for policy, it might be said, 'never sleeps'. Policy in education, perhaps more than in any other area of government activity, is subject to the ebb and flow of political whim. While patterns over time can be detected and analysed, there are sometimes subtle surprises that appear to go against the grain of policy orthodoxy and these can provide helpful starting points for deeper philosophical investigation.

The restlessness engendered by a commitment to the critic and conscience role is indicative of what lies in store for those who take the task of philosophy

---

5   See, for example: Codd (1993, 2001, 2004); Devine (2004); Fitzsimons, Peters, and Roberts (1999); Locke (2015); Marshall (1996); Olssen (2001); M. A. Peters (2001, 2011); Peters and Marshall (1996); Roberts and Peters (2008); Tesar (2013).

of education seriously. To be a philosopher of education means being willing to accept a certain discomfort that comes with asking critical questions. Educational, epistemological, and ethical problems become not easier to solve but seemingly more difficult and complex than ever before. Committing to philosophy of education can create doubt and even, at times, a sense of despair (Roberts, 2013). But these possibilities are there for anyone who confronts the challenges associated with education. Education is an inherently risky process (Biesta, 2014). With education, and critical education in particular, there is 'no going back'. A critical consciousness, once developed, cannot simply be 'switched off'. There is thus a special need for clarity, sensitivity, and care when contributing, through teaching, to the emergence of these qualities in others. But accepting the risk of being educated also opens up the possibility of new perspectives, new forms of knowledge, new ways of being in the world. The suffering that sometimes forms part of the educational process need not be 'useless pain' (Ozolins, 2003). Hard intellectual work can be satisfying—even joyful—and when we take the time to slow down, pay attention, and wait, beauty can be found all around us (Caranfa, 2010; Murdoch, 2001; Teschers, 2018; Weil, 1997, 2001).

Becoming educated is, in part, a matter of learning to accept that we are necessarily unfinished beings. It also involves learning how to work constructively with uncertainty and unpredictability. Through philosophy of education, we can come to appreciate that much of what matters most in teaching and learning, and in human life more generally, does not lend itself well to the logic of measurement, monitoring, and management. Immeasurability becomes not something to resist or fear but rather something to embrace and celebrate. A critical philosophical education can lead us to believe that some of the most significant questions we face as human beings will never be finally and fully addressed. Many philosophers of education would have it no other way. Philosophy of education is not just a form of academic exercise; it is, or can be, a *way of life*. This notion is consistent with the attitude adopted by the early Greeks, who saw themselves as engaged not just in abstract inquiry but in the practical process of learning how to live (Hadot, 1995). A similar attitude is evident among many existentialist thinkers (Webster, 2009). Søren Kierkegaard (2009), for example, argued for a passionate inwardness that would recover our central task of learning how to exist; Miguel de Unamuno (1972) placed a premium on the question of whether there was life after death; and Simone de Beauvoir (1948) urged us to face up to the ethical ambiguities at the heart of human existence. These thinkers are but a few of the examples that could be named in demonstrating the importance of pondering 'big' questions: Who are we? Why are we here? What should we do? These philosophers, and many others, show us that it is not always the easiest educational path that is best; what seems complex, difficult, even impossible, can sometimes be precisely what we need to make progress, to grow, and to learn.

Concluding comments

It has been possible in this chapter to provide only a brief glimpse of what philosophy of education has to offer. Given space constraints, the primary focus has been on a small number of selected themes and theorists. But it must be stressed: there is much more that could be said about the field, both internationally and in New Zealand specifically. New Zealand scholars have brought distinctive Indigenous voices to bear on wider philosophical conversations; they have addressed some of the most pressing global problems of our time (for example, terrorism, the environmental crisis, and the emergence of post-truth politics); and they have made a notable contribution to theoretical knowledge in the different sectors of education (with their influence being particularly marked in early childhood education).[6] Organisations such as the Philosophy of Education Society of Australasia have provided a sense of community, solidarity, and support for educational theorists in this country, with opportunities to share and debate ideas with others from elsewhere in the world via conferences and other events. Over the last half century, philosophy of education has become more diverse in its methods, theoretical orientations, and areas of focus, but the questions identified in the introduction to this chapter have remained central for many scholars throughout this period. Philosophy of education, it has been argued in this chapter, is not merely an abstract activity; it is also a practical endeavour, relevant to the everyday lives of teachers and learners. A philosophical approach to education can help us to more deeply understand ourselves, our commitments and ideals, and the wider contexts that structure and shape pedagogical possibilities.

---

6   Among many other sources that could be cited here, see Arndt & Tesar (2019); Farquhar (2010); Farquhar & Fitzsimons (2008); Farquhar & White (2014); Gibbons (2007); Irwin (2010); Mika (2012, 2015); Mika & Stewart (2016); M. A. Peters (2004, 2017); Stewart (2018a, 2018b); Stratford (2019); Tesar (2013, 2015); and E. J. White (2014, 2015, 2016).

Recommendations for further reading

Noddings, N. (2012). *Philosophy of education* (3rd ed.). Boulder, CO: Westview Press.

Quay, J., Bleazby, J., Stolz, S., Toscano, M., & Webster, S. (Eds.). (2018). *Theory and philosophy in education research: Methodological dialogues*. New York, NY: Routledge.

Siegel, H. (Ed.). (2009). *The Oxford handbook of philosophy of education*. Oxford, UK: Oxford University Press.

References

Aristotle. (1976). *Ethics* (J. A. K. Thomson, Trans.). Harmondsworth, UK: Penguin.

Aristotle. (1981). *The politics* (T. A. Sinclair, Trans.). Harmondsworth, UK: Penguin.

Arndt, S., & Tesar, M. (2019). Posthuman encounters in New Zealand early childhood teacher education. In C. A. Taylor & A. Bayley (Eds.), *Posthumanism and higher education: Reimagining pedagogy, practice and research* (pp. 85–102). Cham, Switzerland: Palgrave Macmillan.

Beauvoir, S. de. (1948). *The ethics of ambiguity* (B. Frechtman, Trans.). New York, NY: Citadel Press.

Beckett, D. (2008). Holistic competence: Putting judgements first. *Asia Pacific Education Review*, *9*(1), 21–30.

Beckett, K. S. (2011). R. S. Peters and the concept of education. *Educational Theory*, *61*(3), 239–255.

Benade, L. (2012). *From technicians to teachers: Ethical teaching in the context of globalised education reform*. New York, NY: Continuum.

Besley, T., & Peters, M. A. (2008). *Subjectivity and truth: Foucault, education and the culture of the self*. New York, NY: Peter Lang.

Biesta, G. (2009). Pragmatism's contribution to understanding learning-in-context. In R. Edwards, G. Biesta, & M. Thorpe (Eds.), *Rethinking contexts for teaching and learning: Communities, activities and networks* (pp. 61–73). New York, NY: Routledge.

Biesta, G. J. J. (2014). *The beautiful risk of education*. Boulder, CO: Paradigm Publishers.

Boler, M. (1999). *Feeling power: Emotions and education*. New York, NY: Routledge.

Boler, M. (2000). An epoch of difference: Hearing voices in the 1990s. *Educational Theory*, *50*(3), 357–381.

Bowles, S., & Gintis, H. (1976). *Schooling in capitalist America*. New York, NY: Basic Books.

Boyd, W., & King, E. J. (1964). *A history of Western education* (7th ed.). London, UK: Adam & Charles Black.

Burbules, N., & Rice, S. (1992). Dialogue across differences: Continuing the conversation. *Harvard Educational Review*, *61*(4), 393–417.

Burbules, N. C. (1991). Two perspectives on reason as an educational aim: The virtues of reasonableness. *Philosophy of Education 1991* (pp. 215–224). Normal, IL: Philosophy of Education Society.

Caranfa, A. (2010). Contemplative instruction and the gifts of beauty, love, and silence. *Educational Theory*, *60*(5), 561–585.

Carr, W. (2004). Philosophy and education. *Journal of Philosophy of Education*, *38*(1), 55–73.

Clark, J. (2006). Philosophy of education in today's world and tomorrow's: A view from "down under". *Paideusis, 15*(1), 21–30.

Codd, J. (1993). Neo-liberal education policy and the ideology of choice. *Educational Philosophy and Theory, 24*(2), 31–48.

Codd, J. (2001). The Third Way for tertiary education policy: TEAC and beyond. *New Zealand Annual Review of Education, 10,* 31–57.

Codd, J. (2004). Export education and the commercialisation of public education in New Zealand. *New Zealand Annual Review of Education, 13,* 21–41.

Confucius. (1979). *The analects* (D. C. Lau, Trans.). Harmondsworth, UK: Penguin.

Curtis, S. J., & Boultwood, M. E. A. (1965). *A short history of educational ideas* (4th ed.). London, UK: University Tutorial Press.

Darder, A. (2002). *Reinventing Paulo Freire: A pedagogy of love.* Boulder, CO: Westview Press.

Dearden, R. F., Hirst, P. H., & Peters, R. S. (Eds.). (1972). *Education and the development of reason.* London, UK: Routledge and Kegan Paul.

Devine, N. (2004). *Education and public choice: A critical account of the invisible hand in education.* Westport, CT: Bergin and Garvey.

Dewey, J. (1966). *Democracy and education.* New York, NY: Free Press.

Dewey, J. (1997). *Experience and education.* New York, NY: Touchstone.

Dewhurst, D. (1997). Education and passion. *Educational Theory, 47*(4), 477–487.

Ellsworth, E. (1989). Why doesn't this feel empowering? Working through the repressive myths of critical pedagogy. *Harvard Educational Review, 59*(3), 297–324.

Farquhar, S. (2010). *Ricoeur, identity and early childhood education.* Lanham, MD: Rowman and Littlefield.

Farquhar, S., & Fitzsimons, P. (Eds.). (2008). *Philosophy of early childhood education: Transforming narratives.* Oxford, UK: Wiley-Blackwell.

Farquhar, S., & White, E. J. (2014). Philosophy and pedagogy of early childhood. *Educational Philosophy and Theory, 46*(8), 821–832.

Feinberg, W. (2006). "Back to the future": Philosophy of education as an instrument of its time. *Education and Culture, 22*(2), 7–18.

Fitzsimons, P., Peters, M., & Roberts, P. (1999). Economics and the educational policy process in New Zealand. *New Zealand Journal of Educational Studies, 34*(1), 35–44.

Freeman-Moir, J., & Scott, A. (Eds.). (2003). *Yesterday's dreams: International and critical perspectives on education and social class.* Christchurch: Canterbury University Press.

Freeman Butts, R. (1955). *A cultural history of Western education: Its social and intellectual foundations* (2nd ed.). New York, NY: McGraw-Hill.

Freire, P. (1972). *Pedagogy of the oppressed.* Harmondsworth, UK: Penguin.

Freire, P. (1976). *Education: The practice of freedom.* London, UK: Writers and Readers.

Freire, P. (1985). *The politics of education.* London, UK: Macmillan.

Freire, P. (1994). *Pedagogy of hope.* New York, NY: Continuum.

Freire, P. (1996). *Letters to Cristina: Reflections on my life and work.* London, UK: Routledge.

Freire, P. (1997). *Pedagogy of the heart.* New York, NY: Continuum.

Freire, P. (1998a). *Teachers as cultural workers: Letters to those who dare teach.* Boulder, CO: Westview Press.

Freire, P. (1998b). *Pedagogy of freedom: Ethics, democracy, and civic courage.* Lanham, MD: Rowman and Littlefield.

Freire, P. (2004). *Pedagogy of indignation.* Boulder, CO: Paradigm Publishers.

Freire, P. (2007). *Daring to dream.* Boulder, CO: Paradigm Publishers.

Freire, P., & Macedo, D. (1987). *Literacy: Reading the word and the world.* London, UK: Routledge.

Freire, P., & Macedo, D. (1995). A dialogue: culture, language, and race. *Harvard Educational Review, 65*(3), 377–402.

Freire, P., & Shor, I. (1987). *A pedagogy for liberation.* London, UK: Macmillan.

Gaon, S. (2002). Education *qua* Enlightenment: On the rationality of the principle of reason. *Philosophy of Education 2002* (pp. 285–292). Normal, IL: Philosophy of Education Society.

Gibbons, A. (2007). *The matrix ate my baby.* Rotterdam, The Netherlands: Sense Publishers.

Glanz, J. (1997). The Tao of supervision: Taoist insights into the theory and practice of educational supervision. *Journal of Curriculum and Supervision, 12*(3), 193–211.

Hadot, P. (1995). *Philosophy as a way of life.* (M. Chase, Trans.). Oxford, UK: Blackwell.

Hansen, D. T. (1997). Being a good influence. In N. C. Burbules & D. T. Hansen (Eds.), *Teaching and its predicaments* (pp. 163–174). Boulder, CO: Westview Press.

Harris, K. (1979). *Education and knowledge.* London, UK: Routledge & Kegan Paul.

Harris, K. (1982). *Teachers and classes.* London, UK: Routledge & Kegan Paul.

Hirst, P. H. (1974). *Knowledge and the curriculum.* London, UK: Routledge and Kegan Paul.

Hirst, P. H., & Peters, R. S. (1970). *The logic of education.* London, UK: Routledge and Kegan Paul.

Howe, K. R. (2014). Philosophy of education and other educational sciences. *Theory and Research in Education, 12*(1), 77–87.

Irwin, R. (Ed.). (2010). *Climate change and philosophy: Transformational possibilities.* London, UK: Continuum.

Johnson, I. (2002). The application of Buddhist principles to lifelong learning. *International Journal of Lifelong Education, 21*(2), 99–114.

Kierkegaard, S. (2009). *Concluding unscientific postscript* (A. Hannay, Trans.). Cambridge, UK: Cambridge University Press.

Kirylo, J. D. (2011). *Paulo Freire: The man from Recife.* New York, NY: Peter Lang.

Lao Tzu. (1963). *Tao Te Ching* (D. C. Lau, Trans.). London, UK: Penguin.

Laverty, M. J. (2014). Conceiving education: The creative task before us. *Theory and Research in Education, 12*(1), 109–119.

Liston, D., & Garrison, J. (Eds.). (2004). *Teaching, learning, and loving: Reclaiming passion in educational practice.* New York, NY: RoutledgeFalmer.

Locke, K. (2015). Performativity, performance and education. *Educational Philosophy and Theory, 49*(3), 247–259.

Loreman, T. (2011). *Love as pedagogy.* Rotterdam, The Netherlands: Sense.

Lyotard, J.-F. (1984). *The postmodern condition: A report on knowledge* (G. Bennington & B. Massumi, Trans.). Minneapolis, MN: University of Minnesota Press.

Mackinnon, A. (1996). Learning to teach at the elbows: The Tao of teaching. *Teaching and Teacher Education, 12*(6), 653–664.

Marshall, J. (1996). The autonomous chooser and "reforms" in education. *Studies in Philosophy and Education, 15*, 89–96.

Martin, J. R. (1981). The ideal of the educated person. *Educational Theory, 31*(2), 97–109.

Martin, J. R. (1985). *Reclaiming a conversation: The ideal of the educated woman*. New Haven, CT: Yale University Press.

Martin, J. R. (1986). Redefining the educated person: Rethinking the significance of gender. *Educational Researcher, 15*(6), 6–10.

Marx, K. (1970). *A contribution to the critique of political economy*. Moscow, USSR: Progress Publishers.

Mayo, P. (1999). *Gramsci, Freire and adult education: Possibilities for transformative action*. London, UK: Zed Books.

McLaughlin, T. H. (2000). Philosophy and educational policy: Possibilities, tensions and tasks. *Journal of Education Policy, 15*(4), 441–457.

Mika, C. (2015). Counter-colonial and philosophical claims: An indigenous observation of Western philosophy. *Educational Philosophy and Theory, 47*(11), 1136–1142.

Mika, C., & Stewart, G. (2016). Māori in the kingdom of the gaze: Subjects or critics? *Educational Philosophy and Theory, 48*(3), 300–312.

Mika, C. T. H. (2012). Overcoming 'being' in favour of knowledge: The fixing effect of 'mātauranga'. *Educational Philosophy and Theory, 44*(10), 1080–1092.

Moshman, D. (2009). The development of rationality. In H. Siegel (Ed.), *The Oxford handbook of philosophy of education* (pp. 145–161). New York, NY: Oxford University Press.

Murdoch, I. (2001). *The sovereignty of good*. London, UK and New York, NY: Routledge.

Noddings, N. (1992). *The challenge to care in schools*. New York, NY: Teachers College Press.

Noddings, N. (2003). *Happiness and education*. Cambridge, UK: Cambridge University Press.

Noddings, N. (2012). *Philosophy of education* (3rd ed.). Boulder, CO: Westview Press.

Olssen, M. (2001). *The neo-liberal appropriation of tertiary education policy in New Zealand: Accountability, research and academic freedom*. Palmerston North: New Zealand Association for Research in Education.

Openshaw, R., & Clark, J. (Eds.). (2012). *Critic and conscience: Essays in memory of John Codd and Roy Nash*. Wellington: NZCER Press.

Ozolins, J. (2003). Suffering: Valuable or just useless pain? *Sophia, 42*(2), 53–77.

Papastephanou, M. (2001). Reformulating reason for philosophy of education. *Educational Theory, 51*(3), 293–313.

Peters, M. (Ed.). (1995). *Education and the postmodern condition*. Westport, CT: Bergin and Garvey.

Peters, M. A. (2001). *Poststructuralism, Marxism and neoliberalism; Between theory and politics*. Lanham, MD: Rowman & Littlefield.

Peters, M. A. (Ed.). (2004). *Education, globalization and the state in the age of terrorism*. Boulder, CO: Paradigm Publishers.

Peters, M. A. (2011). *Neoliberalism and after? Education, social policy and the crisis of capitalism*. New York, NY: Peter Lang.

Peters, M. A. (2017). Education in a post-truth world. *Educational Philosophy and Theory, 49*(6), 563–566.

Peters, M., & Marshall, J. (1996). *Individualism and community: Education and social policy in the postmodern condition*. London, UK: Falmer Press.

Peters, R. S. (1970). *Ethics and education*. London, UK: Allen and Unwin.

Peters, R. S. (1973). *Authority, responsibility and education* (revised ed.). London, UK: George Allen and Unwin.

Phillips, D. C., & Soltis, J. F. (2009). *Perspectives on learning* (5th ed.). New York, NY: Teachers College Press.

Plato. (1949). The Meno (F. Sydenham, Trans.). In Plato, *Five dialogues* (pp. 82–132). London, UK: Everyman's Library.

Plato. (1974). *The republic* (H. D. P. Lee, Trans.). Harmondsworth, UK: Penguin.

Plato. (1975). *The laws* (T. J. Saunders, Trans.). Harmondsworth, UK: Penguin.

Pring, R. (2000). *Philosophy of educational research*. London, UK: Continuum.

Roberts, P. (1996a). Critical literacy, breadth of perspective, and universities: Applying insights from Freire. *Studies in Higher Education, 21*(2), 149–163.

Roberts, P. (1996b). Defending Freirean intervention. *Educational Theory, 46*(3), 335–352.

Roberts, P. (1996c). Structure, direction and rigour in liberating education. *Oxford Review of Education, 22*(3), 295–316.

Roberts, P. (1999). A dilemma for critical educators? *Journal of Moral Education, 28*(1), 19–30.

Roberts, P. (2003). Epistemology, ethics and education: Addressing dilemmas of difference in the work of Paulo Freire. *Studies in Philosophy and Education, 22*(2), 157–173.

Roberts, P. (2007). Intellectuals, tertiary education and questions of difference. *Educational Philosophy and Theory, 39*(5), 480–493.

Roberts, P. (2013). Happiness, despair and education. *Studies in Philosophy and Education, 32*(5), 463–475.

Roberts, P. (2015). "It was the best of times, it was the worst of times": Philosophy of education in the contemporary world. *Studies in Philosophy and Education, 34*(6), 623–634.

Roberts, P. (2016). *Happiness, hope, and despair: Rethinking the role of education*. New York, NY: Peter Lang.

Roberts, P. (2018). Theory as research: Philosophical work in education. In J. Quay, J. Bleazby, S. Stolz, M. Toscano, & S. Webster (Eds.) *Theory and philosophy in education research: Methodological dialogues* (23–35). New York, NY: Routledge.

Roberts, P., & Freeman-Moir, J. (2013). *Better worlds: Education, art, and utopia*. Lanham, MD: Lexington Books.

Roberts, P., & Peters, M. A. (2008). *Neoliberalism, higher education and research*. Rotterdam, The Netherlands: Sense Publishers.

Roberts, P., & Saeverot, H. (2018). *Education and the limits of reason: Reading Dostoevsky, Tolstoy and Nabokov*. New York, NY: Routledge.

Robertson, E. (1999). The value of reason: Why not a sardine can opener? In R. Curren (Ed.), *Philosophy of education 1999* (pp. 1–14). Normal, IL: Philosophy of Education Society.

Rusk, R. R. (1956). *The doctrines of the great educators*. London, UK: Macmillan.

Saevi, T. (2011). Lived relationality as fulcrum for pedagogical–ethical practice. *Studies in Philosophy and Education, 30*(5), 455–461.

Scheffler, I. (1960). *The language of education*. Springfield, IL: Charles C. Thomas.

Scheffler, I. (1973). *Reason and teaching*. London, UK: Routledge & Kegan Paul.

Scheffler, I. (1991). *In praise of the cognitive emotions*. New York, NY: Routledge.

Schugurensky, D. (2011). *Paulo Freire*. London, UK: Continuum.

Shim, S. H. (2007). A philosophical investigation of the role of teachers: A synthesis of Plato, Confucius, Buber, and Freire. *Teaching and Teacher Education, 24*, 515–535.

Siegel, H. (1988). *Educating reason: Rationality, critical thinking, and education*. New York, NY: Routledge.

Siegel, H. (1992). Two perspectives on reason as an educational aim: The rationality of reasonableness. In M. Buchmann & R.E. Floden (Eds.) *Philosophy of Education 1991* (pp. 225–233). Normal, IL: Philosophy of Education Society.

Siegel, H. (Ed.). (1997a). *Reason and education: Essays in honor of Israel Scheffler*. Dordrecht, The Netherlands: Kluwer.

Siegel, H. (1997b). *Rationality redeemed? Further dialogues on an educational ideal*. New York, NY: Routledge.

Siegel, H. (Ed.). (2009). *The Oxford handbook of philosophy of education*. Oxford, UK: Oxford University Press.

Snook, I. (1972a). *Indoctrination and education*. London, UK: Routledge and Kegan Paul.

Snook, I. (Ed.). (1972b). *Concepts of indoctrination*. London, UK: Routledge and Kegan Paul.

Standish, P. (2007). Rival conceptions of the philosophy of education. *Ethics and Education, 2*(2), 159–171.

Stewart, G. (2018a). What does 'indigenous' mean, for me? *Educational Philosophy and Theory, 50*(8), 740–743.

Stewart, G. (2018b). From both sides of the indigenous-settler hyphen in Aotearoa New Zealand. *Educational Philosophy and Theory, 50*(8), 767–775.

Stratford, R. (2019). Educational philosophy, ecology and the Anthropocene. *Educational Philosophy and Theory, 51*(2), 149–152.

Tan, C. (2013). *Confucius*. London, UK: Bloomsbury.

Tesar, M. (2013). Lessons of subversion: Ethics and creativity in neoliberal academia. In M. A. Peters & T. Besley (Eds.), *The creative university* (pp. 111–118). Dordrecht, The Netherlands: Sense Publishers.

Tesar, M. (2015). Reconceptualising the *Child*: Power and resistance within early childhood settings. *Contemporary Issues in Early Childhood, 15*(4), 360–367.

Teschers, C. (2018). *Education and Schmid's art of living: Philosophical, psychological and educational perspectives on living a good life*. New York, UK: Routledge.

Unamuno, M. de. (1972). *The tragic sense of life in men and nations* (A. Kerrigan, Trans.). Princeton, NJ: Princeton University Press.

Vokey, D. (2006). What are we doing when we are doing philosophy of education? *Paideusis, 15*(1), 45–55.

Webster, S. (2009). *Educating for meaningful lives through existential spirituality*. Rotterdam, The Netherlands: Sense Publishers.

Weil, S. (1997). *Gravity and grace* (A. Wills, Trans.). Lincoln, NE: Bison Books.

Weil, S. (2001). *Waiting for God* (E. Craufurd, Trans.). New York, NY: Perennial Classics.

Weiler, K. (1991). Paulo Freire and a feminist pedagogy of difference. *Harvard Educational Review, 61*(4), 449–474.

Weiss, R. (2006). Learning without teaching: Recollection in the *Meno*. *Interpretation: A Journal of Political Philosophy, 34*(1), 3–21.

White, E. J. (2014). 'Are you 'avin a laff?' A Bakhtinian response to pedagogical carnivalesque in early childhood education. *Educational Philosophy and Theory, 46*(8), 898–913.

White, E. J. (2015). *Introducing dialogic pedagogy: Provocations for the early years*. New York, NY: Routledge.

White, E. J. (2016). A philosophy of seeing: The work of the eye/'I' in early years educational practice. *Journal of Philosophy of Education, 50*(3), 474–489.

White, J. (2013). Philosophy, philosophy of education, and economic realities. *Theory and Research in Education, 11*(3), 294–303.

Wilson, J. (2003). Perspectives on the philosophy of education. *Oxford Review of Education, 29*(2), 279–303.

Wong, E. (2004). *Nourishing the essence of life: The outer, inner, and secret teachings of Taoism*. Boston, MA: Shambhala.

Zembylas, M. (2002). "Structures of feeling" in curriculum and teaching: Theorizing the emotional rules. *Educational Theory, 52*, 187–208.

Zembylas, M. (2007). *Five pedagogies, a thousand possibilities*. Rotterdam, The Netherlands: Sense Publishers.

Chapter 3
Education and history

David Small

Who do we think we are?

> *If you are in a comfortable majority, you really don't know what privilege that gives you, because you don't get the daily reminder that your ancestral legacy is less worthy, or that your ancestral language is something that's worthless, or that the ideas of your ancestors might have nothing to contribute to society.*
>
> Dame Anne Salmond[1]

In her response to the terrorist attacks on the Al Noor Mosque and the Linwood Islamic Centre on 15 March 2019, New Zealand's Prime Minister, Jacinda Ardern, declared "this is not who we are". It was a sentiment picked up by many New Zealanders who sought to distance themselves from the atrocity of the act as well as the white supremacist ideology that motivated it.

The notion that, as white people, they are superior to those who are not white, is one that the vast majority of Pākehā New Zealanders would totally reject. The discussions about white supremacy in New Zealand that were sparked by the mosque massacre were mostly focused on why the extensive

---

1   *Marae*, TVNZ, 17 March, 2019.

powers and resources of New Zealand's intelligence and security agencies were keeping the country's Muslim population under close surveillance and paying no attention to the violent underbelly of neo-Nazi white supremacists. Yet if those same people were asked why Māori were grossly over-represented among the prison population and why they underachieved in education, the explanations would likely be centred around the characteristics, attitudes, and behaviours of Māori people, families, and communities; that is, shortcomings within Māori and not within the social institutions.

Among other functions, a society's education system distributes rewards and the criminal justice system distributes punishments. Because they so fundamentally shape people's life chances, these social institutions must operate in a fair way according to principles that are applied to everyone equally without fear or favour. The rewards and punishments administered by these institutions should be those that individuals deserve. The integrity of society depends on this being the case and being seen to be the case. A social system that is designed to ensure that everyone gets what they deserve is called a meritocracy. In this system, educational success comes to those who apply themselves to develop their talents at school and beyond. They merit the rewards that educational achievement brings them just as those who do not succeed in education merit their failure.

This chapter will argue that New Zealand's legal and educational systems have not been giving everyone an equal chance in life; that there are reasons that Pākehā have been obtaining far more of the benefits of education and featuring far less in criminal punishment than Māori. Those reasons do not lie in any innate differences in intelligence or criminality between Māori and Pākehā. Rather, they can be found in the historical origins of the institutions that have formed the basis of New Zealand society. To develop this argument requires a critical analysis of how New Zealand society and its people have been, and continue to be, shaped by the process of settler colonialism. This chapter will examine how New Zealanders have learnt to think of themselves and each other and will argue that assumptions about white superiority or supremacy, although seldom expressed in those terms, have always been part of who we are as New Zealanders. It will be argued that, by assuming and imposing the idea of Pākehā as the norm and the ideal, New Zealand's settler colonial context has been, and continues to be based on, what Sayyid calls "the uncontested universality of the Western project" (2000, p. 268). At the heart of this project is education.

Settler colonialism

In 2014, the Waitangi Tribunal concluded that when the Māori chiefs signed Te Tiriti o Waitangi, the Māori language version of the Treaty of Waitangi, they "did not cede their sovereignty" to Britain (Waitangi Tribunal, 2014, p. xxii). The Tribunal's reasons for coming to this view are well argued and documented, and not surprising, given the significant discrepancies between Te Tiriti in te reo Māori which the chiefs signed, and The Treaty in English which the Crown has always held to be the definitive text. The English version of the Treaty of Waitangi contained the one element that the Crown required above all else, and one that was absent from Te Tiriti—the cession of sovereignty by the Māori chiefs to the British Crown. On the basis of this claim to sovereignty, the Crown assumed absolute authority over the country. What that meant was that all Māori people and institutions became answerable to the Crown. The colonial authorities unilaterally established laws that would apply to everyone living in New Zealand, along with institutions with the power to administer and enforce those laws. From that point on, the Crown ceased to act as a Treaty partner and wherever it was in dispute with Māori, even over matters related to the Treaty, the Crown asserted its purported authority to determine the outcome and to enforce it. The Crown had helped itself to what every modern state requires, what Weber referred to as a "monopoly of the legitimate use of physical force in the enforcement of its orders" (Weber, 1947, p. 154).

The colonisation of New Zealand is an example of settler colonialism, a form of colonisation in which, with the backing of a colonial power, large numbers of settlers seek to gain sovereignty over and make permanent new homes on the lands of Indigenous peoples. A defining characteristic of settler colonialism, one that sets it apart from other 'classical' forms of colonialism, is the imperative to control and own land. The land becomes what is

> most valuable, contested, required … because the settlers make indigenous land their new home and source of capital and also because the disruption of indigenous relationships to land represents a profound epistemic, ontological, cosmological violence. (Tuck & Yang, 2012, p. 5)

In settler colonialism where the value of a new colony is in the land, not in the people who inhabited it, the "dominant feature is not exploitation but replacement" (Wolfe, 1999, p. 163). For the colonial project to succeed in New Zealand, therefore, Māori needed to be removed from their lands.

Tuck and Yang make the point that, under settler colonialism, "land is made into property and human relationships to land are restricted to the relationship of the owner to his property" (2012, p. 5) The removal of Māori from their land and the disruption of Māori identity, culture, and social organisation that resulted from this was, as Mikaere (2005) has argued, "no mere by-product of colonisation, but an integral part of the process" (p. 19). Across much of the North Island, the Crown's exercise of what it claimed to be its sovereign authority over all things Māori led to active resistance and ultimately warfare. The wars that ensued began just 5 years after the signing of the Treaty and lasted until 1872, although not included in this period were the invasion of Parihaka in 1881 and the operations against Tūhoe leader, Rua Kēnana, as recently as 1916. With a total population of only around 60,000, Māori were confronted and ultimately defeated by as many as 12,000 professional colonial soldiers. The percentage of North Island land in Māori ownership fell from around 80% in 1860 to 40% in 1890 and to 27% by 1910. Almost all of the South Island had been lost to Māori by the 1870s.

The impact on Māori of the wars and loss of land cannot be overstated. The financial value of the land that was taken is immense—far more than the amounts that have been offered in compensation by the Crown in recent years. The loss of land removed the productive base from Māori communities that was necessary to sustain themselves and to develop and prosper. Beyond that direct economic impact, the loss of the land as well as the other impacts of the wars affected Māori in the most profound ways. To alienate Māori from their lands, their mountains, their rivers, the places they reference in the same breath as their family and ancestral histories impacts Māori in ways that it can be difficult for those from non-indigenous contexts to comprehend. So deeply does this colonial project strike at the essence of the being of Māori, Moana Jackson refers to it as an "attack on the indigenous soul" (1992, p. 4).

Māori had their authority extinguished, and were only able to retain and exercise remnants of rights to the extent that Pākehā authority recognised and permitted them. Symbolic of the inability of Māori to assert what they considered to be Treaty rights was the dismissal of their attempt in 1877 to reference the Treaty in the case of *Wi Parata v The Bishop of Wellington*.[2] Chief Justice

---

2   *Wi Parata v The Bishop of Wellington* [1877] NZJurRp 183; (1877) 3 NZ Jur (NS) 72 (SC); 1 NZLRLC 14 (17 October 1877).

Prendergast dismissed the Treaty as "a legal nullity" as it had not been (and still has not been) enacted into law. In naming this ruling, the legal system, which was established by a state that derived its authority from the Treaty, held that the Treaty had no legal standing. Māori sovereignty had been completely usurped. As Jackson put it:

> Colonization demanded and still requires, that Māori no longer source their right to do anything in the rules of their own law. Rather they have to have their rights defined by Pākehā; they have to seek permission from an alien word to do those things which their philosophy had permitted for centuries. (1992, p. 6)

Creating the New Zealand identity

The defeat and the decline in the population of Māori in the second half of the 19th century followed a pattern common to other colonial encounters around the world. In a period when *The Origin of Species* was proving influential, the concept of "survival of the fittest" was deployed by Social Darwinists to both explain and present as somehow natural, the dramatic population decline of Indigenous peoples in contexts of colonialism. No longer a threat, Māori were pitied as "a dying race". In 1899, Rudyard Kipling expressed a common perception of this relationship between coloniser and colonised in his poem "The White Man's Burden"—the solemn responsibility of the European to enlighten and civilise the "darker races".

For the political leaders of early New Zealand, the challenge became not only one of dispossessing and subduing Māori but also incorporating and assimilating them into a nation-building project. It remained essential for the Pākehā authorities to be able to assert political power backed by military force—a power projection that they demonstrated as late as 1916 with the arrest of Tūhoe leader Rua Kēnana. However, the ongoing presence of resentful and antagonistic Māori was incompatible with the sort of hegemonic power that was needed for the entrenchment of a stable nation state. Beyond physical resistance, the priority for Māori became survival. This involved trying to keep intact as much of their world as they could at the same time as accepting and adapting to the realities of the emergent New Zealand nation. As Linda Tuhiwai Smith put it, this involved "our attempts to survive, as Māori, in the world being constructed for us, a world which was dehumanising" combined with "attempts by Māori to remain as Māori as possible in the circumstances, that is, a struggle for our humanity or rangatiratanga" (L. T. Smith, 1996, p. 359). In practice, this Māori imperative for survival and adaptation was not incompatible with the nation-building policy agenda of the political authorities. Māori were being transformed from a Treaty partner to, in effect, an interest group that the state had a responsibility towards. The relationship between Māori and state increasingly took the form of Māori engagement with Pākehā institutions.

It was through these institutional connections that the Pākehā authorities sought to assimilate Māori into colonial society—they determined what institutions would exist, the rules by which they would operate, and the ways that Māori would be allowed or required to interact with them. They were not called Pākehā institutions, of course, but that is what they were. State agencies exercised power and responsibility in a wide range of areas including housing, land, welfare, health, and education. Alongside this, the police, the courts, and the prison system ensured the laws of the land were adhered to. The laws themselves were enacted by a technically democratic but overwhelmingly Pākehā parliament. The procedures by which these institutions operated and the rules and policies that they applied were determined with little or no reference to Māori. Nevertheless, in keeping with dominant beliefs about the governance of modern Western societies, the assumption was that these institutions represented the neutral management of public services and functions for the common good of society.

What this meant in practice was that Māori were required to subject themselves to the operation of institutions that were established by, and in order to advance, the interests of the Pākehā settler project. A century later, in the 1980s, this model was labelled "institutional racism". A report into social welfare by the Māori Perspective Advisory Committee (1988) that used the term and is still cited with authority defines institutional racism as

> the outcome of mono-cultural institutions which simply ignore and freeze out the cultures of those who do not belong to the majority. National structures are evolved which are rooted in the values, systems and viewpoints of one culture only. (p. 19)

Within the colonial project, the power of institutional racism is not just that it operates according to cultural assumptions and political contexts that are circumscribed by and promote the interests of the colonial power, but also that it manufactures the belief that these processes are normal, natural, and in the common interest of all members of society. Education is the institution where this normalising of the universal Western project is most effectively advanced.

Other than in circumstances of open hostility, Māori embraced European schooling. They saw it as an opportunity to acquire the knowledge and consequent benefits of European society which were obviously attractive and which could be obtained first by the missionaries and later by the state. Māori aspirations from colonial education were different from, but not incompatible with, the goals of the missionaries and the state, which, quoting comments from government officals of the day, Walker described as "civilising the natives and pacifying the country" (2016, p. 23). This made education one of the institutions that was embraced by coloniser and colonised alike but for quite divergent reasons. As Simon (1994) put it:

> Māori embraced schooling as a means to maintain their sovereignty and enhance their life-chances. The government, on the other hand, sought control over Māori and their resources through schooling. Māori wanted to extend their existing body of knowledge. The government, with its assimilation policy, intended to replace Māori culture with that of the European. (pp. 58–59)

Colonial education is inherently corrosive of culture and identity. In the early stages, while Indigenous languages, cultural practices and beliefs, and sense of identity were strong, colonial education promised obvious advantages and few disadvantages. The colonial school was not seen as a site for the reproduction and transmission of important beliefs, attitudes, practices, knowledge, language, and other elements that comprised cultural identity. Those processes took place within noncolonised spaces and institutions. The use of English as a language of instruction in schools is an illustration of this. The formal prohibition of Māori in schools around the turn of the century caused major anguish for Māori entering school at a time when an estimated 90% of them spoke Māori at home. However, this policy had significant support among Māori. Although he became a supporter of schools teaching Māori language, in 1930 the influential leader Āpirana Ngata said "Māori parents do not like their children being taught in Māori, even in the Māori schools, as they argue that the children are sent there to learn English and the ways of the English" (Barrington & Beaglehole, 1974, p. 206).

For Māori, colonial schooling was Europeanisation. As such, it was part of a process of what Māori scholars have referred to in Freirean terms as "cultural invasion" (L. T. Smith & Reid, 2000, p. 20). Whatever else they learnt at school,

Māori were taught that everything that was worth knowing was European, and that anything that their parents or grandparents knew was of no value in the modern world. This was an essential component of the hidden curriculum in schooling for Māori. As Freire (2000) put it:

> In cultural invasion, it is essential that those who are invaded come to see their reality with the outlook of the invaders rather than their own ... For cultural invasion to succeed, it is essential that those invaded become convinced of their intrinsic inferiority. (p. 114)

Alongside this there emerged an overt curriculum about the nature of New Zealand and their place in it. The notion of one New Zealand people was first expressed by Hobson at the time of the signing of the Treaty when he said in Māori "We are now one people" (Phillips, 2009, p. 5). In 1901, the suffragette leader Kate Sheppard articulated this more explicitly when she said "Māori and Pākehā have become one people, under one Sovereign and one Parliament, glorying alike in the one title of New Zealander" (Phillips, 2009, p. 5). This theme and its component parts can be seen echoed through the school curriculum in the early part of the 20th century.

If the task for the schooling of Māori was to make them feel inferior, the socio-political task for the schooling of non-Māori was to conceal from them or make them forget about or reconceptualise their colonial history and the society to which it gave birth. A significant component of this was a highly racialised account of Māori and Pākehā shaped by Victorian notions of racial hierarchy, allied to comparisons between New Zealand and Australia. In contrast to Australia's history as a penal colony, New Zealand settlers saw themselves as superior stock who were "not only British but the 'best British'" (Irvine & Alpers, 1902, p. 421). As school children were told in their textbooks:

> The New Zealander of today is proud to remember that no colony of the British Empire has ever received such splendid colonists as came to the New Zealand settlements both in the north and in the south. (*Our Nation's Story*, 1931, p. 135)

It was also common for Māori to be described as superior to indigenous Australians. In 1897, the American writer Mark Twain toured Australasia and described Māori as looking "intellectual" and "noble", in camparison to Australian Aboriginals whom he said "looked the savage". Around the same time, *Longman's School Geography for Australasia* was using similar terms describing Māori as "the most intelligent of all natives whom the Europeans met with on the Australasian colonies" (Chisholm, 1901, p. 113). Pākehā society's patronising praise of Māori and pejorative perceptions of indigenous Australians were coupled with self-congratulatory accounts of just settlement and an example of noble, enlightened, and benign colonisation. Particularly instructive are the accounts of the colonial wars that are found in materials used in schools such as this comment in a turn of the century school reader, in which a Māori boy is the interlocuteur for a grateful race:

> The men of our race sometimes complain because the white people have taken away so much of their land; but I am sure that our teacher is right when he tells us that we have more land left than we can use. He says, too, that the white men have given us peace and order, and a thousand blessings that we could never have enjoyed but for their coming to settle among us. (*Imperial Readers*, 1899, p. 20)

Even where it was acknowledged that colonial wars had taken place, they were couched in imagery of mutual respect and admiration. This can be seen in the following passage from the primary school text, *Our Nation's Story*:

> You will also, if you hear the story aright, feel a warm admiration for the courage and determination of the Maoris against whom we fought in some of the Maori wars. It is because of our great respect for the Maoris that white man and brown man now live side by side as friends and fellow citizens of New Zealand. (1929, pp. 11–12)

The Māori were categorised as people "we" fought against. The victors, who wrote the history, present themselves as magnanimous, displaying a respectful and admiring view of the vanquished. O'Malley (2016) traces the origin of this discourse to 1914 and the 50th anniversary of Ōrākau, the most famous battle of the Waikato conflict. An official ceremony organised to mark the occasion was attended by a very large Pākehā crowd and, not surprisingly, very few Māori. *The New Zealand Herald* described Ōrākau as representing "the final acceptance of British mana by a heroic and warlike native people" and said that it had given rise to "a just and generous reciprocity which is everywhere regarded as an example to the civilised world". Continuing in a tone that one might expect in the after-match speech of a gracious captain of a winning sports team as competitors from both sides shared a drink at the clubrooms, *The New Zealand Herald* wrote:

> This freedom, this equality, may be unhesitatingly ascribed to the possession by the Maori of the heroic qualities which make Orakau historic and to the whole-hearted appreciation of those qualities by the Pakeha people. ('The fruit of Orakau'. *The New Zealand Herald*, 31 March, 1914)

O'Malley (2016) identifies this event and the official version of history that emerged from it as the origin of the pervasive national myth that New Zealand had the greatest race relations in the world. As McGeorge (1993) noted, this all contributed to the idea that New Zealanders told ourselves and others that

> race relations in New Zealand were a shining example to the rest of the Empire; and white New Zealanders in their dealings with Maoris once again displayed the purity of their heritage, their sense of justice and their characteristically British appreciation of courage and chivalrous conduct in war. (p. 71)

The middle decade of the 20th century saw a massive urbanisation of Māori. The departure of the youth led to the "breaking up [of] what was left of the papakāinga which early colonists had so fervently wished to destroy" (L. T. Smith, 1996, p. 348). In the cities, state assistance for Māori housing involved "pepper-potting", a practice of allocating housing to ensure that Māori were relatively evenly sprinkled among houses occupied by non-Māori (Woods, 2002). This exacted a high price, as Walker (1979) stated:

> Without grandparents and elders, the traditional teachers and minders of children in the extended family arrangement, the urban family unit is culturally cut off and disorganized ... They know they are stuck with minority status as Maoris but they know little or nothing about Maori values and pride in their cultural heritage. (p. 38)

The urbanisation of Māori led to more Māori being enrolled in public schools than in Māori schools which were eventually incorporated into the mainstream schooling system in 1969. Throughout the post-War period, the long economic boom and the shortage of labour—even unskilled labour—meant that the standards of living of Māori continued to rise despite their educational failure. Although there were some aspects of 'Māoritanga' incorporated into the state schools as early as the 1930s, the emphasis remained on the assimilation and later the integration of Māori into Pākehā society.

In 1966, the study of the Treaty of Waitangi and the New Zealand Wars, and much more of New Zealand's colonial history, were effectively removed from the school curriculum in New Zealand by the decision of the Education Department to introduce a new history prescription for School Certificate, in which the history of New Zealand began in 1870 (Evison, 2010, p. 404). Educational resources were produced to support the new curriculum which contained nothing of the important period immediately following the signing of the Treaty, a move that turned New Zealand into what Evison called "a nation without a memory".

Although primary schooling had been free and compulsory for all New Zealand children since 1894, the education of Māori and non-Māori in the same institutions reinforced the prevailing myths of meritocracy. Although education actually meant Pākehā education, the school system was presented as neutral. Explanations for Māori educational under-achievement relied on cultural deficit theory. The UNESCO report into New Zealand education demonstrated this theory with its comment that the lack of Māori representation in the professions in New Zealand was largely because "not all Maori take advantage of the educational opportunities that are available" (UNESCO, 1972, p. 67). The fault lay not with the education system but with the Māori who failed to make use of the opportunities it offered.

New Zealand society confronted by Māori radicalism

Māori radicals were having none of that. In the late 1960s, young Māori started to become politically aware and active through groups such as Ngā Tamatoa. They analysed the wide inequalities between Māori and Pākehā and located the problem with the way Aotearoa New Zealand society was organised. From the outset, the education system was a target of the activists' criticism with one group describing it as a site of "cultural murder" (Walker, 1990, p. 210). The power of institutional racism had created a newly urbanised generation of Māori who were largely cut off from their Māori heritage but also unable to succeed in Pākehā society. Many of this generation had one or more parents who could speak te reo Māori but didn't. This was a time when te reo was largely absent from public discourse and was seen as an impediment to educational success.

The radicalism of Māori activists was based on a recognition that the entire foundation of Aotearoa New Zealand society was fundamentally unjust and that, without radical change, Māori would be condemned to exist only in its margins and within the constraints that were the product of historical and ongoing injustice. The Māori activism that emerged and grew in strength through the 1970s saw the emergence of a radical reassessment of Aotearoa New Zealand society and the myths and ideology that sustained it. It was the beginning of Māori refusing to accept that their future lay in trying to improve their position within a society that Pākehā had created. In addition to protests and marches, the new generation of Māori activists was undeterred by legal sanctions. Led by Ngāti Whātua, the occupation of Takaparawhā (Bastion Point)—an area of contested land in Auckland that was destined to become an upmarket housing development—began in 1977 and lasted 506 days before it was eventually ended by mass eviction of the protestors by a combined police and army operation that resulted in 222 arrests, the largest number of arrests for a political event in modern times (Locke, 2012).

The second largest number of people arrested for political reasons on one day was during protests against the Springbok rugby tour in 1981. The anti-apartheid movement mobilised unprecedented numbers of people in months of protest activities. With such a wide cross-section of people involved in and transformed by the anti-tour protests, many people's attitudes towards radical political action and radical views changed. Māori activists who saw large numbers of non-Māori taking political action including breaking the law to make a stand against racism in South Africa began to question where the commitment of those people was to fighting racism in New Zealand. An underlying theme of 1981 was that the mostly white anti-tour movement was against racism and against the system of apartheid that the racist white South African people and government were imposing on the black majority. At the time, however, Pākehā consciousness of racism was very low. Few would have considered themselves or their country racist. While it was clear how white South Africans were benefiting from apartheid, it was much less clear to the Pākehā protestors how they were also benefiting from colonisation. Most of what people thought they knew about New Zealand's colonial past was distorted by the various fragments that were used to construct the national myths that all New Zealanders had been raised on. Many Pākehā had had very little first-hand interaction with Māori and where their lives did intersect in Pākehā society—at the pub, on a worksite, on the sports field—they commonly encountered the popularised image of Māori as fun, friendly, and gregarious.

The politicisation of Māori shocked Pākehā society to the core. The progressive Pākehā community first felt the full force of the radical Māori challenge in their institutions in 1979 at the United Women's Convention. The flagship national gathering of what was a big, vibrant feminist movement in New Zealand was disrupted by radical Māori women who, saying that they had been excluded, branded the gathering a "white women's convention" (Dann, 1985, p.23). The challenge to Pākehā feminists was just the beginning. Through the 1980s, no progressive organisation was left untouched by this rewriting of the political script as all over the country groups were confronted about where they positioned themselves in relation to Māori political demands. Peace groups, environmental groups, aid organisations, trade unions, women's groups, and many others were unable to avoid the issue. Nothing could prepare the membership of these progressive groups for the politicised Māori who were waking up to the reality of colonialism and realising the extent of its legacy of dispossession and alienation. Māori experienced institutional exclusion not only from agencies of the state, but also from nongovernmental organisations and community groups, many of which saw themselves as upholding principles that they considered supportive and inclusive of Māori aspirations. Educated, liberal, well-meaning Pākehā were shocked to realise how little they understood the cultural politics of their own personal history and that of their country. Juliet Seule, a participant at the 1979 United Women's Convention, expressed a common feeling when she said "I felt ashamed of my ignorance of their cause … I had neglected the genuine oppressed minority group of the convention" (Seule, 1979, p. 22). Feelings of shame and guilt were common responses by progressive Pākehā as they became aware of the nature and impact of settler colonialism. For many Māori, the response was anger. The mix was volatile.

As the myth of New Zealand's harmonious race relations unraveled, Pākehā individuals and groups found themselves in largely uncharted territory. Even those who were immediately seized by the truth and urgency of what they were being confronted with struggled to respond in an adequate and appropriate way. Although the term did not exist at the time, many turned to what is now referred to as "epistemic exploitation". That is, they expected Māori to invest their time and energy educating Pākehā about the nature of the problem and the solutions. Berenstain describes epistemic exploitation as "occurring when privileged persons compel marginalized persons to produce an education or explanation about the nature of the oppression they face" (2016, p. 570). Although for a while some Māori activists did run decolonisation workshops for Pākehā, the message was clear; that the role of Pākehā in the decolonisation project was to alert other Pākehā to the situation and work at an individual and structural level to identify and transform the attitudes, policies, and practices that were preventing a just resolution of the country's colonial legacy.

Māori had their own urgent issues to attend to, a priority of which was education. The educational underachievement of Māori had been documented as early as 1960 in the Hunn Report which described it as a "statistical blackout". By the time the Department of Education introduced a cultural awareness programme called Taha Māori, few saw it as the answer. It introduced "aspects of Māori language and culture" in the hope that they would "be a normal part of the school environment with which all pupils and staff should feel comfortable and at ease" (Department of Education, 1984). Taha Māori was never embraced as passionately as it was rejected. Māori educationalists such as Linda Tuhiwai Smith referred to the introduction of Māoritanga into schools as "tokenism", arguing that

> it reduced a culture to a set of classroom topics, and complex values could be reduced to short definitions. Māoritanga failed to address the deeper issues which were being discussed concurrently in Māori politics, and it failed to address the educational tendencies which continued to undermine Māori language, knowledge and culture". (L. T. Smith, 1996, p. 365)

Graham Hingangaroa Smith branded it a "sticking plaster solution" which was "a Pākehā defined, initiated and controlled policy which serves the needs and interests of Pākehā people" (G. H. Smith, 1990, p. 183). Others criticised it from a conservative perspective. The Concerned Parents Association, for example, called it "politically-motivated social engineering" which they said would lead to racial divisions and "a strife-ridden society" (cited in Spoonley, 1988, p. 56). The polarisation of responses was an indication of growing social discord that was being provoked by the political assertiveness of Māori.

A similar level of polarisation emerged with the launch in 1982 of Kōhanga Reo, the first step towards what became a comprehensive movement in kaupapa Māori education. This Māori initiative was designed to address the crisis in the loss of te reo Māori, the consequences of acculturation and assimilation, Māori educational underachievement, and the loss of Māori self-determination in relation to the education of their own children. It profoundly reshaped the educational, cultural, and political landscape. However, like any initiative that is focused specifically on Māori needs and is not fully inclusive of other

New Zealanders, it was branded as "separatist" and interpreted as anathema to the concept of nationhood to which some New Zealanders continue to cling dearly.

The separatist label is commonly applied to attempts by Māori to question and challenge their forced inclusion into a notion of one New Zealand in which they are not permitted to define their own participation. This opposition emanates from organised political groups such as Hobson's Pledge which advances a view first popularised in the Orewa speech of Don Brash (2004) as leader of the National Party. As King (2012) points out, this notion is underpinned by an ideology of meritocracy which views everyone as equal and therefore holds that nobody should receive special privileges.

> The egalitarian idea behind the one-people discourse obscures the fact that proponents of the one-people discourse tend to envisage an ideal context in which everyone behaves and treats each other like Pākehā, while ignoring that the advantages denied to non-Pākehā people mean we do not all start out on a level playing field. (p. 51)

But it can also be found clearly articulated in the comments of individual parents reflecting on the schooling of their children (Doerr, 2004).

The past and the future

Societies divided around their experience of colonialism and racism are also divided about history. Dillon (2017) advocates leaving the past behind, arguing that focusing on the historical damage done by settler colonial societies can be extraordinarily damaging and sap their motivation to make a difference in their lives. This perspective characterises those who continue to make appeal to Treaty guarantees as being "stuck in grievance mode" and motivated by the financial returns available from what has been called the grievance industry. Others warn of the dangers of societies being unaware of their colonial past. Stuart Hall refers to a "profound historical forgetfulness … the loss of historical memory, a kind of historical amnesia, a decisive mental repression which has overtaken the British people about race and Empire" (1978, p. 26). Others call it racial amnesia or "white amnesia" (Hesse, 1997, p. 91). Jackson (2019) goes further, arguing that "in this country, there has been a deliberate misremembering of history that has obscured the reality of what colonization really was and is".

Knowing more about New Zealand's colonial past is an important first step, and one to which the education system was challenged to commit itself. In 2015, the New Zealand History Teachers' Association called for colonial history to be taught in schools. Two years later, a 12,000-strong petition organised by pupils at Ōtorohanga College was presented to Parliament calling for the inclusion of teaching about the New Zealand Wars as a compulsory part of the curriculum. An historian from the Ministry of Education, which opposed the petition, made the point that many teachers would find it confronting, challenging, and risky to teach this content not least because it "represents a big gap in their own education and training" (Watters, 2017). In 2019, the Prime Minister, Jacinda Ardern, announced that by 2022, New Zealand history, including colonial history, will be taught in all New Zealand schools (Ardern, 2019).

A 2015 survey of secondary school maths teachers in Auckland revealed that there were clear racial biases in their expectations of pupils and a persistent resorting to deficit explanations for the underachievement of Māori and Pacific students, while rarely applying deficit theories to underachieving Pākehā or Asian students (Turner, Rubie-Davies, & Webber, 2015). This is consistent with the 2018 findings of the Children's Commissioner and the School Trustees Association which canvassed the views of 1,678 children and young people. Māori and Pacific students reported experiences of racism they encountered from other students and from their teachers whom they feel judge them, underestimate them, and even set them up for failure (New Zealand School Trustees Association & Office of the Children's Commissioner, 2018, pp. 18–21). The report used the word "racism" to describe the experiences relayed by these children because that was the word the children used themselves. However, as Rata (2017) points out, palatable euphemisms for racism are commonly deployed such as the Department for Corrections referring to "unconscious bias", the Police conceding "a disparity in the way we applied some of our discretion" and, in reference to the example above, "negative cognitive bias in teachers' judgements" (Rata, 2017).

The New Zealand education system has been built on and sustained by institutional racism since its inception. Most of the teachers that system employs were themselves educated in ways that were informed by institutional racism. This makes the task of addressing the sorts of concerns cited above very challenging. The sort of educational transformation that is required which goes well beyond that which can be transmitted by textbooks and formal instruction has become known as decolonising education. According to Norris (2019), engaging in this form of education calls for "innovative pedagogical strategies that examine the underlying beliefs that operate to reject or constrain one's understanding of institutional and structural racist practices" (p. 3).

There is now widespread acceptance at a policy level of the need for a bicultural orientation to public policy, including education. This is, in part, a process of identifying and removing practices, policies, and beliefs that assume the universality and superiority of Pākehā knowledge over Māori knowledge and is to be encouraged. These assumptions operate at a deep level and are not easy for individuals or institutions to confront. However, there is also a tendency within bicultural discourse to package things into a palatable nonthreatening vision that is less likely to be contested—"the promise of a better nation: a nation not only free of guilt but harmonious, a happy society without the scourge of racial tension" (Kolig, 2004, pp. 97–98). There is also a danger that some forms of biculturalism can collapse into versions of cultural appropriation and careerism. Norris warns that without a critical grappling with the ongoing impact of colonialism's legacy, cultural inclusion can be reduced to little more than being "viewed or used as a good to be consumed by whites to fulfil an individual desire or to market themselves as more attractive in the market place" (Norris, 2019, p. 8) Further, as Jones (1999) put it, the pursuit of cross-cultural understanding needs to avoid the "colonising impulses" of seeking to know the other and focus instead on "a deeper understanding of one's own culture, society and history, and their political relation to those of others, [which] is crucial to any desirable future and any just structural social change" (p. 314).

Beyond biculturalism, there is also a need for a decolonising education. This involves helping Pākehā to have a consciousness of their own assumptions and perspectives in order to recognise and examine their origins and identify elements of privilege that may have remained hidden or disguised. This sort of decolonising education helps to address what King refers to as whiteness gaining "a significant sort of power in New Zealand", a power that in her view is related to a lack of awareness "of the way that educational, religious, legal, political, social, media and cultural institutions may be organised to suit Pākehā perspectives to the disadvantage of non-Pākehā people" (King, 2012, p. 38). The advantage of this approach is that it broadens the inquiry beyond a question of what can be done about Māori education towards an orientation that tasks us all with the responsibility to create an education system that aims to meet the needs of everyone.

In her analysis of "the invisible knapsack" of white privilege, Peggy McIntosh says that she did not see herself as racist because she "was taught to recognise racism only in individual acts of meanness by members of (her) group, never in systems conferring racial dominance on her group from birth" (McIntosh, 2018, p. 98). What she did not see was the way that her whiteness made her feel at home in the world, escape fear, anxiety, insult, or injury, not having to hide or be in disguise or feel sick or crazy, and avoid penalties and dangers that others suffer. As Jackson (2019) says, "they might acknowledge certain discrete injustices done to Māori but not the overarching injustice of colonization itself".

The task of unpacking the knapsack, examining its contents, and working out how educators can individually and collectively use it as a starting point is a challenging one. Its need was identified and articulated as early as 1987 by Nairn and more recently by Milne (2019). Each offered conceptual clarity and practical suggestions for what is required and how we might work towards it. In her article identifying white supremacy in the classroom, Milne puts the challenge in these terms:

> We need to be looking towards pedagogies that intentionally critique, in fact are brutally honest about, our existing systems that perpetuate and foster linguistic, literate, and cultural pluralism as part of schooling for positive social transformation, that critically enrich strengths rather than replace deficits and that deliberately de-centre whiteness and offer potential for challenging and dismantling racism and oppression. (Milne, 2019, n.p.)

On 12 September 2019, the day it was announced that New Zealand history would be a compulsory part of the curriculum, legislation was introduced in Parliament to pardon the Tūhoe prophet, Rua Kēnana. At the same time, the occupation of Ihumātao was continuing to challenge the legacy of colonial conquest and dispossession. Neither the pardon nor the occupation nor any of the other ongoing unresolved issues of our past can be understood in ignorance of the historical contexts that gave rise to them. New Zealand's colonial past is inextricably linked to the present. The decision to require New Zealand's formal education system to address the most challenging issues of the country's colonial past was brave and important. It can be a radically transformational and inclusive move, a step towards decolonizing our education system and society. It provides an opportunity for future generations of New Zealanders to consider in an informed way a basic question of national identity–who do we think we are?

Recommendation for further reading

Hutchings, J., & Lee-Morgan, J. (2016). *Decolonisation in Aotearoa: Education, research and practice.* Wellington: NZCER Press.

References

Ardern, J. (2019). *NZ history to be taught in all schools.* Retrieved from: https://www.beehive.govt.nz/release/nz-history-be-taught-all-schools.

Barrington, J. M., & Beaglehole, T. H. (1974). *Māori schools in a changing society: An historical review.* Wellington: New Zealand Council for Educational Research.

Berenstain, N. (2016). Epistemic exploitation. *Ergo: An Open Access Journal of Philosophy, 3*, 569–590.

Brash, D. (2004). *Nationhood.* Retrieved from: http://www.scoop.co.nz/stories/PA0401/S00220.htm

Chisholm, G. G. (1901). *Longman's School Geography for Australasia.* London, UK: Longman.

Department of Education. (1984). *Taha Māori: Suggestions for getting started.* Wellington: Author.

Dann, C. (1985). *Up from under: Women and liberation in New Zealand 1970–1985.* Wellington: Allen and Unwin.

Dillon, A. (2017). *On Leaving the Past Behind.* Retrieved from: https://quadrant.org.au/opinion/bennelong-papers/2017/08/leaving-past-behind/

Doerr, N. M. (2004). Desired division, disavowed division: An analysis of the labeling of the bilingual unit as separatist in an Aotearoa/New Zealand school. *Anthropology & Education Quarterly, 35*(2), 233–253.

Evison, H. C. (2010). *New Zealand racism in the making. The life and times of Walter Mantell.* Christchurch: Panuitia.

Freire, P. (2000). *Pedagogy of the oppressed.* New York, NY: Continuum.

Hall, S. (1978). Racism and reaction. In *Commission for Racial Equality. Five views of multi-racial Britain* (pp. 23–35). London, UK: Commission for Racial Equality.

Hesse, B. (1997). White governmentality: Urbanism, nationalism, racism. In S. Westwood & J. M. Williams (Eds.), *Imagining cities. Scripts, signs, memory* (pp. 93–110). London, UK: Routledge.

Hunn, J. K. (1961). *Report on the Department of Māori Affairs: with statistical supplement, 24 August 1960.* Wellington: Government Printer.

Imperial readers: Second reader. (1899). Christchurch: Whitcombe and Tombs.

Irvine, R. F., & Alpers, O. T. J. (1902). *The progress of New Zealand in the Nineteenth Century.* Edinburgh, UK: W and R Chambers.

Jackson, M. (1992). The Treaty and the word: The colonization of Māori philosophy. In G. Oddie & R. W. Perrett (Eds), *Justice, ethics and New Zealand society* (pp. 1–10). Auckland: Oxford University Press.

Jackson, M. (2018). *Respecting what we're prepared to share and not share.* Retrieved from: https://e-tangata.co.nz/comment-and-analysis/respecting-what-were-prepared-to-share

Jackson, M. (2019). *The connection between white supremacy and colonisation.* Retrieved from: https://e-tangata.co.nz/comment-and-analysis/the-connection-between-white-supremacy/

Jones, A. (1999). The limits of cross-cultural dialogue: Pedagogy, desire, and absolution in the classroom. *Educational Theory, 49*(3), 299–316.

King, M. (2012). *The Flesh Coloured Bandaid: Whiteness, dominance and Pākehā cultural normativity in television news.* Unpublished doctoral thesis, The University of Auckland. Available at: https://researchspace.auckland.ac.nz/bitstream/handle/2292/20324/whole.pdf

Kipling, R. (1998) The white man's burden. *Peace Review. 10*(3), 311–312.

Kolig, E. (2004). Deconstructing the Waitangi Treaty narrative: Democracy, cultural pluralism, and political myth making in New Zealand/Aotearoa. *Sites: A Journal of Social Anthropology and Cultural Studies, 1*(2), 84–118.

Locke, C. (2012). *Workers in the margins. Union radicals in post-war New Zealand.* Wellington: Bridget Williams Books.

Māori Perspective Advisory Committee. (1988). *Puao-te-ata-tū*. Wellington: Department of Social Welfare.

McGeorge, C. (1993). Race, empire and the Maori in the New Zealand primary school curriculum 1880–1940", In J. A. Mangan (Ed.), *The Imperial Curriculum: Racial images and education in the British colonial experience* (pp. 64–78). London, UK: Routledge.

McIntosh, P. (2018). White privilege and male privilege. In Lee, J. & Shaw, S. M. (Eds.), *Women's voices, feminist visions: Classic and contemporary readings* (pp. 91–98). London, UK: McGraw-Hill.

Mikaere, A. (2005). Introduction. In A. Mikaere (Ed.), *Yearbook of New Zealand Jurisprudence, Special Issue, 8*(2), 1–35. Retrieved from: https://www.waikato.ac.nz/__data/assets/pdf_file/0003/32799/Yearbook-of-NZ-Jurisprudence-vol-8-issue-2-2005.pdf

Milne, A. (2019). *White supremacy in our classrooms.* Retrieved from: https://educationcentral.co.nz/opinion-ann-milne-white-supremacy-in-our-classrooms

Nairn, M. (1987). *Taha Māori—The Māori dimension in education.* Retrieved from: https://trc.org.nz/content/taha-Māori-Māori-dimension-education

Norris, A. (2019). Discussing contemporary racial justice in academic spaces: Minimizing epistemic exploitation while neutralizing white fragility. In S. Ratuva (Ed.), *The Palgrave handbook of ethnicity* (pp. 1–14). Singapore: Palgrave Macmillan.

New Zealand School Trustees Assn & Office of the Commissioner for Children. (2018). *Education matters to me: Key insights.* Wellington: Author. Retrieved from: https://www.occ.org.nz/publications/reports/education-matters-to-me-key-insights/

O'Malley, V. (2016). *The great war for New Zealand: Waikato 1800–2000.* Wellington: Bridget Williams Books.

Our Nation's Story: A Course of British History: Standard IV. (1929). Christchurch: Whitcombe and Tombs Primary History Series.

Our Nation's Story: A Course of British History: Standard VI. (1931). Christchurch: Whitcombe and Tombs Primary History Series.

Phillips, J. (2009). *The New Zealanders–Māorilanders.* Te Ara. Retrieved from: http://www.TeAra.govt.nz/en/the-new-zealanders/5

Rata, A. (2017). *Watered-down biculturalism—How avoiding the 'r-word' undermines our liberation movement.* http://www.scoop.co.nz/stories/HL1705/S00017/how-avoiding-the-r-word-undermines-our-liberation-movement.htm

Sayyid, S. (2000). Bad faith, anti-essentialism, universalism and Islamism. In A. Brah & A.E. Coombes (Eds.). *Hybridity and its discontents. Politics, science, culture* (pp. 257–271), London, UK: Routledge.

Seule, J. (1979). After the Convention's over: Reports on the United Women's Convention 1979. *Broadsheet 70*, 20–22. Retrieved from: https://broadsheet.auckland.ac.nz/docs/1979/Broadsheet-1979-070.pdf

Simon, J. (1994). Historical perspectives on education. In E. Coxon, K. Jenkins, J. Marshall, & L. Massey (Eds.), *The politics of learning and teaching in Aotearoa/New Zealand* (pp. 34–81). Palmerston North: Dunmore.

Smith, G. H. (1990). Taha Māori: Pākehā capture. In J. Codd, R. Harker & R. Nash (Eds.), *Political issues in New Zealand education* (pp. 183–197). Palmerston North: Dunmore.

Smith, L. T. (1996). *Ngā aho o te kakahu matauranga: The multiple layers of struggle by Māori in education*. Unpublished doctoral thesis, The University of Auckland.

Smith, L. T., & Reid, P. (2000). *Māori research development: Kaupapa Māori principles and practices*. Wellington: Te Puni Kokiri.

Spoonley, P. (1988). *Racism and ethnicity*. Auckland: Oxford University Press.

Tuck, E., & Yang, K. W. (2012). Decolonization is not a metaphor. *Decolonization, Indigeneity, Education & Society, 1*, 1–40.

Turner, H., Rubie-Davies, C. M., & Webber, M. (2015). Teacher expectations, ethnicity and the achievement gap. *New Zealand Journal of Educational Studies, 50*(1), 55–69.

UNESCO. (1972). *Compulsory education in New Zealand* (2nd ed.). Paris, France: Author.

Waitangi Tribunal. (2014) *He whakaputanga me te Tiriti. The declaration and the Treaty: The report on stage 1 of the Te Paparahi o Te Raki inquiry*. Retrieved from: https://waitangitribunal.govt.nz/assets/Documents/Publications/WT-Part-1-Report-on-stage-1-of-the-Te-Paparahi-o-Te-Raki-inquiry.pdf.

Walker, R. (1979). *The urban Māori. He matapuna: Some Māori perspectives*. Wellington: New Zealand Planning Council.

Walker, R. (1990). *Ka whawhai tonu mātou*. Auckland: Penguin Books.

Walker, R. (2016). Reclaiming Māori education. In J. Hutchings & J. Lee-Morgan, *Decolonisation in Aotearoa: Education, research and practice* (pp. 19–38). Wellington: NZCER Press.

Watters, S. (2017). *Should teaching the New Zealand Wars be compulsory?* Retrieved from: https://nzhistory.govt.nz/classroom/conversations/new-zealand-wars/should-teaching-new-zealand-wars-compulsory

Weber, M. (1947). *The theory of social and economic organisation*. A.M. Henderson and T. Parsons, trans. New York, NY: Oxford University Press. (Original work published 1904).

Wolfe, P. (1999). *Settler colonialism and the transformation of anthropology*. London, UK: A&C Black.

Woods, M. C. (2002). *Integrating the nation: Gendering Māori urbanisation and integration, 1942–1969*. Unpublished doctoral thesis, University of Canterbury, Christchurch.

Chapter 4
Sociology of education

Annelies Kamp

Introduction

Sociology involves the study of social relationships and institutions. The sociology of education is a contested body of work—"a diverse, messy, dynamic, somewhat elusive and invariably disputatious field of work" (Apple, Ball, & Gandin, 2010, p. 1)—that is, in itself, a 'construction' (Apple, 1996), forged by debates between unequal actors in educational contexts (including, but not limited to, the academy). What unifies this discipline is the purpose of understanding how social action is shaped by, and shapes, cultural and social structures in a given time and place, or across time and place, and what the consequences of this shaping might be for individuals, communities, and societies. Within this field of study, the sociology of education is concerned with how relationships between factors of the social world—political, cultural, economic—and schools "affect the way people think, live and work, their place in society and their chances for success or failure" (Sadovnik, 2007b, p. xiii). In particular, it examines the educational achievement and outcomes that flow from individual experiences in education systems, and the personal, and political, implications of variations in achievement and outcomes.

This chapter provides a necessarily limited overview of theory and method in the sociology of education. It does not claim to give a comprehensive overview of the field. Even if the boundaries of such a diverse field were able to be fixed, such an endeavour would be beyond the limits of any one chapter. However, I do introduce some key theorists of sociology—the 'founding fathers'— and flag the work of those who have sought to open spaces for readings from positions other than that of the white male voice, including women, people of colour, and people living with diverse abilities. This more recent scholarship has challenged the conditions of the production of knowledge about 'the social', in productive ways. The section closes with a consideration of the potential contribution of postmodern sensibilities for the sociology of education.

The chapter then moves to consider a particular shift in contemporary global education policy networks. Since the latter years of the 20th century, in a context of globalisation, there has been an increasing uptake of various forms of collaboration in education systems in pursuit of more equitable educational achievement and outcomes. The genesis of this policy direction in the global context, and its manifestation in the local context as Kāhui Ako | Communities of Learning, with be sketched. I will then consider the insights that sociology of education can offer to Kāhui Ako. Contemporary social theory will be used to imagine a more powerful mobilisation of the policy agenda through consideration of the role of human and nonhuman actors, in realising the potential of the forms of capital that exist in, and can be generated by, collaborative endeavours.

Sociology of education in retrospect and prospect

While the sociology of education has schooling as its predominant focus, and while accepting that 'education' and 'schooling' often slip in usage to be applied interchangeably, such a slippage is, for my purposes here, unproductive. On the one hand, 'schooling' privileges learning that happens in various kinds of classrooms (see Chapter 14 in this collection) and loses sight of the learning that happens between and beyond those spaces. While non-school sites of learning have long been acknowledged—although often not particularly understood or valued (e.g., Kamp & Black, 2014)—they are increasingly a core component of the process of formal education in the context of 21st century education. On the other hand, a singular focus on schools in isolation makes excessive demands on what schools and teachers—individually or collectively—can achieve. Given the contemporary focus on interorganisational collaboration, education can and does happen in the context of formalised learning collaborations that reach beyond classrooms, in pursuit of the wellbeing, and optimal achievement, of all students.

Education for social cohesion

Any overview of the sociology of education must reference the work of Émile Durkheim, Professor of the Science of Education and Sociology at the University of Paris from 1902. Durkheim was the first person to study the sociology of education systematically. In part, this was a consequence of the time and place in which he undertook his work: the breakdown of a sense of national unity in France in the later decades of the 19th century and, in part, the role of an increasing individualism that could be traced to the French Revolution of the late 18th century. Using social realism as his lens—a belief that social realities exist externally to the individual and can be studied objectively—Durkheim argued that these external realities had causal powers over individual acts (Morrison, 2006). In part, this power was exerted by a shared consciousness that was held in common by the citizens of a given society. Thus, social groups such as clans, families, or religions played a functional role in uniting members of a particular society through the creation of a "collective consciousness" (Durkheim, 1893).

Education played a role in reinforcing social cohesion—the degree to which individuals and society are integrated. For Durkheim, two types of cohesion reflected different forms of society: primitive (or mechanical) and industrialised (or organic). In primitive societies, given a high level of homogeneity, collective consciousness would form through shared systems of belief, often religious. This provided for strong levels of cohesion and, thereby, responsibility to the broader community. However, industrialised contexts were more complex and more individualistic and, accordingly, needed the state to impose rules and norms to ensure individual differences could be resolved, and cohesion built (Durkheim, 1897). In the process of this, a state of 'anomie' can be experienced where imposed norms do not enable individuals to meet their individual needs or societal goals. Formal education systems are central to the perpetuation of society values and beliefs, regulating society, and contributing to stability and wellbeing. For Durkheim, "educational transformations are always the result and the symptom of the social transformations in terms of which they are explained" (Durkheim, 2006, p. 166). Change happens in social institutions, such as educational systems, because societal changes—in ideas and needs—emerge to which the old system can no longer respond. These were 'functionalist' theories of education that emphasised the interdependence of the components of the social system as a kind of machine to 'make society work'. As a paradigm for the sociology of education, they were the dominant until the 1960s, when theories focused on how schools served the needs, and generated the sustained educational achievement, of some societal groups over others became dominant (Sadovnik, 2007a).

Education, conflict, and social change[1]

This shift in the sociology of education to a concern with conflicting needs—and of the role of education in social change—has 19th century German-born Karl Marx as its "intellectual founder" (Sadovnik, 2007a, p. 6). Marx, writing with his countryman Friedrich Engels, argued that human societies develop through class struggle, and education played a role in this struggle given its close connection with social class. In capitalism as an economic system, there is conflict between the ruling classes (the 'bourgeoisie', as controllers of the means of production) and the working classes (the 'proletariat', who enable the bourgeoisie by selling their labour power in return for wages). The relationship between the classes is, for Marx and Engels, inherently antagonistic. Schooling, as a system, was used to perpetuate bourgeois ideologies; the ruling class creates an ideology, which becomes accepted by society as a whole, not least through its inculcation in the minds of the young through education. Yet, that education also offers the opportunity for social change:

> And your education! Is not that also social, and determined by the social conditions under which you educate, by the intervention, direct or indirect, of society, by means of schools, etc.? The Communists have not invented the intervention of society in education; they do but seek to alter the character of that intervention, and to rescue education from the influence of the ruling class. (Marx & Engels, 2017/1848, p. 21)

Accordingly, in the measures that they present to change the mode of production, Marx and Engels argued that all children should receive free, and equal, education, in public schools (Marx & Engels, 2017/1848, p. 27). While the overtly economic focus of Marxism has led to claims of over-determination, it has retained resonance for 20th century sociologists of education (e.g., Bowles

---

1 Given the limits of this chapter, I am not engaging with a third group of 'interactionist' theories, which extend the functionalist and conflict arguments. See, for example, the body of work of Erving Goffman.

& Gintis, 1976). For Max Weber, while conflict was accepted as central to the structure of society, this was not solely related to class conflict; Weber argued that status cultures, bureaucracy, and bureaucratic thinking were at work in setting the limits and possibilities for educational reform (Roth & Wittich, 1978; Weber, 1947).

What occurs in the course of the provision of public education is, for the conflict theorists, a matter of contestation, as is surveyed in the discussion on curriculum in Chapter 6 of this collection. This concern with the 'what' of education is the focus of the extensive body of work of British linguist Basil Bernstein in the 20th century. Bernstein argued that individuals occupy different positions within society, each position having specific patterns of language use which influenced the ability of group members to succeed in public schools. In this, Bernstein argued that education should be about effective democracy and three interrelated, pedagogic democratic rights (Bernstein, 1996, p. 6): the right to enhancement, including the "right to the means of critical understanding and to new possibilities", the right to inclusion, and the right to participation. Theory and analysis were central to the achievement of these rights, having two key roles:

> The first is to grasp the real, as it is ... But the real itself is to be understood not in a static sense but in a dynamic one; every actually existing real nurtures within it a series of logical alternative possible futures. This second, pre-eminent role of theory is to grasp the real as the realization of only one of a series of logical possibilities. That is, the task is always not only to map an existing state of affairs but to understand that state as an actualized possibility, with determinate features of variation, alongside other virtual possible worlds with equally determinate features of variation. It is these possible worlds, when delineated, which offer themselves up for political choice and action. (Muller, 2004, p. 3)

This possibility of "other virtual possible worlds" is, according to Zygmunt Bauman (1990, p. 44), increasingly difficult in Western education systems. Bauman suggests that modern schools reflect society's 'solid' form, a neoliberal, vocationalist agenda, and a belief in unproblematic meritocracy through sustained educational engagement, rather than reflecting the ambivalence that sits at the heart of our late modern society:

> Among the millions of those punished, there are hundreds of thousands of [young people] who believed, or were given no choice but to behave as if they

believed, that the room at the top is boundless, that a university diploma is all you need to be let in, and that once you were there the repayment of the loans you took out along the way would be childishly easy … They are now facing the prospect of scribbling innumerable job applications which are hardly ever answered, of infinitely long unemployment, and of the acceptance of wobbly jobs without a future, miles below the top room, as their sole alternative.

This notion of the exchange value of sustained engagement with education heralds a concern with education as a form of capital.

Education and the forms of capital

In this section, I am focusing on three sociological concepts of particular concern to the sociology of education in the context of the turn to collaborative policy surveyed in the next section of the chapter: habitus, cultural capital, and social capital (Bourdieu, 1977, 1986; Coleman, 1988). Habitus is a concept that is most commonly connected with French sociologist Pierre Bourdieu, notwithstanding its origins in the work of Aristotle and its appearance in various sociologies over time. For Bourdieu (1977), habitus provided a way to engage with the tension between agency and structure; with how particular patterns of behaviour in given social classes—speech, conduct, dress, manner, values, and so on—are instilled over time by everyday social experiences within families and peer groups. Habitus operates below the level of consciousness, accumulating over time and providing individuals with an intuitive sense of how to act in the contexts they encounter, including educational contexts. Given these contexts are shaped by the culture of the dominant group in society—the group that control access to resources—those whose habitus aligns with the "field"[2] benefit in terms of their "feel for the game" (Bourdieu, 1990). In schooling, differences in achievement are often attributed to individual characteristics and ability rather than being attributed to "the greater or lesser affinity between class cultural habits and the demands of the educational system or the criteria which define success within it" (Bourdieu & Passeron, 1977, p. 22). While Bourdieu's early work on habitus has been subject to criticism for its perceived determinism, his later work (Bourdieu, 1999) illustrates the potential for

---

2 A "field" is a system of formal and informal norms in a particular social sphere of activity, where certain forms of capital, or combinations of capital, are recognised, and used (Bourdieu, 1993).

resistance (see Edgerton & Roberts, 2014; C. Mills, 2008, for an overview of this critique and a counter reading).

From Bourdieu's perspective, capital is a force inscribed in the objectivity of things so that everything is not equally possible or impossible (Bourdieu, 1986, pp. 241–242); Bourdieu argues that we cannot consider the social world unless that consideration moves beyond a singular focus on economic capital to consider capital in all three "fundamental guises": economic capital, cultural capital, and social capital (Bourdieu, 1986, p. 243). To explore how education, as a social institution, favours those from middle and upper class backgrounds, Bourdieu developed the concept of cultural capital. While economic capital—the wealth that is used in making profit in the capitalist economic system—is connected to access and use of resources such as land, money, and buildings, Bourdieu was interested in the considerable influence of other forms of capital. Cultural capital takes three forms: embodied, objectified, and institutionalised. Embodied cultural capital is acquired over time, through socialisation processes within family, culture, and tradition. Objectified cultural capital relates to objects that an individual might own such as property; objectified cultural capital can be sold—that is, exchanged for economic capital—or can be retained as used as a means to symbolically convey one's cultural capital by way of both ownership *and* appreciation. Institutionalised cultural capital is the institutional recognition of one's cultural capital, usually in the form of professional or academic awards (Shusterman, 1999). In all its forms, cultural capital refers to a way of thinking and disposition to life that smooth the way into, through, and beyond education:

> Expected behaviours, expected language competencies, the explicit and implicit values, knowledge, attitudes to and relationship with academic culture required for success in school are all competencies which one class brings with them to school. (Henry, Knight, Lingard, & Taylor, 1990, p. 233)

Research suggests teachers come from middle class backgrounds, often having had little experience of people with backgrounds other than their own, and unable to accommodate diversity in their educational practice (Aragón, Dovidio, & Graham, 2017; Hinojosa Pareja & López López, 2018; Leavy, 2005; Specht & Metsala, 2018; see also Chapter 13 in this collection). In this, schools continue to work in accord with middle class behaviours, competencies, and so on; "any other background, however rich in experiences, often turns out to be a liability" (Henry et al., 1990, pp. 142–143). The alignment of cultural capital with the capital of the structures of education contexts is further institutionalised through the achievement of higher levels of educational qualification which, in turn, can—according to the dominant narrative—be converted into economic capital by way of more profitable employment, a point to which I will return.

By contrast, social capital is made up of connections. Bourdieu defines social capital as

> the aggregate of the actual or potential resources which are linked to possession of a durable network of more or less institutionalized relationships of mutual acquaintance and recognition—or in other words, to membership in a group. (Bourdieu, 1986, p. 248)

Social capital—commonly defined as networks, norms, and trust (Putnam, 1993, 1995)—enables us to explain the "work of connections" which are evident when different individuals profit differently from apparently equivalent economic and/or cultural capital by way of their ability to "mobilize by proxy the capital of a group" (Bourdieu, 1986, p. 256). Social capital depends not only on a network of connections with a volume of capital, but also on the ability to effectively mobilise those connections; social capital is not independent of, and "exerts a multiplier effect" on, capital possessed by an individual or groups in their own right (Bourdieu, 1986, p. 249). In the context of late-modern times and the increasing complexity of education—young people remain in education for longer periods of time, with a broader curricula offering, and in school communities with more cultural diversity in the context of a globalised world (Giddens, 2002)—the potential of this "work of connections" has increasingly been taken up as an education policy instrument.

Sociologists were the first to explore how different forms of connection 'act' in different ways: most people have a blend of strong, and weaker, connections (Granovetter, 1973, 1983). The important point here is that it is the *weak* ties that form bridges for the network, allowing it to reach into social worlds that would otherwise remain "distant and ... quite alien" (Buchanan, 2002, p. 44). At the same time, within *strong* ties, clusters will be apparent: if one person is strongly linked to two others, it is likely these two will also be strongly linked and the connection will be 'closed', in the same way a triangle is closed. Strong links protect connections—if one link in a network of connections breaks, the connection will sustain through the other links that are present—and they 'multiply' influence, as Coleman's work (1988) illustrates. Coleman gives an example of what he refers to as 'intergenerational closure' in school settings where there is a high degree of closure among peers, who see each other daily, have expectations toward each other, and develop norms about each other's behaviour. He notes the impact where the parents' friends are the parents of their children's friends: if parent A is linked to parent B—if there is closure between parents—each of them can multiply the influence they have on both their own child and the child of the other through the ability to impose common sanctions that can shape behaviour (Coleman 1988, p.107).

Coleman identified three forms of social capital: obligations, expectations, and the trustworthiness of structures; information channels; and norms. The first form—obligations, expectations, and trustworthiness of structures—acts like a system of "credit slips" (Coleman, 1988, p. 102). In this, one person or organisation does something for another, on the assumption that this will be reciprocated in the future. This imaginary system of credit slips depends fully on the trustworthiness of the social environment, and the extent of the obligation that is involved in the exchange. The second form of social capital—information channels—recognises that action is based on information. In turn, information is fundamentally connected to social relations. However, the information we get from social relations is often not the primary rationale for the relationship; we secure this information as a by-product of our everyday interactions with others; this has implications for how policy might look to implement initiatives that forge social capital. Coleman's final form of social capital is norms: "if a norm exists, and is effective, it constitutes a powerful, though sometimes fragile, form of social capital" (Coleman, 1988, p. 104). Norms reflect an attempt to "to limit negative external effects or [to] encourage positive ones" (Coleman, 1988, p. 105). All three forms of social capital encourage us to act in certain ways while foreclosing on other acts.

However, while social capital has become an accepted part of the social policy lexicon, it frequently lacks the analytical depth required to achieve its potential. This lack is manifest in, first, the impoverished discussion of the nature of connections between people; and, second, in an undue emphasis on people, to the exclusion of other actors (Kamp, 2013; Salomão Filho & Kamp, 2019). I will return to this issue in the conclusion of the chapter.

The postmodern turn
Postmodernism developed in the 20th century, in response to frustrations concerning the inability of grand narratives around class, gender, and so

forth, and a lessening of confidence in the Enlightenment project of reason. This response implied a move away from the divide between the objective and the subjective, and the embrace of approaches to knowledge that undermined assumptions that reality is both knowable and consistent; that the world has qualities and quantities that relate one to the other in predictable proportions, and that standing opposite these knowable structures is an analysing subject (Mansfield, 2000). For Sadovnik (2007a), critical postmodern theory is assembled from a number of themes:

1. It rejects all metanarratives—all-encompassing explanations of the world—in favour of localised theorisation.
2. It demands a connection between theory and practice.
3. It prioritises a democratic impulse in the face of injustice (Lyotard, 1984).
4. It confronts the domination of Eurocentric and patriarchal thought (Giroux, 1991; Lather, 1992).
5. It is attentive to power relations (Foucault, 1983).
6. It is a commitment to work with difference in productive ways.

Sadovnik (1995) suggests that the postmodern turn has provided a fertile ground for critical education theory such as Paolo Freire's *Pedagogy of the Oppressed* (1972).

Postmodernism remains a contested territory for the sociology of education. In his General Introduction to the extensive collection *Sociology of Education. Major Themes*, Stephen Ball (2000, p. xlii) notes that, as a sensibility, while some sociologists see "new possibilities" in the postmodern for "situated struggles", for others, "postmodernism is 'a problem', even just 'boys games' particularly in that postmodernism critiques the 'oppressions' embedded within the humanist tradition". He quotes Kenway (1997, p. 132) who suggests, in grappling with the implications of the postmodern for the feminist agenda, that "in many senses feminist postmodernism has become 'The New Way' to approach feminist research, pedagogy and politics … [however] when one takes this new way, one confronts many confusions, difficulties, dilemmas and dangers".

From my perspective, the postmodern offers productive spaces for understanding complex social concerns, such as the "wicked problem" (Rittel & Webber, 1973) of enduring educational inequality. Inequalities—in education and other social policy contexts—have increased in the context of an increasingly globalised, neoliberal world. Globally, the need for collaboration to support schools in achieving all they are asked to achieve has become increasingly evident. In the context of Aotearoa, the self-managing policy of Tomorrow's Schools had, over a period of three decades, led to an increasing atomisation of individual schools and a breakdown of a collaborative ethics (Wylie, 2012). From 2013, the introduction of Kāhui Ako | Communities of Learning has been intended to serve as a counterpoint to this atomisation.

A joined-up education policy agenda

Globally, structural reform in education systems is increasingly based on notions of various forms of joining-up: in networking, collaboration, and partnership that can respond to the elevated complexities and inequalities associated with globalisation. Globalisation is a term that conveys a number of intertwined phenomena (Axford, 2013; Giddens, 2002; McCarthy, Miller, & Skidmore, 2004; Urry, 2003). It involves the growth and increasing influence of supra-national political bodies such as the United Nations and the Organisation for Economic Cooperation and Development (OECD), and the formation of global education policy communities (M Henry, Lingard, Rizvi, & Taylor, 2001). Particularly since the second half of the 20th century—with the rapidly increasing impact of information, communication, and transport technologies—it has revolutionised how economies and labour markets interact (see Castells, 1996, for a detailed thesis). While far from a complete project, not only being the subject of political contestation but also being patchy in the strength of its impact in local communities, globalisation has changed our lives through its influence on mobility and migration, family structures and gender roles, the form and shape of employment, and our forms of communication and entertainment (Hutton & Giddens, 2001). Thus, while globalisation has fostered economic, technical, and cultural integration, it has also contributed to fragmentation and competition at a local level (Beck, 1992). While the world might now be conceptualised as a 'space of flows' (Castells & Ince, 2003), a space that keeps information, money, people, consumer goods, ideas, and so on moving around, much community life—including that which occurs within and around schools—is fundamentally based in a sense of place. It is to a consideration of this shift to collaboration in our place that I now turn.

Kāhui Ako | Communities of Learning

In Aotearoa, the shift towards a joined-up ethos in education policy is currently mobilised through Kāhui Ako | Communities of Learning. Kāhui Ako are one of three components of the government's 2014 policy initiative *Investing in Educational Success*. The policy intent was to "raise the learning (ako) and achievement of all our children and young people, particularly for ākonga/students that are most at risk of underachieving" (Ministry of Education, 2016, p. 2); this was to be achieved by way of early learning services, schools and kura, and tertiary providers working together in a process of collaboration, inquiry, evaluation, and improvement. As a consequence, the intervention logic suggests that on-the-ground change will be evident in:

1. shared accountability and collective responsibility for students
2. "deliberate" collaboration
3. building and sharing teaching and leadership expertise
4. new career pathways for "good" teachers and "outstanding" principals
5. evidence-driven action
6. productive partnerships with families, iwi, employers, and the community. (Ministry of Education, 2018, p. 5)

Each community sets shared goals—achievement challenges—based on the needs of its children and young people. The intent is that the community works with students, their parents, whānau, iwi, and communities to achieve those challenges. State and state-integrated schools and kura within a Kāhui Ako are funded to allow teachers and principals time to work together on meeting the achievement challenges. How might the insights provided by a sociology of education benefit this policy initiative?

In connection to the first shift of *shared accountability and collective responsibility* for students, social capital's reference to the ability to *mobilise* the capital in the group rests in the effectiveness of obligations, expectations, trustworthiness, and norms. The most recent research (Ministry of Education, 2018, p. 1) suggests that between 20% (approved Kāhui Ako) and 70% (endorsed Kāhui Ako) took responsibility for students in schools other than their own. This trajectory from approved to endorsed[3] communities suggests the culture of shared

---

3   Endorsement here refers to the process whereby a Kāhui Ako has had its proposed achievement challenges endorsed by the Secretary for Education. Once endorsement is gained, Kāhui Ako can access the full range of available resources.

accountability is one that is learnt over time (Schein, 1989). In mobilising this learning, the factors that mobilise engagement are pivotal:

> When the mindset of members is to use the group as a vehicle to get resources, the goals of the Kāhui Ako will tend to be set with funders in mind. The group is likely to take an approach of 'satisficing': adopting goals that only commit the group to the minimum effort needed to do what is required, and measured, by the Ministry of Education. (Ramsey & Poskitt, 2019, p. 11)

Here, an understanding of the strength of the closed network and its ability to exert influence on human actors around expectation through bonded connections and "credit slips" is where leadership can be applied. At the same time, maintaining awareness of the influence being exerted by nonhuman actors, such as funding mechanisms, and how these might be mediated, is valuable.

In terms of the aspiration for *deliberate collaboration*, sociology of education speaks to the function of collaboration. In the context of vocationalism—the perspective that the purpose of education is workplace preparation (Grubb & Lazerson, 2005)—and mindful of the risks of young people experiencing anomie (an inability to reconcile imposed norms and individual needs), it would seem to me that Kāhui Ako have immense potential. In 2016, the defining characteristics of Aotearoa New Zealand that were ranked highest by New Zealanders were "freedom, rights, and peace" and "environment" (mean rating 9.1), followed by "the people in New Zealand" (mean rating 8.5) (StatsNZ, 2016). Beyond this, the commitments and opportunities that inhere in the Treaty of Waitangi and the growing embrace of, for instance, tikanga, whanaungatanga, and kotahitangai, offer an invitation to a collaborative ethos that of necessity includes the range of ties that Granovetter (1973) demonstrated. At the current time, the most common foci of deliberate collaboration in Kāhui Ako centre on meetings and administration, professional development, deliberate inquiry into practice, and strategic planning. All of these have potential to mobilise the agenda but seem to suggest an overt focus on the deliberate, the formal, and the structured which obscures the importance of the organic, the informal, and the everydayness of embedded commitment. For Coleman (1988), so much of the information we need for social capital comes to us as a by-product of our everyday interactions.

Building and sharing teaching and leadership expertise is the third change on the ground that is sought. A sociology of education can offer insights into the question of leadership expertise in the context of collaborative endeavours

(Kamp, 2018). The insights here would suggest a troubling of the idea that leadership inheres in one human, whether or not they occupy a position of leadership. Thus, leadership should be understood to emerge in contextually-relevant ways in the course of the flow of practice (Lovett, 2018); should be acknowledged to move beyond a dualism of leader/follower, being more aligned to a "collaborative professionalism" (Hargreaves & O'Connor, 2018); and be understood to not solely be the domain of human actors. From this perspective, leadership involves "active hybrids composed of networks of associations" (Grint, 2004, p. 5). Those associations include nonhuman actors such as funding, school timetables, bus routes, employment contracts, position descriptions, reputations, and so on. Secondly these associations should be understood by way of a 'flat' analytical basis—in other words, in our research on what is going on we must not only focus on a principal, or other nominated human 'leader', notwithstanding the key creative role that humans play as 'first among equals' (Grint, 2004, p. 8). (See Chapter 12 in this collection for a further discussion on the possibilities for education leadership.)

Consider *new career pathways* for 'good' teachers and 'outstanding' principals. From the perspective of a sociology of education, the suggestion here would be to reflect on the conflict theorists' call for "free, equal, public education" (Marx & Engels, 2017/1848, p. 21) and the question of "what counts as important knowledge" (Apple et al., 2010, p. 6) within an 'equal' education. Thus, the measures of how we categorise 'good' teachers and 'outstanding' principals becomes essential to setting the conditions of possibility for what might be achieved. The 2017 survey suggests that 80% of principals and board chairs felt that "people with sufficient skills and expertise had been appointed" to the various roles of positional leadership in Kāhui Ako (Ministry of Education, 2018, p. 2). The nature of the skills and expertise that are deemed 'sufficient' would be a productive arena for research. At the same time, the evidence suggesting a lack of clarity around how to use the positional leadership roles, and the inability to secure cover to conduct the roles (cited by up to 50% of respondents), indicates some very real limitations in potential.

In regard to the fifth change area of *evidence-driven action*, a sociology of education has a long history, and a continuing concern, with the question of what 'counts' in education. For Michael Apple (2006), one of the seven tasks of the critical analyst is an expansion of the kinds of research that inform practice. This is not to speak against the value of numerical data—the dominant form of evidence accepted in the neoliberal context—but, rather, to give equal weight to "thick descriptions of critically democratic school practices" (Apple et al., 2010, p. 5). The survey indicates a great deal of intent to use data, including data that moves beyond student achievement in isolation and concerns itself with student and staff feedback and measures of their wellbeing (Ministry of Education, 2018, p. 3). Here, Coleman's commentary on the importance of information channels is pertinent. The range of data that is available in the current context, and the confidence expressed by endorsed Kāhui Ako about their expertise in working with it, offers immense possibility; attention to the concerns flagged in the survey concerning the reliability of data and the privacy and security of data management systems, according to Coleman (1988) and Wittel (2001), would seem to be areas for productive investment by government in the context of the realisation of the Education Work Programme (Office of the Minister of Education, 2018).

The sixth, and final, on-the-ground change that is sought is *productive partnerships with families, iwi, employers, and the community.* The most recent research indicates that there is much work to be done on this change on-the-ground. While Kāhui Ako *are* working in partnership, that partnership work is most frequently with an 'external expert' rather than parents, whānau, iwi, or other community stakeholders (Ministry of Education, 2018, p. 3). From a sociological perspective, this suggests the question of whose knowledge is valued, and in what ways, remains an issue of concern. It also indicates a productive space for research in regard to mapping the bonding, bridging and linking networks of various Kāhui Ako. A reliance on external experts suggests somewhat impoverished linking partnerships at this time. The position of government, in the form of the Ministry of Education, in the network of Kāhui Ako is also pivotal, given the role of bureaucracy in setting the limits and possibilities on what can be imagined as possible at the level of the local.

Concluding thoughts

This chapter has presented a necessarily limited review of the highly diverse collection of work that identifies itself as sociology of education. I have presented the genesis of this body of work, and some of its contemporary concerns. From my perspective, the development of a sociology of education since the 19th century and through to its most recent concerns with the postmodern, places the contemporary drive for the joined-up policy agenda in education in focus; it offers an array of tools to explore, and potentially intervene in, the persistent failure of schooling to deliver educational equity. As has been encountered throughout this chapter, the limits of the current configuration of our education system are not 'real'; they are an effect of one actualised possibility, an actualised possibility that can be remade in other, potentially more productive, ways.

In part, this is about a persistent call to maintain what C. Wright Mills (1959) would refer to as a "sociological imagination"—an ability to understand the relationship between experience and society and to place ourselves outside of the routines that inhabit our everyday lives, in the process being able to imagine new possibilities. Given our commitment in Aotearoa New Zealand to the moral purpose of schooling, and the consistent failure of our education system to deliver on that commitment, sociology offers a range of tools to support each one of us in making progress, individually and in our collaborative endeavours. As I have argued elsewhere, seeing ourselves as social beings, continuously learning new ways of being and acting is central to that endeavour. The ability to work productively with the tension that inheres in boundary crossing is essential to this process; without the tension, innovation of the kind needed to achieve the kind of system-level change (Ministry of Education, 2018) intended by the policy is unlikely to be achieved (Kamp, 2013). We will remain within the limits of 'what is' in our system of schooling.

As well, engagement with the sociology of education reminds us to be fully attentive to the range of actors who are involved in the formation of "the social" (Latour, 2007). Sociology of education has always been attentive to how social action acts on, and is acted on by, a wide range of actors and structures, and what the consequences of this shaping have been, in classrooms, in school departments, in organisations, and in the education system as a whole. A sociology of education offers a rich and diverse body of research that renders the full range of actors present and prompts us to remain attentive to the limits and possibilities that every one of those actors offers.

Recommendations for further reading

Bauman, Z. (2012). *On education*. Cambridge, UK: Polity Press.
Sadovnik, A. R. (2007). *Sociology of education. A critical reader*. New York, NY: Routledge.

References

Apple, M. W. (1996). Power, meaning and identity: Critical sociology of education in the United States. *British Journal of Sociology of Education, 17*, 125–144.
Apple, M. W. (2006). Rhetoric and reality in critical education studies in the United States. *British Journal of Sociology of Education, 27*, 679–687.

Apple, M. W., Ball, S. J., & Gandin, L. A. (2010). Mapping the sociology of education: Social context, power and knowledge. In M. W. Apple, S. J. Ball, & L. A. Gandin (Eds.), *The Routledge international handbook of the sociology of education* (pp. 1–12). London, UK: Routledge.

Aragón, O. R., Dovidio, J. F., & Graham, M. J. (2017). Colorblind and multicultural ideologies are associated with faculty adoption of inclusive teaching practices. *Journal of Diversity in Higher Education, 10*(3), 201–215.

Axford, B. (2013). *Theories of globalisation*. Cambridge, UK: Polity Press.

Ball, S. J. (2000). General introduction. In S. J. Ball (Ed.), *Sociology of education. Major themes* (Vol. 1, pp. xxxi–xlvi). London, UK: RoutledgeFalmer.

Bauman, Z. (1990). *Modernity and ambivalence*. Cambridge, UK: Polity Press.

Beck, U. (1992). *Risk society. Towards a new modernity. Theory, culture & society*. London, UK: Sage.

Bernstein, B. (1996). *Pedagogy, symbolic control and identity: Theory, research, critique*. London, UK: Taylor & Francis.

Bourdieu, P. (1977). *Outline of a theory of practice*. Cambridge, UK: Cambridge University Press.

Bourdieu, P. (1986). The forms of capital. In J. G. Richardson (Ed.), *Handbook of theory and research for the sociology of education* (pp. 241–260). New York, NY: Greenwood Press.

Bourdieu, P. (1990). *In other words: Essays towards a reflexive sociology*. Cambridge, UK: Polity Press.

Bourdieu, P. (1993). *The field of cultural production*. Cambridge, UK: Polity Press.

Bourdieu, P. (1999). *The weight of the world: Social suffering in contemporary society*. Cambridge, UK: Polity Press.

Bourdieu, P., & Passeron, J. (1977). *Reproduction in education, society and culture*. London, UK: Sage.

Bowles, S., & Gintis, H. (1976). *Schooling in capitalist America*. New York, NY: Basic Books.

Buchanan, M. (2002). *Small world. Uncovering nature's hidden networks*. London, UK: Weidenfeld Nicolson.

Castells, M. (1996). *The rise of the network society* (2nd ed. Vol. 1). Oxford, UK: Blackwell.

Castells, M., & Ince, M. (2003). *Conversations with Manuel Castells*. London, UK: Polity Press.

Coleman, J. (1988). Social capital in the creation of human capital. *American Journal of Sociology, 94*, Supplement S95–120.

Durkheim, E. (1893). *The division of labour in society*. Glencoe, IL: The Free Press.

Durkheim, E. (1897). *Suicide*. New York, NY: Free Press Imprint.

Durkheim, E. (2006). *Émile Durkheim selected writings on education. The evolution of educational thought*. Abingdon, UK: Routledge.

Edgerton, J. D., & Roberts, L. W. (2014). Cultural capital or habitus? Bourdieu and beyond in the explanation of enduring educational inequality. *Theory and Research in Education, 12*(2), 193–220.

Foucault, M. (1983). The subject and power. In H. L. Dreyfus & P. Rabinow (Eds.), *Michel Foucault: Beyond structuralism and hermeneutics* (pp. 208–226). Chicago, IL: University of Chicago Press.

Freire, P. (1972). *Pedagogy of the oppressed*. Harmondsworth, UK: Penguin.

Giddens, A. (2002). *Runaway world: How globalisation is reshaping our lives*. London, UK: Profile.

Giroux, H. (1991). *Postmodernism, feminism, and cultural politics: Redrawing educational boundaries*. New York, NY: SUNY Press.

Granovetter, M. (1973). The strength of weak ties. *American Journal of Sociology, 78*, 1360–1380.

Granovetter, M. (1983). The strength of weak ties: A network theory revisited. *Sociological Theory, 1*, 203–233.

Grint, K. (2004). *Actor network theory*. In G. Goethals, G. Sorenson, & J. M. Burns (Eds.), *Encyclopedia of leadership*. (pp. 5–8). London, UK: Sage.

Grubb, W. N., & Lazerson, M. (2005). The education gospel and the role of vocationalism in American education. *American Journal of Education, 111*(3), 297–319.

Hargreaves, A., & O'Connor, M. T. (2018). *Collaborative professionalism. When teaching together means learning for all*. Thousand Oaks, CA: Corwin.

Henry, M., Knight, J., Lingard, R., & Taylor, S. (1990). *Understanding schooling: An introductory sociology of Australian education*. Florence, SC: Routledge.

Henry, M., Lingard, B., Rizvi, F., & Taylor, S. (2001). *The OECD, globalisation and policy making in education*. Oxford, UK: Pergamon/Elsevier.

Hinojosa Pareja, E. F., & López López, M. C. (2018). Interculturality and teacher education. A study from pre-service teachers' perspective. *Australian Journal of Teacher Education, 43*(3), 74–92.

Hutton, W., & Giddens, A. (2001). *On the edge. Living with global capitalism*. London, UK: Vintage.

Kamp, A. (2013). *Rethinking learning networks: Collaborative possibilities for a Deleuzian century*. Oxford, UK: Peter Lang.

Kamp, A. (2018). Assembling the actors: Exploring the challenges of 'system leadership' in education through Actor-Network Theory. *Journal of Education Policy, 33*(6), 778–792. https://doi.org/10.1080/02680939.2017.1380231

Kamp, A., & Black, D. (2014). *3 ply: Exploring the potential of transformative workplace learning for and by teachers*. Research report. Armagh, UK: SCoTENS.

Kenway, J. (1997). Having a postmodern turn or postmodernist angst: A disorder experienced by an author who is not yet dead or even close to it. In A. H. Halsey, H. Lauder, P. Brown, & A. S. Wells (Eds.), *Education: Culture, economy, society* (pp. 131–143). Oxford, UK: Oxford University Press.

Lather, P. (1992). Critical frames in educational research: Feminist and post-structural perspectives. *Theory into Practice, 31*(2), 87–99.

Latour, B. (2007). *Reassembling the social. An introduction to Actor-Network-Theory*. Oxford, UK: Oxford University Press.

Leavy, A. (2005). "When I meet them I talk to them": The challenges of diversity for preservice teacher education. *Irish Educational Studies, 24*(2), 159–177.

Lovett, S. (2018). *Advocacy for teacher leadership. Opportunity, preparation, support and pathways*. Cham, Switzerland: Springer.

Lyotard, J. F. (1984). *The postmodern condition: A report on knowledge*. Manchester, UK: Manchester University Press.

Mansfield, N. (2000). *Subjectivity: Theories of the self from Freud to Haraway.* New York, NY: New York University Press.

Marx, K., & Engels, F. (2017/1848). *The communist manifesto.* Minneapolis, MN: Lerner Publishing Group.

McCarthy, H., Miller, P., & Skidmore, P. (2004). *Network logic. Who governs in an interconnected world?* London, UK: DEMOS.

Mills, C. (2008). Reproduction and transformation of inequalities in schooling: The transformative potential of the theoretical constructs of Bourdieu. *British Journal of Sociology of Education, 29*(1), 79–89. https://doi.org/10.1080/01425690701737481

Mills, C. W. (1959). *The sociological imagination.* New York, NY: Oxford University Press.

Ministry of Education. (2016). *Communities of Learning guide for schools and kura.* Wellington: Author. Retrieved from: https://www.education.govt.nz/assets/Documents/col/Communities-of-Learning-Guide-for-Schools-and-Kura-web-enabled.pdf

Ministry of Education. (2018). *Communities of Learning | Kāhui Ako 2017 survey.* Wellington: Author.

Morrison, K. (2006). *Marx, Durkheim and Weber. Formations of modern social thought.* London, UK: Sage.

Muller, J. (2004). Introduction. The possibilities of Basil Bernstein. In B. Davies, A. Morais, & J. Muller (Eds.), *Reading Bernstein, researching Bernstein* (pp. 1–14). London, UK: RoutledgeFalmer.

Office of the Minister of Education. (2018). *Education portfolio work programme: Purpose, objectives and overview.* Wellington: New Zealand Government. Retrieved from: http://www.education.govt.nz/assets/Documents/Ministry/Information-releases/R-Education-Portfolio-Work-Programme-Purpose-Objectives-and-Overview.pdf

Putnam, R. D. (1993). The prosperous community. Social capital and public life. *The American Prospect, 4*(13), 1–6.

Putnam, R. D. (1995). Bowling alone: America's declining social capital. *Journal of Democracy, 6*(1), 65–78.

Ramsey, P., & Poskitt, J. M. (2019). Understanding leadership dynamics 'within' and 'across school' roles—and moving forward. *New Zealand Principals' Federation Magazine, 34*(1), 10–12.

Rittel, H. W. J., & Webber, M. M. (1973). Dilemmas in a general theory of planning. *Policy Sciences, 4*(2), 155–169.

Roth, G., & Wittich, C. (1978). *Max Weber. Economy and society.* Berkley, CA: University of California Press.

Sadovnik, A. (1995). Postmodernism and the sociology of education: Closing the rift among scholarship, research, and practice. In G. W. Noblit & W. Pink (Eds.), *Continuity and contradiction: The futures of the sociology of education* (pp. 309–326). Cresskill, NJ: Hampton Press.

Sadovnik, A. (2007a). Theory and research in the sociology of education. In A. Sadovnik (Ed.), *Sociology of education: A critical reader* (pp. 3–21). New York, NY: Routledge.

Sadovnik, A. (Ed.). (2007b). *Sociology of education. A critical reader.* New York, NY: Routledge.

Salomão Filho, A., & Kamp, A. (2019). Performing mundane materiality: Actor-network theory, global student mobility and a re/formation of 'social capital'. *Discourse: Studies in the Cultural Politics of Education, 40*(1), 122–135.

Schein, E. H. (1989). Organizational culture: What it is and how to change it. In P. Evans, Y. Doz, & A. Laurent (Eds.), *Human resource management in international firms* (pp. 56–82). Basingstoke, UK: Macmillan.

Shusterman, R. (1999). *Bourdieu. A critical reader.* Oxford, UK: Blackwell Publishers.

Specht, J. A., & Metsala, J. L. (2018). Predictors of teacher efficacy for inclusive practice in pre-service teachers. *Exceptionality Education International, 28*(3), 67–82.

StatsNZ. (2016). *Well-being statistics: 2016.* Wellington: Author.

Urry, J. (2003). *Global complexity.* Cambridge, UK: Polity Press/Blackwell Publishing.

Weber, M. (1947). *The theory of social and economic organization.* London, UK: Oxford University Press.

Wittel, A. (2001). Toward a network sociality. *Theory, Culture and Society, 18*(6), 51–76.

Wylie, C. (2012). *Vital connections: Why we need more than self-managing schools.* Wellington: NZCER Press.

Chapter 5
Psychology of education

Valerie Sotardi and Myron Friesen

Introduction

In this chapter, we offer an understanding of the learner—in early and middle childhood, and adolescence—through an integrated perspective of educational and developmental psychology. We draw on a range of national and international literature to highlight key competencies related to the emerging mind and behaviour of students from early childhood to adolescence in Aotearoa New Zealand. To narrow the scope, we focus our attention on recent educational research where students are participants.

While preparing this chapter, we conducted a systematic literature search to identify trends in student-focused educational research from 2009 to 2019 in Aotearoa New Zealand (see Appendix). A clear trend was that 48% of the sources involved students at the tertiary education level, overshadowing what is known about students in early childhood education (5%), primary education (17%), and secondary education (30%).[1]

---

1 Using NVivo software with all sourced abstracts, the five most frequently used keywords were assessment, achievement, support, engagement, and culture. Moreover, a variety of methodologies was employed, with questionnaires, interviews, and case studies as the most commonly reported.

Throughout the chapter, we comment on research gaps within the student-focused literature in Aotearoa New Zealand (see also Zhang, 2015). We do so with the intent that such gaps could be opportunities for future research agendas, an ultimate goal of improving the learning and holistic development of students in early childhood, middle childhood, and adolescence.

Understanding learners in early childhood

A primary goal of early childhood education (ECE) is to provide young children with interactive opportunities where they have a sense of agency and are able to develop as confident, competent lifelong learners. In Aotearoa New Zealand, such aims are woven into the national curriculum—*Te Whāriki*. The curriculum adopts a holistic, culturally diverse, and child-centred approach to support learning and development in supporting tamariki (young children) (Ministry of Education, 2017b; see also, Lee, Carr, Soutar, & Mitchell, 2013). Still considered as one of the more progressive early childhood curricula worldwide (see, for example, Duhn, 2006; Mutch, 2013), *Te Whāriki* frames successful outcomes for young children based on mana atua (wellbeing), mana whenua (belonging), mana tangata (contribution), mana reo (communication), and mana aotūroa (exploration). The curriculum is flexible in that it takes a descriptive, rather than prescriptive, pedagogical approach. It draws on philosophies arguing that children should learn as natural opportunities arise rather than by outside forces (a view contended by Rousseau).

A secondary goal of ECE is to prepare young children for the demands of formal schooling through informal pedagogies (Csibra & Gergely, 2009; Tomasello, 1999; Yu, Bonawitz, & Shafto, 2019). In Aotearoa New Zealand, various philosophies for ECE are embraced and, therefore, different approaches are implemented (see, for example, Reggio Emilia, Montessori, Steiner, and Kōhanga Reo[2]). An overarching theme across these approaches is that young children should have opportunities to interact with and learn from the social and cultural environment. Although there is little consensus on how school readiness is defined (Lewit & Baker, 1995), ECE and its preparation for school remain underlying issues in Aotearoa New Zealand. For instance, researchers highlight the influences of ECE on young children on short-term circumstances

---

2   Kōhanga Reo supports the holistic development of young children from te ao Māori (Māori philosophical worldview). Specifically, it follows an approach in which te reo Māori and tikanga Māori (Māori language, knowledge, and culture) are transmitted from kaumātua (respected elders) to mokopuna (grandchildren).

(e.g., social interactions and encouraging a love for learning) but also long-term circumstances (e.g., school entry, school achievement, and future employment; Brooks-Gunn, 2003; Entwisle & Alexander, 1993; Magnuson, Ruhm, & Waldfogel, 2007; Rimm-Kaufman, Pianta, & Cox, 2000). Not all ECE settings are the same in terms of quality; however, they play a critical—often underappreciated—role in communities and the children within them.

Te Whāriki has considerable overlap with developmental systems theory (DST) (Cantor, Osher, Berg, Steyer, & Rose, 2018), a framework broadly stating that children develop from the shared contributions from genetics, epigenetics,[3] and the environment. First, the curriculum emphasises the agentic quality of human development, thus empowering children and helping them to nurture their intrinsic interests. Secondly, *Te Whāriki* acknowledges the interplay between developmental domains (e.g., physical, cognitive, affective, social, and spiritual) and considers how these interdependent systems give rise to certain behaviours. Thirdly, *Te Whāriki* and DST recognise the diverse ecological contexts that may enhance or impede development and learning, namely contributions from family, whānau, and community. Importantly, these contexts include kaiako (teachers) and the early childhood setting.

Te Whāriki regards early childhood as ranging from birth to school entry. The early years of life could be considered the most varying and important in a child's life. In the next section, we focus our attention to emerging competencies in the period representing "young children" (2.5 years old to school entry). This is not to exclude the fundamental significance of earlier years; rather, this is to engage with the literature on preschool learners with adequate depth.

Key competencies of young children (2.5 years to school entry)

In this section, we highlight three key competencies that offer an emergent understanding of learners in the later years of early childhood: (1) attachment; (2) self and others; and (3) communication, language, and play. Attachment is a behavioural system in which the child uses the caregiver as a source of comfort and security in times of distress and a secure base for exploration (Ainsworth, 1989). The attachment a child forms with his or her primary caregiver (typically a parent) sets an essential foundation for development (see Bowlby, 2004). Just as is the case with infancy and toddlerhood, warm, sensitive, and responsive

---

3   Epigenetics generally refers to heritable, physical variations caused by modifications to one's gene expression rather than the alteration of one's DNA.

caregivers are associated with secure child-caregiver relationships (Howes & Ritchie, 2002). In Aotearoa New Zealand, Drewery and Bird (2004) explain that secure attachment relationships are those in which the child and caregiver are both motivated to maintain and deepen their shared connection. By integrating traditional Māori hapū, Aotearoa New Zealand researchers (see, for example, Durie, 1985; du Plessis, 2009; Metge, 1995) highlight the importance of considering young children's attachment bonds not only with biological parents but also with group members who accept equal responsibility for the care of an individual child.

A core feature of attachment theory is that the behavioural system of attachment slowly becomes internalised over the early childhood and primary years to become an internalised model or an interpretive filter that helps children to make sense of their relational experiences. In ECE, young children's social circles expand to include teachers and peers and, although they usually do not represent the full-fledged attachment bonds children have with primary caregivers, teachers and peers can offer structure, warmth, and haven (Verschueren & Koomen, 2012). In a supportive environment, young children learn to share and express concern for each other's welfare. Indeed, it can be both an opportunity and a challenge for young children to forge relationships with members of a new environment (Howes, Sanders, & Lee, 2008). These demands include building partnerships with the teacher, peer groups, and the setting (McCaslin, Sotardi, & Vega, 2015).

Increased skills in language and the utilisation of other cultural tools with the teacher aid children's abilities to detect everyday problems and respond through joint coping and co-regulation. For instance, teachers' inductive support and encouragement of language to express and understand emotion are critical during this time. This occurs by teachers using terms such as "use your words" and "how would you feel if ...?" (Kim, Boldt, & Kochanska, 2015). Such interactions are crucial yet challenging: the teacher must strike a balance between standing back to empower and enable discovery while also scaffolding the "shaky test-drives" of the child's early efforts for self-regulation (Skinner & Zimmer-Gembeck, 2016). Indeed, watching young children struggle with a problem may not be easy for adults; however, a lack of challenge also denies children the opportunity to learn how to adjust their emotions, thoughts, and behaviour, and to learn how to recover should they fail to do so (McCaslin et al., 2015).

A secure child–caregiver relationship is known to yield positive effects, including children's educational outcomes (Bergin & Bergin, 2009). Just as in the home, the social and emotional climate of an early childhood learning environment can enhance or impede the social development of young children (Howes, 2010). Children who enter ECE with insecure child-caregiver attachment relationships may lag behind their securely attached peers in terms of developing academic skills and social competence; however, some studies have found that teachers who are sensitive to these children's needs can ameliorate these potential setbacks (Buyse, Verschueren, & Doumen, 2011; Mitchell-Copeland, Denham, & DeMulder, 1997). Indeed, large-scale observational studies indicate two characteristics of sensitive teachers: instructional support and social-emotional support (Hamre & Pianta, 2005; Mashburn & Pianta, 2006; Pianta, Downer, & Hamre, 2016). Such learning environments are vibrant places teeming with dialogue and joy as children and teachers participate in different activities (Howes, 2010). They have clear (but also adaptable) rules, expectations, and routines.

Understanding self and others develops between the ages of 3 and 5, when children typically acquire Theory of Mind (ToM)—an ability to anticipate and explain the actions and feelings of others based on mental states like beliefs and perceptions (Astington, 1993; Wellman, 2002). With ToM, children understand that behaviour reveals underlying intentions, beliefs guide behaviour even when they are not based on reality, and people's words may have multiple meanings (Wellman Fang, & Peterson, 2011; Wellman, 2018). ToM develops at about the same time in most children around the world (see, for example, Liu, Wellman, Tardif, & Sabbagh, 2008). However, its rate of development is linked to children's environment such as attachment and parenting styles (Carpendale & Lewis, 2004), as well as the number of adults and peers a young child interacts with on a day-to-day basis (Lewis, Freeman, Kyriakidou, Maridaki-Kassotaki, & Berridge, 1996; Ruffman, Perner, Naito, Parkin, & Clements, 1998).

The emergence of ToM has far-reaching implications for learning and development in early childhood. ToM starts early in ECE and fundamentally represents children's drive to ask questions, evaluate the reasons behind others' actions, and provide reasons for their behaviours. As a result of this early form of inquiry, ToM is related to pretend play (Taylor & Carlson, 1997), school adjustment (Dunn, 1995), and the understanding of multiple identities and roles (Lalonde & Chandler, 1995).

In the early childhood learning environment, ToM accompanies increased levels of emotional awareness and expression (see, for example, Thompson, 2015). Through dialogue, children are able to identify and describe how they feel. Teachers are essential contributors: they support academic success and serve as socialisers of learners' emotional competence (Denham, Bassett, & Zinsser, 2012). In Aotearoa New Zealand, McLaughlin, Aspden, and Clarke (2017) have identified core themes and strategies for educators to support young children in ECE: aro ki ngā kare ā-roto (emotional literacy), whakatau puehu (social problem solving), whakatau wairua (calming down), pūkenga whakahoahoa (social skills and friendships), and kia ū ki te pai (preventing and addressing challenging behaviour). Research conducted by Bateman (2013) also highlights the particular importance of respecting young children's contributions through question–answer sequences as a co-constructed means of demonstrating responsive reciprocal relationships valued in *Te Whāriki*. ToM and emotional competence are, therefore, critical to advancements in communication, equipping young children with a culturally-coded vocabulary for different situations (Skinner & Zimmer-Gembeck, 2016).

In regard to communication, language, and play, infants are active communicators months before they start using language, and the gains in language development between 12 months and the preschool years have long been recognised. In the early childhood years, advances in language happen in concert with the development of other cognitive processes such as working memory and cognitive control (Deak, 2014). One aspect of language development is private speech, where young children talk to themselves while engaged in an activity, a function which then also facilitates the development of inner speech.[4] Children begin using private speech around 2 years of age, and this increases through early childhood and then gradually decreases in the later primary years; however, private speech does not disappear completely, as adults will sometimes use private speech when faced with cognitively demanding tasks (Alderson-Day & Fernyhough, 2015).

Play is a clear example of how language connects to other developmental domains in ECE. For instance, sociodramatic play is a joint role-play in which children choose a specific social context (e.g., enjoying a meal), negotiate roles

---

4   Inner speech is what most people consider thinking, and is described as the "subjective experience of language in the absence of overt and audible articulation" (Alderson-Day & Fernyhough, 2015, p. 931).

(cooks and guests), and interact together through imitation based on their individual experiences. Researchers in Aotearoa New Zealand add that the physical learning environment supports the principles of *Te Whāriki* (and thus, the development of young children) when the ECE setting represents authentic aspects of the home, community, and culture (see, for example, Guo, 2017; Hedges, Cullen, & Jordan, 2011). Play in learning environments outside of the ECE setting, such as museums and the natural environment, also support communication and language where co-constructed knowledge can take place (Clarkin-Phillips, Carr, Thomas, Tinning, & Waitai, 2018; Mawson, 2014; Sargisson & McLean, 2012). Indeed, play interactions are more than entertaining games. Play holds cultural and social meaning and serves as direct preparation for later school behaviour since it represents core aspects of readiness: motivation, self-regulation, symbolic thought, and language (Karpov, 2014).

By the end of early childhood, learners undergo a considerable shift from an inter-personal to an intra-personal means in how they perceive and respond to the world around them (Skinner & Zimmer-Gembeck, 2016). In earlier years, children's thoughts and actions would typically have been co-regulated in close interaction with primary caregivers and other adults (Fogel, 1993). However, children are usually able to interpret situations and cope with problems using their perceptions, judgements, and behaviours. As a result, children's attempts to complete tasks without the aid of others become a central theme. In ECE, the formation and maintenance of new social relationships (shaped by attachment relationships), the advancement of ToM with its ties to higher-order thinking and emotional competence, and the ability to communicate in cultural terms give rise to social needs for independence, agency, and autonomy. Each of these elements is valued in *Te Whāriki* and remains a priority for effective ECE settings in Aotearoa New Zealand.

Understanding learners in middle childhood

In Aotearoa New Zealand, children transition into primary school between 5 and 6 years of age. All state and state-integrated schools[5] follow the national curriculum: *The New Zealand Curriculum* (*NZC*) (Ministry of Education,

---

5   State schools are funded and operated by the New Zealand government, and are free to citizens and permanent residents. State-integrated schools are former private schools that have chosen to integrate into the state education system.

2007) for English-medium schools, and *Te Marautanga o Aotearoa* (TMoA) (Ministry of Education, 2017a) for Māori-medium schools. At present, *NZC* comprises eight levels and eight major learning areas: English, the Arts, Health and Physical Education, Learning Languages, Mathematics and Statistics, Science, Social Sciences, and Technology. TMoA incorporates a ninth learning area, Māori Language.

Broadly, the first few years of primary school are a time of unbridled discovery for children (Sotardi, 2018). This schooling transition includes not only the emergence of discipline-specific content (e.g., the eight major learning areas in *NZC*) but also an introduction to the role of a student. As learners progress from year to year, they are socialised in a way to know what "being a student" entails as well as its role in different learning environments. With time, children in primary school encounter new ways to think, interact, and comprehend according to expectations imposed by others. This can be challenging as the acculturative process is driven by demands, change, and stress (Sotardi, 2016).

In Aotearoa New Zealand, school curricula and pedagogy are among the most devolved in the world and, correspondingly, tend to be progressive in the modernisation of educational practices (see Deborah, Dany, John, & Paulo, 2012). However, regular revising of "how things are done" can be a double-edged sword. Modifications can introduce opportunities to ensure that all learners are supported—especially those from marginalised populations. Conversely, change can also introduce a sense of unpredictability and inefficiencies in where and how learning takes place. For example, an increasing number of state and state-integrated primary schools have moved towards educational environments that utilise physical learning spaces that are more open and flexible in their design (e.g., modern, innovative, and flexible learning environments) (Ministry of Education, 2015). Such contemporary topics are discussed elsewhere in Chapter 14 of this collection. However, we agree with researchers such as Alansari (2018) who comment that there is considerable research exploring pedagogical approaches to these learning environments in Aotearoa New Zealand, yet there is an alarming deficit in research involving students' experiences in these learning environments. In our literature search, we were unable to locate any peer-reviewed articles documenting the impact of such learning environments on students in Aotearoa New Zealand. More broadly, we highlight that learners may struggle, academically and personally, if educational reforms—especially those that directly affect students—lack thorough inspection and analysis.

Key competencies of children (5–6 to 12 years)

In this section, we highlight three key competencies that offer an emergent understanding of children in the primary years: (1) self-regulation; (2) emotional competence; and (3) executive function. Self-regulation is an umbrella term for a suite of cognitive, emotional, and social skills that allow people to manage behaviour, pursue goal-directed tasks, and successfully interact with others. Olson and Lunkenheimer (2009, p. 58) define self-regulation as "an ongoing process of modulating attentional, behavioral, and emotional responding in ways that potentiate socially adaptive outcomes". Implicit within this definition are two manifestations of self-regulation: inhibition of immediate response (i.e., thinking before acting), and activation of controlled, cognitive, and behavioural skills when striving to reach a desirable goal.

In middle childhood, learners become more competent in their ability to handle demanding (and stressful) situations. Through greater self-regulation, children can experiment with a range of coping strategies when faced with obstacles, difficulties, and setbacks. This advancement includes new cognitive strategies such as mental distraction and cognitive reframing, as well as the increasing reliance on friends as sources of emotional support (Skinner & Zimmer-Gembeck, 2007). On the one hand, learners become proficient in their ability to handle learning and inter-personal challenges at school with greater independence, efficiency, and effectiveness. On the other hand, learners also become proficient in their ability to conceal possible concerns and shameful experiences from likely sources of support, such as teachers, counsellors, and family members (Skinner & Zimmer-Gembeck, 2016). This is of particular concern for vulnerable children who might lack the necessary support systems outside the school setting.

Within the classroom, learners face increasingly more complex cognitive tasks from year to year (e.g., paying attention for lengthier periods and completing multi-step tasks), which places higher demands on self-regulation. For children who struggle with these expectations, such as those with attention deficit hyperactivity disorder, the school can become an increasingly challenging environment in which to function. To address these challenges, researchers in Aotearoa New Zealand have developed an intervention based on cognitively stimulating games and exercise (Healey & Halperin, 2015; Healey & Healey, 2019). The ENGAGE intervention has been tested with preschoolers in two trials and found to reduce children's symptoms of attention deficit hyperactivity disorder and improve self-regulation with effects sustained up to 12 months.

Because self-regulation provides children with greater autonomy and a sense of resilience, a central objective for many primary school teachers is to encourage learners to operate within a "zone of proximal development" (Vygotsky, 1980). This refers to a process where teachers aim to identify what each learner can and cannot (yet) do independently, and thus each task is designed to be beyond the learner's current level of competence (van der Veer, 2007). From a practical stance, however, this is no easy feat. In primary school classrooms, each individual's zone lies within the broader setting; thus, what a teacher does to elicit challenge will vary (a) between students based on personal histories, knowledge, and goals, and (b) within students over time, therefore requiring continual readjustment.

The affective component of self-regulation is emotional competence. It is defined as a set of essential social skills for people to identify, appraise, and respond to emotional states in themselves and others (Saarni, 1999). In early childhood, learners begin to develop emotional competence through co-regulated attachment bonds at home and in ECE settings. In middle childhood, learners build on these skills by further monitoring their attention and emotional states but also by adjusting emotions through their own mental control (Skinner & Zimmer-Gembeck, 2007). According to Stegge and Terwogt (2007), emotions begin as fragmented experiences and, with practice and integration, they give rise to predictable (and modifiable) patterns.

Typically, it is often not until later in primary school (9–11 years old) in which learners can analyse and reflect upon a situation from various perspectives (Pons, Harris, & de Rosnay, 2004). This competence triggers complex—and often conflicting—feelings, and also offers greater self-control over children's emotions (Stegge & Terwogt, 2007). In the classroom, if a learner is able to comprehend that (a) emotions change over time and across situations, (b) emotions can be expressed in numerous ways, and (c) it may be better to think before (re)acting, such skill is applicable to a wide range of school situations that call for adjustment (Skinner & Zimmer-Gembeck, 2016). Indeed, children's emotional competence is linked to school-related factors such as greater social skills and peer acceptance, less aggressive behaviours, and higher classroom performance (Arsenio, Cooperman, & Lover, 2000; Denham et al., 2003; Eisenberg et al., 2001; Izard et al., 2001).

In middle childhood, learners are likely to deploy emotion-focused strategies when faced with school-related challenges, academic setbacks, and social difficulties (Lau, 2002; Skinner & Zimmer-Gembeck, 2016). Specifically, children will typically have acquired sufficient language to express feelings but can also calm themselves down rather than relying on others (Aldwin, 2007). Such emotion-focused strategies have implications for primary school. Even in best-case scenarios where children learn within a supportive environment, daily hassles and the emotions associated with them are a natural part of classroom and school life (Boekaerts, 1993). Such hassles may include learning new content, managing a fast-paced curriculum and workload, forming and maintaining friendships, and experiencing (or witnessing) bullying and malicious teasing (Sotardi, 2017). Research has shown that children who are unable to manage distressing emotional situations are at risk of physical and psychological health complications (Compas, Connor-Smith, Saltzman, Thomsen, & Wadsworth, 2001; Fallin, Wallinga, & Coleman, 2001; Hampton, 2006). There is a collective priority for educators to provide learners with opportunities to develop and practise adaptive means of self-regulation (Rohrkemper & Corno, 1988; Sotardi, 2016, 2017).

Finally, executive functioning can be thought of as the cognitive aspect of self-regulation and includes a variety of interrelated higher-order mental processes that are primarily supported by the prefrontal cortex in the brain (see, for example, Zelazo, Carlson, & Kesek, 2008). Meta-analyses of cross-sectional and longitudinal studies of executive functioning have identified developmental trajectories suggesting rapid periods of growth from ages 5 to 8, moderate to strong improvements from 8 to 12, and slower development and refinement in adolescence (Romine & Reynolds, 2005).

In primary classrooms, children must be able to manage information and avoid distractions to accomplish learning tasks. The ability to do this depends on three components of executive functioning: working memory, inhibitory control, and mental flexibility (see, for example, Miyake et al., 2000). Imagine, for example, that children in a small group are directed to perform a task together. Each child needs to have enough control to stop and listen to what others have to say (inhibitory control). However, when it is one's turn to contribute, the child must also remember what the task requires as well as what the child wants to say or do (working memory). If other group members do something unpredictable, such as shifting to an off-topic conversation, the child needs to be able to adjust their actions accordingly (mental flexibility).

With these advancements, learners will typically have practised skills with assessing problems, generating solutions, planning for action, and evaluating the consequences of a decision (Zelazo et al., 2008). At this point, children can manage situations flexibly and proactively. No longer is the child a reaction to causal events: the child can anticipate and avoid circumstances that might otherwise lead to distress. Executive functioning sets the groundwork for primary students to stop, think, manage a heated moment, and identify strategies that could work under controllable circumstances such as most academic tasks and learning difficulties.

During this time, reactions from teachers and criticisms from peers carry a heavy emotional weight. Especially in public settings, children unable to cope effectively with everyday school challenges may experience disappointment, shame, and embarrassment. However, Skinner and Zimmer-Gembeck (2016) explain that, within the boundaries of safety, it can be beneficial for teachers to create a learning environment in which students are free to make mistakes, test out their limits, give in to their feelings, and give up. They explain that a positive climate is one in which failure is tolerated, there are secure opportunities to persist in the face of difficulty, and children learn to hold themselves accountable for mistakes and are encouraged to fix them. Children, therefore, can learn "how to fail, feel bad, and recover" (p. 182).

In Aotearoa New Zealand, there has been an emphasis on understanding student difficulties in primary school. An example involves the high rates of bullying reported by New Zealand children (Adair, 1999; Carroll-Lind 2009). Research by Raskauskas and colleagues (see, for example, Raskauskas & Stoltz, 2007) has shown that 16% of students aged 8–13 years in Aotearoa New Zealand were bullied once a week or more. In the primary school classroom, it is shown that how teachers manage peer aggression varies considerably (Yan, 2009) and that children do not feel confident that teachers will act decisively when bullying is reported (Raskauskas, Gregory, Harvey, Rifshana, & Evans, 2010). In a positive climate through direct instruction and modelling from the teacher, learners can acquire effective, socially appropriate ways of responding to everyday challenges (Raskauskas et al., 2010). Practising emotional competence, self-regulation, and executive functioning is valuable for not only classroom situations in primary school but also for life in secondary school, where a host of challenges and changes lie ahead.

Understanding learners in adolescence

In Aotearoa New Zealand, secondary school students build on *NZC* according to its specified values, key competencies, and learning areas. From Years 11 to 13, *NZC* is designed to offer students choice and specialisation as they construct ideas about their future directions after completing school. Learners can select courses within the specified learning areas or take courses across or outside learning areas, depending on what schools offer.

Within *NZC*, key competencies were designed to support student wellbeing and resilience (Hipkins, 2006) and promote adaptive coping strategies (Naglieri, LeBuffe, & Shapiro, 2013). From a student-focused perspective, however, there is some evidence that secondary students generally value these key competencies but have difficulty grasping what such dimensions mean in practical terms (Brudevold-Iversen, Peterson, & Cartwright, 2013).

Perhaps the most significant educational adjustment during secondary school in Aotearoa New Zealand is the National Certificate of Educational Achievement (NCEA). NCEA is a qualification that awards credit for high achievement in the learning areas from Years 11 to 13. Credits can be transferred later to tertiary study. In its current version, NCEA uses a criterion-referenced assessment framework to measure student competence. For every enrolled subject, one's performance is compared against two general types of learning outcomes referred to as achievement standards: (a) external standards (e.g., exams and portfolios assessed by the New Zealand Qualifications Authority [NZQA] at the end of the year), and internal standards (assessed internally by teachers during the year).

Key competencies of adolescents (13–18 years)

We highlight three key competencies that offer an emergent understanding of adolescents in secondary school: (1) risk-taking behaviours; (2) self and identity; and (3) metacognition. Adolescence involves considerable developmental changes in physical, psychological, and social domains (American Psychological Association, 2002; Dahl, 2004; Lesham, 2016). Whereas middle childhood is a relatively sturdy time in one's life, this is typically not the case in adolescence (Skinner & Zimmer-Gembeck, 2016).

At the onset of puberty, adolescents undergo considerable changes in hormones and neurological structures that underpin risk-taking activities (see Casey, 2015; Pellegrini & Bartini, 2001). To explain such behaviours, it is beneficial to understand the limbic system of the brain and its development during adolescence. The limbic system includes pathways relating memory, primary emotions, motivation, and learning (Casey, Jones, & Hare, 2008; Steinberg, 2010); it is, therefore, a central hub for relaying sensory information to higher-order processing in the brain. The limbic system is also responsible for reward-seeking and is stimulated during particularly emotional states. Because the system develops earlier than that of the prefrontal cortex (which oversees complex cognition such as self-regulation and executive function), adolescent desires for rewards often supersede rational thinking (Casey et al., 2008; Galvan, Hare, Voss, Glover, & Casey, 2007). Metaphorically, this developmental gap is like supercharging a car's engine and then waiting a few years to improve the brakes, suspension, and handling!

There are two critical points to make about risk-taking behaviours. First, although such actions can have potential dangers (e.g., substance abuse and having unprotected sex), not all risks are dangerous per se. In everyday life, young people may need to take risks to achieve their goals. For example, the decision to perform on stage in a school event requires some risk beyond their boundaries of comfort. Secondly, it is important to highlight that such behaviours should not be attributed solely to hormones and neurobiology, since such complex actions also have psychological, social, and cultural underpinnings (Skinner & Zimmer-Gembeck, 2016). During this developmental period, associations exist between adolescent pressures, mitigating risks, and a sense of self.

Adolescence is also a stage in life where an emerging sense of self and identity take place (McLean & Syed, 2016). Although identity is defined in various ways, self-identity broadly comprises adolescents' understanding of (a) their personal strengths and weaknesses as goal-directed, motivated agents (skills directly related to the subsequent sub-section on metacognition), (b) how they interact with their physical, social, and spiritual milieu (social actor), and (c) their life narrative from past experiences to future possibilities (autobiographical author) (Erikson, 1950, 1968; McAdams & Zapata-Gietl, 2015). Adolescents develop multiple roles, including their identity as a secondary student, friend, family and community member, romantic partner, and supporter of particular social and cultural beliefs. It is typical during adolescence that individuals experiment with who they are (actual self), who they could be (possible self), and their perceived compatibility or conflict with societal ideals and expectations (Markus & Nurius, 1986; Oyserman, Destin, & Novin, 2015).

In secondary school, adolescents face many new experiences that may challenge the self. Typical examples include school performance and attendance, peer pressure, romantic relationships, and financial pressure (Byrne, Davenport, & Mazanov, 2007). In Aotearoa New Zealand, Sotardi and Watson (2019) sought to identify the everyday stressors experienced by a large sample of adolescents in Auckland and Canterbury regions. Findings revealed that school performance, the conflict between school and leisure, and the uncertainty about the future were particular concerns. These were stronger among students later in secondary school, namely those in Years 11, 12, and 13—when the NCEA process commences. These everyday challenges have implications for identity development, as they are associated with weaker self-perceptions of school achievement and reduced satisfaction with life.

Adolescents often experience a desire for peer relationships and reluctance to seek guidance and support from adults (Allen & Miga, 2010). In Aotearoa New Zealand, secondary students who are bullied may be cautious in reporting such behaviours to teachers (Denny et al., 2015). A need for belongingness within one's social circle could help to explain the dramatic rise in risk-taking behaviours due to increased anxieties about not fitting in and rejection (Galvan et al., 2007; Steinberg, 2010). Researchers in Aotearoa New Zealand report that school belonging is vital to a positive sense of identity (Sanders & Munford, 2016) and that positive friendship groups could help to reduce the likelihood of risky and dangerous behaviours (Buckley, Chapman, Sheehan, & Cunningham, 2012). Longitudinal research in Aotearoa New Zealand indicates that poor self-esteem in childhood is linked to problems in adolescence (e.g., eating problems, suicidal ideation, depressive and anxiety disorders, and poor health) and social issues such as criminal convictions, early school departure, and long-term unemployment (see, for example, McGee & Williams, 2000; Trzesniewski et al., 2006). Given concerns about wellbeing (Boden, Sanders, Munford, Liebenberg, & McLeod, 2016; Fleming et al., 2014; UNICEF, 2017), there are opportunities for more psychological research in schools to support the holistic development of students in Aotearoa New Zealand.

Furthermore, adolescence is a period of increasing capability in complex reasoning, perspective-taking, and logical and abstract thinking, all of which contribute to more advanced problem-solving capabilities; that is, metacognition. Building on developments in theory of mind (ToM) during early childhood and executive functioning during middle childhood, advancements in cognitive abilities in adolescence contribute to the ability to reflect on one's thinking: metacognition. Mainly within the prefrontal cortex, metacognition represents one's active control over the process of thinking (Flavell, Miller, & Miller, 1993; Schneider, 2008). Metacognition is often referred to as thinking-about-thinking in that learners consider their mental processes within the context of performing cognitive activities.

Not surprisingly, metacognition has vast implications for secondary education (see, for example, Palincsar, 1986; see also Schneider, 2008), and particularly in Aotearoa New Zealand. First, the ability to identify students' learning strengths and weaknesses provides valuable information about which skills can be performed well and which areas need improvement (this corresponds to the development of self and identity, as previously noted). Secondly, the more sophisticated ability to plan, monitor, and evaluate situations aids students to flexibly modify their thoughts, feelings, and behaviours when needed. Thirdly, metacognition and its close connection to learning are always a cultural process in which students are acquiring skills and knowledge that will be useful to their culture (Arnett, Chapin, & Brownlow, 2018). Last, but not least, metacognitive knowledge and the self-regulated deployment of learning strategies can be modelled and taught by more knowledgeable others from late childhood on (Schneider, 2008). Unsurprisingly, research has consistently shown that metacognitive skills tend to be associated with better academic performance in secondary school even after individual differences in intellectual abilities are taken into account (see, for example, Veenman, Kok, & Blöte, 2005).

Development of metacognition, however, has trade-offs that are relevant to adolescents. On the one hand, metacognition can help learners to reflect on the self, set personal goals, and detect when help is needed to achieve these goals. On the other hand, metacognition can lead learners to more harshly judge and criticise the self, feel worried and anxious when personal goals appear unattainable, and trigger shame and rumination which hinders the likelihood of seeking help from others (Skinner & Zimmer-Gembeck, 2016). Metacognitive awareness, therefore, can give rise to concerns the student is continually judged by others (imaginary audience) and that others cannot understand them (personal fable) (Elkind, 1967). For better or worse, such dynamics collectively form an identity through continuous evaluation of personal values, beliefs, and the rewards desired by each individual. Within the social milieu of secondary school, learners compare their identities not only to personal standards but also social-prescribed norms. Together, these elements contribute to an evolving—often daunting—process toward self-discovery.

Concluding thoughts

In this chapter, we have provided an introductory overview of the psychology of education by bearing in mind an often overlooked cohort: the learners themselves. We agree that understanding the student is at the heart of developmental and educational psychology. We have highlighted literature that may be useful to educators—both pre-service and in-service—and to researchers and policy makers. One observation is that there seems to be an overall lack of peer-reviewed research involving learners as participants in Aotearoa New Zealand, especially in early childhood and primary education sectors. This empirical gap has direct implications for effective classroom practice in Aotearoa New Zealand, as incomplete or inaccurate understandings of how young people develop and learn may create problems for both the teacher and students. We believe that this is a gap worth filling, as the learner's voice is a powerful one when considering teaching, curriculum, and policy development. We encourage educators to collaborate with educational researchers and advocate for students in efforts to promote wellbeing and academic success in learners across Aotearoa New Zealand.

Appendix

Our search began with EBSCOHost in which all Education and Psychology databases were included. To gain an accurate picture of contemporary research, we limited our search to 10 years: 2009 to 2019. Upon inspecting the literature, our final search criteria included the following: (student* or learner*) AND (new zealand or aotearoa or nz) AND (early childhood or university or higher education or tertiary or primary school or elementary school or middle school or intermediate school or high school or secondary school or preschool or kindergarten) NOT (inpatient or outpatient or program* evaluation or mental health services or curricul* or teacher education or professional development or inservice teacher* or clinical or pre-service teacher* or education system or comparative or comparative education or social work* or public health or nursing or histor* or sociolog* or medic* or policy). This search generated 4,075 references. We further refined the search to set the search Geography to "New Zealand" among only source types of peer-reviewed academic journals. These refinements resulted in a manageable set of 1,231 references. To search for other potential references, we conducted a parallel search in the databases Web of Science and Index New Zealand (INNZ). These searches generated 112 and 41 references, respectively. Most, however, were duplicates of the previous search. A total of 38 new references were added. With this set of 1,269 references, we individually inspected all titles and abstracts. We removed any references which (a) were theoretical rather than empirical, (b) did not include students as participants of the research, and (c) included students as participants for empirical research but were not related to education (e.g., students used a convenience sample for unrelated research). This resulted in 467 references for review in NVivo.

Recommendations for further reading

Drewery, W., & Bird, L. (2004). *Human development in Aotearoa: A journey through life* (2nd ed.). Auckland: McGraw Hill.

Healey, D., & Healey, M. (2019). Randomized controlled trial comparing the effectiveness of structured-play (ENGAGE) and behavior management (TRIPLE P) in reducing problem behaviors in preschoolers. *Scientific Reports, 9*(1), 3497.

Skinner, E. A., & Zimmer-Gembeck, M. J. (2007). The development of coping. *Annual Review of Psychology, 58*, 119–144.

Zhang, Q. (2015). The voice of the child in early childhood education research in Australia and New Zealand: A systematic review. *Australasian Journal of Early Childhood, 40*(3), 97–104.

References

Adair, V. A. (1999). No bullies at this school: Creating safe schools. *Children's Issues, Journal of the Children's Issues Centre, 3*(1), 32–37.

Ainsworth, M. D. S. (1989). Attachments beyond infancy. *American Psychologist, 44*, 709–716.

Alansari, M. (2018, May 17). *Modern classrooms won't fix education*. Retrieved from: https://www.auckland.ac.nz/en/about/perspectives/opinion

Alderson-Day, B., & Fernyhough, C. (2015). Inner speech: Development, cognitive functions, phenomenology, and neurobiology. *Psychological Bulletin, 141*(5), 931–965.

Aldwin, C. M. (2007). *Stress, coping, and development: An integrative perspective*. New York, NY: Guilford.

Allen, J. P., & Miga, E. M. (2010). Attachment in adolescence: A move to the level of emotion regulation. *Journal of Social and Personal Relationships, 27*(2), 181–190.

American Psychological Association. (2002). *Developing adolescents: A reference for professionals*. Washington, DC: Author.

Arnett, J., Chapin, L., & Brownlow, C. (2018). *Human development: A cultural approach*. Melbourne, VIC: Pearson Australia.

Arsenio, W. F., Cooperman, S., & Lover, A. (2000). Affective predictors of preschoolers' aggression and peer acceptance. *Developmental Psychology, 36*, 438–448.

Astington, J. W. (1993). *The child's discovery of the mind* (Vol. 31). Cambridge, MA: Harvard University Press.

Bateman, A. (2013). Responding to children's answers: Questions embedded in the social context of early childhood education. *Early Years: An International Journal of Research and Development, 33*, 275–288.

Bergin, C., & Bergin, D. (2009). Attachment in the classroom. *Educational Psychology Review, 21*(2), 141–170.

Boden, J. M., Sanders, J., Munford, R., Liebenberg, L., & McLeod, G. F. (2016). Paths to positive development: A model of outcomes in the New Zealand youth transitions study. *Child Indicators Research, 9*(4), 889–911.

Boekaerts, M. (1993). Being concerned with well-being and with learning. *Educational Psychologist, 28*(2), 149–167.

Bowlby, R. (2004). *Fifty years of attachment theory*. London, UK: Karnac.

Brooks-Gunn, J. (2003). Do you believe in magic? What we can expect from early childhood intervention programs. *SRCD Social Policy Report, 17,* 3–14.

Brudevold-Iversen, T., Peterson, E. R., & Cartwright, C. (2013). Secondary school students' understanding of the socio-emotional nature of the New Zealand key competencies. *Teachers and Curriculum, 13,* 56–63.

Buckley, L., Chapman, R. L., Sheehan, M., & Cunningham, L. (2012). Keeping friends safe: A prospective study examining early adolescent's confidence and support networks. *Educational Studies, 38*(4), 373–381.

Buyse, E., Verschueren, K., & Doumen, S. (2011). Preschoolers' attachment to mother and risk for adjustment problems in kindergarten: Can teachers make a difference? *Social Development, 20*(1), 33–50.

Byrne, D. G., Davenport, S. C., & Mazanov, J. (2007). Profiles of adolescent stress: The development of the adolescent stress questionnaire (ASQ). *Journal of Adolescence, 30*(3), 393–416.

Cantor, P., Osher, D., Berg, J., Steyer, L., & Rose T. (2018). Malleability, plasticity, and individuality: How children learn and develop in context. *Applied Developmental Science, 22*(2), 1–31.

Carpendale, J. I., & Lewis, C. (2004). Constructing an understanding of mind: The development of children's social understanding within social interaction. *Behavioral and Brain Sciences, 27*(1), 79–96.

Carroll-Lind, J. (2009). *School safety: An inquiry into the safety of students at school*. Wellington: Office of the Children's Commissioner.

Casey, B. J. (2015). Beyond simple models of self-control to circuit-based accounts of adolescent behavior. *Annual Review of Psychology, 66,* 295–319.

Casey, B. J., Jones, R. M., & Hare, T. A. (2008). The adolescent brain. *Annals of the New York Academy of Sciences, 1124*(1), 111–126.

Clarkin-Phillips, J., Carr, M., Thomas, R., Tinning, A., & Waitai, M. (2018). Fostering the artistic and imaginative capacities of young children: Case study report from a visit to a museum. *International Journal of Early Childhood, 50*(1), 33–46.

Compas, B. E., Connor-Smith, J. K., Saltzman, H., Thomsen, A. H., & Wadsworth, M. E. (2001). Coping with stress during childhood and adolescence: Problems, progress, and potential in theory and research. *Psychological Bulletin, 127*(1), 87–127.

Csibra, G., & Gergely, G. (2009). Natural pedagogy. *Trends in Cognitive Sciences, 13*(4), 148–153.

Dahl, R. E. (2004). Adolescent brain development: A period of vulnerabilities and opportunities. Keynote address. *Annals of the New York Academy of Sciences, 1021*(1), 1–22.

Deak, G. O. (2014). Interrelations of language and cognitive development. In P. J. Brooks & V. Kempe (Eds.), *Encyclopedia of language development* (pp. 284–291). Thousand Oaks, CA: Sage.

Deborah, N., Dany, L., John, M., & Paulo, S. (2012). *OECD reviews of evaluation and assessment in education: New Zealand 2011* (Vol. 2012). OECD Publishing.

Denham, S., Bassett, H., & Zinsser, K. (2012). Early childhood teachers as socializers of young children's emotional competence. *Early Childhood Education Journal, 40*(3), 137–143.

Denham, S. A., Blair, K. A., DeMulder, E., Levitas, J., Sawyer, K., Auerbach-Major, S., & Queenan, P. (2003). Preschool emotional competence: Pathway to social competence? *Child Development, 74*, 238–256.

Denny, S., Peterson, E. R., Stuart, J., Utter, J., Bullen, P., Fleming, T., ... & Milfort, T. (2015). Bystander intervention, bullying, and victimization: A multilevel analysis of New Zealand high schools. *Journal of School Violence, 14*(3), 245–272.

Drewery, W., & Bird, L. (2004). *Human development in Aotearoa: A journey through life* (2nd ed.). Auckland: McGraw Hill.

Duhn, I. (2006). The making of global citizens: Traces of cosmopolitanism in the New Zealand early childhood curriculum, Te Whāriki. *Contemporary Issues in Early Childhood, 7*(3), 191–202.

Dunn, J. (1995). Children as psychologists: The later correlates of individual differences in understanding of emotions and other minds. *Cognition & Emotion, 9*(2–3), 187–201.

Durie, M. H. (1985). A Māori perspective of health. *Social Science & Medicine, 20*(5), 483–486.

du Plessis, K. (2009). Early childhood teacher–child attachment: A brief review of the literature. *He Kupu—The Word, 2*(1), 45–53.

Eisenberg, N., Cumberland, A., Spinrad, T. L., Fabes, R. A., Shepard, S. A., Reiser, M. et al. (2001). The relations of regulation and emotionality to children's externalizing and internalizing problem behavior. *Child Development, 72*, 1112–1134.

Elkind, D. (1967). Egocentrism in adolescence. *Child Development, 38*(4), 1025–1034.

Entwisle, D. R., & Alexander, K. L. (1993). Entry into school: The beginning school transition and educational stratification in the United States. *Annual Review of Sociology, 19*(1), 401–423.

Erikson, E. (1950). *Childhood and society.* New York, NY: Norton.

Erikson, E. (1968). *Youth: Identity and crisis.* New York, NY: Norton.

Fallin, K., Wallinga, C., & Coleman, M. (2001). Helping children cope with stress in the classroom setting. *Childhood Education, 78*(1), 17–24.

Flavell, J. H., Miller, P. H., & Miller, S. A. (1993). *Cognitive development.* Englewood Cliffs, NJ: Prentice-Hall.

Fleming, T. M., Clark, T., Denny, S., Bullen, P., Crengle, S., Peiris-John, R., ... Lucassen, M. (2014). Stability and change in the mental health of New Zealand secondary school students 2007–2012: Results from the national adolescent health surveys. *Australian & New Zealand Journal of Psychiatry, 48*(5), 472–480.

Fogel A. (1993). *Developing through relationships: Origins of communication, self, and culture.* Chicago, IL: University of Chicago Press.

Galvan, A., Hare, T., Voss, H., Glover, G., & Casey, B. J. (2007). Risk-taking and the adolescent brain: Who is at risk? *Development Science, 10*(2), F8–F14.

Guo, K. (2017). Immigrant children in the context of multicultural early childhood education. *Journal of Cultural Diversity, 24*(1), 13–19.

Hampton, T. (2006). Effects of stress on children examined. *Journal of the American Medical Association, 295*(16), 1888.

Hamre, B. K., & Pianta, R. C. (2005). Can instructional and emotional support in the first-grade classroom make a difference for children at risk of school failure? *Child Development, 76*(5), 949–967.

Healey, D. M., & Halperin, J. M. (2015). Enhancing neurobehavioral gains with the aid of games and exercise (ENGAGE): Initial open trial of a novel early intervention fostering the development of preschoolers' self-regulation. *Child Neuropsychology, 21*(4), 465–480.

Healey, D., & Healey, M. (2019). Randomized controlled trial comparing the effectiveness of structured-play (ENGAGE) and behavior management (TRIPLE P) in reducing problem behaviors in preschoolers. *Scientific Reports, 9*(1), 3497.

Hedges, H., Cullen, J., & Jordan, B. (2011). Early years curriculum: Funds of knowledge as a conceptual framework for children's interests. *Journal of Curriculum Studies, 43*(2), 185–205.

Hipkins, R. (2006). *The nature of the key competencies. A background paper*. Wellington: New Zealand Council for Educational Research.

Howes, C. (2010). Children's social development within the socialization context of child care and early childhood education. In Smith, K., & Hart, C (Eds), *The Wiley-Blackwell Handbook of Childhood Social Development* (pp. 246–262). Oxford, UK: Blackwell Publishing.

Howes, C., & Ritchie, S. (2002). *A matter of trust: Connecting teachers and learners in the early childhood classroom* (Vol. 84). New York, NY: Teachers College Press.

Howes, C., Sanders, K., & Lee, L. (2008). Entering a new peer group in ethnically and linguistically diverse childcare classrooms. *Social Development, 17*(4), 922–940.

Izard, C., Fine, S., Schultz, D., Mostow, A., Ackerman, B., & Youngstrom, E. (2001). Emotion knowledge as a predictor of social behavior and academic competence in children at risk. *Psychological Science, 12*, 18–23.

Karpov, Y. V. (2014). *Vygotsky for educators*. Cambridge, UK: Cambridge University Press.

Kim, S., Boldt, L. J., & Kochanska, G. (2015). From parent–child mutuality to security to socialization outcomes: Developmental cascade toward positive adaptation in preadolescence. *Attachment & Human Development, 17*(5), 472–491.

Lalonde, C. E., & Chandler, M. J. (1995). False belief understanding goes to school: On the social-emotional consequences of coming early or late to a first theory of mind. *Cognition & Emotion, 9*(2–3), 167–185.

Lau, B. W. K. (2002). Does the stress in childhood and adolescence matter? A psychological perspective. *The Journal of the Royal Society for the Promotion of Health, 122*(4), 238–244.

Lee, W., Carr, M., Soutar, B., & Mitchell, L. (2013). *Understanding the Te Whāriki approach: Early years education in practice*. London & New York: Routledge.

Leshem, R. (2016). Brain development, impulsivity, risky decision making, and cognitive control: Integrating cognitive and socioemotional processes during adolescence—An introduction to the special issue. *Developmental Neuropsychology, 41*(1/2), 1–5.

Lewis, C., Freeman, N. H., Kyriakidou, C., Maridaki-Kassotaki, K., & Berridge, D. M. (1996). Social influences on false belief access: Specific sibling influences or general apprenticeship? *Child Development, 67*(6), 2930–2947.

Lewit, E. M., & Baker, L. S. (1995). School readiness. *The Future of Children, 5*(2), 128–139.

Liu, D., Wellman, H. M., Tardif, T., & Sabbagh, M. A. (2008). Theory of mind development in Chinese children: A meta-analysis of false-belief understanding across cultures and languages. *Developmental Psychology, 44*(2), 523–531.

Magnuson, K. A., Ruhm, C., & Waldfogel, J. (2007). Does prekindergarten improve school preparation and performance? *Economics of Education Review, 26*(1), 33–51.

Markus, H., & Nurius, P. (1986). Possible selves. *American Psychologist, 41*(9), 954–969.

Mashburn, A. J., & Pianta, R. C. (2006). Social relationships and school readiness. *Early Education and Development, 17*(1), 151–176.

Mawson, W. B. (2014). Experiencing the 'wild woods': The impact of pedagogy on children's experience of a natural environment. *European Early Childhood Education Research Journal, 22*(4), 513–524.

McAdams, D. P., & Zapata-Gietl, C. (2015). Three strands of identity development across the human life course: Reading Erik Erikson in full. In K. C. McLean & M. Syed (Eds.), *The Oxford Handbook of identity development* (pp. 81–94). New York, NY: Oxford University Press.

McCaslin, M., Sotardi, V. A., & Vega, R. I. (2015). Self-regulated learning and classroom management. In E. T. Emmer & E. J. Sabornie (Eds.), *Handbook of classroom management* (2nd ed., pp. 322–343). New York, NY: Taylor & Francis.

McGee, R. O. B., & Williams, S. (2000). Does low self-esteem predict health compromising behaviours among adolescents? *Journal of Adolescence, 23*(5), 569–582.

McLaughlin, T., Aspden, K., & Clarke, L. (2017). How do teachers support children's social–emotional competence? Strategies for teachers. *Early Childhood Folio, 21*, 21–27.

McLean, K. C., & Syed, M. (2016). Personal, master, and alternative narratives: An integrative framework for understanding identity development in context. *Human Development, 58*(6), 318–349.

Metge, J. (1995). *New growth from old: The whānau in the modern world.* Wellington: Victoria University Press.

Ministry of Education. (2007). *The New Zealand curriculum for English-medium teaching and learning in years 1–13.* Wellington: Learning Media. Retrieved from: http://nzcurriculum.tki.org.nz/The-New-Zealand-Curriculum

Ministry of Education. (2015). *Flexible learning spaces in schools.* Retrieved from: http://www.education.govt.nz/school/property/state-schools/design-standards/flexible-learning-spaces/

Ministry of Education. (2017a). *Te Marautanga o Aotearoa.* Wellington: Ministry of Education.

Ministry of Education. (2017b). *Te whāriki: He whāriki mātauranga mō ngā mokopuna o Aotearoa: Early childhood curriculum.* Wellington: Author.

Mitchell-Copeland, J., Denham, S. A., & DeMulder, E. K. (1997). Q-sort assessment of child–teacher attachment relationships and social competence in the preschool. *Early Education and Development, 8*(1), 27–39.

Miyake, A., Friedman, N. P., Emerson, M. J., Witzki, A. H., Howerter, A., & Wager, T. D. (2000). The unity and diversity of executive functions and their contributions to complex "frontal lobe" tasks: A latent variable analysis. *Cognitive Psychology, 41*(1), 49–100.

Mutch, C. (2013). Progressive education in New Zealand: A revered past, a contested present and an uncertain future. *International Journal of Progressive Education, 9*(2), 98–116.

Naglieri, J. A., LeBuffe, P. A., & Shapiro, V. B. (2013). Assessment of social–emotional competencies related to resilience. In Goldstein, S., & Brooks, R. (Eds), *Handbook of resilience in children* (pp. 261–272). Boston, MA: Springer.

Olson, S. L., & Lunkenheimer, E. S. (2009). Expanding concepts of self-regulation to social relationships: Transactional processes in the development of early behavioral adjustment. In A. Sameroff (Ed.), *The transactional model of development: How children and contexts shape each other* (pp. 55–76). Washington, DC: American Psychological Association.

Oyserman, D., Destin, M., & Novin, S. (2015). The context-sensitive future self: Possible selves motivate in context, not otherwise. *Self and Identity, 14*(2), 173–188.

Palincsar, A. S. (1986). The role of dialogue in providing scaffolded instruction. *Educational Psychologist, 21,* 73–98.

Pellegrini, A. D., & Bartini, M. (2001). Dominance in early adolescent boys: Affiliative and aggressive dimensions and possible functions. *Merrill-Palmer Quarterly,* 142–163.

Pianta, R., Downer, J., & Hamre, B. (2016). Quality in early education classrooms: Definitions, gaps, and systems. *The Future of Children, 26*(2), 119–137.

Pons, F., Harris, P. L., & de Rosnay, M. (2004). Emotion comprehension between 3 and 11 years: Developmental periods and hierarchical organization. *European Journal of Developmental Psychology, 1*(2), 127–152.

Raskauskas, J. L., Gregory, J., Harvey, S. T., Rifshana, F., & Evans, I. M. (2010). Bullying among primary school children in New Zealand: Relationships with prosocial behaviour and classroom climate. *Educational Research, 52*(1), 1–13.

Raskauskas, J., & Stoltz, A. 2007. Relations between traditional and internet bullying among adolescent females. *Developmental Psychology, 43*(3), 564–575.

Rimm-Kaufman, S. E., Pianta, R. C., & Cox, M. J. (2000). Teachers' judgments of problems in the transition to kindergarten. *Early Childhood Research Quarterly, 15*(2), 147–166.

Rohrkemper, M., & Corno, L. (1988). Success and failure on classroom tasks: Adaptive learning and classroom teaching. *The Elementary School Journal, 88*(3), 297–312.

Romine, C. B., & Reynolds, C. R. (2005). A model of the development of frontal lobe functioning: Findings from a meta-analysis. *Applied Neuropsychology, 12*(4), 190–201.

Ruffman, T., Perner, J., Naito, M., Parkin, L., & Clements, W. A. (1998). Older (but not younger) siblings facilitate false belief understanding. *Developmental Psychology, 34*(1), 161–174.

Saarni, C. (1999). *The development of emotional competence.* New York, NY: Guilford Press.

Sanders, J., & Munford, R. (2016). Fostering a sense of belonging at school—five orientations to practice that assist vulnerable youth to create a positive student identity. *School Psychology International, 37*(2), 155–171.

Sargisson, R. J., & McLean, I. G. (2012). Children's use of nature in New Zealand playgrounds. *Children, Youth and Environments, 22*(2), 144–163.

Schneider, W. (2008). The development of metacognitive knowledge in children and adolescents: Major trends and implications for education. *Mind, Brain, and Education, 2*(3), 114–121.

Skinner, E. A., & Zimmer-Gembeck, M. J. (2016). *The development of coping: Stress, neurophysiology, social relationships, and resilience during childhood and adolescence.* Springer.

Skinner, E. A., & Zimmer-Gembeck, M. J. (2007). The development of coping. *Annual Review of Psychology, 58,* 119–144.

Sotardi, V. A. (2016). Understanding student stress and coping in elementary school: A mixed-method, longitudinal study. *Psychology in the Schools, 53*(7), 705–721.

Sotardi, V. A. (2017). Exploring school stress in middle childhood: Interpretations, experiences, and coping. *Pastoral Care in Education, 35*(1), 13–27.

Sotardi, V. A. (2018). Bumps in the road: Exploring teachers' perceptions of student stress and coping. *The Teacher Educator, 53,* 208–228.

Sotardi, V. A., & Watson, P. W. S. J. (2019). A sample validation of the Adolescent Stress Questionnaire (ASQ) in New Zealand. *Stress and Health, 35*(1), 3–14.

Stegge, H., & Terwogt, M. M. (2007). Awareness and regulation of emotion in typical and atypical development. In Gross, J. (Ed.), *Handbook of Emotion Regulation* (pp. 269–286). New York, NY: The Guilford Press.

Steinberg, L. (2010). A dual systems model of adolescent risk-taking. Developmental psychobiology. *The Journal of the International Society for Developmental Psychobiology, 52*(3), 216–224.

Taylor, M., & Carlson, S. M. (1997). The relation between individual differences in fantasy and theory of mind. *Child Development, 68*(3), 436–455.

Thompson, R. A. (2015). Relationships, regulation, and early development. *Handbook of Child Psychology and Developmental Science, 3*(6), 1–46.

Tomasello, M. (1999). *The cultural origins of human cognition.* Cambridge, MA: Harvard University Press.

Trzesniewski, K. H., Donnellan, M. B., Moffitt, T. E., Robins, R. W., Poulton, R., & Caspi, A. (2006). Low self-esteem during adolescence predicts poor health, criminal behavior, and limited economic prospects during adulthood. *Developmental Psychology, 42*(2), 381–390.

UNICEF. (2017). *Building the future: Children and the sustainable development goals in rich countries.* Innocenti Report Card 14. Florence, Italy: UNICEF Office of Research.

van der Veer, R. (2007). *Lev Vygotsky.* New York, NY: Bloomsbury.

Veenman, M., Kok, R., & Blöte, A. (2005). The relation between intellectual and metacognitive skills in early adolescence. *Instructional Science, 33,* 193–211.

Verschueren, K., & Koomen, H. M. (2012). Teacher–child relationships from an attachment perspective. *Attachment & Human Development, 14*(3), 205–211.

Vygotsky, L. S. (1980). *Mind in society.* Cambridge, MA: Harvard University Press.

Wellman, H. (2018) Theory of mind: The state of the art. *European Journal of Developmental Psychology, 15,* 728–755.

Wellman, H. M. (2002). Understanding the psychological world: Developing a theory of mind. *Blackwell Handbook of Childhood Cognitive Development,* 167–187.

Wellman, H. M., Fang, F., & Peterson, C. C. (2011). Sequential progressions in a theory-of-mind scale: Longitudinal perspectives. *Child Development, 82*(3), 780–792.

Yan, E. (2009). *The classroom emotional environment: Observing teachers' interactions with their students.* Unpublished honours thesis, Massey University, Palmerston North, New Zealand.

Yu, Y., Bonawitz, E., & Shafto, P. (2019). Pedagogical questions in parent–child conversations. *Child Development, 90*(1), 147–161.

Zelazo, P. D., Carlson, S. M., & Kesek, A. (2008). The development of executive function in childhood. In C. A. Nelson & M. Luciana (Eds.), *Developmental cognitive neuroscience. Handbook of developmental cognitive neuroscience* (pp. 553–574). Cambridge, MA: MIT Press.

Zhang, Q. (2015). The voice of the child in early childhood education research in Australia and New Zealand: A systematic review. *Australasian Journal of Early Childhood, 40*(3), 97–104.

Chapter 6
Curriculum studies

Jane Abbiss

Introduction

Curriculum studies is a field of educational endeavour that presents a wide range of issues and questions about curriculum. These include, but are not restricted to, questions about: the nature and moral purpose of curriculum; curriculum policy and influences on national curriculum development; curriculum design and the curriculum in practice, in particular educational contexts; teacher and learner curriculum experiences; and pedagogical approaches and challenges in specific sectors, learning areas, or subjects.

Curriculum and curriculum-related concerns are the focus of research across different fields—for example, in analysis of curriculum policy; research on teaching and learning, pedagogy, and assessment; and engagement with questions of equity and social justice in education. Yet some have argued that it is only relatively recently that curriculum has become a substantial field of educational studies, and that across the decades curriculum has been under-theorised and poorly understood (Hargreaves, 1994; Mutch, 2009; Snook, 1995). A contemporary challenge, then, in curriculum studies is to highlight the relevance of inquiry that focuses intentionally on curriculum and curriculum issues, which means making explicit and inviting discussion and debate about the contemporary and emerging curriculum challenges that confront those involved in curriculum policy development, curriculum design, and in shaping the learning experiences for children and young people.

Every day, learners and teachers engage with, shape, respond to, and experience curriculum in a variety of forms. Curriculum and curriculum issues are of keen public interest. The news and popular media often carry stories relating to concerns about what is taught in schools and how it is taught—witness the persistent discussion and debates relating to: students' performance in mathematics (e.g., in PISA [Programme for International Student Assessment] test results), and questioning of what and how mathematics is taught; the nature and appropriateness of literacy teaching and learning within primary and early childhood contexts; sexuality education and sensitivities about what should be taught in schools, and by whom; policy developments and priorities that emphasise STEM (Science, Technology, Engineering, and Mathematics) education; the teaching of New Zealand history in schools, and, more specifically, history relating to the New Zealand Wars and colonisation; and concerns about the underachievement of particular groups of learners and whether or not the curriculum, and how it is taught and experienced by learners, serves those learners well. These matters are just illustrative of a wide range of curriculum-related debates. While some curriculum concerns may be specific to the Aotearoa New Zealand context, many are represented in international debate even as they are given local expression.

Broadly speaking, curriculum studies relate to the key question, "What knowledge is of most worth?" (Pinar, 2012, p. xv) and those engaged in exploration of curriculum issues ask questions about what, how, and for whom (Mutch, 2009). Curriculum researchers question who makes curriculum decisions, the intentions and messages contained within curriculum policies and practices (both explicit and implicit), the consequences of these decisions, and tensions that may exist within and between policies and practices. These questions reflect and illuminate global concerns about curriculum that play out in different ways at the local level. This chapter provides an overview of some different ways of thinking about and understanding curriculum and examines some contemporary curriculum issues in Aotearoa New Zealand, paying particular attention to emerging issues and placing these within broader contexts. The intention is to provide background and signpost contemporary and emerging curriculum challenges for those involved in curriculum development and the design of teaching and learning experiences for the children and young people of Aotearoa New Zealand.

Understanding curriculum

There are different ways of thinking about and engaging with the notion of 'curriculum'. Curriculum theory helps make sense of people's experiences with curriculum, of curriculum reform, and of a complex curriculum landscape. One way of thinking about curriculum is through schemas or classifications of types of curriculum. Examples of different curriculum types derived from such classification include, but are not restricted to, notions of:

Official curriculum: the authorised, formal curriculum that establishes priorities and provides foci for teaching and learning. This includes national curriculum policies for early childhood, primary, and secondary education, encompassing *Te Whāriki* (Ministry of Education, 2017b, early childhood curriculum), *Te Marautanga o Aotearoa* (Ministry of Education, 2017a, curriculum for Māori-medium education in primary and secondary education), and *The New Zealand Curriculum (NZC)* (Ministry of Education, 2007, primary and secondary English-medium curriculum).

Assessment curriculum: the assessment policies and frameworks that specify what needs to be taught for assessment purposes at different levels, which includes the high-stakes National Certificate of Educational Achievement (NCEA) assessment framework at secondary level. Assessment frameworks impact what is actually taught, as assessment requirements may drive teaching and learning in an educational setting and act as default or de facto curricula.

Enacted curriculum: the curriculum in practice—how curriculum policy and assessment frameworks are given effect through enactment of teaching and learning programmes and design for learning. This occurs as teachers follow through on their plans to convey ideas, engage with content, and develop learners' skills or competencies through the actual teaching and learning activities in educational settings. The curriculum in practice includes classroom-based and "education outside the classroom" (EOTC) learning opportunities.

Experienced curriculum: the curriculum that is the lived experience of learners. The focus is on learners, what they encounter, and how they make sense of their engagements in learning contexts, what they really learn, and the messages they take with them from their learning experiences.

Hidden curriculum: relates to the values, ideological elements, social structures, routines, and practices of educational establishments that are taken for granted but which provide subtle and potent messages about what is really important. These messages tend to have a marginalising effect, in providing signals about whose and what knowledge is valued—and whose and what knowledge doesn't really count.

Outside curriculum: non-school influences on learning, where learning takes place outside of early childhood centres or schools. These include shadow education, a concept that encapsulates a range of tutoring and classes that take place outside of mainstream education, as well as more informal influences relating to culture, families and home, mass and social media, communities and community-based organisations (Abbiss, 2019; McGee, 1997; McGee & Fraser, 2001; Schubert, 2008; Young, Gough, & Jung, 2018).

As a corollary to recognition that there are different types of curriculum, curriculum may also be examined in relation to curriculum developments, or the accounting of where and how particular curricula (e.g., national or subject-specific official and assessment curricula) came to be, or where and how particular curricula are enacted or experienced in different educational contexts. Curriculum may also be examined for the ideas contained within documents or programmes and the knowledge or values that are conveyed. For example, in a survey of international trends in curriculum developments within selected English-speaking countries and focusing at the policy level, Sinnema and Aitken (2013) identified common goals and emphases relating to curriculum developments. These common goals relate to the use of curriculum as a lever for educational improvement, curriculum development in the service of equity for particular groups of learners and equity as a focus of teaching, a future focused orientation relating to the preparation of students for uncertain economic futures, and a search for curriculum coherence. Within curriculum policies, emphasis is given to the development of learner competencies, values, and agency, and providing guidance for teachers relating to desirable pedagogy, strengthening partnerships between school and home, and reduced curriculum prescription, all as a means to achieve the common goals. Tensions are evident between the rhetoric of aspirational goals and the contextual realities of teachers' work.

Another way of engaging with the concept of curriculum is through curriculum discourses, which may be represented through metaphorical or symbolic understandings of "curriculum as …"; for example, curriculum as institutionalised, gender, racial, political, historical, or autobiographical/biographical text

(Pinar, Reynolds, Slattery, & Taubman, 2004). Focusing on the idea of curriculum 'texts' emphasises the discursive nature of human reality, constituted through language. Paying attention to curriculum discourses highlights the way in which understandings of curriculum reflect changing ways in which people engage with ideas about curriculum, how particular ideas of curriculum might be the focus of attention at a particular historical juncture, and how these ideas shift. This is a way of understanding the curriculum field that takes account of people's perspectives and challenges the notion of a 'master' or single narrative for understanding curriculum and the field of curriculum studies. By way of illustration, the 'curriculum as political text' discourse emphasises the politically charged, non-neutral nature of curriculum and the notion that "curriculum can be understood in any comprehensive sense only if it is contextualized socially, economically, and politically" (Pinar et al., 2004, p. 244); whereas the discourse of 'curriculum as autobiographical or biographical text' draws attention to and emphasises personal experience in the ways in which curriculum is encountered, experienced, and negotiated by people. Curriculum actors are understood to have a sense of self and bring their own biographies and life experiences to their engagement with curriculum. Curriculum discourses intersect, while also providing distinct ways of thinking about and understanding curriculum. There is, for example, an element of the historical in the autobiographical, and the notion of curriculum as gender or racial text carries political overtones in attention that is given to reproductions of power and challenges that may be made to power relations.

For some teachers, researchers, and developers, it might be tempting to see curriculum simply as policy that has to be implemented and adhered to, in order to meet specified educational outcomes, learning goals, or assessment results. While this essentially technocratic view of curriculum might reflect the political realities of teachers' work within accountability regimes, a broader view of curriculum provides a deeper and richer understanding of curriculum and teachers' agency in shaping curriculum and the learning experiences of children and young people. A more nuanced understanding of curriculum comes with recognition of the political nature of curriculum and the importance of not separating curriculum from the structures and wider political changes within which it is embedded (Hargreaves, 1989; Roberts, 2003), along with recognition of the ideological nature of curriculum and the contestability of curriculum in relation to claims for knowledge that is worth knowing (Pinar, 2012). The ideological nature of curriculum is similarly highlighted in recognition of ways that hidden curricula operate, where norms, values, and beliefs are consciously and unconsciously conveyed through social interactions and organisational structures (Giroux & Penna, 1979).

Considering the role of teachers in relation to curriculum, a nuanced understanding of curriculum highlights different assumptions and conflicting expectations of teachers in positions as both 'curriculum implementers' and 'curriculum designers'. As implementers, teachers are held responsible for the enactment of the official curriculum and the execution of assessment procedures. As designers, they are positioned as active in curriculum development as they interpret, reconstruct, and co-construct curriculum in context and practice (Elliott, 1998; McGee, 1997). In an implementer role, teachers might be seen more as technicians. In a designer role, they are agentic in shaping, framing, and opening up possibilities for knowledge that is worth knowing. In acknowledging the role of teachers as curriculum designers, though, it is also important to recognise that curriculum is a structure that constrains the activities of learners, teachers, and curriculum developers alike (Young, 2014). It both sets limits and makes things possible. Teachers navigate for themselves, in specific contexts, the tensions between the different roles they perform, expectations placed on them, and the nature of their curriculum agency (Biesta & Tedder, 2007; Biesta, Priestley, & Robinson, 2015).

Contemporary and emerging curriculum issues

Teachers across sectors (early childhood, primary, secondary) engage with curriculum challenges every day. They do this as they engage in the development of learning activities, in lesson and course design, and as they make decisions about what learners need to know, understand, or be able to do. They face challenges in making sense of official or prescribed curricula and the messages these present, as they design subject curricula or learning programmes and enact these in practice. Curriculum issues may be very particular and context specific, for example, relating to what aspect of a science topic to emphasise, and what kinds of learning activities will best support learning with a particular group of children or young people. There are, though, some broad and interconnected curriculum themes that are evident in a range of curriculum debates. These include: questions about the nature of knowledge; 21st century learning and future-focused curriculum; tight–loose curriculum reform; and the relationship between curriculum and assessment. This is a list of selected rather than definitive curriculum themes. Rather than representing problems that can be solved by teachers, curriculum developers, or policy makers, these themes represent dilemmas that need to be constantly negotiated, worked through, resolved, and reconsidered by these people in their work and interactions with curriculum policies and materials, colleagues, learners, and communities.

Knowledge and curriculum

If it is accepted that curriculum debates ultimately come down to questions of what knowledge is most valued, then explicit engagement with questions about whose knowledge is valued, what type of knowledge is valued, who gets or should get to decide, how this is decided, and whose interests are served and should be served, is important for those involved in curriculum development and design. These are broad questions for educational theorists and philosophers that transcend national boundaries. In Aotearoa New Zealand, these questions are manifest in relation to debates about the nature and valuing of Indigenous Māori knowledge, Western knowledge, the cultural knowledges of diverse ethnic communities and learners, and discipline and subject knowledge. These questions and debates are both moral and political: moral in the sense that they involve consideration of values, and political in how they invite a political stance by those who make decisions about that which is important to defend or about that which it is important to advocate for change. Justice cannot be done to the breadth, depth, and nuance of the debates in a section within a chapter, but examples of these provide a taste of how questions of knowledge and curriculum have emerged as contemporary educational issues of relevance for curriculum developers and teachers.

The aspirations for nurturing a bicultural society, underpinned by Te Tiriti o Waitangi, have led scholars to question how Indigenous Māori knowledge is and is not valued in curriculum, and how this knowledge may sit in contrast with and alongside Western and traditional disciplinary knowledge. For example, in reflecting on the significance of *Te Marautanga o Aotearoa* and its relationship with *NZC*, Stewart, Trinick, and Dale (2017) highlight the "contested" nature of this relationship and tensions in development processes across two decades that historically belie the rhetoric of a commitment to similar valuing of English-medium and Māori-medium curricula. They explain that the Māori-medium curriculum for schools was developed on a different time-frame than its English-medium counterpart, and that the structures of the English-medium version were applied to the Māori-medium curriculum—some elements being imposed and some elements and models being voluntarily adopted. They also identify challenges for the curriculum writers of *Te Marautanga o Aotearoa* in defining the knowledge base and the nature and purpose of learning within the curriculum where there is a range of goals or motivations. These aims include advancing Māori goals for te reo learning as part of a broader language revitalisation movement, articulating a Māori world view and philosophy, and revitalising Māori knowledge, while also seeking to maintain the "rights of Māori-medium students to access all the benefits of global knowledge represented by NZC" (Stewart, Trinick & Dale, 2017, p. 12) and ensure that Māori learners are not disadvantaged in relation to future career and study pathways.

Questions have also been asked about the valuing of Pasifika knowledge in curriculum (relating to those of Pacific heritage, who have immigrated to or were born in New Zealand), and the inclusion of Pacific people in the development of curriculum. For example, focusing on the development of the process for the development and review of a national curriculum for early childhood, Leaupepe, Matapo, and Ravlich (2017) emphasise the importance of acknowledging the multicultural, Pasifika fabric of Aotearoa New Zealand society and of affirming the culture and identity of Pacific children and reflecting Pasifika perspectives in curriculum. For them, this needs to extend beyond superficial naming of examples of ethnic-specific ways of knowing within curriculum to provide deeper understanding of meaning. It calls for a richer image of the Pacific child within curriculum. While there will be debate amongst curriculum developers about the nature of national curriculum documents and the level of detail these should provide, both within official curriculum documents and in support materials, a key point is that questions are raised about the valuing of different cultural knowledges within curriculum, where these are seen to be undervalued or unrecognised in curriculum policy and the curriculum in practice.

Turning attention to subjects in the school-level curriculum—which have foundations in parent disciplines and are the traditional building blocks for learning in schools—there has been a shift in emphasis within curriculum whereby developments over the past 20 years have given prominence to key competencies and values over subject content (Benade, 2013, 2014; Hipkins & Boyd, 2011; Sinnema & Aitken, 2013). For some, this represents a hollowing out or downgrading of the content and knowledge foundations of subjects or learning areas in *NZC*; whereas for others, it represents a vehicle for change, responsiveness to shifting social and economic needs, and a future-focused curriculum that suits the needs of 21st century learners. Tensions relating to the nature of knowledge and relative emphasis placed on knowledge, competencies, and learning processes take specific form in relation to particular subjects and learning areas, including, for example, music (McPhail, 2014, 2016), science (Hipkins & Bull, 2015; Stewart & Buntting, 2015), and social sciences (Abbiss, 2011, 2013; Aitken, 2006; Harcourt, Milligan, & Wood, 2018; Ormond, 2012). They are articulated in questions about the purpose of education; the emphasis that is or should be given to skills development, subject content, or substantive knowledge, and core conceptual understandings within subjects; and how broadly framed competencies may intersect and interact with processes by which knowledge is built within subjects through disciplinary forms of reasoning.

In the context of specific subjects or learning areas, teachers negotiate the tension between subject knowledge and competencies, in the process of deciding the emphasis they should give to the theoretical or conceptual foundations of subjects, which provide access to the systems of meaning within subjects, and to practical, inquiry, experiential, and competency-related elements, which help make connections with real-world contexts and problems and enhance the relevance of learning. At the same time, teachers also take into account the interests, experience, and knowledge of the learners in their care and for whom they design and enact the curriculum through pedagogical practices. In negotiating this tension, teachers make decisions about the type of knowledge that is worth knowing, which are value judgements that may be made consciously or unconsciously. Rather than engaging with the knowledge–competencies nexus in oppositional terms, challenges for teachers relate more to how they might draw on different forms of knowledge to develop curricula in practice that support social justice goals by providing access to knowledge and skills that are important and relevant for learners, in specific subjects and across subjects.

There is, though, always a need for educators to be conscious that national curricula represent knowledge valued by those with power and that any curriculum negotiations involve power—including decisions made about curriculum development at the national level and school levels. In the words of Young and Muller (2019) "we recognise that no knowledge, including specialised knowledge, when used in the real world of contending interests, can remain innocent of power relations" (p. 208). In making curriculum design decisions, curriculum developers and teachers engage with knowledge–power relations in the decisions they make about what is relevant, what is important, and what is possible.

Twenty-first century learning and future-focused curriculum

Already hinted at within the discussion of knowledge and curriculum, 21st century learning and future-focused curriculum is a prominent theme in contemporary curriculum debate, both nationally and internationally. For more than a decade, education policies in Aotearoa New Zealand have been directed towards the development of knowledge societies, 21st century learning, and 'modern' or 'innovative' schooling environments and pedagogies (Abbiss, 2015; Benade, Gardner, Teschers, & Gibbons, 2014; see also Chapter 14 of this collection). This echoes an international trend, both at governmental level and the level of supra-national organisations, such as the OECD. The OECD (2006, 2013) has strongly advocated for education oriented towards 21st century learning and innovative learning environments, to support the education of knowledge workers for the future. In reviewing national curricula for different nations, and including Aotearoa New Zealand in the review, Sinnema and Aitken (2013) highlight commonalities across newly developed curricula in different countries that include a move beyond content and skills to focus on competencies for 21st century learners.

So, what is 21st century learning and a future-focused curriculum? The discourses of 21st century learning, future-focused curriculum, knowledge societies, and innovative learning environments are interconnected. Discussion about 21st century learning and skills emphasises components of 'deep learning', where students are empowered to have autonomy over and take responsibility for their own learning (Mahat, Bradbeer, Byers, & Imms, 2018). However, while emphasis is placed on elements such as student-centred, inquiry-based, personalised, collaborative, authentic, and active learning, these are not necessarily new ideas or pedagogical approaches and nor are they exclusive to the 21st century learning discourse. What distinguishes 21st century learning is the contextualisation of curriculum and learning in a highly connected digital world. In seeking to define 21st century learning, Benade (2014) distinguishes it as "teaching and learning that prepares young people for engaging in complex socioeconomic and political contexts that are deeply influenced by globalisation and the revolution in digital technology" (p. 338). The idea of future-oriented learning, also framed as 21st century learning, assumes the ubiquity of digital technologies in many societies and an important role for new technologies in shaping teaching and learning (Benade et al., 2014; Istance & Kools, 2013). There is also recognition that the learners of today will work in a rapidly changing and digitally connected world. The world of the future in which today's learners will live may be hard to imagine.

Given impetus by Gilbert's (2005) examination of the knowledge society and the future of education, educators in Aotearoa New Zealand have questioned the nature of learning and efficacy of teaching practices for 21st century learners. Advocates of future-oriented education envisage a paradigm shift in education and the transformation of teaching and learning in ways that are increasingly responsive to the needs and interests of new millennium learners (Bolstad et al., 2012). This involves a shift in thinking about teaching and learning, and about knowledge. Distinguished from other views on knowledge, such as social constructivist and social realist views, futures thinkers' views of knowledge are characterised by the rejection of the idea of knowledge being 'stuff' or content to be learnt and of knowledge structures based in discipline silos, and advocacy for a view of knowledge as a problem-solving process. While disciplinary or subject knowledge is still valued as raw material, the way in which students engage with this knowledge and build their knowledge base is reconceptualised; understanding how disciplinary knowledge systems work and ability to move between disciplines become more important than just knowing and being able to recall detailed facts related to a subject (Benade, 2014; Bolstad et al., 2012).

A future-focused curriculum, then, is one that is oriented towards 21st century learning and transformation of education. In the official curriculum, *NZC*, there is emphasis on key competencies, learning directed towards problem solving, and the development of learning dispositions for lifelong learning. As a curriculum in practice and experienced by learners, it is one where learning is highly personalised, learners have more say over the focus of learning and how they will engage with content and subject material, and where curriculum is organised in interdisciplinary and integrated ways. Learners experience the curriculum through digitally mediated learning platforms and collaborative learning networks.

The orientation towards 21st century learning and a future-focused curriculum is accompanied by a 'spatial turn' in educational policy (Benade, 2019). Redesigning learning environments is seen as a way of the future, which promotes change in the 'pedagogical core' of education and promotes increased educational effectiveness (Istance & Kools, 2013) and which focuses on use of space in relation to 'activity systems' (Alterator & Deed, 2018). In Aotearoa New Zealand, as in other countries, the spatial turn is characterised by building designs that remove traditional classroom cells in favour of more permeable, open plan spaces that support multiple and different types of educational activities taking place at the same time and which have digital connectivity. These are variously labelled 'modern', 'flexible' and 'innovative' learning environments and they are intended to support facilitative styles of teaching, where teachers work in collaborative teams, with multiple groups of students, in shared learning spaces. These environments are intended to shift the way in which curriculum is organised in practice and experienced by learners.

For teachers as curriculum designers, there are significant implications for changes in practice as they are required to work differently in the new spaces, design integrated curricula and personalised learning opportunities, and teach in different ways—through digital platforms, in collaboration with other teachers, and interacting with and facilitating learning for different groups of learners who may or may not constitute their 'class'. In thinking about the relationship between space and pedagogy, it is important to distinguish flexible learning pedagogy from the flexible space itself: while flexible learning spaces may be designed to support pedagogical practices that may not easily be enacted within traditional single-cell classrooms, it is possible to teach in traditional ways within the flexible space. Likewise, it is possible to enact innovative pedagogies within single-cell classroom spaces. Also, 'personalised learning' may be understood differently by teachers, who may place greater or lesser emphasis on individualised and independent learning or on whole-class learning programmes that enable students as a group to engage with real-life problems, topics, or contexts that are of interest and relevance to them, or to collaborate with others on problems or topics. Human factors relating to the valuing of different and particular pedagogical practices will likely impact the use of space and nature of the enacted curriculum. However, research around the relationships between learning spaces and teacher mind frames, the learning experiences of children and young people, and the nature of learning and achievement of diverse learners within flexible learning environments is emergent. These are aspects of curriculum research that are gaining increasing attention.

Tight–loose curriculum reform

A perennial curriculum theme is the relationship between prescription or compulsory curriculum requirements (tightness) and flexibility or curriculum choice (looseness). Thompson and Wiliam (2007) offered the "Tight but Loose" (p. 2) framework to theorise tensions between opposing factors in scalable school reform, which can also act as a tool to support the design and implementation of classroom interventions as part of reform agendas. The idea of a tight–loose relationship highlights a simultaneous need to maintain fidelity with the core principles or ideas that drive reform while also ensuring enough flexibility is built into the system so that people can take advantage of local opportunities and be responsive to local contexts. Although Thompson and Wiliam were concerned with assessment reform, the tight–loose relationship can also be applied to curriculum reform and regulation. Curriculum is a lever of reform, through which governments shape schooling, teaching, and learning. The tight–loose dynamic accounts for the way in which national curriculum policy and official curriculum documents regulate teaching and learning in ways that serve a broad reforming purpose but where the curriculum in practice is locally developed, varied, and context-related.

Official curricula provide a degree of prescription through mandated requirements. These requirements may relate to broad competencies, skills or knowledge that learners must engage with across the curriculum and in subjects or learning areas; also, what learning areas or subjects students should engage with at different levels. National curricula can be 'tighter' or 'looser' in their degree of prescription. In the international curriculum scheme of things, *NZC* is recognised as a conceptual, permissive, high-autonomy, and intentionally broad national curriculum (Abbiss 2011; Priestley & Sinnema, 2014; Sheehan, 2017). It provides a conceptual guide for teaching and learning, rather than a detailed prescription of subject content, and emphasises school-level autonomy and flexibility that places considerable responsibility on teachers for school-level curriculum development and design of the curriculum in practice. At the same time, it presents challenges for teachers in their professional decision making about the nature and design of the curriculum at school levels, as they seek to enact curriculum values and frameworks for learning in schools in ways that are responsive to their learners.

While the flexibility that is offered by *NZC* for teachers to be responsive to learners is generally seen as a good thing, there are critics who suggest that the broad and briefly described or vague nature of guidance provided in the official curriculum may not necessarily be helpful. For example, Zohar and Hipkins (2018) suggest that there is a looseness in the national curricula in both New Zealand and Israel that is "associated with a lack of clear criteria for teaching, assessing and designing interventions that include a focus on knowledge-building practices in the disciplines, i.e. an epistemic focus" (p. 44). They suggest there is a need for clearer explication of knowledge-building practices, development of more models of instruction and assessment for teachers, and provision of professional development that supports teachers' understanding of disciplinary practices, modes of inquiry, and associated higher order thinking in disciplinary context. In examining specific examples of a global 'new curriculum' that is characterised by emphasis on development of more generic skills, capacities, or competencies and flexibility of content, Priestley and Sinnema (2014) note that the professional space given to teachers in Aotearoa New Zealand and Scotland to determine content might signal a shift towards higher levels of professional trust and autonomy for curriculum decision making in their local contexts. However, a lack of specification of process for deciding what content is important in context also presents risks relating to the downgrading of content knowledge, or of content being specified for poorly considered reasons. The 'looseness' of curriculum is seen as a source of possible confusion.

The tight–loose relationship gives rise to a wide variety of practice challenges or dilemmas. In the process of developing official curriculum policy documents, curriculum policy makers and writers contend with content aspects of curriculum (what teachers should teach and learners should learn), process elements (how content should be taught and learnt), and theoretical foundations of curriculum development (the purpose of curriculum reform). Challenges arise in how they signal shifts in purpose of national curricula and how they avoid excessive prescription while also supporting sense-making by teachers and others who interpret and design curriculum in practice (Aitken, 2006). At the level of schools and classrooms, dilemmas for teachers include how to make sense of a sometimes wide array of official curriculum and allied support documents, how to balance breadth and depth of learning, and how to decide what is essential for all learners as opposed to that which can be a matter of learner choice (relating to topics, nature of learning activities and assessments, and modes of engagement with learning materials). Teachers also grapple with how to resolve pressures within national qualification and assessment frameworks to 'teach to the test' against a desire to provide rich learning experiences and intelligible learning programmes, and how to develop learners' higher order cognitive thinking, key competencies, and learning dispositions while simultaneously engaging with and deepening knowledge and understanding.

Examples of how teachers may 'work out' the prescription–choice dilemma include the extent to which, and ways that, they enable learners to pursue topics or questions that learners themselves decide are relevant, within the parameters of compulsory topics or processes specified in national curricula or assessment frameworks; also, how learners get to engage with content, competencies, or skills and learning materials, and how they get to show what they know. As a matter of school-wide policy, some subjects, learning areas, or knowledge domains may be prioritised over others in the design of school curricula and learning programmes. In the primary schooling context, literacy and STEM-related learning may be given more focused time in the curriculum than social studies or music, or project-based learning may be designed to focus on particular curriculum elements as matters of priority. At the secondary level, the nature of curriculum choices provided for learners may mean they have little engagement with some subjects or learning areas. Whether or not the prioritising of some learning areas or subjects is seen as a problem, though, depends on people's views on the worth of different subjects and the place of disciplinary knowledge in curriculum design. It is important to recognise that disciplinary knowledge is not the same as subjects and it is possible to have rigorous and logically connected teaching and learning programmes that are not framed as traditional subjects (Priestley & Sinnema, 2014).

The 'new curriculum', combined with a 'spatial turn' in school design and future-focused learning movement, has seen a trend towards more integrated, interdisciplinary learning and curriculum design in Aotearoa New Zealand. The tightness of curriculum supports reform agendas, which involve an emphasis on development of learner competencies and knowledge acquisition associated with specified learning areas. The looseness of curriculum enables the curriculum in practice to be shaped in ways that are responsive to learners, in local contexts, and firmly positions teachers as key curriculum developers and designers. Tight–loose curriculum dynamics have influenced and will continue to be a feature of national and local curriculum development and decision making, although policy changes may see changes in the tight–loose balance.

Curriculum and assessment relationship

Curriculum and assessment are interconnected. Assessment frameworks are designed to find out what learners know or understand from engagement with curriculum, but they also shape the curriculum by influencing what is taught and learnt. The relationship between curriculum and assessment highlights the political nature of curriculum and how it needs to be understood in the context of political, social, and economic change. Internationally, curriculum has increasingly become the business of national governments and supra-national organisations, especially through assessment structures such as PISA (Programme for International Students Assessment) which is an OECD assessment programme that provides international comparisons of student achievement (Biesta & Priestley, 2013). The government in Aotearoa New Zealand, along with other governments, looks to PISA results as a marker of national educational success. Slipping PISA rankings are a cause for concern and lead to questioning about the nature of curriculum-related learning and perceived failings in teaching. There is evidence that as school curricula, including those of Aotearoa New Zealand, have become increasingly flexible and generic, they have also narrowed in contexts where there is high-stakes assessment and strengthening accountability pressures (Crooks, 2011; Priestley & Sinnema, 2014). Pressure exerted through high-stakes assessment in Aotearoa New Zealand reflects international trends.

Taking the position that curriculum represents what is taught and learnt in practice, assessment can be seen as a driver of curriculum, and in some contexts it is a very powerful driver. It is broadly accepted that 'assessment for learning' is an important element of teachers' pedagogical practice—to deepen learner understanding, support learners to identify and achieve next learning steps, and help children and young people to develop skills and commitment to learning (Black & Wiliam, 1998; Crooks, 2011; Thompson & Wiliam, 2007). Beyond localised assessment practice, though, there is a range of assessment regimes that influence what is taught and learnt. There is evidence that these frameworks exert a strong influence on the enacted curriculum.

High-stakes assessment may be used as a tool to influence teaching and learning and it also may have unintended impacts on the enacted and experienced curriculum. The process whereby assessment influences teachers and learners is referred to as 'washback' (Mizutani, Rubie-Davies, Hattie, & Philp, 2011). At the primary school level, the requirement introduced in 2010 (and removed from 2018) for compulsory assessment and reporting of children's achievement against national standards for literacy and numeracy was seen to produce performative effects, including a tightening focus on literacy and numeracy in teaching programmes, curriculum narrowing, and reinforcement of a two-tier curriculum, although there was also push back against these effects from teachers (Thrupp, 2018). At the secondary school level, assessment for NCEA not only has a potent influence on the curriculum in Years 11 to 13, it also influences the curriculum in earlier secondary school years as teachers and learners look to the requirements of assessment in the senior school for models of how to assess learning and ideas about what is valuable learning (Taylor, 2011).

A dilemma for teachers relates to how they can negotiate different assessment pressures, to recognise where and how assessment is valuable and embed it within pedagogical practice while also countering a tendency for high-stakes assessment requirements to inadvertently become the 'real curriculum'. However, it is all very well to say that assessment shouldn't drive the curriculum, but the political reality of schools and educational systems is that teachers and schools are judged on assessment results and these results are used by some schools as a marketing tool. It is, then, inevitable that assessment will influence and be an integral part of curriculum. What is not inevitable, though, is that assessment will necessarily become the main or sole curriculum driver. Teachers play an important role in navigating the space between official and assessment curricula for learners, in the ways that they design assessment to support learning, enable learners to achieve within different and particular assessment regimes, and push back against assessment practices and pressures that may be negative for their learners.

Conclusion

In considering a range of interconnected contemporary and emerging curriculum issues, the question emerges: "What is an Education Studies for Aotearoa New Zealand in relation to curriculum?" It is evident that curriculum studies is a complex and broad-ranging field and that there is a wide range of foci for curriculum inquiry, which extend from particular, localised challenges of curriculum design, implementation, and curriculum-based teaching and learning, to considerations of broad policy developments at a national level and international trends. The very breadth of the field may make it difficult to grasp and understand what curriculum studies is and might be, while simultaneously providing rich and varied possibilities for curriculum inquiry.

Underpinning any consideration of the nature of the field, though, is an understanding that all curriculum is ideological. It is ideological in the way that it requires decisions to be made about knowledge that is most valuable—by teachers as they make daily decisions about the focus for learning and the types of learning and assessment activities that will be incorporated into learning programmes, by policy makers as they decide on levels of prescription in official curricula and define what should be taught, learnt, and assessed and how this will be done, and by researchers as they decide those curriculum questions and issues that are relevant or important to examine. It is the job of curriculum scholars, then, to make visible the ideological tensions inherent in curriculum issues and the dilemmas these present. It is the job of curriculum developers to make broad policy decisions, and of teachers to make daily, practice-related decisions, in the knowledge and understanding of how their resolutions present particular, values-based, moral, and political curriculum-related choices about what students need to know and knowledge that is valued. Curriculum studies for Aotearoa New Zealand encompasses a range of theoretical and practice-oriented endeavours, drawing on international theorising about curriculum while focusing on the specific sociocultural, political, and educational contexts within which official curriculum is developed, how this is made sense of and enacted by teachers, and how it is experienced by learners.

Further reading

Pinar, W., Reynolds, W., Slattery, P., & Taubman, P. (2004). *Understanding curriculum: An introduction to the study of historical and contemporary curriculum discourses*. New York, NY: Peter Lang.

Curriculum Matters, a journal published by the New Zealand Council for Educational Research (NZCER), provides an overview of curriculum research undertaken in Aotearoa New Zealand and gives readers an idea of the kinds of curriculum issues and questions that interest and are addressed by curriculum scholars, researchers, and practitioners. See https://www.nzcer.org.nz/nzcerpress/curriculum-matters

References

Abbiss, J. (2011). Social sciences in the New Zealand curriculum: Mixed messages. *Curriculum Matters, 11*, 118–137.

Abbiss, J. (2013). Social sciences and '21st century education' in schools: Opportunities and challenges. *New Zealand Journal of Educational Studies, 48*(2), 5–18.

Abbiss, J. (2015). Future-oriented learning, innovative learning environments and curriculum: What's the buzz? *Curriculum Matters, 11*, 1–9.

Abbiss, J. (2019). Becoming a teacher. In M. Hill & M. Thrupp (Eds.), *The professional practice of teaching in New Zealand* (6th ed., pp. 1–19). South Melbourne, VIC: Cengage Learning Australia.

Aitken, G. (2006). Signalling shifts in meaning: The experience of social studies curriculum design. *Curriculum Matters, 2*, 6–25.

Alterator, S., & Deed, C. (Eds.). (2018). *School space and its occupation: Conceptualising and evaluating innovative learning environments*. Leiden, The Netherlands: Brill Sense.

Benade, L. (2013). Review of 'The politics of knowledge in education' by E. Rata. *New Zealand Sociology, 28*(1), 204–206.

Benade, L. (2014). Knowledge and educational research in the context of 'Twenty-first century learning'. *European Educational Research Journal, 13*(3), 338–349.

Benade, L. (2019). Flexible learning spaces: Inclusive by design? *New Zealand Journal of Educational Studies, 54*(1), 53–68.

Benade, L., Gardner, M., Teschers, C., & Gibbons, A. (2014). 21st century learning in New Zealand: Leadership insights and perspectives. *Journal of Educational Leadership, Policy and Practice, 29*(2), 47–60.

Biesta, G., & Priestley, M. (2013). A curriculum for the twenty-first century. In M. Priestley & G. Biesta (Eds.), *Reinventing the curriculum: New trends in curriculum policy and practice* (pp. 229–236). London, UK: Bloomsbury.

Biesta, G., Priestley, M., & Robinson, S. (2015). The role of beliefs in teacher agency. *Teachers and Teaching: Theory and Practice, 21*(6), 624–640.

Biesta, G., & Tedder, M. (2007). Agency and learning in the lifecourse: Towards an ecological perspective. *Studies in Education of Adults, 39*(2), 132–149.

Black, P., & Wiliam, D. (1998). Inside the black box: Raising standards through classroom assessment. *Phi Delta Kappan, 80*(2), 139–148.

Bolstad, R., Gilbert, J., McDowall, S., Bull, A., Boyd, S., & Hipkins, R. (2012). *Supporting future oriented teaching and learning: A New Zealand perspective*. Wellington: Ministry of Education.

Crooks, T. (2011). Assessment for learning in the accountability era: New Zealand. *Studies in Educational Evaluation, 37*, 71–77.

Elliott, J. (1998). *The curriculum experiment: Meeting the challenge of social change*. Buckingham, UK: Open University Press.

Gilbert, J. (2005). *Catching the knowledge wave: The knowledge society and the future of education*. Wellington: NZCER Press.

Giroux, H., & Penna, A. (1979). Social education in the classroom: The dynamics of the hidden curriculum. *Theory and Research in Social Education, 7*(1), 21–42.

Harcourt, M., Milligan, A., & Wood, B. (Eds.). (2018). *Teaching social studies for critical, active citizenship in Aotearoa New Zealand*. Wellington: NZCER Press.

Hargreaves, A. (1989). *Curriculum and assessment reform*. Milton Keynes, UK: Open University Press.

Hargreaves, A. (1994). Critical introduction. In I. Goodson (Ed.), *Studying curriculum* (pp. 1–11). Buckingham, UK: Open University Press.

Hipkins, R., & Boyd, S. (2011). The recursive elaboration of key competencies as agents of curriculum change. *Curriculum Matters, 7*, 70–86.

Hipkins, R., & Bull, A. (2015). Science capabilities for a functional understanding of the nature of science. *Curriculum Matters, 11*, 117–133.

Istance, D., & Kools, M. (2013). OECD work on technology and education: Innovative learning environments as an integrating framework. *European Journal of Education, 48*(1), 43–57.

Leaupepe, M., Matapo, J., & Ravlich, E. (2017). Te Whāriki a mat for "all" to stand: The weaving of Pasifika voices. *Curriculum Matters, 13*, 21–41.

Mahat, M., Bradbeer, C., Byers, T., & Imms, W. (2018). *Innovative learning environments and teacher change: Defining key concepts*. Melbourne, VIC: University of Melbourne.

McGee, C. (1997). *Teachers and curriculum decision-making*. Palmerston North: Dunmore Press.

McGee, C., & Fraser, D. (Eds.). (2001). *The professional practice of teaching* (2nd ed.). Palmerston North: Dunmore Press.

McPhail, G. (2014). Music teachers talking: Views on secondary school curriculum content. *Curriculum Matters, 10*, 32–55.

McPhail, G. (2016). The future just happened: Lessons for 21st century learning from the secondary school music classroom. *Curriculum Matters, 12*, 8–28.

Ministry of Education. (2007). *The New Zealand curriculum*. Wellington: Ministry of Education.

Ministry of Education. (2017a). *Te marautanga o Aotearoa*. Wellington: Ministry of Education.

Ministry of Education. (2017b). *Te whāriki: He whāriki mātauranga mō ngā mokopuna o Aotearoa: Early childhood curriculum*. Wellington: Ministry of Education.

Mizutani, S., Rubie-Davies, C., Hattie, J., & Philp, J. (2011). Do beliefs about NCEA and its washback effects vary depending on subject? *New Zealand Journal of Educational Studies, 46*(2), 47–59.

Mutch, C. (2009). Curriculum: What, how and for whom? *Curriculum Matters, 5*, 1–4.

OECD. (2006). *21st century learning environments*. New Milford, CT: OECD Publications.

OECD. (2013). *Innovative learning environments*. Paris: Educational Research and Innovation, OECD. http://dx.doi.org/10.1787/9789264203488-en

Ormond, B. (2012). Aligning curriculum and assessment—divergent processes in the framing of knowledge. *Curriculum Matters, 8*, 9–32.

Pinar, W. (2012). *What is curriculum theory?* (2nd ed.). New York, NY: Routledge.

Pinar, W., Reynolds, W., Slattery, P., & Taubman, P. (2004). *Understanding curriculum: An introduction to the study of historical and contemporary curriculum discourses*. New York, NY: Peter Lang.

Priestley, M., & Sinnema, C. (2014). Downgraded curriculum? An analysis of knowledge in new curricula in Scotland and New Zealand. *The Curriculum Journal, 25*(1), 50–75.

Roberts, P. (2003). Contemporary curriculum research in New Zealand. In W. Pinar (Ed.), *International handbook of curriculum research* (pp. 495–516). Mahwah, NJ: Lawrence Erlbaum Associates.

Schubert, W. (2008). Curriculum inquiry. In F. M. Connelly, M. F. He, & J. Phillion (Eds.), *The SAGE handbook of curriculum and instruction* (pp. 399–419). Los Angeles, CA: Sage Publications.

Sheehan, M. (2017). A matter of choice: Controversial histories, citizenship, and the challenge of a high-autonomy curriculum. *Curriculum Matters, 13*, 103–114.

Sinnema, C., & Aitken, G. (2013). Emerging international trends in curriculum. In M. Priestley & G. Biesta (Eds.), *Reinventing the curriculum: New trends in curriculum policy and practice* (pp. 141–163). London, UK: Bloomsbury.

Snook, I. (1995). Re-forming the curriculum in New Zealand. In D. Carter & M. O'Neill (Eds.), *International perspectives on education reform and policy implementation* (pp. 158–168). London, UK: Falmer Press.

Stewart, G., & Buntting, C. (2015). Teachers, curious minds, and science education. *Curriculum Matters, 11*, 98–116.

Stewart, G., Trinick, T., & Dale, H. (2017). Te Marautanga o Aotearoa: History of a national Māori curriculum. *Curriculum Matters, 13*, 8–20.

Taylor, R. (2011). Trickle down effects: How have developments in senior secondary school social studies shaped practice in junior secondary social studies? *Curriculum Matters, 7*, 195–212.

Thompson, M., & Wiliam, D. (2007, April). *Tight but loose: A conceptual framework for scaling up school reforms.* Paper presented at the annual meeting of the American Educational Research Association (AERA), Chicago. Retrieved from: https://www.dylanwiliam.org/Dylan_Wiliams_website/Papers.html

Thrupp, M. (2018). *The search for better educational standards: A cautionary tale.* Cham, Switzerland: Springer.

Young, C. K., Gough, N., & Jung, J-H. (2018). Shadow education as an emerging force in worldwide curriculum studies. *Curriculum Matters, 14*, 8–30.

Young, M. (2014). What is curriculum and what can it do? *The Curriculum Journal, 25*(1), 7–13.

Young, M., & Muller, J. (2019). Knowledge, power and powerful knowledge revisited. *The Curriculum Journal, 30*(2), 196–214.

Zohar, A., & Hipkins, R. (2018). How "tight–loose" curriculum dynamics impact the treatment of knowledge in two national contexts. *Curriculum Matters, 14*, 31–47.

Chapter 7
Student engagement in flexible and distance learning in Aotearoa New Zealand

Cheryl Brown, Niki Davis, and William Eulatth-Vidal

Introduction

The chapter provides a critical overview of distance students' engagement in online modes of education. We examine the influence of technology enhanced learning on distance education and explore the way this has shaped student engagement in learning in schools and higher education in Aotearoa New Zealand, including a case of flexible learning for initial teacher education. Reflecting on key issues and developments, we identify innovative pedagogies that facilitate student engagement. Approaches for better engaging students in flexible and distance learning are identified through an exploration of the evolutionary processes of technology enhanced learning, educational practice and policy, and their interactions. This chapter brings together an overview of research into student engagement in flexible and distance learning in both schools and in higher education.

Student engagement is a common concern and is often spoken of in everyday learning and teaching discourse. It is of concern in schools because improved engagement is likely to lead to better student outcomes and also because disengaged students are likely to disrupt compulsory schooling for themselves and others. In higher education, engagement has also been linked with quality assurance of courses and their teaching staff. The increasing utilisation of digital devices in innovative learning environments and in online and blended learning has brought new opportunities and challenges for student engagement.

The chapter begins by considering the different ways the literature discusses student engagement. In doing so, the multifaceted and contested nature of the term is presented. Moving to the way engagement has been discussed in relation to flexible and distance learning, four common perspectives about engagement, which emerged from research literature, are outlined. The way engagement is conceptualised in Aotearoa New Zealand by the Ministry of Education and in research conducted in schools and higher education is outlined. The influence of organisations on student engagement is foregrounded and discussed in relation to flexible and distance learning and some of its perceived challenges. Institutional approaches to collecting data on student engagement are then described. Drawing on two key reports on trends in education, relevant issues in relation to student engagement are highlighted. Some of the complexities are illustrated with a case study of student engagement in initial teacher education, which is at the intersection of schooling and higher education. Recognising that, during the first decades of the 21st century the digital world has become part of everyday life, important concerns for education in Aotearoa New Zealand are introduced.

What is student engagement?

One of the reasons we care so much about engagement as educators is that engagement is seen as an important precursor to learning (Handlesman, Briggs, Sullivan, & Towler, 2005; Zyngier, 2008). In a schooling context, the association between student engagement and a number of educational and social outcomes has been noted as a statistically significant relationship (Wylie & Hodgen, 2011). An OECD report on engagement in schools has linked engagement to students' economic success and long-term health and wellbeing (Willms, 2003). As such, Willms argues that it "deserves to be treated alongside academic achievement as an important schooling outcome" (p. 9). Engagement has increasingly been positioned "as a defining characteristic of high-quality teaching and learning in higher education" (Ashwin & McVitty, 2015, p. 343). In this context, engagement has been increasingly tied to academic success of students and the institutional benefits from student engagement are seen to be both reputational and financial (Trowler, 2010; Zepke, 2015).

Table 7.1: **Perspectives on student engagement and its opposite, disengagement**

Perspective on student engagement	Perspective on student disengagement
Academic achievement/performance	Inactivity
Affective states (e.g., belonging)	Negative emotions (e.g., overwhelmed, frustrated)
Approaches to interacting with instructional resources	Disinterest
Behaviour in the classroom	Disruption
Metacognitive ability	Dependent, non-reflective
Social learning	Anti-social
Features of instructional and learning contexts designed to facilitate learning	Lack of participation
Motivational beliefs	Unmotivated
Persistence	Helplessness
Self-regulation	Off-task behaviours (e.g., distracted)
Students' self-perceptions of beliefs in handling individual and contextual aspects of learning situations	Isolated
Teacher's role and practice in learner-centred classrooms	Passivity

One of the challenges for teachers is that lack of clarity about the concept makes it difficult to know exactly how student engagement can be improved. There is a wide range of perspectives about what counts as student engagement (Azevedo, 2015). We grapple with its antithesis—the lack of engagement in learning both in face-to-face and virtual contexts; distraction (McCoy, 2016), lack of attendance (Edwards & Clinton, 2018), and 'passivity' (both online and offline) are all areas of concern for teachers. This lack of clarity also foregrounds questions as to how the concept could and should be measured

(Louwrens & Hartnett, 2015). Generally, engagement is understood as the extent to which students actively participate in learning by talking, thinking, and interacting with academic content and interacting with classmates/peers and teachers. However, what is meant by engagement varies with both the theoretical perspective of the researcher and the context of learning and teaching. Thus, defining the concept of engagement has been problematic (Henrie, Halverson, & Graham, 2015; Louwrens & Hartnett, 2015; engagement is often constructed through reference to its opposite, disengagement (Donovan, Green, & Hartley, 2010; Hayden, Ouyang, Scinski, Olszewski & Bielefeldt 2011; Rowe, Shores, Mott, & Lester, 2011). In Table 7.1, although the perspectives on engagement and disengagement can be contrasted, they should not be viewed as polar opposites but as alternative ways of thinking about this multifaceted concept.

What is engagement in flexible and distance learning?

There has also been a significant amount of research that has shown that technology can have a positive influence on students' engagement in learning (Chen, Lambert, & Guidry, 2010; Kahn, Everington, Kelm, Reid, & Watkins 2017). In undertaking a literature review of how the concept of engagement has been described over the past decade in online and blended learning (using the search terms 'distance learning', 'online learning', 'blended learning', 'engagement', 'concept, definition and framework') we identified 66 articles (Brown, Davis, Sotardi, & Eulatth-Vidal, 2018). Some of these were themselves systematic literature reviews on the concept (Henrie et al., 2015; Nortvig, Petersen & Balle, 2018; Schindler, Burkholder, Morad & March 2017; Trowler, 2010) and demonstrated to us that engagement can mean many different things to different people. We categorised these as follows:

1. **Social perspective:** Definitions were based on a constructionist and community of inquiry approach, active learning, and student identity/belonging. Engagement is understood as a result of social interactions (20 articles).

2. **Individual perspective:** Definitions were based on the individual's involvement with activities and conditions likely to generate high-quality learning (15 articles).

3. **Flow theory perspective:** Definitions are based on the individual's feeling of enjoyment and the extent to which they become immersed in their learning. It is argued that the triggering of interest establishes engagement (11 articles).
4. **Multidimensional perspective:** Definition based on the idea that engagement does not comprise a single dimension but different and interconnected ones (e.g., behavioural, cognitive, emotional, etc.) (12 articles).

The social perspective has as its core the way individuals learn through social interaction. It is based on the premise that students perform better when working collaboratively with others by helping each other to fill in the gaps in each other's knowledge; they learn by observing others' behaviours. In e-learning, that observational learning may occur when students read opinions posted by other students or staff members. There is a need for active learning and interaction, which implies that students need to feel as if they are dealing with real people and belong to an authentic group of learners. From this approach, observational learning (OBL), which involves observing and modeling another's behaviors, attitudes, or emotions, is seen as a learning process that involves taking part and maintaining relations with others. The process comprises actions that occur online and offline, such as communicating, thinking, feeling, and belonging (Carr, Palmer, & Hagel, 2015). Under the community of inquiry approach, three presences are considered: social presence, teaching presence, and cognitive presence.

The individual perspective explores engagement from the extent of students' involvement and active participation in learning activities (Yang, 2011). It is often explained as the quality of effort students themselves devote to educationally purposeful activities that contribute directly to desired outcomes. In terms of e-learning, courseware engagement was defined as the degree of effort and persistence students reported putting forth into digital activities such as videos, tutorial practice problems, guided solutions, and sample tests (Hu & Kuh, 2003; Spence & Usher, 2007).

The flow theory perspective has been used to describe the feelings people experience when they throw themselves into a high-demanding activity to the exclusion of their surroundings. The intense engagement of online gaming is an example of flow theory in action. Whilst it is questionable whether this engagement results in learning, students certainly seem to report being more engaged when they are having fun (Wood & Klosterman, 2012). In e-learning, when students undertake an activity that meets particular conditions of challenge, control, focused attention, and presence they become absorbed in the activity which ultimately translates into positive impact on their academic performance (defined very broadly) (Rodriguez-Ardura & Meseguer-Artola, 2017).

The multidimensional perspective goes beyond learning, teaching, and pedagogy because it extends to recognise the relevance of the individual student's confidence, motivation, culture, and life experiences. It can be aligned with established frameworks such as Handlesman et al. (2005), who have conceptualised engagement as encompassing skills, participation/interaction, emotional engagement, and performance engagement. The multifaceted view often comprises behavioural, cognitive, and emotional facets. In terms of online engagement, behavioural engagement is often measured and discussed through the reports produced by online software (analytics of access and downloads). Cognitive engagement can be visible in online discussions where the deep focused thinking can provide visible evidence of knowledge construction and where understanding can be observed. Emotional engagement is harder to determine online and is seen to be a particularly crucial aspect of flexible and distance learning because learners need to feel connected and comfortable in order to engage well in the online space, with both teachers and peers (Louwrens & Hartnett, 2015).

However, there is also research that has strongly argued the need to move away from frameworks of engagement. Gourlay and Oliver (2018), in re-theorising the concept, move away from the idea of a definition or framework and instead view student digital engagement as a set of socio-material practices that emphasises the everyday interaction between students and technology. They argue that individual student experiences are clearly varied and not reducible into binary contracts such as engaged/disengaged.

Engagement as it is conceptualised in Aotearoa

In Aotearoa New Zealand, the Ministry of Education recognises that e-learning can be applied to personalise schooling and thus improve achievement and engagement in traditional and innovative learning environments as well as increase equity through online distance education (Davis, Mackey, & Dabner, 2018). Te Tāhuhu o Te Mātauranga, the Ministry of Education, has adopted a multidimensional view of engagement including:

- cognitive engagement: students are engaged with the processes and progressions of their learning
- behavioural engagement: students show they are ready and willing to learn
- emotional engagement: students feel secure in their relationships with their teachers, classmates, and the school.

Examining student and teacher perceptions of student engagement in Te Kura,[1] Louwrens and Hartnett (2015) adopted the multidimensional perspective of student engagement. They found that students' behavioural engagement increased when they undertook activities outside of the formal Learning Management System and developed good relationships which enhanced a sense of belonging and connectedness. They noted that giving and receiving feedback particularly enhanced both emotional and cognitive engagement. Where activities and content were interesting and meaningful to students, all three types of engagement were enhanced. This posed a challenge for teachers, as what was perceived by students as fun and enjoyable was not always the best for curriculum requirements.

A different multidimensional framework was developed by Kahu (2013) for student engagement in higher education in Aotearoa New Zealand. This puts the student at the centre of the relationship between engagement, achievement, and outcomes. The individual perspective, with its three dimensions of affect, cognition, and behaviour, was embedded within the sociocultural contexts of both the student and his or her institution. A key strength of framing student engagement in this way was the acknowledgement of the lived reality of each individual as well as the influence of the organisation through which they study.

Organisational approaches to student engagement in Aotearoa

Student engagement in flexible and distance learning varies with the environment in which the student studies, and thus the characteristics and support of the educational organisation and the perspectives of families and communities are important in our understanding of engagement. Ecological frameworks based on human ecology, including Bronfenbrenner's bioecological theory, are

---

1 Formerly known as The Correspondence School, set up in 1922 to increase equity with nationwide distance provision of flexible and distance learning for children.

well known in early childhood education. The more recent Arena Framework of Davis (Davis, 2018) recognises the co-evolution of education in both the physical and digital world at multiple levels, including organisational ecosystems in schools and universities and cloud-based systems of educational services that stretch globally.

The changing roles and responsibilities of collaborating teachers that tend to evolve in technology-rich learning environments that are effectively organised to personalise learning in compulsory schooling are described by Davis et al., (2018). Arrangements for innovative learning environments within which two or more teachers collaborate were contrasted with online distance teaching for students attending different schools (or those home schooled). Both of these arrangements include ongoing facilitation of student engagement. A recent snapshot of online distance education clarified that there is a variety of approaches that include face-to-face interactions to complement the online study (Blewden, Henderson, Tuwhangai, Baldwin, & Butler, 2018). Building student engagement was a strong focus of this report; the most frequent methods used to build student engagement in online teaching and learning were prompt, personalised student feedback (86%), and relationships with students based on high expectations and nondeficit thinking (75%). Flexibility, choice, and connection also featured (Blewden et al., 2018). This closely resonated with Lai's (2017) study of the introduction of 'knowledge building' pedagogy to eTeachers in NetNZ, which acknowledged the importance of fostering motivation and engagement in order to create an engaging learning environment. Drawing on self-determination theory as a theoretical framework, Lai highlighted pedagogical practices such as: enabling student agency (e.g., having choice in the design of learning); providing academic support; providing clear learning structure and constructive feedback which enables students to exercise control and develop a sense of competence; and developing positive teacher/student relationships and student/student relationships.

Among the challenges for flexible and distance learning are the socio-emotional risks that are sometimes associated with high use of digital devices (James et al., 2017). Social media and digital 'addictions' along with other destructive behaviours such as cyberbullying may result in distraction and possibly disengagement from learning (McNaughton & Gluckman, 2018). The importance of wellbeing is acknowledged in Ministry of Education-funded Wellbeing@School toolkit (Lawes & Boyd, 2018) which enables schools and Kāhui Ako / Communities of Learning to monitor their ecosystems to maintain a safe and caring climate that deters bullying, including cyberbullying. This supports research that demonstrates that approaches that build students' social and emotional skills and competencies may lead to improvements across a range of student outcomes, including engagement. Although organisations such as Netsafe[2] have guidance to improve health and safety in the digital worlds of school-aged learners, there is a gap in our knowledge around engagement strategies, including embedding skills and knowledge about wellbeing and healthy constructive approaches to online learning more generally. Understanding and developing successful strategies for developing digital wellbeing is now recognised as an essential part of learning and teaching.

NZCER offers the Me and My School student engagement survey which is designed for Aotearoa New Zealand students in Years 4–10. It focuses on the three dimensions of engagement as conceptualised by the Ministry of Education. The first is behaviour, and the students' actual participation in school and learning. This includes positive conduct, persistence, and involvement in school life. Emotional and cognitive aspects of engagement are a focus with students' emotional responses to teachers, peers, learning, and school as one area of focus and the psychological investment students have in their own learning, willingness to take on learning challenges and self-regulate their learning as another (New Zealand Council for Educational Research, 2019). NZCER runs surveys across schools nationally every 3 years exploring a diverse set of issues including how schools are using the engagement and wellbeing data.[3]

In the context of higher education, research on student engagement has confirmed its influence on both student satisfaction and learning, and has also identified reciprocal and complex interactions between emotions, engagement, and learning (Kahu, Stephens, Leach, & Zepke, 2014). An increased focus on the student experience in higher education has resulted in national surveys of student engagement or course experience in some contexts. These serve as an alternative metric of evaluation for colleges and universities to measure 'quality' on a national platform. For example, in the United States and Canada the National Survey of Student Engagement (NeSSE) is based on four themes: academic challenge, learning with peers, experiences with faculty, and campus environments. The NeSSE draws on 10 Engagement Indicators (EI) that are

---

2   https://www.netsafe.org.nz/
3   See https://www.nzcer.org.nz/research/national-survey

noted for their positive outcomes on student learning and retention (National Survey of Student Engagement, 2017). In Australia and New Zealand, over 30 institutions participated in the Australasian Survey of Student Engagement in 2012 (ACER, 2019). Currently, the Australian Government Department of Education and Training funds the Student Experience Survey (SES). The student engagement section of this survey focuses on belonging, preparedness and strongly on interactions with other students (QILT, 2019). In Aotearoa New Zealand, universities generally have their own survey and evaluation units and explore aspects of students' engagement as part of an overall student experiences survey approach; for example, the Quality Advancement Unit at the University of Otago, or the Learning Evaluation and Academic Development (LEAD) at the University of Canterbury.

One of the unfortunate aspects of this institutional focus on surveying of students' experience, and in particular on surveying engagement, is that it positions universities and schools to be in competition with each other. Too often these measures end up homogenising the student experience and lump people (from a range of diverse/differentiated) contexts into a single entity. Discourse of student experience tends to place a greater emphasis on role of the teachers and the institution and less on students. Underpinning these surveys are particular ideologies about how students should behave—in other words, demonstrating a desired form of engagement. One of the problems with discourse is positioning the student as non-agentive, the passive recipient of a product. As Gourlay and Oliver (2018) note, it leads to a performative culture that uncritically promotes active learning and self-disclosure.

In a higher education context, some institutions have been 'legislating' engagement through the requirement for lecture and tutorial attendance focusing on students' physical presence as a necessary requirement for learning. Innovations such as lecture recording can be met with distrust as a result of concerns that having the option to 'watch' a lecture online will result in low attendance by students (Edwards & Clinton, 2018). In the online context, institutions seek to find ways of monitoring student activities that are similar to attendance, which can result in the allocation of a mark for contributions to forums and requiring students to attend synchronous sessions or undertake particular activities as coursework. A variety of solutions are being developed, and learning analytics—the collection and use of learner-produced data—is seen as a powerful way of identifying students deemed to be at risk (Viberg, Hatakka, Bälter, & Mavroudi, 2018). Whilst this can be an important indicator, it adopts a particular view of engagement as being an observable behaviour. Thus, it renders the practice of individual scholarship (reading, writing, and thinking for an assignment) invisible and perhaps encourages students to direct their activities to more observable interactions than the less visible development of knowledge. Personal mobile devices (PMDs) such as smartphones, laptops, and tablets also have an important role to play in learning. Students often rely on these tools for the informal (and often less visible) aspects of engagement. For example, in one study students used their PMDs for research, reading, thinking, understanding, and preparation. These are the invisible informal strategies and processes of learning, sometimes described as the inner layer of learning (Brown & Haupt, 2018).

Key issues and developments

One of the key trends in education currently is the use of 'big data'. This refers to extremely large data sets that usually need to be analysed by systems and tools and are used to reveal patterns and trends especially relating to human behaviour and interactions. In the education sector this is often referred to as a component of learning analytics, used particularly to examine student achievement with the intent of enriching our understanding of how students learn (Wang, 2016) and identifying patterns of risk (Jokhan, Sharma, & Singh, 2018).

In their annual report on trends and influences shaping how we live, work, and learn, Core Education adopts a broad view of engagement and refers to it in terms of community, pedagogy, and inclusivity. Whilst big data is often discussed as being useful, they foreground the value of small data "being the everyday, nuanced observations and decisions made by teachers/kaiako" as being every bit as useful in providing insights as big data (Core Education, 2019). In foregrounding community and inclusivity, Core Education touches on two other very important issues in the context of Aotearoa New Zealand, namely engaging with whānau, and Māori pedagogical concepts and approaches. This has particular resonance given the emergence of the distributed role of the teacher in flexible and distance learning contexts where learning at school and in the kāinga (home) effectively becomes blended with learning with distant teacher(s) and class(es) (Davis et al., 2018). Distance providers such as Te Kura and the Virtual Learning Network—a group of school clusters operating as a collaborative network using digital technologies—offer extensive online learning for parents who find it challenging to access traditional education services (Roberts, 2010).

Culturally sensitive flexible and distance learning not only enhances equity and increases the cultural capital for the learners' communities, but also increases engagement through relevance and connection (Hunt et al., 2011). Exemplary tertiary teaching has included a case study of a wānanga that adopted e-learning in a way that maintained te ao Māori (the Māori worldview) while building the engagement and capacity of whānau as well as students (Greenwood, Ti Aika, & Davis, 2010). The five overarching principles used by Greenwood and Ti Aika (2008) in their research is instructive in this context and includes

- toko a-iwi a-wānanga—institutional and iwi support
- tikanga—the integration of Māori and iwi values and protocols
- pūkenga—the involvement of suitably qualified educational leadership and staff
- ako—development of effective teaching and learning strategies
- huakina te tatau o te whare—opening up the doors to the house.

Behavioural engagement featured as a mid-term trend in the 2019 Horizon Higher Education Edition report under the topic of "growing focus on measuring learning".[4] Using predictive analytics to capture and measure academic readiness, learning progress, and students' success is becoming an increasing focus of academic institutions. Whilst it is acknowledged that engagement with materials is not a proxy for learning, learning analytics technologies are predicted as having a time to adoption of one year or less (Alexander et al., 2019). Engagement is also noted as being fundamental to student success and support initiatives with Artificial Intelligence (AI) being proposed as a solution working to "bring more human-like connection to those who seek it, whether in a discussion forum or on the other side of a support call" (Alexander et al 2019, p. 27). Whilst this appears a futuristic possibility, time to adoption is positioned at 2 to 3 years, with examples of its application in learning already in practice globally. These include supporting pedagogical approaches through adaptive learning, using algorithms to customise content to the predicted needs of individual students, and working with institutional data to help educational institutions understand retention rates, intervention needs, and programme performance.

---

4   https://library.educause.edu

However, despite its possibilities, it is acknowledged that AI introduces unknown potential ethical challenges about privacy, data use, and learning.

A case study of student engagement

The College of Education, Health and Human Development at the University of Canterbury (UC), which has a long history of distance learning stretching back some 20 years (Astall et al., 2016; Hunt et al., 2011), in 2018 undertook a study of distance students' engagement in flexible and distance learning. The report by Brown et al. (2018) showed that many of the pedagogical practices that students most valued were surprisingly "low tech" in their implementation. These included having simple, organised, and consistent ways of delivering information to students; developing positive relationships between the lecturer and student; addressing different students' needs, making them feel included and valued; and teaching students things that were practical for their future work (such as education applied to real work). These highlight strategies teachers can adopt to increase behavioural engagement (i.e., helping students know what is expected of them), emotional engagement (connectedness and confidence), and cognitive engagement (understanding the relevance of what they were learning). Certainly, as Louwrens and Hartnett (2015) noted, cognitive engagement such as students' personal investment in their own learning was evident in the giving and receiving of feedback as well as the interest and relevance of certain activities generated for learners. Emotional engagement was elicited through the design and facilitation of the activities, and through the ongoing development of a learning community in which students felt safe to contribute.

However, this study at UC challenges the notion that engagement in an online and blended learning should always be visible. With the widespread uptake of social media, students' agency has increased, adding previously unconsidered informal channels to learning interactions. It is widely recognised that social aspects are invisibly mixed with private and informal learning. The visible perspective of engagement should not "wash away" the informal and social aspects so that they are missed. This reminds us that, while engagement with digital tools continues to increase in prominence for staff and students, they are only the more visible of the channels through which students engage in their learning. Students often spoke of their need for learning to be flexible and described activities they undertook offline and in their own space. They also reflected on their own compliance behaviour when asked to watch a recording, or to participate in an online discussion for which they couldn't see the value in terms of learning. In addition to clarifying the benefits of engaging in particular activities, as educators we need to seek ways to acknowledge the variety of tools and channels including the 'invisible' nondigital components that are likely to remain particularly important for the learning of students who engage from a distance (Brown et al., 2018). Given the continuing evolution and co-evolution of flexible and distance learning, we recognise that this commitment will involve all educators in lifelong learning about teaching. It will also involve us in reflective learning and professional learning and development in relation to our commitments under the Treaty of Waitangi, including learning from our students' feedback and our facilitation of their engagement with the Treaty.

Conclusion

Engagement is a multifaceted concept that goes beyond learning, teaching, and pedagogy, given that it intersects with the individual student's confidence, motivation, culture, and life experiences in the context of diverse, interconnected ecosystems (both physical and digital). From an organisational perspective, student engagement in online and blended learning encompasses both the conditions that create an enabling (or disabling) environment for learning, along with the pedagogical strategies that are used in course design and delivery.

In reflecting on the literature and our own research, we believe teachers and institutions need to value the affective aspect of engagement; feelings of interest, belonging, confidence, and motivation (to name just a few) are an important foundation for learning. We need to be aware that visibility does not always equate to engagement in learning, and vice versa. Measuring of presence can be a helpful diagnostic, but needs to be aligned with follow-up support strategies. As educators in the context of Aotearoa New Zealand, we believe we are in a valuable position to build our bicultural confidence and competence, and to develop culturally sensitive ways of supporting engagement in flexible and distance learning contexts.

Recommendations for further reading

Davis, N. E., Mackey, J., & Dabner, N. (2018). *Changes in school culture with the emergence of virtual schooling*. In K. Kennedy & R. Ferdig (Eds.), *Handbook of research on K-12 online and blended learning* (2nd ed., pp. 133–145). Pittsburgh, PA: Carnegie Mellon University ETC Press.

Louwrens, N., & Hartnett, M. (2015). Student and teacher perceptions of online student engagement in an online middle school. *Journal of Open, Flexible and Distance Learning, 19*(1), 27– 43. http://www.jofdl.nz/index.php/JOFDL/article/view/241

Marshall, S., & Shepherd, D. (2016). *E-learning in tertiary education. Highlights from Ako Aotearoa projects*. Wellington: Ako Aotearoa: The National Centre for Tertiary Teaching Excellence. Available from: https://ako.ac.nz/assets/reports/Synthesis-reports/8d322345cb/SYNTHESIS-REPORT-e-Learning-in-tertiary-Education-Highlights-from-Ako-Aotearoa-supported-research.pdf

References

ACER. (2019). *Australasian survey of student engagement* (AUSSE). Australian Council for Educational Research. Retrieved from: https://research.acer.edu.au/ausse/

Alexander, B., Ashford-Rowe, K., Barajas-Murphy, N., Dobbin, G., Knott, J., McCormack, M., Pomerantz, J., et al. (2019). *EDUCAUSE horizon report: 2019 higher education edition*. Louisville, KY: EDUCAUSE.

Ashwin, P., & McVitty, D. (2015). The meanings of student engagement: Implications for policies and practices. In A. Curaj, L. Matei, R. Pricopie, J. Salmi, & P. Scott (Eds.), *The European higher education area*. (pp. 343–359). Cham, Switzerland: Springer.

Astall, C., Abbiss, J., Cunningham, U., Clarke, T., Davis, N., Fickel, L. H., Dunn, K. et al. (2016, April). *Shifting practice in teacher preparation with a poutama and an ePortfolio: Charting our journey*. Paper presented at the DEANZ 2016 conference, University of Waikato, Hamilton, New Zealand.

Azevedo, R. (2015). Defining and measuring engagement and learning in science: Conceptual, theoretical, methodological, and analytical issues. *Educational Psychologist, 50*(1), 84–94. doi:10.1080/00461520.2015.1004069

Blewden, M., Henderson, C., Tuwhangai, R., Baldwin, K., & Butler, R. (2018). *On-line distance education research final report*. Cognition Education.

Brown, C., Davis, N., Sotardi, V., & Eulatth-Vidal, W. (2018, November). *Towards understanding of student engagement in blended learning: A conceptualization of learning without borders*. ASCILITE 2018. Geelong, VIC.

Brown, C., & Haupt, G. (2018). Using personal mobile devices to increase flexibility and equity in learning in resource-constrained contexts. *Journal of Open, Flexible and Distance Learning, 22*(13), 18–31.

Carr, R., Palmer, S., & Hagel, P. (2015). Active learning: The importance of developing a comprehensive measure. *Active Learning in Higher Education, 16*, 173–186.

Chen, P-S., Lambert, A., & Guidry, K. (2010). Engaging online learners: The impact of web-based learning technology on college student engagement. *Computers and Education, 54*(4), 1222–1232.

Core Education. (2019). *Ten trends 2019*. Christchurch: Author. Retrieved from: http://core-ed.org/research-and-innovation/ten-trends/2019/real-time-reporting/

Davis, N. E. (2018). *Digital technologies and change in education. The Arena Framework*. London, UK & New York, NY: Routledge.

Davis, N. E., Mackey, J., & Dabner, N. (2018). Changes in school culture with the emergence of virtual schooling. In K. Kennedy & R. Ferdig (Eds.), *Handbook of research on K-12 online and blended learning* (2nd ed., pp. 133–145). Pittsburgh, PA: Carnegie Mellon University ETC Press.

Donovan, L., Green, T., & Hartley, K. (2010). An examination of one-to-one computing in the middle school: Does increased access bring about increased engagement. *Journal of Computing Research, 42*(4), 423–441.

Edwards, M., & Clinton, M. (2018). A study exploring the impact of lecture capture availability and lecture capture usage on student attendance and attainment. *Higher Education, 7*(3), 403–421.

Gourlay, L., & Oliver, M. (2018). *Student engagement in the digital university: Sociomaterial assemblages*. London, UK: Routledge.

Greenwood, J., & Te Aika, L. H. (2008). *Hei tauira: Teaching and learning for success for Māori in tertiary settings*. Wellington: Ako Aotearoa.

Greenwood, J., Te Aika, L. H. & Davis, N. E. (2010). Māori virtual marae—bicultural adoption of digital technologies within Aotearoa New Zealand: Cultural reconstruction and hybridity. In P. R. Leigh (Ed.), *International explorations of technology equity and the digital divide: Critical, historical and social perspectives* (pp. 58–79). Charlotte, NC: Information Age Press.

Handelsman, M., Briggs, W., Sullivan, N., & Towler, A. (2005). A measure of college student course engagement, *The Journal of Educational Research, 98*(3), 184–192.

Hayden, K., Ouyang, Y., Scinski, L., Olszewski, B., & Bielefeldt, T. (2011). Increasing student interest and attitudes in STEM: Professional development and activities to engage and inspire learners. *Contemporary Issues in Technology & Teacher Education, 11*(1), 47–9.

Henrie, C. R., Halverson, L. R., & Graham, C. R. (2015). Measuring student engagement in technology-mediated learning: A review. *Computers and Education, 90*, 36–53. doi:10.1016/j.compedu.2015.09.005

Hu, S., & Kuh, G. (2003). Diversity experiences and college student learning and development. *Journal of College Student Development, 44*(3), 320–334.

Hunt, A. M., Mackey, J., Dabner, N., Morrow, D., Breeze, D., Walker, L., & Davis, N. (2011, May). Culturally sensitive blended learning for future teachers in challenging times. *Distance Education Association of New Zealand (DEANZ) Magazine*, 1–4.

James, C., Davis, K., Charmaraman, L., Konrath, S., Slovak, P., Weinstein, E., & Yarosh, L. (2017). Digital life and youth well-being, social connectedness, empathy, and narcissism. *Pediatrics, 140* (Supplement 2), 71–75.

Jokhan, A., Sharma, B., & Singh, S. (2018). Early warning systems as a predictor for student performance in higher education blended courses. *Studies in Higher Education* (Online). doi. 10.1080/03075079.2018.1466872

Kahn, P., Everington, L., Kelm, K., Reid, I., & Watkins, F. (2017). Understanding student engagement in online learning environments: The role of reflexivity. *Educational Technology Research and Development, 65*(1), 203–218.

Kahu, E. (2013). Framing student engagement in higher education. *Studies in Higher Education, 38*, 758–773.

Kahu, E., Stephens, C., Leach, L., & Zepke, N. (2013). The engagement of mature distance students. *Higher Education Research & Development, 32*(5), 791–804.

Lai, K-W. (2017). Pedagogical practices of NetNZ teachers for supporting online distance learners. *Distance Education, 38*(3), 321–335.

Lawes, E., & Boyd, S. (2018). *Making a difference to student wellbeing—A data exploration.* Wellington: New Zealand Council for Educational Research. Retrieved from: https://www.nzcer.org.nz/system/files/Student%20Wellbeing%20Report.pdf

Louwrens, N., & Hartnett, M. (2015). Student and teacher perceptions of online student engagement in an online middle school. *Journal of Open, Flexible and Distance Learning, 19*(1), 27–43.

McCoy, B. (2016). Digital distractions in the classroom Phase II: Student classroom use of digital devices for non-class related purposes. *Journal of Media Education, 7*(1), 5–32.

McNaughton, S., & Gluckman, P. (2018). *A commentary on digital futures and education. A report prepared for the Office of the Prime Minister.* https://www.pmcsa.org.nz/wp-content/uploads/18-04-06-Digital-Futures-and-Education.pdf

National Survey of Student Engagement. (2017). *Engagement insights: Survey findings on the quality of undergraduate education.* Retrieved from: https://www.insidehighered.com/sites/default/server_files/files/NSSE%20Annual%20Results%202017-Embargoed.pdf

New Zealand Council for Educational Research. (2019). *Me and my school.* Wellington: Author. Retrieved from: https://www.nzcer.org.nz/system/files/MMS%20-%20The%20research.pdf

Nortvig, A. M., Petersen, A. K., & Balle, S. H. (2018). A literature review of the factors influencing e-learning and blended learning in relation to learning outcome, student satisfaction and engagement. *The Electronic Journal of e-Learning, 16*(1), 46–55.

QILT. (2019). *Student experience. Quality indicators for learning and teaching.* Retrieved from: https://www.qilt.edu.au/about-this-site/student-experience

Roberts, R. (2010). *Increasing access for learners—The virtual learning network.* In V. Ham & D. Wenmoth (Eds.), *e-learnings: Implementing a national strategy for ICT in education, 1998–2010* (pp. 144–152). Christchurch: CORE Education. Available at: https://goo.gl/zhS81s

Rodrīguez-Ardura, I., & Meseguer-Artola, A. (2016). Flow in e-learning: What drives it and why it matters. *British Journal of Educational Technology, 48*(4), 899–915.

Rowe, J., Shores, L., Mott, B., & Lester, J. (2011). Integrating learning, problem solving, and engagement in narrative-centered learning environments. *International Journal of Artificial Intelligence in Education, 21*(1), 115–133.

Schindler, L., Burkholder, G., Morad, O., & March, C. (2017). Computer-based technology and student engagement: A critical review of the literature. *International Journal of Educational Technology in Higher Education, 14*(25), 1–28. doi:10.1186/s41239-017-0063-0

Spence, D. J., & Usher, E. L. (2007). Engagement with mathematics courseware in traditional and online remedial learning environments: Relationship to self-efficacy and achievement. *Journal of Educational Computing Research, 37*(3), 267–288. Retrieved from: https://www.learntechlib.org/p/69211/.

Trowler, V. (2010). Student engagement literature review. The Higher Education Academy: York, UK. Retrieved from: https://www.heacademy.ac.uk/system/files/resources/frameworkforaction_institutional.pdf.

Viberg, O., Hatakka, M., Bälter, O., & Mavroudi, A. (2018). The current landscape of learning analytics in higher education. *Computers in Human Behavior, 89*, 98–110.

Wang, Y. (2016). Big opportunities and big concerns of big data in education. *TechTrends, 60*, 381–384.

Willms, J. D. (2003). *Student engagement at school: A sense of belonging and participation. Results from PISA 2000*. Paris, France: Organisation for Economic Co-operation and Development. Retrieved from: http://www.oecd.org/education/school/programmeforinternationalstudentassessmentpisa/33689437.pdf

Wood, B., & Klosterman, M. (2012). Reflective journal writing and student engagement. In L. McCoy (Ed.), *Studies in teaching 2012 research digest* (pp. 145–150). Winston-Salem, NC: Wake University.

Wylie, C., & Hodgen, E. (2011). *Forming adulthood: Past, present and future in the experience and views of the competent learners @ 20*. Wellington: Ministry of Education. Retrieved from: https://www.educationcounts.govt.nz/publications/ECE/2567/forming-adulthood

Yang, Y-F. (2011). Engaging students in an online situated language learning environment. *Computer Assisted Language Learning, 24*(2), 181–198.

Zepke, N. (2015). Student engagement research: thinking beyond the mainstream. *Higher Education Research and Development, 34*(6), 1311–1323.

Zyngier, D. (2008). (Re)conceptualising student engagement: Doing education not doing time. *Teaching and Teacher, 24*(7), 1765–1776.

Chapter 8
Diversity, education, and inclusion in Aotearoa New Zealand

Christoph Teschers and Trish McMenamin

Introduction

At this moment in our common history, the topic of this chapter "Diversity, education, and inclusion in Aotearoa New Zealand" has a very particular poignancy and pertinence. On 15 March 2019 in Christchurch—where we live—there was an horrendous attack on two mosques that resulted in the deaths of 51 people, injury to many more, and trauma and distress for Muslim communities both in Aotearoa New Zealand and worldwide. While this assault had as its target the Muslim community, its impact was much wider than on that community alone. Across the wider Christchurch community and the whole of Aotearoa, people reeled in shock that an action of such brutality and hatred could occur in their midst. This very recent, and very close, act of terror brings into stark relief the dire consequences that can be the result of a lack of acceptance and understanding of difference and diversity in our societies. This act was a cold-blooded, planned attack designed to foster division and hatred. But what happened in the wake of this attack was quite the opposite. Across the country, and across all walks of life, the community came together in what was not only an outpouring of love and support for the Muslim community, but also a show of defiance against extremism. "They Are Us", the phrase coined by the Prime Minister, Jacinda Ardern, became the banner behind which the country rallied in defence of the values and humanity that we as a country claim to hold dear but are rarely called upon to publicly stand up for. The attack of 15 March has prompted much reflection and discussion about what difference, diversity, and inclusion mean for us in Aotearoa New Zealand; it is in the light of this that we present the ideas here about diversity, education, and inclusion.

In many, if not most, contexts across the world, communities are becoming increasingly diverse. With this has come an increasing focus on diversity in education contexts and settings, as countries respond to what Ainscow (2016) has described as "a global education challenge" (p. 143). Aotearoa New Zealand is no exception. Aotearoa's society is ethnically and culturally diverse with a population that has, according to the 2013 census, "more ethnicities ... than there are countries in the world" (Statistics New Zealand, 2013). But, of course, when we think of the diversity of a society we must consider not only culture and ethnicity, but also aspects such as gender, disability/ability, religious beliefs, socioeconomic status, sexual orientation, age, and more. All these variations are represented in our society and in its educational settings. Aotearoa New Zealand represents itself as a tolerant and friendly society that is respectful and welcoming of diversity and difference. It upholds the rights of its citizens to freedom from discrimination on account of any of these factors through the Human Rights Act 1993 and the New Zealand Bill of Rights 1990. In the context of education, there is a strong commitment to the notion of diversity as a principle that underpins policy and practice in curricula, regulations, and other official Ministry of Education material (e.g., *The New Zealand Curriculum* (Ministry of Education, 2007), *Te Whāriki* (Ministry of Education, 2017), the National Education Goals, and the National Administration Guidelines).

The *principle of inclusion* and the *principle of cultural diversity*, two of the principles that underpin *The New Zealand Curriculum*, speak directly to the demands of diversity, stating respectively that "The curriculum is non-sexist, non-racist, and non-discriminatory; it ensures that [all] students' identities, languages, abilities, and talents are recognised and affirmed and that their learning needs are addressed" (Ministry of Education, 2007, p. 9), and that "[t]he curriculum reflects New Zealand's cultural diversity and values the histories and traditions of all its people" (Ministry of Education, 2007, p. 9). Similar references to valuing and celebrating diversity can be found in other Ministry of

Education resources and materials such as the online resource Te Kete Ipurangi.[1] While it would not be unreasonable to suggest that these factors augur well for the way in which diversity is understood and attended to in Aotearoa New Zealand—particularly as regards the education context—in this chapter, following Burbules (1997) and others, we suggest that we need to think more critically about the notion of diversity and how it is used in public, academic, and educational domains. We begin the chapter by presenting an analysis and critique of diversity and the way it is conceptualised in policy and more broadly. Following this, we examine matters to do with inclusive education as the policy response to diversity and argue that there are some limitations to how this is currently conceived. In the final section of the chapter, we present an alternative holistic approach to diversity and discuss some practices that have promise for developing a different approach to diversity through strengthening awareness that each individual is a unique human being, and so create an understanding of diversity *as the norm*.

Troubling diversity

The concept and term 'diversity', like many such terms, has been used in varied ways in relation to education policy and practices and has multiple meanings that denote differing understandings and positioning of difference. Different interpretations can also be found within the domains of academia and public debate such as between academic disciplines or different political party positions, all of which are informed by changing historical contexts and discourses. It would, however, be fair to say that, in the current education and social context, 'diversity' is most commonly used as an umbrella term that denotes one or more of what Mitchell (2016, p. 2) has described as the 'big five' diversities: sexuality and gender; race, ethnicity, and culture; beliefs and religion; socioeconomic status; and disability/ability.

As noted above, in the context of education, but also more broadly, the discourse around diversity tends to be positive; diversity is something to be respected and celebrated, a resource that enriches not only education settings but society overall. References to encouraging, respecting, celebrating, and valuing diversity are ubiquitous in the education lexicon. At one level, this appears to be a good thing. Ideas associated with celebrating, valuing, and respecting diversity are of themselves both intuitively appealing and, particularly in

---

[1] www.tki.org.nz

the context of education, morally compelling. Programmes and practices that support and develop tolerance, acceptance, and understanding of the many variations among people undoubtedly have improved both the educational experiences and the social environment for many. However, from another point of view, diversity conceptualised in these ways may not be an entirely good thing. When diversity is understood as referring to particular categories of difference—as, for example, Mitchell's 'big five'—these categories of difference are, by implication, being compared to something; something that they all share *being different from*.

The point here is not that differentiation of itself is always a problem—clearly in social contexts we do differentiate among people in various ways, including such as those listed above, and possibly always have. The difficulty here is that a categorical approach to difference implies, firstly, that there is something prior to these categories against which their difference can be positioned, and, secondly, that these differences can be clearly defined and circumscribed as static and unchanging. Burbules (1997) calls this a "presumption of sameness or normalcy" (p. 99), which, he argues, is set as the starting point from which categorical definitions and understanding of diversity are derived. From this perspective, diversity denotes difference from some 'presupposed' norm and names those who fit particular categories of difference from that 'norm'. An almost inevitable consequence of naming particular types of difference or diversities in this way is that those categories are then positioned as deficit. Thus, the effect of the way in which differences are categorised under the umbrella term 'diversity' is not entirely benign and may serve to reinforce negative stereotypes and views of difference. Those groups that are named as diverse are often those very same groups that tend to be over-represented in negative statistics such as poverty, incarceration, suicide rates, and unemployment. They are also the very same groups that are more likely to face significant issues in their education experiences, including low achievement, exclusion, marginalisation, alienation, and so on. The risk, as Todd (2011) suggests, is that a result of this type of positioning of diversity is that it becomes "shorthand for naming precisely those differences that need to be 'managed'" and leads to "the assumption that diversity is a problem" (p. 102): a problem for society, for those who are not diverse, for those who represent the norm and the dominant culture or way of being.

Furthermore, these same ideas can serve to minimise and even trivialise the lived experiences of marginalisation, discrimination, and even oppression of those who fall into the categories of diversity. If accepted unquestioningly, they can, as Burbules (1997) puts it, "domesticate difference" and thus obscure or gloss over the tensions and complexities among people with their many and varied differences. Perhaps more significantly, they may also obscure and gloss over the histories of conflict, struggle, and power imbalance that are the experiences of groups who are categorised as diverse. Diversity is not a neutral state of being, nor are differences neutral; to be different has consequences which often reflect inequalities in social power and position that result in exclusion, stigmatisation, and even, in extreme circumstance, death; being different can be dangerous (Burbules, 1997; Mitchell, 2016). Benjamin (2002) suggests that phrases such as "valuing diversity" are simply clichés that obscure and collude with the maintenance of inequalities in education and fail to highlight injustices or provide for change. Moreover, despite the positive terms associated with it, the model of diversity that specifies categories and types such as 'the big five' is compromised by being, as Swartz (2009) argues, "shackled to the dominant discourse of 'otherness'" (p. 1045) and thus "defined in reference to established norms and categories" (Burbules, 1997, p. 99). Burbules paints a stark picture of the impact of this on the choices of those so categorised as regards education who must decide either to

> abandon or suppress their differences for the sake of conformity or 'fitting in'; or to accept the characterization of one's own differences from the dominant perspective, becoming alienated from oneself; or to reject the standards and norms others have set, and so lose out on the opportunity that education represents—and then often being blamed for it into the bargain. (Burbules, 1997, p. 99)

In the face of all of this, the discourse of celebrating and valuing diversity rings rather hollow and is, not surprisingly, called into question. It would not be unreasonable, given this analysis, to argue that in some situations 'diversity' is simply a euphemism for difference positioned as deficit, something that needs to be managed rather than something to celebrate, value, and respect. Nonetheless, references to encouraging, respecting, celebrating, and valuing diversity are ubiquitous in the education lexicon, particularly as regards inclusive education as we shall discuss in the next section.

Inclusive education: A policy response to diversity

As noted above, there is a commitment to upholding principles and ideals that value and respect diversity set out in policy and curricula in Aotearoa

New Zealand. But here, as in the wider international context, the overarching commitment to such principles and ideals is stated in the aspirations for inclusion in education that are set out in national policy and also agreed to through international conventions and agreements (UNESCO, 1994; United Nations, 2006). While initially more narrowly conceived in relation to the education of disabled children and young people, inclusive education is now conceptualised more broadly as a project for the development of education systems that are welcoming and responsive to all children and young people, irrespective of any differences. In her consideration of diversity as conceptualised within the New Zealand Best Evidence Synthesis (BES) project, Alton-Lee (2003) wrote:

> The concept of 'diversity' is central to the synthesis. This frame rejects the notion of a 'normal' group and 'other' or minority groups of children and constitutes diversity and difference as central to the classroom endeavour and central to the focus of quality teaching in Aotearoa, New Zealand. It is fundamental to the approach taken to diversity in New Zealand education that it honours the Treaty of Waitangi. (p. v)

This quote is germane to the ideals underpinning inclusive education which similarly propose an understanding of diversity that rejects any notion of a "norm" against which difference should be measured and positions difference and diversity as central. The Ministry of Education commissioned Wellbeing@School website states in its *Inclusive Practices Toolbox* that inclusive practices are

> about ensuring all students are made to feel welcome at school and are able to take part in all aspects of school life. Diversity is respected and school-wide practices and classroom programmes respond to students' different needs, skills, interests, cultures, and backgrounds. (Ministry of Education, 2019)

The relationship between the *principle of cultural diversity* and *the principle of inclusion* (Ministry of Education, 2007) is also set out clearly in an Education Review Office report which, referring to the *principle of diversity,* states that "there is a close link between this principle and inclusion. Both require teachers to value students as individuals and celebrate the diversity that they bring" (Education Review Office, 2012, p. 19). Internationally, an understanding that there is a strong connection between inclusion and diversity is also apparent in definitions and descriptions of inclusion and inclusive education. UNESCO (2005) defines inclusion as "a dynamic approach of responding positively to pupil diversity and of seeing individual differences not as problems, but as opportunities for enriching learning". It explains inclusive education as

> an approach that looks into how to transform education systems and other learning environments in order to respond to the diversity of learners ... [that] aims towards enabling teachers and learners both to feel comfortable with diversity and to see it as a challenge and enrichment of the learning environment, rather than a problem. (UNESCO, 2005)

Despite the claims made for inclusive education and inclusion as a way to respond to diversity and difference, the reality is that there are still significant issues to be addressed; the promise of a welcoming and inclusive education system has yet to be realised for many. In the New Zealand context, the educational experiences and social outcomes for those who are disabled, members of ethnic, religious, and cultural minorities, those who are gender diverse, and those from low socioeconomic backgrounds are—still—often characterised by failure, marginalisation, and alienation. A question we want to raise here is whether a discourse of inclusion in itself can be the final aim in the endeavour for equity and social justice in schools and society, or if it is just another step towards these higher values and promises. As discourses are strongly influenced and defined by language, and language has power over the way we think and what it is possible for us to think (that is, "How can we think about something that we have no word for and no conception of?"), one could argue that the term 'inclusion' in itself poses a limitation. If we aim to 'include' someone, then this inevitably raises questions about who we include, and into what do we include them? Csikszentmihalyi (2008) states that

> [s]ocialization, or the transformation of a human organism into a person who functions successfully within a particular social system, cannot be avoided. The essence of socialization is to make people dependent on social controls, to have them respond predictably to rewards and punishments. And the most effective form of socialization is achieved when people identify so thoroughly with the social order that they no longer can imagine themselves breaking any of its rules. (p. 17)

What Csikszentmihalyi is pointing out here is that socialisation into any society comes with a transformation, a change of the individual to bend to commonly agreed social norms and rules. To a point this is unavoidable to enable us to live in social structures, which similarly benefit each individual. However, values, beliefs, and rules are socially constructed and create the 'norms' of society. Arguably, inclusion is about bringing anyone who might be perceived as sitting outside of these norms into society through 'education', socialisation, and/or force (emotional, mental, or physical). Using the lens of social constructivism and considering the processes Csikszentmihalyi indicates, we can see that each society tends to be exclusive of those who are 'other', different, diverse. As Bowles and Gintis (2002) argue, and as surveyed in Chapter 4 of this collection, schools are always shaped by the social structure and society they are embedded within. Therefore, inclusive education is exposed to similar constraints as inclusion on a social level is; that is, the need to include someone into an arbitrary 'norm' of a particular society.

Despite the rhetoric in policy and practice of embracing, celebrating, and valuing diversity, the lived educational experiences of many of those who fall under the umbrella of 'diversity' are not necessarily improved by these policies and practices. But education and schooling have a responsibility of care for all children and young people, and play a significant role in their socialisation and subjectification (Biesta, 2013). This would suggest education policy and practice should be at the forefront of change towards equity and inclusion rather than be complicit in reproducing outdated notions of difference, individual shortcomings, and assumed supremacy of some over others, which is arguably still represented in the lived experiences of students with diverse backgrounds in Aotearoa New Zealand schools (Alton-Lee et al., 2000; MacArthur, 2009; Rietveld, 1994). So what might be done instead?

Ainscow (2016) suggests that "inclusion has to be seen as a never-ending search to find better ways of responding to diversity. It is about learning how to live with difference, and, learning how to learn from difference" (p. 147). But this is no easy matter. We human beings have a long history of difficulty with those we deem to be different, as Tomlinson (2018) so aptly puts: while we may "live in a time when diversity is a hallmark of society", this is also a time in which "one of our greatest challenges is shedding centuries-old suspicions of 'the other'" (p. 10). It is debatable whether our current approach to diversity and ideas about inclusion are sufficient to enable us to break with this enduring habit of suspicion and so to achieve the ideal of inclusion that Tomlinson describes:

inclusion advocates classroom heterogeneity of many kinds, so that students of varied cultures, languages, races, abilities, interests, and approaches to learning can, under the guidance of an informed teacher, create a learning community that mirrors the diversity in society—one in which students have the opportunity to understand human differences as both normal and desirable, and in which students are enriched as they grow to understand and appreciate the elements that all humans have in common as well as the differences that make us individuals. (pp. 8–9)

Perhaps, as Burbules suggests, rather than aiming for tolerance and/or celebration of difference, what is needed in education, and is the task of education, "is the critical re-examination of difference, the questioning of our own systems of difference, and what they mean for ourselves and other people" (1997, p. 99). One approach to this, as we will discuss below, is to think of diversity in reference to each person as a unique human being. Conceptions of diversity that categorise individuals largely fail to acknowledge the unique human being. As Todd (2011) puts it, categorisation turns "a person into an aggregate of her cultural attributes: she bears these attributes like a mantle into encounters with others as though they stand for who she is" (p. 103) so that "what makes 'us' diverse, is rooted in an understanding of what individuals represent and not in an understanding of who they are" (p. 104). By starting with the uniqueness of each human being, we may be able to move from the presumption of sameness as the starting point to a deeper and more nuanced understanding of difference and differences.

A holistic approach to diversity

As mentioned above, the local and historical perspective and the view people take based on their background and experiences influences how diversity might be perceived. A narrow take on diversity may be based, for example, on an individual's cultural background or ability and be strongly informed by a view of limitations and difference from the norm, whatever that norm might be. But considered from a social constructivist perspective, the emphasis is not on the limitations of the individual, such as impairment, but on the limitations of a society in the way it caters for the range of diversity of its members. From this viewpoint, diversity and uniqueness are not seen as a deviation from the norm but rather *as the norm*; what stops some people from fully participating in society in similar ways to others are barriers that result from a limited view of diversity as deficit. What we would like to offer is an alternative approach to diversity that can be seen as holistic, positive, and inclusive.

Diversity, as understood here, builds on the recent developments in the discourse of disability and social construction, as well as the anthropological view of each person as a unique human being (e.g., Biesta, 2010; Teschers, 2018). Diversity is seen holistically here, it is not limited to selected characteristics as in, for example, the 'special needs' discussion, but encompasses all characteristics and attributes of human beings as listed earlier, including a person's different abilities, interests, aspirations, and desires. Part of what makes each human being unique are our interests and what we strive for in life. Taking this position alerts us to the positive implications of diversity for society and humanity. Only a range of diverse interests, abilities, and aspirations allows our societies and humanity to develop the way we do and to enrich our life substantially. Just envision a world in which no one would be interested in making furniture, cars, technology, or art—our way of living would be significantly deprived. Part of this diversity originates in differences in culture, upbringing, norms and values, experiences, and encounters made, as well as abilities and aptitudes—inherent or acquired.

Besides the positive aspects of diversity for society (which cannot be explored in full in this chapter, but arguments can be made that a society diverse in many ways will enrich life for everyone), diversity seen in a holistic way can also be beneficial for classroom teaching and education. For example, it can support students' development of tolerance and empathy, it can broaden students' horizon in terms of cultural diversity and other ways of thinking, believing, and values that are considered as important. Students with different abilities can support each other and can be seen as supportive agents for peer and co-operative learning. However, to engage positively with diversity in society and the classroom alike, a person's/teacher's bias, beliefs, and mindset need to be open to this view. Relevant aspects in this regard are an *acceptance of otherness*, which, one could argue, reaches beyond the notion of tolerance. Where tolerance allows other positions to exist, but not necessarily on equal footing, acceptance of otherness can acknowledge the limits of one's own position and the validity of other ways of thinking and being as equally valid in parallel with one's own position.[2]

---

2   This does not mean to give in to relativism and acceptance of all positions as equally good from a moral perspective, but to acknowledge that different ways of being in the world in a grown up way (Biesta, 2013) exist that do not have to conflict ethically (what can be seen and argued for as universally good), even though maybe morally (social and cultural conventions of a time and place—a local society).

In addition to acceptance of otherness, a certain level of understanding and empathy needs to be developed—understanding of differences and diversity, but also the understanding and acceptance that no one person will ever be able to fully understand the experienced reality, life, and position of another. Through empathy and contextual knowledge, we can develop some approximation of understanding of another's lived reality, but we will always fall short of grasping the full experience and way of being of another person. In fact, it sometimes seems difficult enough to fully understand one's own experiences of life in the current moment as well as retrospectively. Other skills, knowledge, and attitudes that seem relevant in this context would be the ability to critically reflect on one's own and other positions, caring and community focused thinking skills, a general humanistic education that provides a sounding board for the individual to set their own and other ways of being and thinking into perspective, and the development of what Aristotle called *phronesis*: prudence and practical wisdom to 'know' what might be the 'right thing to do' in situations one encounters with others.

These considerations create some questions for education and schooling, such as how to support the development of empathy and understanding, as well as critical, caring, and community thinking; what content areas are important for a rounded humanistic education; and how to support the development of prudence and practical wisdom. Some answers to these questions are discussed in relation to Schmid's (2000) concept of an art of living (Teschers, 2018). Teschers has explored Schmid's notion of a good and beautiful life in relation to education, and substantial links can be established between Schmid's concept, education, and schooling. Schmid's concept, similarly to the understanding of diversity offered above, sees each person as a unique human being and takes into account the complexity of human diversity with a specific focus on human interests, aspirations, and striving. As such, many of the requirements Schmid (2000) and Teschers (2018) identified as relevant to allow each person to develop their own art of living and actively shape their life towards what they perceive a good and beautiful life to be, are reflected in the skills, knowledge, and attitudes indicated above as relevant for engaging with diversity in a holistic and inclusive manner.

In this context, Teschers raises the overarching question of what education, and schooling as a social institution contributing to a person's overall education, are for. He argues that education, in the meaning of knowledge and understanding, plays an important part in the formation and personal development of each individual far beyond the scope of qualification for the job market. In regards to schooling, qualification, as Biesta (2013) agrees, is an important aspect of the function of schooling, but Biesta argues further that socialisation (becoming part of existing social traditions and ways of doing and being) and subjectification (the question of 'How am I?'; the becoming and development of a human being and one's sense of self and identity) are equally important. This resonates strongly with Teschers' argument that the overarching aim of education and schooling should be *"to develop their [students'] own art of living: to live a good and beautiful life, according to their own judgement and under the circumstances they are living in"* (2018, p. 114, italics in original). This acknowledges the fact that human life is more than contributing to a society's industry and economy, which seems often the focus of current neoliberal political agendas, and that it can be conducive to a flourishing society if we enable all members to flourish themselves, considering their unique and diverse interests, abilities, and life pathways.

Some of the practical suggestions for schools and classroom practice made in this context are the use of what are known as "Philosophy for Children" practices, especially the pedagogical method of communities of philosophical inquiry. Communities of philosophical inquiry have been shown (Millett & Tapper, 2012) to support critical, creative, community, and caring thinking; they promote tolerance towards otherness and openness to other opinions and ways of thinking. Evidence also exists that the use of communities of philosophical inquiry in schools further supports the academic achievement of all students, but especially students who are most disadvantaged, which can contribute to social justice and equity in schools. One could argue that such groups and communities that include students in all their diversity can also further a sense of belonging, which sits at the heart of some current understandings of inclusive education (e.g., Carrington & MacArthur, 2016; Thomas, 2013). Further engagement with content areas that show the diversity of humanity and human existence, and which promote understanding of otherness and other ways of being through exposure and familiarity, can also contribute to more tolerance, inclusion, and a reflected position of personal norms, values, and beliefs. Examples of such content areas, which could be approached through communities of philosophical inquiry or otherwise, are suggested by Schmid: *"the human being as individual, the social human being, difficulties and burdens of human life, striving for fulfilment and meaning in life, religions, beliefs and human cultures, and personal life-styles and global perspectives"* (as cited in D'Olimpio & Teschers, 2016, p. 118, italics in original).

If, as discussed above, diversity is seen holistically and each student and person is seen as a unique human being who is part of a widely diverse social community, and if an overarching end of education would be to support all members of society to develop their own good and beautiful lives, arising implications for schooling include that teachers and educators (but also politicians, parents, and individuals) have to reflect critically on the set up of our schools and education system. Further, we have to question whether the current model is conducive, across all age groups and levels, to cater for the uniqueness of individuals and the existing range of diversity in our society. Also, are the pedagogy, teaching practices, curriculum, and assessment procedures appropriate and supportive of developing each student's own art of living? Or could it be that we have allowed structures to develop that support only some and focus more on qualification, job opportunities, and monetary futures of the ruling majority (i.e., most of us reading this chapter) as Biesta (2013) points out?

Conclusion

The focus of this chapter has been to question common conceptions of diversity in public, academic, and policy discourses. We aimed to trouble the notion of 'celebrating diversity', which often can lead to seeing diversity as difference from some kind of norm. Instead, we propose a holistic viewpoint of diversity *as the norm*, recognising that each human being is unique and different. We argued that this holistic perspective aligns well with the notion of inclusive education which acknowledges that all students are different from each other to some extent and learn differently from each other, as well as its aim for a *meaningful participation* (Ballard, 2004; Carrington & MacArthur, 2016) of *all students*, not just some or most (Florian & Black-Hawkins, 2011; Skidmore, 2002), in classrooms and schools and ultimately our wider society. Finally, we argue that to achieve the aspiration of fairness and justice for all people in Aotearoa and beyond, and to realise the promise of inclusive education, societies and schools need to respond to and cater for the uniqueness of each individual in policy and practice.

Recommendations for further reading

Mitchell, D. (2016). *Diversities in education: Effective ways to reach all learners*. Oxford, UK: Routledge.

Thomas, G. (2013). A review of thinking and research about inclusive education policy, with suggestions for a new kind of inclusive thinking. *British Educational Research Journal, 39*(3), 473–490.

References

Ainscow, M. (2016). Diversity and equity: A global education challenge. *New Zealand Journal of Educational Studies, 51,* 143–155.

Alton-Lee, A. (2003). *Quality teaching for diverse students in schooling: Best evidence synthesis*. Wellington: Ministry of Education.

Alton-Lee, A., Rietveld, C., Klenner, L., Dalton, N., Diggins, C., & Town, S. (2000). Inclusive practices within the lived cultures of school communities: Research case studies in teaching, learning and inclusion. *International Journal of Inclusive Education, 4*(3), 179–210.

Ballard, K. (2004). Children and disability: Special or included? *Waikato Journal of Education, 10,* 315–326.

Benjamin, S. (2002). Valuing diversity: A cliché for the 21st century. *International Journal of Inclusive Education, 6*(4), 309–323.

Biesta, G. (2010). *Good education in an age of measurement: Ethics, politics, democracy*. Boulder, CO: Paradigm.

Biesta, G. (2013). *The beautiful risk of education*. Boulder, CO: Paradigm.

Bowles, S., & Gintis, H. (2002). Schooling in capitalist America revisited. *Sociology of Education, 75*(1), 1–18.

Burbules, N. C. (1997). A grammar of difference: Some ways of rethinking difference and diversity as educational topics. *Australian Educational Researcher, 24*(1), 97–116.

Carrington, S., & MacArthur, J. (2016). *Teaching in inclusive school communities*. Hoboken, NJ: John Wiley & Sons.

Csikszentmihalyi, M. (2008). *Flow: The psychology of optimal experience*. New York, NY: Harper Perennial.

D'Olimpio, L., & Teschers, C. (2016). Philosophy for children meets the art of living: A holistic approach to an education for life. *Philosophical Inquiry in Education, 23*(2), 114–124.

Education Review Office. (2012). *The New Zealand curriculum principles: Foundations for curriculum decision-making*. Wellington: Author.

Florian, L, & Black-Hawkins, K. (2011). Exploring inclusive pedagogy. *British Educational Research Journal, 37*(5), 813–828.

MacArthur, J. (2009). *Learning better together: Working towards inclusive education in New Zealand schools*. Wellington: IHC.

Millett, S., & Tapper, A. (2012). Benefits of collaborative philosophical inquiry in schools. *Educational Philosophy and Theory, 44*(5), 546–567.

Ministry of Education. (2007). *The New Zealand curriculum*. Wellington: Learning Media.

Ministry of Education (2017). *Te whāriki: He whāriki mātauranga mō ngā mokopuna o Aotearoa: Early childhood curriculum*. Wellington: Author.

Ministry of Education. (2019). *Inclusive practices toolkit*. Wellington: Wellbeing@School. Retrieved from: https://wellbeingatschool.org.nz/about-inclusive-practices-tools.

Mitchell, D. (2016). *Diversities in education: Effective ways to reach all learners*. Oxford, UK: Routledge.

Rietveld, C. (1994). From inclusion to exclusion: Educational placement of children with Down Syndrome. *Australasian Journal of Special Education, 18*(2), 28–35.

Schmid, W. (2000). *Philosophie der lebenskunst. Eine grundlegung*. [Philosophy of the art of living. A foundation.] Frankfurt, Germany: Suhrkamp.

Skidmore, D. (2002). A theoretical model of pedagogical discourse. *Disability, Culture and Education, 1*(2), 119–131.

Statistics New Zealand. (2013, 10 December), *New Zealand has more ethnicities than the world has countries*. [Press release]. Retrieved from: http://archive.stats.govt.nz/Census/2013-census/data-tables/totals-by-topic-mr1.aspx

Swartz, E. (2009). Diversity: Gatekeeping knowledge and maintaining inequalities. *Review of Educational Research, 79*(2), 1044–1083.

Teschers, C. (2018). *Education and Schmid's art of living*. London, UK: Routledge.

Thomas, G. (2013). A review of thinking and research about inclusive education policy, with suggestions for a new kind of inclusive thinking. *British Educational Research Journal, 39*(3), 473–490.

Todd, S. (2011). Educating beyond cultural diversity: Redrawing the boundaries of a democratic plurality. *Studies in Philosophy of Education 30,* 101–111.

Tomlinson, C. A. (2018). Championing inclusion: A reflection. *Australian Educational Leader, 40*(2), 8–11.

UNESCO. (1994). *The Salamanca statement and framework for action on special needs education*. Paris: Author.

UNESCO. (2005). *Guidelines for inclusion: Ensuring access for all*. Paris, France: Author.

United Nations. (2006). *United Nations convention on the rights of persons with disabilities*. New York, NY: Author.

Chapter 9
Community engagement as a particularly appropriate pedagogy for Aotearoa New Zealand

Billy O'Steen

What makes a teaching and learning innovation stick? This chapter considers that question through the lens of a natural disaster and the development of an academic response to it that had to take into account and address local conditions—an example of acting locally while thinking globally. As such, this contextualised case study provides general guidance to any teacher seeking to implement a new approach, even without the extraordinary circumstances of a series of earthquakes.

Introduction: 1873–2010

In 1873 in the newly emerging city of Christchurch on the South Island of New Zealand, two professors from Cambridge and two professors from Oxford established Canterbury College as the second oldest tertiary institution in the recently formed colony. The College was located in the centre of the downtown district in direct alignment between the Christchurch Cathedral and the Botanic Gardens. Its central position represented the importance that the city planners placed on higher education and the institution itself. Further, naming it Canterbury as opposed to Christchurch ensured that the whole region and not just the city could affiliate with it. Twenty years later in 1903 and several thousand kilometres away in the United States, this regional approach to a university's scope was first given voice with "the Wisconsin idea" whereby "the boundaries of the university are the boundaries of the state" (Benson et al., 2017, p. 71). This idea of universities serving their communities did not begin with Canterbury or Wisconsin, but the events since then have proven its staying power over 100 years later.

While rose-tinted nostalgia hints otherwise, it is safe to say that between 1873 and the 1970s, Christchurch and the University of Canterbury (UC) were not always the best of neighbours but they were neighbours of necessity, as the campus was seamlessly interwoven with the city. "Community engagement" was not a term used during that time period and did not necessarily need to be an explicit institutional strategy—it simply was the result of existing in close proximity with one another. This close 'town and gown' relationship began to disintegrate with the bittersweet solution to the growth of the University and its need for more land and facilities. By the midpoint of the decade, the move was complete and staff and students settled into a new campus located a few kilometers away in the Ilam suburb on the other side of Hagley Park from the downtown area. In exchange for the iconic Gothic campus in the city, new buildings were designed in the Brutalist style of concrete and metal and land was plentiful. A common observation of the Ilam campus to this day is that it has nice grounds.

Another common observation and critique is that the Ilam campus faces inward. This can be seen in the buildings that front the surrounding streets without any obvious or welcoming entrances or pathways in. There is no defined traditional university-style entrance in the form of a gate, drive, or distinguishing building. Thus, one could do a loop around the perimeter of the campus and not really know (or care) what was going on. A former Vice-Chancellor said it resembled a fortress that was not welcoming to those on the outside. In addition to the difficulty with accessing the campus, another potentially negative consequence of the relocation came with thousands of students seeking accommodation nearby. Overnight, a substantial rental house market was created with students infiltrating well-established residential neighbourhoods. To this day, there are family homes interspersed with high-density student flats which often bring a variety of baggage with them—multiple cars parked on yards, broken bottles, the occasional burned couch, and activity at all hours of the day and night. While some students have been responsible neighbours, prior to 2010, many were viewed as a menace to be tolerated and not to be positively engaged with. In 2009, the potential to change this dynamic was suggested by Dr Rod Carr in one of his first actions as new Vice-Chancellor. Coming from a business background, he believed that UC did not have a clear strategic vision or mission. He set about to change that by having cross-campus conversations for input and this resulted in the strategic statement intent of "people prepared to make a difference". Depending on how this was implemented and shared with students, there was the opportunity to have students see themselves differently. However, before this statement had time to be well established, everything changed due to the power of two forces—nature and the students.

Earthquakes: 2010–2011

On Saturday, 4 September 2010, a massive 7.1 earthquake struck just outside of the city limits at 4:35 am. The jolt lasted nearly a minute and disturbed what otherwise had been a quiet period of seismic activity in Christchurch which had lasted for over 100 years. Within seconds, the lives of more than half a million people were significantly affected. However, due to the time of day, no one died. As dawn broke across the region, the damage to a number of buildings and houses was revealed with several brick facades demolished on the sidewalks and many chimneys (including mine) displaced or collapsed altogether. The first hint at how Kiwis were going to respond came from my neighbour who was surveying my teetering chimney with me and immediately offered to help dismantle it. From the vantage point on top of our house, we saw that every other chimney on the street was in disrepair. For the next several hours, I felt useful in helping to take down these other chimneys and it represented the New Zealand impulse to "get stuck in" and fix it yourself. In other parts of town, the most significant damage beyond chimneys was the emergence of liquefaction, which is a grey, quicksand-like substance that comes up as the result of a disturbed water table. In moments, people's cars, houses, and yards were virtually swallowed up within the muck.

An area of town that did not suffer much structural damage or any liquefaction was the UC campus and surrounding environs. Despite this, the senior leadership team at UC announced the immediate suspension of classes for at least 2 weeks in order to check the buildings and to allow staff the time to get resettled. This was met by the students with a quick flurry of Facebook events for after-quake parties. However, one student had a different idea about how to spend the 2-week break. Sam Johnson started quite a different Facebook event that invited fellow students to join him on 7 September to go out to a suburb that was particularly affected by liquefaction. The response to his "Student Base to Provide Relief from the Earthquakes" event was tepidly received, initially garnering fewer than 100 likes. Thus, he was pleased when 100 students showed up at a UC parking lot that Tuesday morning. Equipped with little more than enthusiasm and gumption and not shovels, wheelbarrows, or boots they set out to the Halswell area and ended up using little kids' beach buckets to move the liquefaction from people's yards out to the street. As lunchtime arrived, Sam quickly headed to the grocery store and depleted his bank account to feed the hungry volunteers. Feeling like they had provided some assistance both physically and morally, Sam reposted the event for the next day and had more than 200 volunteers show up. The numbers kept growing throughout the week as did external acknowledgement that these students were doing something meaningful. By the end of the week, Sam had 1,000 volunteers and was receiving donations of equipment, money, and the use of city buses. All told, the 2 weeks of what was soon to be known as the Student Volunteer Army (SVA) involved over 2,000 students moving thousands of tons of liquefaction. As importantly, they were flipping the script on what the public understood what it meant to be a University of Canterbury student.

Throughout their 2-week deployment, I kept thinking that it was going to be a real shame if the student volunteers were to go right back to their statistics, biology, and history classes without an opportunity to reflect on and celebrate their accomplishments. After briefly toying with proposing an academic response in the form of a service learning course related to it, the general vibe in the city and on campus was that we had survived the big one and gotten away with no deaths and no overwhelming damage to the city. In a typical Kiwi approach to the situation, people were ready to move on and not dwell on what happened. Thus, the moment for a course or initiative passed. In the ensuing months after the quake, Sam's Facebook event became an official club that would be devoted to promoting volunteering among students by doing the odd weekend project.

Less than 6 months after getting through the big, once-in-a-lifetime seismic event, on 22 February 2011 at 12:51 pm, Christchurch was hit by a quake that was more violent, shallower, and much closer to the downtown. Unlike the September earthquake, this time there were people all over the city—eating lunch, attending meetings, riding buses, and going to school. Every quake and aftershock has its own personality. In comparison, the 2010 quake was a wave, and this one was a punch. And the city crumbled. Over 80% of the built downtown instantly sent up clouds of dust as buildings collapsed. More than 11,000 homes would be rendered uninhabitable due to poor land conditions. Most unfortunately, 185 people died in the destruction and rubble. The catastrophic nature of this quake immediately put everything on hold. The government, businesses, schools, and the University announced closures for the foreseeable future while first responders descended on what was left of the city. Similar to the first quake, the area around campus appeared to be less affected than other areas so students retained the comforts of housing, power, water, and sewage. It was the second day of the first semester and Clubs Day when student groups recruit new members. Ironically, the SVA had a stand and was making efforts to attract new volunteers when the quake hit.

The leadership of the SVA club met on the night of the 22nd to discuss whether and how they would deploy based on what they had learnt from the September quake. By the next day, they had determined to go all in and quickly ramped up their communications and logistics to be ready to deploy on the 24th. The SVA Facebook page exploded overnight with more than 25,000 likes and thousands of students showing up on that first day. Over the next 3 weeks, nearly all students at UC participated to some extent in the SVA, which again became a highly organised force with advanced communications, equipment, transportation, food, and even entertainment to keep the volunteers' spirits up. In fact, they were the largest non-governmental organisation operating in Australasia at the time. Just as important as their physical labour was, they captured the imagination of the country and parts of the world as a bright spot amidst one of New Zealand's darkest hours. Through their incredible community-building efforts, the SVA erased previous negative connotations of drunken, rowdy students and reset what had been a strained 'town and gown' relationship. As one resident summed it up, "I never thought I'd be happy to see a group of university students walking down my street."

An academic and institutional response: 2011–present

"Isn't it great that these students have put their learning aside to help out."

Little could the news anchor realise that his narration over scenes of the green t-shirted SVA members shovelling liquefaction would launch an academic and institutional response of community engagement at UC. I watched this broadcast on the 24th from the security of a vacation home 90 minutes north of Christchurch, where my family had retreated on the night of the 22nd. We had moved out of our home on the 21st for it to be repaired from the September quake. So, we were living out of suitcases anyway and after seeing the lack of essential services in our area, we joined an exodus from the city. The fact that we were in a safe, functioning house contributed to how I was able to have the head space to do what I did next. Upon seeing the news broadcast and hearing the anchor, I saw this as an opportunity to revisit my thoughts after the September quake about providing students with the chance to bring their volunteering back onto campus. I hurriedly sent an email to the Associate Vice-Chancellor with intimations that I had an idea for a class related to the SVA. Much to my surprise, he quickly and positively responded by saying that they were looking for innovative ideas. He gave me 24 hours to develop my thoughts before pitching them to him and the Vice-Chancellor.

During those hours, I consulted with Vincent Ilustre, Director of the Center for Public Service at Tulane University in New Orleans, Louisiana. Six years prior, in 2005, Hurricane Katrina tore through New Orleans leaving thousands dead and homeless. Tulane was forced to close for a semester and upon reopening they determined to reset their relationship with the city by becoming a partner alongside it through the rebuild. To make good on this promise, Tulane made it a graduation requirement to take two service learning classes related to the rebuild. After losing staff and students when they reopened and for a few years, Tulane eventually had the highest number of applications of any US university in 2010. They attributed that to this new mission of becoming the most civically engaged university in the country. Not only were they getting students who were good academically, they were getting students who wanted to do good. Vincent provided me with great advice and ideas about making the course I was considering part of UC's overall mission of "people prepared to make a difference". Along with Vincent, I spoke with Dr Patti Clayton who had been the Director of Service-Learning at North Carolina State University when I taught there. Patti is a hugely regarded leader in the practice and research of service learning. She has literally defined service learning in a way that is used by everyone in the field. It was her model below that I used for the eventual course design (Clayton et al., 2005). She encouraged me to lean on the research of the effectiveness of service learning and to make the course as academically rigorous as possible as she, correctly, anticipated that I might run into opposition against the idea.

Armed with confidence and a clear vision of what I could see happening with the SVA-inspired course, I had a Skype meeting with the Associate Vice-Chancellor, Vice-Chancellor, and a PhD student, Lane Perry. Lane was completing his doctorate with me and had looked into two service learning classes that we had helped to design at UC. In the following months, his research and a related publication of ours—*Engaging students and teachers through service learning* (O'Steen, Perry, Cammock, Kingham, & Pawson, 2011)—would prove to be critical in that it demonstrated that service learning was effective in the UC context. One minute into the conversation, the Vice-Chancellor responded that he was sold and offered his support to make it happen. In addition to his backing, we leaned on shared cultural beliefs about volunteering within New Zealand but had to be mindful of other cultural norms.

Long before the SVA, volunteering was generally accepted as what Kiwis should do with little fanfare or recognition. This stems from their reticence to self promote due to the "tall poppy syndrome", which holds that New Zealanders should not stand out or promote themselves. The ingrained nature of this quiet form of volunteering has resulted in the country being absolutely dependent on it for the delivery of essential services. Each of the 2,531 schools in the country is similar to a charter school in the United States, in that it is run by parents who are elected to boards of trustees. These parents have complete responsibility for hiring decisions, evaluation of the principal, facilities management, and curriculum implementation. Similarly, of New Zealand's 8,000 firefighters, 7,000 are volunteers. When the fire alarm goes up in our village, we know all 20 members who are leaving their homes to address the situation. The surf lifeguards who patrol the country's extensive coastline are all volunteers who often begin their training at 6 years old and work toward their certification at 14. This embedded notion of stepping up and helping out prompted famed Kiwi movie director Sir Peter Jackson to declare that his homeland is not a small country but a large village. Following with his observations, it is unsurprising that New Zealand was ranked third in the 2018 Charities Aid Foundation's World Giving Index (2018).

Many service learning practitioners and scholars understand that attention to culture and language is vitally important in our field. The assumptions, meanings, foundations for relationships, and application can vary significantly from one context to another and it is unwise to blindly foist what appears to work in one place to a different location. Eight years after the earthquakes, the SVA is the biggest club on campus, the UC Community Engagement Hub was established, and community engagement was adopted as one of four graduate attributes that every student will experience. All of these community engagement accomplishments almost did not happen due to not paying close attention to New Zealand culture.

In addition to the overall support for volunteering in New Zealand that would suggest an environment ripe for community engagement, in 2009–11, PhD student Lane Perry researched two classes at UC that had all of the hallmarks of traditional service learning pedagogy even though the instructors weren't labelling them as such. Lane's findings established that the UC context was indeed conducive to students being more engaged with their academic studies, seeing themselves as active citizens, and growing personally. Thus, when we observed the SVA's actions after the earthquakes, we saw an opportunity to design a post-disaster community engagement course *á la* Tulane's efforts following Hurricane Katrina. By drawing on the extensive research of how to create these kinds of courses by Dr Clayton, and how to do so after a disaster by Vincent Ilustre, we began the work of putting together CHCH101: Rebuilding Christchurch. The course would acknowledge students' volunteering as equating to one-third of the course being complete and then they would engage with academic content and critical reflection for the other two-thirds. During our creation phase, in addition to meeting with senior management and colleagues across campus, we approached the SVA founders to share our idea with them. This is where community engagement at UC was almost stopped in its tracks due to cultural context.

First, some of our colleagues immediately responded that students should not be given credit for volunteering. It took some time and wise use of research and theory in the field of experiential education and service learning / community engagement (e.g., Ash & Clayton, 2009; Clayton et al., 2005; Dewey, 1938; Eyler & Giles, 1999; Stanton, 1999) to clearly establish that the volunteering was only one part of the course and that to receive credit, students would need to engage with content and critically reflect on it and their actions. Fortunately, the strength and rigour of the field's research coupled with Dr Perry's research on our own campus gave us credibility and the space to continue with the development of the course. Secondly, and most importantly, the SVA founders were strongly opposed to the course because they feared that people would regard their incredible efforts as having been done just to get course credit. In this, they were exhibiting all the cultural heritage of unheralded volunteering, the country as a village, and the "tall poppy syndrome". They viewed their post-quake actions as being just what you do and not anything to be held up and regarded.

While the field's research was relevant to our colleagues, we believed it would have less sway with the students so we designed a critical reflection experience for them to demonstrate the value of thinking about their actions within an academic setting. As the students had been so busy with the work of volunteering across the city, they had not had much opportunity to reflect on what they did. After 2 hours of using Ash and Clayton's DEAL (Describe, Evaluate, Articulate Learning) Framework (Ash & Clayton, 2009) with them, each SVA founder was convinced that community engagement and service learning is not about simply doling out credit for volunteering. Because of the power of the reflection experience, they immediately became advocates and encouraged their fellow students to consider taking the course. Eight years later, the course has had over 1,000 students take it and contribute 30,000 hours of service throughout the city. In hindsight, the challenges posed by our colleagues and students about the composition of community engagement and service learning were healthy opportunities to learn how to be clearer about how we talk about this field and how to strategically utilise the rich literature base.

The portrayal of our field to those unfamiliar with it needs to take into account cultural contexts as well as how best to use the existing base of literature and research. This is especially important in international settings where service learning may run counter to existing cultural norms and practices. Despite many shared characteristics between New Zealand and the United States, our experience with introducing service learning demonstrated how assumptions and inattention to unique contextual factors could sabotage the best of intentions. Within this context, the university students in the SVA may have very likely seen themselves as replicating what they had seen their parents and whānau do on school boards, fire brigades, or surf lifesaving crews. Regardless of their motivations and intentions, they made significant contributions to the city and country by peforming compassionate service. This resembled the positive impacts I had seen their counterparts at North Carolina State University contribute through my implementation of service learning into the teacher education programme.

With the support of Dr Clayton, we designed ways for these prospective teachers to experience service learning as students so that they would hopefully be inclined to try it with the students in their future classrooms. Our work took us to a variety of service sites from a Habitat for Humanity ReUse Center deconstruction through voter registration in the presidential election in 2004, to a sanctuary for large cats (cougars and panthers). What I observed across the different contexts was that the benefits of academic engagement, active citizenship, and personal growth were consistent and demonstrable. After heading to UC from North Carolina in 2005, I was excited to see these similar benefits by assisting with the design, implementation, and Lane's study of two existing service learning courses in geography and management. However, despite these courses having all of the hallmarks of traditional service learning, the lead faculty on them did not know the terminology, the vast literature of the field, or the international community. They were simply doing what they thought was effective pedagogy. Lane's findings showed that students in these two classes were overwhelmingly impacted by them and they outpaced their peers on all measures of the National Survey of Student Engagement. Thus, before the earthquakes, all of the pieces were in place at UC to pursue service learning on a bigger scale—a national disposition to volunteering and proof of concept with the two classes.

Beyond the earthquakes

Both the SVA and CHCH101 have maintained positive trajectories since the earthquakes by being adaptive and attuned to further opportunities. For the SVA, they have done so through the establishment of the Volunteer Army Foundation in 2012, which has served as a consistent backdrop for support and vision. Starting with the Great East Japan Earthquake in March of 2011 and continuing with Hurricane Sandy in 2012, Cyclone Pam in Vanuatu in 2015, the Nepalese earthquake of 2015, and the Port Hills wildfires in Christchurch in 2017, the SVA has been called upon to provide on-the-ground assistance as well as strategic consultation. In each instance, the Foundation has helped out with logistical matters and evaluative advice.

Similarly, after the success of CHCH101 for 3 years, the UC Community Engagement Hub was established to provide support and vision for all things community engagement at UC. This intentionally coincided with the adoption of community engagement as one of four attributes for a campus-wide graduate profile. Like the relationship between the SVA and the Foundation, the UC Community Engagement Hub and the graduate profile represent the shift of these two movements born of the earthquake into 'business as usual', being of potential use on an international level. This was poignantly apparent when the SVA and the Hub reached out to the students at Marjory Stoneman Douglas High School in Parkland, Florida following the 14 February 2018 mass shooting there. Those students, like the SVA, were quick to respond to the tragedy in front of them by quickly organising the March for Our Lives a little more than a month after the shooting. We immediately reached out to support them and then invite them to visit us to discuss how to maintain and sustain a youth-led movement. While our tragedies were vastly different, we believed that we could share our experiences and stories of being active citizens for the past 8 years and find common ground in being parts of youth-led movements. As a result, a guidebook was produced at UC by them and the SVA for others who are interested in creating and sustaining youth-led movements regardless of their origin.

Akin to the SVA and Marjory Stoneman Douglas students who wanted to make a difference, Jessica Weston was a student from the University of Illinois doing her study-abroad semester at UC in the first half of 2013 and was taking CHCH101. She was particularly inspired by a guest lecture during one of the classes by Jason Pemberton, one of the founding SVA team members. Because of him, she focused her final project—a Healing Proposal to improve a specific aspect of a specific community—on creating an SVA back in Illinois. Two months after she had been back at the University of Illinois, she watched in horror as her hometown of Washington, Illinois was decimated by a severe tornado. Within 24 hours, she was busy organising a "fill the truck" campaign that eventually obtained enough needed items to fill two tractor trailers, which were on their way to Washington by the end of the week. Jessica directly credits her confidence and motivation to do what she did to CHCH101 and the SVA.

As is evident by the sheer numbers of volunteers and hours contributed since the inception of the SVA in 2010 through its continued existence, CHCH101, and the UC Community Engagement Hub, it is clear that young people want to be involved and connected with their communities. Despite portrayals that they are more consumed with screen time and virtual communities, we have seen that they are ready to motivate, to move, and to make a difference when given the opportunity and that screens can even be utilised to make it happen, as shown by Sam Johnson's original Facebook event.

Conclusions and implications

The actions of the SVA resonated with people around the world—including visits with them by Prince Harry and Dr Jane Goodall—because they represented the best instincts of humankind in the face of tragedy and displayed a particularly bold approach to Kiwi ingenuity. This resembles the "window of utopia" that Rebecca Solnit observed through exploring people's reactions to disasters in her book, *A Paradise Built in Hell* (2010): the 1906 earthquake in San Francisco, the Halifax munitions cargo ship explosion in 1917, the 1985 earthquake in Mexico City, 9/11, and Hurricane Katrina in New Orleans in 2005. Her description of these reactions as a "surge in citizenship" connects disaster response with fully engaging one's self in the issues and concerns of the day. Many years before these disasters and her observations, the Ancient Greeks described citizenship in a similar fashion by stating that everyone was born an idiot—the Greek word idios means solely concerned with one's self—and it is only through education that one becomes a citizen. As the first group of people to attempt a democracy, this notion of moving someone from self concern to public concern was critical. Likewise, the SVA and 9/11 first responders and New Orleans Red Cross volunteers were all demonstrating active citizenship. It is the goal of the CHCH101 course and many other service learning courses to provide that important aspect of education and movement toward citizenship. Even though this idea is evident in *The New Zealand Curriculum's* key competency of *contributing and participating* (Ministry of Education, 2007) it does not automatically transfer to students through its mere mention or by osmosis. And, despite the fact that the essential services of school governance, surf lifesaving, and fire fighting continue to function, there is no guarantee that the next generations will be ready, willing, and able to step into our places and take part in these community-based organisations. Thus, the Greeks, Solnit, and the SVA have much to teach us with regard to preparing our descendants.

What could this look like in contexts other than post-quake Christchurch? As was demonstrated in our situation, local conditions and cultural norms must be taken into account when planning for service learning and community engagement. At its core, this practice is intertwined with the community and must, therefore, be fully cognizant and responsive to its needs, desires, and capabilities. Ideally, service learning and community engagement will focus on doing *with* the community and not simply doing something *to* it. A good example of this are the 2 years worth of locally based community engagement projects initiated by over 2,000 primary school classrooms across New Zealand. They have been participating in an "SVA in a box" initiative whereby students and teachers are given the basic tools of planning a community engagement project with an emphasis on ideas that are mutually designed and implemented by all involved. Similarly, two other actions stemming from the SVA are suggesitive of the transportability of the community engagement ethos to other contexts beyond the earthquakes. For 3 years, the Serve for New Zealand (SFNZ) campaign has taken place on Anzac Day and has provided thousands of participants with ways to contribute to their communities through locally derived efforts. And, just this year the SVA Service Award has been launched at high schools around the country to enable students to achieve badges based on their work in their communities. Taken together, these three post-quake initiatives are successful due to their emphasis on doing things that are relevant and desired by local communities (O'Steen & Johnson, 2016). While the immediate achievements of the SVA and the development of CHCH101 were rooted in the specific post-quake context, the effectiveness of community engagement beyond that time period indicates the appropriateness of this teaching and learning approach to the wider, non-quake cultural backdrop of New Zealand.

Recommendations for further reading

Ash, S. L., & Clayton, P. H. (2009). Generating, deepening, and documenting learning: The power of critical reflection for applied learning. *Journal of Applied Learning in Higher Education*, *1*(1), 25–48.

Dewey, J. (1938). *Experience and education*. New York, NY: Simon & Schuster.

Jacoby, B., & Mustacio, P. (Eds.). (2010). *Looking in reaching out: A reflective guide for community service learning professionals*. Boston, MA: Campus Compact.

References

Ash, S. L., & Clayton, P. H. (2009). Generating, deepening, and documenting learning: The power of critical reflection for applied learning. *Journal of Applied Learning in Higher Education*, *1*(1), 25–48.

Benson, L., Harkavy, I., Puckett, J., Hartley, M., Hodges, R., Johnston, F., & Week, J. (2017). *Knowledge for social change: Bacon, Dewey, and the revolutionary transformation of research universities in the twenty-first century*. Philadelphia, PA: Temple University Press.

Charities Aid Foundation. (2018). *World Giving Index 2018: A global view of giving trends*. Retrieved from https://www.cafonline.org/about-us/publications/2018-publications/caf-world-giving-index-2018

Clayton, P. H., Ash, S. L., Bullard, L. G., Bullock, B. P., Moses, M. G., Moore, A. C., O'Steen, W. L., Stallings, S. P., & Usry, R. H. (2005). Adapting a core service learning model for wide-ranging implementation: An institutional case study. *Creative College Teaching Journal*, *2*(1), 10–27.

Dewey, J. (1938). *Experience and education*. New York, NY: Simon & Schuster.

Eyler, J., & Giles, D. (1999). *Where's the learning in service learning?* San Francisco, CA: Jossey-Bass.

Ministry of Education. (2007). *The New Zealand curriculum*. Wellington: Learning Media.

O'Steen, B., & Johnson, S. (2016). Just get out of their way! Enabling young Kiwis to make a difference. *Set: Research Information for Teachers*, *3*, 58–59.

O'Steen, B., Perry, L., Cammock, P., Kingham, S., & Pawson, E. (2011). Engaging students and teachers through service learning. In P. Coolbear & K. Weir (Eds.), *Good practice publication grants e-book*. Wellington: Ako Aotearoa.

Solnit, R. (2010). *A paradise built in hell: The extraordinary communities that arise in disaster*. New York, NY: Penguin Books.

Stanton, T., Giles, D., & Cruz, N. (1999). *Service-learning: A movement's pioneers reflect on its origins, practice, and future*. San Francisco, CA: Jossey-Bass.

Chapter 10
The role of emotions in education in Aotearoa

Veronica O'Toole and Rachel Martin

Introduction

The emotional impact of the Christchurch 15 March, 2019 terrorist attack was felt throughout Aotearoa, and reported around the world. When Prime Minister Jacinda Ardern visited a school that had lost two students, with another badly injured, a moving Tahu Pōtiki haka was performed by the grieving student body of "heartbroken children" (Wilkie, 2019). One of the students asked Ardern, "How are you feeling?" She replied, "I'm sad", adding that, "it's okay to grieve; it's okay to ask for help". Media shared clinical psychologist Karen Nimmo's caution that traumatic emotions such as shock, sadness, fear, anxiety, and anger would "likely be running high in workplaces and schools" as a result of the attack (Tso, 2019). Emotional flashbacks might also occur, revisiting emotional trauma generated from the earthquakes that had shaken Christchurch in 2010 and 2011.

In the aftermath of the terrorist attack, senior Muslim leader Farid Ahmed publicly expressed his forgiveness of the terrorist, saying "I do not hate him, I love him" (Mead, 2019). This forgiveness resonates with the Māori concept of aroha, which is "like breathing in all the mamae (pain), hurt and worries of another and breathing out love, joy, and hope".[1] Ardern thanked the Muslim community for their open-hearted response in rejecting anger and instead inviting the community to "grieve with them" (Wetherell, 2019, p. 8). Ardern's response that "they are us", has "spread aroha, trying to mitigate hate through love, empathy and compassion" (p. 7).

This chapter explores the role of emotion in education in Aotearoa. First, we provide an overview of current perspectives on emotions in education: emotional intelligence, emotion regulation, emotional labour theories, and Māori perspectives of emotion in education, including historical influences of colonisation. We present two worldviews of emotion in education, in a shift that eschews the "culturalism" through which Western knowledge and ideologies are treated as the universal norm, with Indigenous knowledges positioned only as differing from this norm (Andreotti & de Souza, 2008). Culturalism homogenises Western and Indigenous cultures (Battiste, 2004); in education, children, whānau (family), and teachers are treated as a single entity instead of culturally and linguistically located peoples. Secondly, we discuss research findings on students', teachers', and whānau emotions during and beyond the February 2011 Christchurch earthquake. We take the "He Awa Whiria—Braided River" approach (Macfarlane, Macfarlane, & Gillon, 2015, p. 52; see also Chapter 1 in this collection), drawing on and blending Māori and Western streams of knowledge to facilitate a more culturally appropriate understanding of the role of emotion in education in Aotearoa New Zealand.

The origin of emotion—Western perspectives

The importance of emotions to life has relatively recently been reaffirmed by scholars and researchers from phenomenological, psychological, developmental, biological, philosophical, evolutionary, functional, and clinical theoretical perspectives (Strongman, 2003). Daniel Goleman's (1995) bestselling book, *Emotional Intelligence: Why it Matters More Than IQ*, popularised interest in emotions by sharing Salovey and Mayer's (2004) theory of emotional intelligence. This new conversation resonated internationally and crystalised the growing challenge to the centuries-old debate on the conflict between a person's thoughts and their feelings: a Western perspective that viewed intellect as superior to emotions (Barrett & Salovey, 2002).

---

1   http://etuwhanau.org.nz/our-values/aroha/

Emotions are complex. They are integral to mental wellbeing, and play a key role in decision making, learning, creativity, and relationships (Brackett, Caruso, & Stern, 2013). While these roles were evident in oral and written traditions dating back thousands of years, Western philosophical traditions over the past two millennia regarded emotions as "less sophisticated, more primitive ways of seeing the world, especially when juxtaposed with loftier forms of reason" (Keltner, 2009, p. 50), demonstrating the longevity of influence of the early ethical philosophers. Aristotle (384–322 BC) was one of the first to propose that emotions are related to our thoughts, defining emotions as "all those feelings that so change [people] as to affect their judgements, and are also attended by pain or pleasure" (Oatley & Jenkins, 1996, p. 12).

Following Aristotle's death, two contrasting philosophical traditions gained traction. Epicurean philosophy suggested humans should pursue pleasure and happiness through simple living, not seeking things that would cause anxiety or anger. The Stoic philosophers held a more radical view: emotions result from desires; thus, in order to prevent personally and socially destructive emotions such as anger, anxiety, and greed, most desires should be "disciplined out of daily experience" (Keltner, Oatley, & Jenkins, 2014, p. 13). This discipline enabled Stoics to endure pain or hardship without complaint. Stoicism was acceptable to the Romans and persisted alongside the spread of Christianity following the Christian conversion of the Roman Emperor Constantine in the 4th century. The problematic desires that should be avoided became known as the "seven deadly sins" (Sorabji, 2000, cited in Oatley, Keltner, & Jenkins, 2006, p. 393). St. Paul (1st century), St. Augustine (4th to 5th century), and the Puritans (16th and 17th centuries) advised against emotional indulgence if one wanted to live an ethical life. Following the Reformation (1517–1648) and the Thirty Years' War (1618–1648), in the early Enlightenment, it became safer to think and publish without threat of persecution. In the 16th and 17th centuries, Descartes identified six basic emotions (wonder, desire, joy, love, hatred, sadness) as "passions of the soul" (1649, in Keltner et al., 2014, p. 14). Although separate from and not totally controlled by our thoughts, it was argued that our thoughts might manage these passions.

Twenty-first century re-understandings of emotion owe much to the 19th century work of Charles Darwin (the evolutionary approach), William James (the psychological approach), and Sigmund Freud (the psychotherapeutic approach) (Keltner et al., 2014). Darwin's interest in facial expressions of emotion inspired Tomkins' (1962) theory that emotions are hardwired, genetically-transmitted, human physiological responses that are distinctly experienced and facially-expressed for nine basic emotions. Tomkins' students, Izard and Ekman, visited remote cultures to test this theory. Izard later focused on the physiology of emotion. Ekman and Friesen (1978) designed the anatomically based Emotion Facial Action Coding system which focuses on the contraction of specific facial muscles for specific emotions and is used to this day (Keltner et al., 2014). William James explored the experiential and physiological aspects of emotion, and Sigmund Freud highlighted the role that past emotions play in present-day illness (see Keltner et al., 2014, for a comprehensive overview). Although early 20th century researchers continued on occasion to regard emotions as "disruptive, regrettable and obsolete" (Oatley & Nundy, 1996, p. 267)—possibly influenced by the then focus on emotional disorders—later 20th century psychological research has brought emotions back into favour, positioned as central to individual mental wellbeing and the conduct of social life.

The origins of emotion—Māori perspectives

In Aotearoa, the word Māori refers to an Indigenous New Zealander, but the application of this collectivist term by Pākehā (European New Zealanders) through colonisation has resulted in the loss of tribal histories and traditions, including mātauranga ā iwi. Mātauranga ā iwi refers to the important knowledges from different iwi, whānau, and hapū, the social organisation before the arrival of Pākehā (Rangihau, 1981). Colonisation resulted in the loss of te reo Māori (Māori language), tikanga (tradition), and te ao (Māori ways of being). Colonisation practices, theoretical perspectives, and the historical and political context of language assimilation have caused intergenerational effects on how emotions are expressed as a collective, and as iwi Māori. Being Māori, and expressing iwi Māori emotions in te reo Māori, is complex and will be expressed differently according to iwi, hapū, and whānau.

Te reo Māori is a taonga (treasure), guaranteed protection under Te Tiriti o Waitangi (the Treaty of Waitangi). A Te Tiriti relationship acknowledges that te reo Māori words have more power and influence than a simple translation in te reo Pākehā (European) text. Assimilation practices have changed the terminology describing Māori mātauranga (knowledge). This is demonstrated in Māori cultural narratives containing information about whakapapa (lineage), historical events, landmarks, geographical features, symbols, relationships with flora and fauna, and the label in English of "myths and legends". Pūrākau—the traditional forms of Māori narratives—cannot be relegated to the position of myths and legends, or a fiction or fable from the past, because they contain "philosophical thought, epistemological constructs, cultural codes and worldviews that are fundamental to our identity as Māori" (Lee, 2009, p. 1). Similarly, translating atua to mean Māori Gods denies their significance and minimises their role as "spiritual beings who ran from the major pantheon of deities such as Rangi and Papa, to the mountains and other monumental geographic entities, right through to lesser spirits and beings whose power is more localised and defined" (Pōtiki, 2018, p. 138). These examples demonstrate the complexity of Māori emotions and the importance of localised contexts, and iwi and hapū mātauranga Māori in the teaching and learning of the expression of emotion.

Māori emotions come from our atua, from the creation of the world and the beginning of people (humanity) and these emotions are represented in our stories. There are many different versions of the creation stories of te timatanga o te ao (the beginning of the world) (Reilly et al., 2018) which can be summarised into the following shorter version of the whakapapa of this story as retold by Tame Kuka (2009):

Ko te kore (the void, energy, nothingness, potential)

Ko te pō (from the void of the night)

Ko te whai ao (to the glimmer of dawn)

Ko te ao marama (to the bright light of day)

Ko te ao (the world)

Tīhei mauriora (there is life)

Within this whakapapa there are many other ways of describing the states and depth of layers within te kore, te pō, and te ao Marama. Each concept is expressed further with descriptions of these states in te reo Māori (Reilly et al., 2018) and contains mātauranga Māori that is taught within each whānau, iwi, and hapū. The creation story contains elements for teaching emotional wellbeing and aroha for humanity. There is much to learn from these stories in a contemporary world and these cultural narratives are taonga tuku iho; that is, teachings handed down from our ancestors in order for future generations to learn.

Theories of emotion—Western perspectives

There are more than 150 theories of emotion (Strongman, 2003). One of the more comprehensive psychological theories to have persisted is Lazarus's (1991) theory. Lazarus defines emotions as "cognitive–motivational–relational configurations" (p. 38) that change according to how we appraise the effect of any change in our environment in relation to our goals or priorities, at any given moment. Lazarus addresses the inter-relationship between thought and emotion, expanding the idea of three entwined functions of mind, namely: motivation, cognition, and emotion (Snow, Corno, & Jackson, 1996). Lazarus's theory underlies emotional intelligence (Salovey & Mayer, 2004) and emotion regulation theories (Gross, 2013).

Emotions are biologically complex, comprising "neuromuscular/expressive and experiential aspects" (Izard, 1991, p. 42). The biological complexities in the entwining of the emotion, endocrine, autonomic (unconsciously regulates heart rate and breathing), and somatic (connects the central nervous system to the muscles and organs of the body) systems, are captured by Lazarus's (1991) theory. The *neuromuscular/expressive* component underlies the behavioural responses or action tendencies (private impulses) that are associated with different emotions, such as the fight, flight, or freeze response in fear. In anxiety, the dominant action tendency is avoidance, and in anger it is primarily to attack. When feeling pride, love, or unity, there may be a tendency to express "expansiveness, by telling people" (p. 272). People may not necessarily follow their instinctive action tendency, but muscle tension towards that action may still be observable, such as clenching one's hands, instead of lashing out in anger. The *experiential* aspect refers to the individual's subjective experience of their physiology, such as an increased heart rate in fear, or heightened energy in excitement. Experiential aspects may be referred to as affect or feelings. In sadness and grief, the action tendency is to withdraw. Because this experience may merge with one's quality of life over a period of time, becoming more "diffuse" (p. 251), this might be considered a mood. Mood and emotion have the same biological and cognitive origins, differing mainly in the intensity and duration of the experience. Moods are maintained states that "… typically last for hours, days or weeks, sometimes as a low-intensity background. When it starts or stops may be unclear" (Oatley et al., 2006, p. 30).

From the cognitive perspective, Lazarus has identified the typical thoughts associated with 15 basic emotions. For example, anger tends to be experienced in response to a perceived demeaning offence to oneself or loved ones, or when our goals are perceived as unfairly thwarted (e.g., road rage); happiness tends to indicate that things are progressing well towards our goals, such as "I'm fine". Lazarus's theory helps us understand the moment by moment, ebb and flow of our emotions in daily life, and why different people may respond differently to the same event. This adaptational response also provides a diagnostic perspective, in that "emotions are a valuable source of information about persons and how they are getting along in their worlds" (Lazarus, 1991, p. 40). If we ask how someone is feeling, this is often a first step in identifying whether all is well or not. We saw the effectiveness of this when the student asked Ardern how she was feeling.

From the social perspective, emotions are communicative both to the self and to others, and are socially and culturally constructed (Averill & Nunley, 1992). In the next section, we explore these sociocultural understandings of emotion through the lenses of Māori emotion theories. Bridging from the Western perspective to this discussion, Strongman (2003, p. 3) sums up the various emotion perspectives as follows:

> Emotion permeates life, it is there as a sub-text to everything we do and say. It is reflected in physiology, expression and behaviour; it interweaves with cognition; it fills the spaces between people, interpersonally and culturally. Above all emotion is centred internally in subjective feelings.

Theories of emotion—Māori perspectives

In 2016, Te Kotahi Research Institute held a conference where invited speakers presented and debated examples of concepts of emotion in te reo Māori, such as aroha and riri (anger). Tom Roa (Te Kotahi Research Institute, 2016) presented two important ideas about emotion from his Waikato–Maniapoto viewpoint. He first expressed caution with the interpretation of emotions in te reo Māori as they are descriptions, not prescriptions, and should not be taken as a literal definition to be used as the only way that an emotion is experienced or expressed. His second point was that describing emotions was preferable to defining them, because expressed emotions impact both the individual and others. Roa explained the concept of hopo which describes feelings of being fearful, apprehensive, superstitious, or overawed in the event of a transgression of tapu (sacred tradition) or tikanga (protocol). Hopo may impact either the transgressor or someone else connected to the person, resulting in sickness. Hopo can be healed through a process whereby a skilled person with the iwi mātauranga vocalises karakia (incantations), and uses wairua (spirituality) to help the transgressor understand what has occurred, therefore lifting the tapu. This process heals both the sickness and the emotions. Roa emphasised that emotions have mauri or an essence that makes us human, and that the two main senses used in te ao Māori are te kite me te rongo; that is, to see and to feel.

Matamua (Te Kotahi Research Institute, 2016) proposed that there are universal principles and elements in te ao Māori that Māori collectively understand about emotions, such as the concept of whakamā (shame or embarrassment), and exceptions to this rule. Matamua is Ngāi Tūhoe and explained that the emotions we experience will differ according to the connections we feel to the specific location, context, and environment in which we live, and the associated atua. For example, riri is a broad context-dependent state which can be expressed in a variety of ways. Riri can be expressed in short moments of anger or can be carried intergenerationally. From a relationship perspective, some historical events may cause feelings of discontent in the environment where someone was raised or through an iwi perspective. Matamua expressed the importance of te reo Māori in the expression of individual emotions when he presented at least 13 words in te reo Māori to describe the state of riri including pukuriri (livid with anger), whakatakariri (outraged), and the kīwaha (idiom) puku te rae, used to express anger. We can see, therefore, that the emotional concepts of hopo, aroha, and riri come from Māori deities and whakapapa, whānau, hapū, iwi, and reo Māori contexts. This whakapapa confirms the importance of Māori language and Māori worldviews in the way that all emotions are valued and expressed, formed and experienced at all stages of growth and development and within relationships.

Emotions in education

Education, as a formal system, brings thousands of individuals into socially interactive spaces on a daily basis. Despite the potentially emotional nature of classrooms, the study of emotions in education was "slow to emerge" (Schutz & Pekrun, 2007, p. 3). Student test anxiety was an early research topic, with more widely encompassing emotion research in education latterly confirming the significance of emotion in student cognition, motivation, learning engagement, and outcomes. An extensive literature review focusing on the content, sources, and functions of academic emotions of secondary school and university students found that "there was virtually no major human emotion not reported by participants, disgust being the notable exception" (Pekrun, Goetz, Titz, & Perry, 2002, p. 93). Students' academic emotions may be elicited prior to, during, and following learning activities, such as anticipatory joy or anxiety, concurrent enjoyment or boredom, and retrospective relief or disappointment. Students' social interactions with their teachers and peers bring a further range of interpersonal emotional triggers.

Research into students' social emotions has been conducted under the Social Emotional Learning (SEL) umbrella. SEL refers to various programmes introduced usually (but not exclusively) into schools, for the purpose of improving students' social and emotional wellbeing. Recent international meta-analyses (e.g., Taylor, Oberle, Durlak, & Weissberg, 2017) provide robust evidence that when young children successfully learn and practise how to understand and manage their emotions, the improvement in their social emotional wellbeing, academic outcomes, and life path trajectories can persist, even up to 18 years later. This success also depends on the preparatory provision of SEL for teachers delivering the programme. Within SEL, students with emotional intelligence—defined as the capacity to both reason about and use emotion to enhance thinking and problem solving (Salovey & Mayer, 1990)—experience less anxiety and depression, are less likely to abuse drugs, alcohol, and cigarettes, are less aggressive, and less likely to bully others. They also have greater leadership skills, are more attentive and less hyperactive in school, and perform better academically, compared to other students (Brackett et al., 2013). Emotional intelligence can be learnt through emotional literacy programmes that include developing students' emotion vocabularies.

Teachers' emotions in education were highlighted by Hargreaves' (1998) finding that teaching is an emotion laden profession with emotions at its "very heart" (p. 835). Teachers experience a wide range of emotions on a daily basis, from joy, excitement, and satisfaction, through to frustration, guilt, and anger (Sutton, 2004). These emotions usually occur in response to their cognitive appraisals (Lazarus, 1991) about their students' successes and failures, and their social interactions with students, parents, colleagues, and administrators (Sutton, 2004). Such a range of emotional experiences in the public eye, where teachers need to appear and act professionally, contributes to the emotional labour of teaching, often leading to emotional exhaustion and burnout.

Emotional labour refers to the expectation that employees in caring professions and public domains should express certain emotions during their social interactions as part of the job (Hochschild, 1983). Many teachers see this positively as "a labour of love" (Hargreaves, 1998, p. 840). Emotional labour requires planning and effort, using surface or deep acting strategies. Surface acting involves pretending or faking the appropriate emotion while hiding any inappropriate emotions. Deep acting involves a more genuine expression of the appropriate emotions by sincerely feeling these, and is less taxing of a person's emotional energy (Hargreaves, 1998). Emotional labour demands can be job focused (such as workload, time pressure, lack of professional opportunities, and lack of perceived support) or employee focused, referring to the individual's emotional responses to their job-focused demands (Brotheridge & Grandey, 2002). Teaching involves extensive emotional labour, with teachers continually drawing on "their regulatory resources" (Keller et al., 2014, p. 2). Surface acting tends to drain these resources more readily, leading to emotional exhaustion, which is highly prevalent in teaching (Taxer & Frenzel, 2015). In te ao Māori, burnout can be augmented by the inability to identify as Māori, that is to teach or live as Māori in the professional or cultural aspects of a dominant Western educational system (Naylor, 2006).

Specific emotions contributing to teachers' emotional exhaustion include frustration, anger, anxiety, guilt, shame and sadness and the experiential intensity of these (Keller, Chang, Becker, Goetz, & Frenzel, 2014). Frustration and anger usually occur when teachers feel they have little or no control over a situation, or as a result of conflict. Anxiety and guilt usually relate to ongoing stress (Chang, 2009). Emotional exhaustion is "feeling emotionally overextended and having depleted one's emotional resources" (Chang, 2009, p. 218); it is an early symptom of burnout, which is associated with chronic stress and is prevalent in teaching (Näring, Briët, & Brouwers, 2006). However, teachers with higher emotional intelligence experience less stress and burnout, more self-efficacy, more positive emotions, and greater job satisfaction (Brackett et al., 2013). Within emotional intelligence, higher emotion management (regulation) was significant in reducing burnout in British secondary school teachers (Brackett, Palomera, Mojsa-Kaja, Reyes, & Salovey, 2010).

Emotion regulation refers to "the processes by which individuals influence which emotions they have, when they have them, and how they experience and express these emotions" (Gross, 1998, p. 271). Teachers continually regulate their emotions (Sutton, 2004). They may do this consciously or unconsciously before (preventative), during, or after (responsive) an emotional response. For example, teachers may generate enthusiasm *before* an unpleasant task by saying something motivating to themselves, or they might imagine "putting on my teacher's hat" as they start their day. *During* an emotional experience that cannot be avoided, teachers might fake or mask (suppress) their emotion through their facial expression. Suppression involves resisting the action tendency of an emotion (Lazarus, 1991), such as holding down a smile when amused, or clenching a fist instead of throwing something in frustration. After an experience, teachers might reappraise the situation in order to feel more positive about it (Jiang, Vauras, Volet, & Wang, 2016). Reappraisal involves rethinking or re-evaluating a situation in order to change the emotional response (Lazarus, 1991). A teacher might try to think differently about a student's late assignment, so that the initial anger or frustration dissipates naturally (Sutton, 2004). Reappraisal is a preferable regulation strategy for health and wellbeing because it tends to decrease stress-related physiology (sympathetic nervous system activation), such as increased heart rate in anger, to a more optimal physiology when no longer angry, and feeling calm (parasympathetic nervous system activation) (Gross, 2013). Emotion suppression has the opposite effect and, if habitually used, leads to chronic health problems (see Gross, 2013).

Emotion and the impact of disaster

As outlined in our introduction to this chapter, experiencing a natural disaster in the school environment may anchor traumatic emotional triggers to the school environment. Highly significant and sudden events that elicit intense emotional responses have the potential to create "flashbulb memories" (Brown & Kulik, 1977), whereby that moment is stored in memory as a highly detailed and highly vivid "snapshot" which we might later recall in absolute detail and fully experience emotionally, as though we are back in that moment. This can be reactivated years later in new trauma, as expressed by Karen Nimmo at the start of this chapter.

The magnitude 6.3 earthquake that struck Christchurch in February 2011 was not the first earthquake-related trauma for Christchurch children, it being part of the aftershock sequence of a 7.1 magnitude earthquake that had struck the city at 4.35 am on 4 September the previous year, violently thrusting people from their beds shortly before dawn. Five months later, the more devastating and fatal February earthquake struck in the middle of a school day, reactivating previous trauma and exacerbating this for children who were placed in extreme danger, or who witnessed death. Some children were reluctant to re-enter school classrooms 3 weeks later because they had been so frightened at the time (O'Toole, 2017). Both earthquakes contributed to an unusually prolonged and intensive aftershock sequence, leading to hypervigilance and everyone feeling "on edge" as one teacher put it.

This was the 'new normal' for several years, with more than 11,000 earthquake aftershocks recorded in the first 2 years up to September 2012 (Wilson, 2013). A significant education-related impact was the temporary or permanent relocation and closure of many schools. This created further upheaval for whānau and students, who required additional pastoral care from teachers (Mutch, 2015). These impacts were reflected in 2012 survey data from the Youth 2000 National Project (Fleming et al., 2013). Christchurch secondary school students who had experienced the earthquakes reported higher levels of stress, emotional health difficulties, lower emotional wellbeing, fewer positive experiences in some aspects of schooling, and less involvement in some positive daily activities, compared to secondary school students from similar backgrounds nationally across Aotearoa.

Liberty, Tarren-Sweeney, Macfarlane, Basu, and Reid (2016) found that primary school children's behaviour problems as reported by teachers in schools serving heavily damaged neighbourhoods had more than doubled after the earthquakes, with associated increased rates of post-traumatic stress disorder. One significant finding counter to this was that Māori children did *not* show a significant increase in post-traumatic stress disorder, consistent with other research findings that Māori adults were less affected by anxiety and stress (Hogg, Kingham, Wilson, Griffin, & Ardagh, 2014).

Teachers as first responders

Veronica O'Toole's research into Christchurch teachers' emotional coping as first responders when the February 2011 earthquake struck showed that their first priority was their students' physical and emotional safety (O'Toole & Friesen, 2016). Their emotion perception and emotion regulation factors (extracted from an emotional intelligence self-report) (Schutte, Malouff, & Bhullar, 2009) contributed to their recalled management of their immediate fear response, in order to respond to the disaster. In line with the emotional labour perspective, several teachers explained that, in that moment, being in their professional role in front of the children helped them cope with the first response demands, because they simply *had* to regulate their emotions. One teacher said "I think the kids did me a favour really, because if they weren't there, I could have gone to pieces" (O'Toole & Friesen, 2016, p. 62).

The majority of the teachers recalled cognitive reappraisal as their main emotion regulation strategy to "put aside" their shock and fear, so as to appear calm, trying to stay standing so that the children could see them. Cognitive strategies included self-talk, "pull yourself together", "you're a professional practitioner", "get on with it". Behavioural strategies included taking deep breaths, creating a calm face, "faking it till you make it", "squash the emotion", "stamp down the emotion". Taking a deep breath is an intuitive way to activate the parasympathetic nervous system towards a genuine calmness, whereas the latter methods suggest emotional suppression. While emotional suppression works well for the emergency response, for health reasons, a subsequent debrief and cognitive reappraisal (as occurs for professional first responders) is required (Cicognani, Pietrantoni, Palestini, & Prati, 2009; Gross, 2013). Some teachers recalled responding automatically, or "running on adrenaline". Almost half the teachers were in imminent danger, with several experiencing a realistic, genuine, and immediate fear of death, both their own and their children's; such intense peritraumatic fear presents a risk of subsequent post-traumatic stress (Grimm, Hulse, & Schmidt, 2012).

Eighteen months later, Christchurch teachers' levels of emotional exhaustion and burnout were associated with personal, school, and citywide disaster impacts, along with an increased workload, while also having to balance home and school demands, especially school relocation which was the most significant predictor of burnout (O'Toole & Friesen, 2016). This was consistent with international (Qi & Wu, 2014) and local findings (Kuntz, Näswall, & Bockett, 2013). There was also a modest negative association with emotion perception: less emotion perception as a component of teachers' emotional intelligence correlated with higher levels of burnout (O'Toole & Friesen, 2016).

At a qualitative level, two teachers whose burnout scores (Milfont, Denny, Ameratunga, Robinson, & Merry, 2008) were amongst the highest, and who also reported lower emotion perception and emotion regulation, used the term "stoic", to describe how they were feeling 18 months on. One teacher said, "You've got to keep reminding yourself that there's always people worse off, being *stoic* about it." The other teacher said:

> We used to joke about it you know before it became super popular and it's a bit overused now, 'keep calm and carry on' sort of thing. I think it was that kind of *stoic* feeling like, 'this isn't great, but I just have to do it'.

The teachers experiencing the most intense imminent danger at the time also reported their greater appreciation for life, indicating some post-traumatic growth. However, their burnout data indicated more tiredness and exhaustion. Qualitative descriptions included: "my [emotional] reservoir isn't filling up as fast as I've used draining it"; "I've lost my mojo"; "presenting an image"; "normalising for the children". Positive emotions such as their continued love of teaching, excitement, and anticipation of improvement were also expressed.

One teacher who reported the lowest level of burnout, alongside higher levels of emotion perception and emotion regulation, said she was "recharging", having requested and obtained time out from school and spending time in the bush. This teacher explained how she maintained her positive energy for teaching 18 months on:

> I'd call it 'good old kiwi' actually, well, 'just get on with it'. 'Kia kaha' actually was very powerful too, like 'We can do it!' I love that sense of Papatūānuku you know, the land and us. At first, there was a lot of blame for the ground, like I was feeling for the first time in my life, quite vulnerable with the ground. I was always quite a land girl, and just realising that there was this fragility between me and the ground, Papatūānuku. And then I just had to let go of that and—nature will do what it has to do, so that was also a really bizarre thing for my love of the land.
>
> With 'kia kaha' I could feel a sense of my grandfathers who had been through the war. I could feel a sense of other people that I admire in the world that have been courageous and coped through things, so that is why my point is being in the now, and I'll try and be as better a person I can be, in the best way that benefits me, and other people and the environment.

Thus, this teacher of European descent referred to "kia kaha" (be strong) as reminding her of her grandfathers' historic trauma, and her connectedness with the land. This was an improvement from feeling "in the void" (O'Toole, 2018) in the early earthquake aftermath. Her narrative resonates with the Māori creation story, moving from ko te kore (the void) to recharging her energy to rejoin ko te ao (the world) and celebrating her enjoyment of life "my life is good"—tīhei mauriora (there is life). This early childhood teacher's narrative was expressed naturally without any overt reference to *Te Whāriki* (Ministry of Education, 2017), the bicultural early childhood curriculum document, perhaps reflecting her internalisation of its Māori values. Her narrative also gave insight into her burnout score, which was the lowest in the group, compared to the higher burnout scores reported by the two teachers who were feeling stoic.

Historical trauma and emotion in education

Maria Yellow Horse Brave Heart (2003) defines historical trauma as the "cumulative emotional and psychological wounding, over the lifespan and across generations, emanating from massive group trauma experiences" (p. 7). Iwi Māori have experienced similar wounding and "cultural and spiritual genocide" (Wirihana & Smith, 2014, p. 198) through the colonisation practices outlined earlier in this chapter. While the healing of the loss of stories, tikanga, language, and cultural ways of being is ongoing in Aotearoa, iwi Māori continue to struggle to maintain their cultural and linguistic identities (Martin, 2017). If emotions are embedded in oral traditions of language and culture, which are subsequently lost, how can those affected support and express their emotional wellbeing? In Aotearoa, trauma is evident not only in loss and stress due to colonisation, but also the loss and stress of collective trauma with a large group experiencing the same dilemmas, caused by disaster such as that experienced by the people of Christchurch.

The long-term effects of disaster trauma experienced in the Christchurch earthquakes have meant changes in the whole community and environment. Emergent bilinguals still learning te reo Māori further lost the ability to understand and express their language identities due to losing their homes and whānau, and shifting away, leaving the city or moving overseas to escape the disaster (Martin, 2017). This affected their psychosocial wellbeing as they experienced present day loss of community connectedness on top of historic losses. This has compounded the earthquake impact for those Māori still in the revitalisation mode of learning Māori language. Ruhia is an emergent bilingual and her narrative below expresses these feelings, demonstrating collective and historical trauma due to language loss as she realises that she has lost the support of her reo Māori community. Ruhia laments:

> But who am I? What is that to me now? I don't feel very connected to my roots and culture, that was such a journey for me my seven years at home in New Zealand. I actually find it really hard now. There's lots of tikanga that I know the do's and don'ts about for different things but I don't really know the legends and I can't tell them the reason why it is this when it comes to Te Ao Māori and that makes me sad, that I'm not really knowledgeable of my own culture. Becoming connected in New Zealand, I was learning more and feeling more me and now I'm feeling a little bit disconnected. (Martin, 2017, p. 135)

Ruhia's narrative typifies the experience of the emergent bilinguals in Rachel Martin's study. In contrast, skilled bilinguals in her study experienced the disaster trauma differently. They knew the importance of sharing whakapapa stories about Ranginui and Papatūānuku and their child Ruāumoko (deity of earthquakes and volcanoes) to demonstrate the connection between land, atua, and language. Bilingual participants told the story of Ruāumoko, created songs and poems, and wrote about Ruāumoko using te reo Māori and te ao Māori as a way of healing disaster trauma. This was a way to share emotions, wairua (spirituality), and whakapapa connections from the environment to the layering of people and connections to atua. There was a shift in awareness from the feelings of terror experienced during the earthquakes to understanding the physical environment created by Ruāumoko and how iwi Māori are connected. This Indigenous method of healing, sharing of emotions, and viewing the world is using the spiritual as well as physical aspects of disaster trauma and demonstrates emotional strength in identity and language. This holistic approach to wellness is advocated by Durie in his Whare Tapa Whā model of health and wellbeing (1982, in Durie, 1997). Taha wairua—the spiritual domain and self-management—were critical for emotional wellbeing during trauma, alongside taha hinengaro (personal empowerment, self-esteem, and resilience), and taha tinana (personal and collective safety) which was lost during disaster trauma and required whole community healing and taha whānau (development and implementation of healthy relationships).

Sonja Macfarlane (in McCrone, 2014) suggests that Māori children in Liberty et al.'s (2016) study cited above, coped better psychologically with disaster trauma because of the close support of whānau, a spiritual approach, and the narratives associated with Ruāumoko, shared from the whakapapa perspective. Macfarlane said that earthquakes were explained to children in a human context, not as a science lesson in plate tectonics (McCrone, 2014). The use of Māori values and the support of the community collective, language, and identity response during the disaster period supported their trauma healing. Martin (2017) adds reo ā iwi and taonga tuku iho to Durie's health and wellness model because, without the inclusion of te reo Māori in all of these aspects, wellness would not be achievable. Additionally, Glover et al. (2017) recommend inclusion of te ao tūroa, the long-standing environment, to situate Durie's model "within the wider sociohistorical political environmental context. The four sides of the house and its environment are interdependent"

(p. 2). This acknowledges the ao Māori connection to the land environment that needs protection now, as the world continues to have environmental catastrophes. Iwi Māori are returning to using traditional mātauranga to heal long-term practices that have changed or taken away mātauranga connected to the land and wellbeing.

Confluence in the riverbed

In this chapter, we have followed two streams of knowledge, inspired by He Awa Whiria, and we have arrived at the riverbed together. We have reviewed historical perspectives of emotion from both Western and Māori streams of knowledge. We have shared findings that can mutually inform and contribute to this interdependent stream, where emotion regulation methods reported in Western research as beneficial for daily and post-disaster emotion management can only benefit from the richness of mātauranga Māori narrative methodologies, such methodologies demonstrating potential in helping Māori children, whānau, and teachers understand and manage their emotions. The narratives shared in this chapter help us understand our links to whakapapa, atua, cultural narratives, and te ao Māori as healing practices, as a resource for emotion regulation for all in Aotearoa. In an Aotearoa and Te Tiriti context, teachers, parents and whānau, hapū, and iwi are part of a whole community as demonstrated in the Christchurch disasters. While emotions are present and experienced by all in different ways, there are aspects that improve wellbeing and sharing and caring experienced in te ao Māori through aroha, and manaakitanga, the arts, and storytelling. Ka'ai and Higgins (2004) refer to ngā rā o mua, meaning the days are in front of us to move forward, and the future is ngā rā kei muri, meaning the days after. This creates a Māori worldview where the past guides the future and the past is carried with us. Based on what we have learnt on our journey down these two streams, the inflow of mātauranga Māori narrative emotional healing practices blending with the inflow from the Western stream to this braided river will augment and enhance the wairua and energy resources, for all involved in education in Aotearoa. Accordingly, we conclude with a well-known whakataukī in te ao Māori: ka mua, ka muri (walk backwards into the future). In the education context of Aotearoa, we can return to the past; a vision of the importance of history, and learning from those who have gone before us, as future pathways are mapped.

Acknowledgements

Dr Veronica O'Toole's research was supported with funding from CEISMIC Canterbury Earthquakes Digital Archive, University of Canterbury (ceismic.org.nz), (Grant No. 210). A sincere thank you to the teachers who shared their stories. Dr Rachel Martin thanks her participants who volunteered their time, especially those who needed to be re-interviewed after the 2011 earthquakes, and Dr Mere Skerrett.

Recommendations for further reading

Keltner, D., Oatley, K., & Jenkins, J. M. (2018). *Understanding emotions* (4th ed.). Hoboken, NJ: Wiley.

Reilly, M., Duncan, S., Leoni, G., Paterson, L., Carter, L., Rātima, M., & Rewi, P. (2018). *Te Kōparapara: An introduction to the Māori world*. Auckland: Auckland University Press.

References

Andreotti, V., & De Souza, L. M. (2008). Translating theory into practice and walking minefields; lessons from the project "Through other eyes". *International Journal of Development Education and Global Learning, 1*(1), 23–36.

Averill, J. R., & Nunley, E. P. (1992). *Voyages of the heart: Living an emotionally creative life*. New York, NY: Free Press.

Barrett, L. F., & Salovey, P. (Eds.) (2002). *The wisdom in feeling: Psychological processes in emotional intelligence*. New York, NY: The Guilford Press.

Battiste, M. (2004). Bringing Aboriginal education into the contemporary education: Narratives of cognitive imperialism reconciling with decolonization. In J. Collard & C. Reynolds (Eds.), *Leadership, gender and culture. Male and female perspectives* (pp. 142–148). Maidenhead, UK: Open University Press.

Brackett, M., Caruso, D. R., & Stern, R. (2013). *Anchors of emotional intelligence*. Port Chester, NY: Dude Press.

Brackett, M. A., Palomera, R., Mojsa-Kaja, J., Reyes, M. R., & Salovey, P. (2010). Emotion-regulation ability, burnout, and job satisfaction among British secondary-school teachers. *Psychology in The Schools, 47*(4), 406–417.

Brave Heart, M. Y. H. (2003). The historical trauma response among natives and its relationship with substance abuse: A Lakota illustration. *Journal of Psychoactive Drugs, 35*(1), 7–13. doi:10.1080/02791072.2003.10399988

Brotheridge, C. M., & Grandey, A. A. (2002). Emotional labor and burnout: Comparing two perspectives of "people work". *Journal of Vocational Behavior, 60*, 17–39. Brown, R., & Kulik, J. (1977). Flashbulb memories. *Cognition, 5*(1), 73–99. doi:10.1016/0010-0277(77)90018-X

Chang, M. (2009). An appraisal perspective of teacher burnout: Examining the emotional work of teachers. *Educational Psychology Review, 21*(3), 193–218.

Cicognani, E., Pietrantoni, L., Palestini, L., & Prati, G. (2009). Emergency workers' quality of life: The protective role of sense of community, efficacy beliefs and coping strategies. *Social Indicators Research, 94*(3), 449–463. http://dx.doi.org/10.1007/s11205-009-9441-x

Durie, M. H. (1997). Māori cultural identity and its implications for mental health services. *International Journal of Mental Health, 26*(3), 23–35. https://www.tandfonline.com/doi/abs/10.1080/00207411.1997.11449407

Ekman, P., & Friesen, W. V. (1978). *The facial action coding system*. Palo Alto, CA: Consulting Psychologists Press.

Fleming, T., Clark, T. C., Denny, S., Robinson, E., Rossen, F., Bullen, P., Crengle, S., Fortune, S., Peiris-John, R., Teevale, T., Utter, J., & The Adolescent Health Research Group. (2013). *The health and wellbeing of secondary school students in Christchurch: Findings from the Youth'12 national youth health and wellbeing survey*. Auckland: The University of Auckland.

Glover, M., Kira, A., Kira, G., McRobbie, H., Breier, B. H., Kruger, R. et al. (2017). An innovative team-based weightloss competition to reduce cardiovascular and diabetes risk among Māori and Pacific people: Rationale and method for the study and its evaluation. *BMC Nutrition, 3*(78), 1–9.

Goleman, D. (1995). *Emotional intelligence: Why it can matter more than IQ*. New York, NY: Bantam Books.

Grimm, A., Hulse, L., & Schmidt, S. (2012). Human responses to disasters: A pilot study on peritraumatic emotional and cognitive processing. *Europe's Journal of Psychology, 8*(1), 112–138.

Gross, J. J. (1998). The emerging field of emotion regulation: An integrative review. *Review of General Psychology, 2*(3), 271–299. doi:10.1037/1089-2680.2.3.271

Gross, J. J. (2013). Emotion regulation: Taking stock and moving forward. *Emotion, 13*(3), 359–365. https://psycnet.apa.org/doi/10.1037/a0032135

Hargreaves, A. (1998). The emotional practice of teaching. *Teaching & Teacher Education, 14*(8), 835–854.

Hochschild, A. R. (1983). *The managed heart: Commercialization of human feeling*. Berkley, CA: University of California Press.

Hogg, D., Kingham, S., Wilson, T. M., Griffin, E., & Ardagh, M. (2014). Geographic variation of clinically diagnosed mood and anxiety disorders in Christchurch after the 2010/11 earthquakes. *Health & Place, 30*, 270–278

Izard, C. (1991). *The psychology of emotions*. New York, NY: Plenum Press.

Jiang, J., Vauras, M., Volet, S., & Wang, Y. (2016). Teachers' emotions and emotion regulation strategies: Self- and students' perceptions. *Teaching and Teacher Education, 54*, 22–31.

Ka'ai, T., & Higgins, R. (2004). Te ao Māori—Māori worldview. In T. Ka'ai, M. Reilly, J. Moorfield, & S. Mosely (Eds.), *Ki te whaiao: An introduction to Māori culture and society* (pp. 13–25). Auckland: Pearson Education.

Keller, M. M., Chang, M., Becker, E. S., Goetz, T., & Frenzel, A. C. (2014). Teachers' emotional experiences and exhaustion as predictors of emotional labor in the classroom: An experience sampling study. *Frontiers in Psychology, 5*, 1442.

Keltner, D. (2009). *Born to be good: The science of a meaningful life*. London, UK: W. W. Norton & Company.

Keltner, D., Oatley, K., & Jenkins, J. M. (2014). *Understanding emotions* (3rd ed.). Hoboken, NJ: Wiley.

Keltner, D., Oatley, K., & Jenkins, J. M. (2019). *Understanding emotions* (4th ed.). Hoboken, NJ: Wiley.

Kuka, T. (2009). *National reo Māori workshops*. Wellington: Ministry of Education. https://tereomaori.tki.org.nz/Professional-learning/National-Reo-Maori-Workshops-Video-archives

Kuntz, J., Näswall, K., & Bockett, A. (2013). Keep calm and carry on? An investigation of teacher burnout in a post-disaster context. *New Zealand Journal of Psychology, 42*(2), 57–67.

Lazarus, R. S. (1991). *Emotion and adaptation*. New York, NY: Oxford University Press.

Lee, J. (2009). Decolonising Māori narratives: Pūrākau as a method. *MAI Review, 2*. Retrieved from: http://www.review.mai.ac.nz/index.php/MR/article/view/242/268

Liberty, K., Tarren-Sweeney, M., Macfarlane, S., Basu, A., & Reid, J. (2016). Behavior problems and post-traumatic stress symptoms in children beginning school: A comparison of pre- and post-earthquake groups. *PLoS currents, 8*. http://dx.doi.org/10.1371/currents.dis.2821c82fbc27d0c2aa9e00cff532b402

Macfarlane, S., Macfarlane, A., & Gillon, G. (2015). Sharing the food baskets of knowledge: Creating space for a blending of streams. In A. Macfarlane, S. Macfarlane, & M. Webber (Eds.), *Sociocultural realities: Exploring new horizons* (pp. 52–67). Christchurch: Canterbury University Press.

Martin, R. (2017). *Te whakarauora reo nō tuawhakarere: Giving our children what we missed out on: Māori language revitalisation for Māori/English bilingualism*. Unpublished doctoral thesis, University of Canterbury, Christchurch.

McCrone, J. (2014). *Quake stress hurting our young*. Retrieved from: http://www.stuff.co.nz/the-press/news/christchurch-earthquake-2011/9674021/Quake-stress-hurting-our-young

Mead, T. (2019, 17 March). *'I don't hate him, I love him': Widower forgives Christchurch gunman who killed his wife*. Newshub. https://www.newshub.co.nz/home/new-zealand/2019/03/i-don-t-hate-him-i-love-him-widower-forgives-christchurch-gunman-who-killed-his-wife.html

Milfont, T., Denny, S., Ameratunga, S., Robinson, E., & Merry, S. (2008). Burnout and wellbeing: Testing the Copenhagen burnout inventory in New Zealand teachers. *Social Indicators Research, 89*(1), 169–177.

Ministry of Education. (2017). *Te whāriki: He whāriki mātauranga mō ngā mokopuna o Aotearoa—Early childhood curriculum*. Wellington: Author. Retrieved from: https://www.education.govt.nz/early-childhood/teaching-and-learning/te-whariki/

Mutch, C. (2015). The role of schools in disaster settings: Learning from the 2010–2011 New Zealand earthquakes. *International Journal of Educational Development, 41*, 283–291. https://doi.org/10.1016/j.ijedudev.2014.06.008

Näring, G., Briët, M., & Brouwers, A. (2006). Beyond demand-control: Emotional labour and symptoms of burnout in teachers. *Work and Stress, 20*(4), 303–315. doi:10.1080/02678370601065182.

Oatley, K., & Jenkins, J. M. (1996). *Understanding emotions*. Cambridge, MA: Blackwell.

Oatley, K., Keltner, D., & Jenkins, J. M. (2006). *Understanding emotions* (2nd ed.). Malden, MA: Blackwell Publishing.

Oatley, K., & Nundy, S. (1996). Rethinking the role of emotions in education. In D. R. Olson & N. Torrance (Eds.), *The handbook of education and human development: New models of learning, teaching and schooling* (pp. 257–274). Malden, MA: Blackwell Publishing.

O'Toole, V. M. (2017). "I thought I was going to die": Teachers' reflections on their emotions and cognitive appraisals in response to the February 2011 Christchurch Earthquake. *New Zealand Journal of Psychology, 46*(2), 71–86.

O'Toole, V. M. (2018). "Running on fumes": Emotional exhaustion and burnout of teachers following a natural disaster. *Social Psychology of Education, 21*(5), 1081–1112.

O'Toole, V. M., & Friesen, M. D. (2016). Teachers as first responders in tragedy: The role of emotion in teacher adjustment eighteen months post-earthquake. *Teaching and Teacher Education, 59*, 57–67.

Pekrun, R., Goetz, T., Titz, W., & Perry, R. P. (2002). Academic emotions in students' self-regulated learning and achievement: A program of qualitative and quantitative research. *Educational Psychologist, 37*(2), 91–105.

Pōtiki, M. (2018). Takiauē (Tangihanga): Death and mourning. In M. Reilly, S. Duncan, G. Leoni, L. Paterson, L. Carter, M. Rātima & P. Rewi (Eds.), *Te Kōparapara: An introduction to the Māori world*. (pp. 137–154). Auckland: Auckland University Press.

Qi, Y., & Wu, X. (2014). The effect of job characteristics on teachers' burnout and work engagement after Wenchuan earthquake: Comparison over times. *Chinese Journal of Clinical Psychology, 22*(2), 301–305.

Rangihau, J. (1981). Being Māori. In M. King (Ed.), *Te ao Hurihuri: The world moves on* (3rd ed., pp. 165–175). Auckland: Longman Paul.

Reilly, M., Duncan, S., Leoni, G., Paterson, L., Carter, L., Rātima, M., & Rewi, P. (2018). *Te Kōparapara: An introduction to the Māori world*. Auckland: Auckland University Press.

Salovey, P., & Mayer, J. D. (2004). Emotional intelligence. In P. Salovey, M. A. Brackett, & J. D. Mayer (Eds.), *Emotional intelligence: Key readings on the Mayer and Salovey model* (pp. 1–27). Port Chester, NY: Dude Publishing.

Salovey, P., & Mayer, J. D. (1990). Emotional Intelligence. *Imagination, Cognition and Personality, 9*(3), 185–211.

Schutte, N. S., Malouff, J. M., & Bhullar, N. (2009). The Assessing Emotions Scale. In C. Stough, D. H. Saklofske, & J. D. A. Parker (Eds.), *Assessing emotional intelligence: Theory, research, and applications* (pp. 119–134). New York, NY: Springer Science+Business Media.

Schutz, P. A., & Pekrun, R. (2007). Introduction to emotion in education. In P. A. Schutz & R. Pekrun (Eds.), *Emotion in education* (pp. 3–10). San Diego, CA: Elsevier Academic Press.

Snow, R. E., Corno, L., & Jackson, D., III. (1996). Individual differences in affective and conative functions. In D. C. Berliner & R. C. Calfee (Eds.), *Handbook of educational psychology* (pp. 243–310). New York, NY and London, UK: Macmillan.

Strongman, K. T. (2003). *The psychology of emotion: From everyday life to theory* (5th ed.). Oxford, UK: Wiley.

Sutton, R. E. (2004). Emotional regulation goals and strategies of teachers. *Social Psychology of Education, 7*(4), 379–398.

Taxer, J. L., & Frenzel, A. C. (2015). Facets of teachers' emotional lives: A quantitative investigation of teachers' genuine, faked, and hidden emotions. *Teaching and Teacher Education, 42*, 78–88.

Taylor, R. D., Oberle, E., Durlak, J. A., & Weissberg, R. P. (2017). Promoting positive youth development through school-based social and emotional learning interventions: A meta-analysis of follow-up effects. *Child Development, 88*(4), 1156–1171.

Te Kotahi Research Institute. (2016). *He Ngākau Māori | Kare-ā-roto Hui—day one and day two. 'He Ngakau Māori: Investigating Māori cultural constructions of emotions'*. https://www.waikato.ac.nz/rangahau/video-hub

Tomkins, S. S. (1962). *Affect, imagery, consciousness: Vol. I The positive affects*. Oxford, UK: Springer.

Tso, M. (2019). *How to look after yourself and others after the Christchurch mosque shootings*. Retrieved from https://www.stuff.co.nz/national/health/111347842/how-to-look-after-yourself-and-others-after-the-christchurch-mosque-shootings

Wetherell, M. (2019). Understanding the terror attack: Some initial steps. *New Zealand Journal of Psychology, 48*(1), 6–8.

Wilkie, K. (2019). *Heartbroken children perform a haka for Jacinda Ardern as she visits school that was home to two teenagers who died in the Christchurch mosque massacre*. Retrieved from: https://www.dailymail.co.uk/news/article-6828569/Heartbroken-children-perform-haka-Jacinda-Ardern-visit-victims-school.htm

Wilson, G. A. (2013). Community resilience, social memory and the post-2010 Christchurch (New Zealand) earthquakes. *Area, 45*(2), 207–215.

Wirihana, R., & Smith, C. (2014). Historical trauma, healing and well-being in Māori communities. *MAI Journal, 3*(3), 197–210.

Chapter 11
Media literacy and digital citizenship in Aotearoa New Zealand

Christoph Teschers and Cheryl Brown

Introduction

In this chapter, we explore the concepts of media literacy and digital citizenship in the context of 21st century Aotearoa New Zealand, and beyond. Focusing on the role criticality and technology play in the current New Zealand mindset, different interpretations of media literacy are discussed and its relevance to primary and secondary education explained. This chapter links theoretical perspectives, such as D'Olimpio's *critical perspectivism*, with the reality of teaching and curriculum in contemporary New Zealand school environments. It explores the importance of digital media literacy in enabling our young generation to become critically reflective, well informed, media and online savvy digital democratic citizens in the information age of internet and social media.

Media and society

Media in many forms has widely influenced people's cultures, beliefs, and life circumstances since the invention of the phonetic alphabet, if not before. Since Gutenberg invented the printing press in the 15th century, information has been increasingly circulated in written form, which led to cultural and technological advancements through widely shared knowledge and ideas. Printed newspapers have informed citizens of social and political ongoings locally, nationally, and internationally, and have drawn attention to grievances and social injustices alike. Until today, newspapers provided one of the most important, and often most rigorously investigated, information avenues. Quality papers are directed by a strong editorial team and spend considerable resources on fact-checking and review before printing news stories and disseminating information.

However, the critical notion that one cannot simply believe what is written or presented in some form has been emphasised since the Enlightenment, particularly with the notion of critical thinking and the ideal of the politically mature human being (see Kant's *Metaphysics of Morals*). The need for these qualities increases as the reach of media grows. Publicist papers and magazines have existed for many years and the influence and power of huge publishing houses on newspapers and magazines in their fold has reached worrisome dimensions. Consider the reach that some family empires have on public opinion today, such as Murdoch's influence in North America, the United Kingdom, Australia, and beyond; the influence of the Springer family on news and academic publishing in Europe and worldwide; and the influence on public opinion Silvio Berlusconi has as a politician through controlling a large part of Italian media, to name only a few examples. Hence, the need for critical thinking and media literacy skills to engage critically with the written word has risen because of increasing availability of information and ease of access. This need has further increased with each new form of media that has brought mass-information to the public.

The invention of radio in the 19th century, and television in the 20th century, have been the latest milestones in information distribution. One could argue that these technologies allowed quicker and more immediate distribution of information, but at the same time, due to the nature of these mediums, information has been largely presented in truncated form. News flashes, running news, and live reporting with vivid pictures, while at the same time limiting actual information, have increasingly become the norm. The epitome of 'infotainment', the entertainment business through news and information (validated or not), can be observed every day in United States' television, as well as in many other countries' television outlets. Even the best reporting on television hardly reaches the quality and depth of information provided by quality newspapers. Hence, the call for media literacy skills and warnings of potential negative impacts of the mass media on public opinion have been around since the mid-20th century (e.g., Adorno & Benjamin, as discussed by D'Olimpio,

2018). Being able to engage critically with information provided in such forms, and the need to inform oneself on pertinent issues through multiple sources for confirmation and background information, has further increased since the advent of the internet and the World Wide Web.

The final milestones in information distribution to date have been reached through the development of the internet in the late 20th-century and the Web 2.0 (allowing interactive online content) in the early-21st century. The invention of social media has changed the way people engage with each other and share information, ideology, and (fake) news. For example, the mass networking capabilities of social media, coinciding with the massification of the internet, provide a suitable channel for a type of politics that appeals to the people typical of populism (ordinary people who feel that established elite groups ignore their concerns) (Gerbaudo, 2018). Similarly, Engesser et al. (2017) confirm that social media has given populism the freedom to articulate their ideologies and spread their messages.

Today, young people are often referred to as 'digital natives', which implies the belief that they have a good understanding of the internet and digital technologies as they have grown up with such technologies from birth (Prensky, 2001). However, considering the wide spread of misinformation and hoaxes (e.g., Mintz, 2012; Shao et al., 2018) in social media, and reports from some studies that the majority of young people receive most of their information from Facebook, Twitter, and similar sources (Marchi, 2012), paints a different, more worrisome, picture of a potential lack of critical engagement with unfiltered, and often unedited, information found online. Some of the latest examples of how social media campaigns have influenced the public arguably against their own best interest, would be the influence Russia has apparently taken on forming public opinion leading up to the 2016 United States' elections (e.g., Dillian, 2019), the influence of false information spread, among others, through the internet and targeted social media in the lead-up to the Brexit (the United Kingdom's exit from the European Union) vote in the United Kingdom (Wintour, 2018), and irresponsible consumption and spread of the live-video taken by the shooter in the Christchurch Mosque attack here in Aotearoa New Zealand in 2019.

Although this account might seem to paint a somewhat negative picture so far, this short summary is not meant to follow the condemnation and often-repeated warnings of the negative impact the internet and social media might have on the development of young people. More positive examples that contribute greatly to active democratic citizenship in the 21st century will be discussed shortly. However, it is necessary, from an educational perspective, to raise awareness of some of the challenges that accompany the latest developments in digital media to create a balanced educational response to the new digital, and partly virtual, reality that many people—and especially the younger generations—live in today. After all, following Dewey (1916), education has the function to support democratic citizenship through enabling people to effectively inform themselves and actively take part in democratic processes. What has changed is the environment and the way information is provided and accessed. Some of the challenges that we see emerge from the examples above are:

1. the ability to distinguish between lies, fake-news, and actual validated information
2. the lack of professional editors and sufficient filters of untrue information and potentially harmful content
3. the potentially polarising effects of algorithms that promote information that fits into a person's existing belief system (i.e., the lack of exposure to other ways of thinking and diverse ways of experiencing the world—see, for example, Chapters 1 and 8 of this collection), and
4. the social and ethical challenges that social media create and can be seen today, such as depersonalisation, bringing out 'the worst' in people, cyber-bullying, and the harmful effects of gossip which now has a permanent digital footprint instead of a 'word-of-mouth behind closed doors' character.

In this chapter, we argue that *digital media literacy*, in combination with D'Olimpio's notion of *critical perspectivism*, are essential skills for digital democratic citizenship in the 21st century, which have their place in schools and need to be part of a modern curriculum.

We wish to emphasise that, despite significant challenges for the positive social and emotional development of younger generations, and active threats to proper independent democratic processes in societies today, the internet and Web 2.0 have contributed a range of positive gains for people and societies today. Some of these we see, for example, in the constant, widespread, and easily accessible availability of information and knowledge, nearly everywhere and all the time. The added benefit to democratic processes through instant reporting and live journalism (if provided by responsible professionals who adhere to ethical conduct) is another benefit, as is the growing phenomenon of digital activism. The latter can be seen in weekly—and sometimes daily—new petitions filed online through government and/or activist sites, such as ActionStation Aotearoa,[1] 350Aotearoa,[2] or Greenpeace[3] to name only three local examples; as well as online voting functions that increase access to democratic procedures in societies today. The internet further gives voice to groups that have not been represented well in the past, such as youth activism[4] and minority groups. One could argue that it has never been easier to be well informed on whatever topic one desires, while at the same time it has never been more difficult to distinguish between actual and fake information on any given topic.

In an educational context, whilst media education has been around as a concept since the 1930s, it was not until the 1970s, that the term 'literacy' was used in relation to media (Buckingham, 2013). So what do we mean by *digital media literacy* and what is implied by using terms like media literacy, digital literacy, multiliteracies, and "mediacy" (as proposed by Hoechsmann & Poyntz, 2012)? The crux is that these concepts overlap and many definitions are in use. Media texts are by nature multimodal, encompassing an array of communication modes, such as writing, images, and sound. Media literacy therefore overlaps with a range of other concepts, such as visual, audio, video, and multimodal literacy. Luke (2000) has suggested that media literacy entails the acquisition of a "metalanguage": a way of describing different modes of communication; understanding the broader social, economic, and institutional contexts in which it occurs; and how these affect people's experiences and practices.

In grappling with the concept, some have attempted to define media itself as encompassing a range of communication channels, including television, cinema, video, radio, photography, advertising, newspapers and magazines, recorded music, computers, and the internet (Buckingham, 2013). Others have endeavoured to describe a media-literate person as one who "can decode, evaluate, analyze and produce both print and electronic

---

1   www.actionstation.org.nz
2   350.org.nz
3   www.greenpeace.org/new-zealand/
4   See, for example, https://educatorinnovator.org/how-young-activists-deploy-digital-tools-for-social-change/

media" (Aufderheide, 1992, cited in Koltay, 2011, p. 211). An attempt to define media literacy at large as a starting point for this discussion is presented by Hoechsmann and Poyntz:

> Media literacy is a set of competencies that enable us to interpret media texts and institutions, to make media of our own, and to recognize and engage with the social and political influence of media in everyday life. (2012, p. 1)

Hoechsmann and Poyntz point out that this definition by no means does justice to the varied facets of understandings of media literacy, but it provides a starting point we can expand on. As seen in the quote, media literacy—similarly to related terms we use in this chapter—includes, but goes far beyond, the skills necessary to *use* media and technology. It highlights the ability of interpretation, of making sense of what one sees—in the literal meaning, but also evaluating the hidden meaning and information media provides (hence the reference to 'institutions' as sources of information and media). The social and political significance of media is also mentioned, which implies a moral and ethical engagement with media content. This, along with social implications of being able to successfully engage with and *create* media content as a means of social status and capital (e.g., ability to create PowerPoint presentations for interviews, or make use of social media to promote personal agendas) are key components.

As indicated above, media literacy as a concept has been discussed since the mid-20th century. Although many of the key ideas of interpretation and critical engagement are still relevant, with the changed landscape of interactive media—in which every child/young person can be not only consumer but also *producer* of media content shared with the world—the original focus of media literacy on the written and spoken word, and known, edited sources of information (newspaper, radio, TV) needs to be adjusted. This has led to the creation of a range of terms, which are equally elusive and not well defined, other than their shared attempt to address the range of media sources today. Terms in use, which all have their own emphasis but roughly try to capture the same experienced reality, are: multiliteracies, mediacy, digital media literacy, and media literacy 2.0. As we focus on online media in the discussion of this chapter, for clarity we have opted to use the term *digital media literacy*. This, however, does not mean that the aspects we discuss, such as critical perspectivism, are less relevant for engaging with other media. On the contrary, it seems that D'Olimpio's (2018) notion of critical perspectivism offers a valuable approach to all forms of media engagement, and especially online communication.

Strengthening digital democratic citizenship through media literacy

Digital media literacy—as, we propose, should be explicitly implemented in school curricula today—is the sum of skills needed to engage meaningfully and ethically with online media. This includes websites and online content, social media sites, as well as online services on smart devices, such as Messenger and communication-type apps. By 'meaningful engagement' we mean the ability to create, as well as access, content relevant to one's own life circumstances; being able to distinguish (in the majority of cases) quality content from fake information; being able to critically engage with opinions and information portrayed online in any form (written, audio recorded, video content, or images); and communicate ethically and compassionately with others in the online, non-face-to-face environment. For us, a key aspect of digital media literacy is the development of D'Olimpio's (2018) attitude of *critical perspectivism*. Critical perspectivism includes the ability to critically engage with content online but also with the online medium (or media) themselves. She advocates for critically engaging with others' perspectives, but, simultaneously, engaging with *compassion*, remembering the person on the other side of the screen one communicates with. We support the notion of compassion rather than empathy (although it is more commonly used in the literature around media literacy) following Andrew Peterson's (2017) argument that compassion adds the component of taking action to the notion of empathy, which, in contrast, can be understood as a passive emotion. It seems important, from an ethical perspective and for a society that aims towards the wellbeing and flourishing of their members, that action should be taken on the basis of compassion and awareness of the feelings of others rather than leaving injustices and hurtful engagements online unchallenged.

D'Olimpio, similar to Hoechsmann and Poyntz (2012), points out the need for an ethical awareness when engaging with mass media and especially with social media. This applies to both sides, the one creating content but also the one receiving/consuming it. Therefore, she also advocates for the ability to engage creatively as well as collaboratively with online media as an important aspect of multiliteracy skills, which resonates with our understanding of digital media literacy. We will discuss in the final section of this chapter how the development of relevant skills for digital media literacy, including *critical, creative, collaborative, and compassionate engagement* as portrayed as aspects of critical perspectivism, can be supported in contemporary school settings in Aotearoa and internationally.

As digital technology has become more common, affordable, and portable, more and more people from all parts of society are increasing their online and digital participation. The concept of the digital divide is shifting from those who 'have' or 'have not' to those who 'can' and 'can-not' (McIntyre, 2014). Understanding the new opportunities, affordances, rules, and potential pitfalls of the digital world does not necessarily come automatically with long-term use. Not everyone using digital technology knows how to handle the range of available tools to their best extent, and even experienced digital technology users can fall prey to hackers, lose control of how they are represented online, or otherwise fail to maintain their digital identity in an optimal manner. This divide in media literacy is centred on the "knowledge of how to effectively use digital technologies for valued social, economic and political practices" (McIntyre, 2014, p. 92).

The internet has further provided a vehicle for people to transcend geography and political borders by interacting with information and communities from across the world. The notion of *global citizenship* has taken on a new meaning in educational contexts as a worldview, or a set of values, that prepares students for a global or world society. We need to develop students' skills in *critically assessing* the information they read. Information and knowledge have significant roles in supporting and maintaining the power structures of the modern world. We should be aware that just because information may be available and accessible, this does not mean it is equitable and without bias. As McGillivray, McPherson, Jones, and McCandlish (2015) propose, understanding issues associated with

> the ownership of data, privacy, platform convergence and the space for creative reinvention are now necessary to underpin digital media use in a networked society whilst facilitating movement across different media platforms and social networks, safely and with confidence. (p. 5)

In addition to a critical engagement, a *compassionate* attitude is needed for students to become aware of other people's perspectives. It is important that we are aware of ourselves and our place in the world, and of others' places in the world, in order to begin to form an understanding of other people's perspectives. Students need to understand that the tools we use are not neutral: for example, commercial providers, with profit-making intentions, may not (and often do not) have their users' best interests in mind and may make ethically questionable choices. Similarly, the content we share and the comments we make are not sitting neutral in the 'ether' but form part of the engagement and experience of other users in the shared space of the internet.

As noted, digital media literacy includes the skills to effectively use but also *create* content in the online space. Online content creation has been viewed as an opportunity to "promote a democratic and diverse public sphere in which elite voices no longer dominate" (Schradie, 2011, p. 146). However, studies from the global North point out that online content creators are a minority of internet users; in effect, this participation gap challenges existing notions of the internet as an egalitarian public space (Brake, 2014; Schradie, 2011). This is a world-wide reality as shown by the annual undergraduate study conducted by the EDUCAUSE Centre for Analysis and Research (ECAR) across 15 different countries. This study shows just how dominant consumption—rather than production—practices are amongst university students (Dahlstrom & Bichsel, 2014). In addition, one just has to look at a map of Wikipedia contributors[5] to realise how dominant particular geographic areas are in terms of the production of global internet content.

Collaborative skills, as D'Olimpio (2018) argues, are increasingly important in today's connected and networked online space. Drawing on shared experiences, knowledges, and skills to engage with the online space, both for content creation and consumption (e.g., raising awareness of certain content in one's circle of friends), seems a necessary skill to have in the social space of the internet today. Digital media can play a central role in connecting young people, enable activism movements such as the so-called Arab Spring,[6] and allow for social campaigns such as #BlackLivesMatter and #MeToo. Framed as an expanded conceptualisation of digital citizenship, there appears to be some calling for global digital citizenship. For example, the Global Digital Citizen Foundation—a non-profit organisation with a mission statement to "cultivate responsible, ethical, global citizens for a digital world"—proposes that this would involve "recognizing and respecting how 21st century technology and digital media have eliminated boundaries between citizens of the world by enabling communication, collaboration, dialogue, and debate across all levels of society" (Global Digital Citizen Foundation, n.d., p. 3). Considering this call for global digital citizenship in a digital world with the challenges and

---

5   https://en.wikipedia.org/wiki/Wikipedia:Who_writes_Wikipedia%3F#/media/File: Enwiki-map.png

6   https://www.thecairoreview.com/essays/the-revolution-will-be-tweeted/

opportunities that the digital space poses for societies, nations, and humanity, the importance of digital media literacy education in today's schools in Aotearoa and internationally becomes apparent.

However, research exploring safety and risk with the use of digital technologies, especially by primary school-aged students in Aotearoa New Zealand, appears to be still at the emergent stage. McDonald-Brown, Laxman, and Hope (2016) conducted what was described as the first study of the online practices of Aotearoa pre-teenage children, and Webster (2016) explored pre-teenagers' concepts and development of privacy in relation to the decisions and actions they were undertaking in online environments. McDonald-Brown et al. noted that schools and parents were often relying on "popular opinion and media speculation which can tend towards a focus on sensational anecdotes and moral panic" (2016, p. 2). However, whilst young people were aware of issues around privacy and internet safety, there did appear to be some disconnect between their perceived capabilities to do so and their actual competencies and knowledge (Webster, 2016).

Schools have a legal responsibility to minimise risk and ensure the safety of the children and staff within the school environment. The Ministry of Education states that the safe and responsible use in schools is achieved by "fostering a positive culture of digital technology use where challenges are understood to exist" (Ministry of Education, 2014, p. 4) and suggests preventing issues is preferable to having to respond to them. It proposes two aspects to this, namely *promotional* (i.e., guiding young people's learning in and about the digital world) and *protective* (i.e., mitigating risk by prevention, support, or intervention) (Ministry of Education, 2014, p. 14). In terms of the 'guiding' strategy, there is an awareness about the value of digital citizenship programmes as an effective way to address digital safety and responsible use with young people in educational contexts (Netsafe, 2018; UNESCO, 2015). Netsafe has developed a digital citizenship model that is contextualised within Aotearoa New Zealand, including principles that are described in terms of Māori values. The Netsafe model identifies skills, knowledge, attitudes, and values; however, it lacks specificity in relation to the technology-related elements, or domains, that students in schools should learn about.

Unsurprisingly, an increasing number of schools are reacting to the negative influence of digital technologies, and particularly mobile devices, by taking preventative measures such as banning cell phones (e.g., Rotorua Intermediate, Tararua College, and Wainuiomata High School at the time of writing). Sadly, whilst this prevents issues arising during school time and mitigates against the risk for schools, it does not build and develop young people's skills and capabilities in digital technology. In a study exploring the social and emotional wellbeing of young people online, YoungMinds and Ecorys (2016) advocate for building digital resilience, which they define as "the social and emotional literacy, and digital competency, to positively respond to and deal with any risks they [young people] might be exposed to when they are using social media or going online" (p. 8). This is a call to action for schools to respond to, we would argue.

The role of schooling and education in developing digital media literacy

Digital technologies are becoming increasingly commonplace in New Zealand schools. With computational thinking becoming part of the technology curriculum from 2020, complemented by the *Hangarau Matihiko* Māori version, schools are in rapid transition to fully digital environments (McNaughton & Gluckman, 2018). However, despite these advances, McNaughton and Gluckman still suggest two areas of focus for optimising benefits and mitigating risks—namely critical thinking and critical literacies, and self-control and social skills. This links with the critical and compassionate aspects of critical perspectivism outlined above and demonstrates that in the Aotearoa context there are others who recognise and acknowledge the importance of (digital) media literacy in education. Computational thinking is clearly valuable in developing the use aspect of digital literacy (Shin, Hwang, Park, Teng, & Dang, 2019) but it does not engage young people in thinking critically or compassionately when it comes to media literacy.

Clearly, resources for schools are sorely needed to support the development of digital citizenship skills in our young generation. Even commercial companies have recognised this need and some examples are available, such as Microsoft's 'promote digital civility' programme[7] and Ryerson University's digital citizenship toolkit.[8] Common sense media[9] teaches youth to thrive in a digital age with research-based lesson plans as well as reviews on everything digital (which incorporate not just parent and teacher views but youth voice as well).

---

7   https://www.microsoft.com/en-us/digital-skills/digital-civility

8   As an open textbook for self-paced study by college/ university students: https://pressbooks.library.ryerson.ca/digcit/

9   https://www.commonsense.org/education/

However, these resources do not suggest what pedagogical approach to adopt in developing young people's capabilities for being critical and compassionate. D'Olimpio (2018) advocates for a Philosophy for Children (P4C) approach drawing on a Community of Inquiry (CoI) pedagogy. P4C is viewed as a holistic practice and is not simply about training of vocational skills. It is more concerned with preparing children for life, strengthening critical, creative, collaborative, and caring thinking. In terms of developing digital media literacy, this approach is more concerned with providing children with abilities and capabilities that they can use in the future than teaching them how to use a computer. The CoI P4C approach is a promising one, especially in a New Zealand context where kaupapa Māori values, such as ako (i.e., the reciprocal role of teacher and learner) are valued. However, an approach like this needs a basis of trust and a skilled teacher/facilitator in order to create a safe space for these kinds of conversations. Making use of the local P4C network[10] and resources to upskill teachers in the CoI pedagogy can make a significant contribution in supporting students and our young generation to learn critical skills that are relevant for life in general and for the development of an attitude of critical perspectivism in the context of digital media literacy.

Similarly, others have tried to grapple with how to develop digital citizens. Maha Bali, in commenting on the political upheaval in Egypt in 2013, has reflected on the role of higher education and urges institutions to move beyond critical thinking (which, she says, is in short supply anyway) and community service and to focus on critical citizenship (Bali, 2013). She then explores ways of developing critical digital citizenship based on premises of empathy and social justice, and argues that social media can be used positively in this regard, particularly in relation to intercultural learning experiences (Bali, 2016). In 2018, Bali, Zamora, and Cronin provided one such model for undertaking this when three classes of students spanning three continents joined together for Equity Unbound courses,[11] an emergent, collaborative curriculum which aims to create equity-focused, open, connected, intercultural learning experiences across classes, countries, and contexts. These are some examples of how adults (teachers or students) can develop digital media literacy in a way that is critical, collaborative, creative, and compassionate to support digital democratic citizenship in Aotearoa and internationally.

---

10   For example, www.p4c.org.nz
11   http://unboundeq.creativitycourse.org/about/

Conclusion

In this chapter, we have made a case for the need for digital media literacy in the 21st century that adopts a critical perspectivist approach to strengthen the digital democratic citizenship of future generations. We argue that this should sit firmly within the Aotearoa New Zealand educational context but that current endeavours to develop critical digital citizens with (digital) media literacy skills are limited. We offer pointers towards a range of resources that address aspects of digital media literacy including two pedagogical approaches for ways to engage with these concepts, namely the P4C CoI approach of D'Olimpio and the open connected learning approach of Bali, Zamora, and Cronin. Supporting our young generation to develop digital media literacy skills and an attitude of critical perspectivism will support not only their ability to use digital media as an enriching aspect of their lives, but also strengthen their role as democratic citizens in the digital age of the 21st century in Aotearoa and the international community.

Recommendations for further reading

D'Olimpio, L. (2018). *Media and moral education: A philosophy of critical engagement*. London, UK: Routledge. https://doi-org.ezproxy.canterbury.ac.nz/10.4324/9781315265452

Schwartz, M. (Ed.). (2019). *Digital citizenship toolkit*: Ryerson University Pressbook. Retrieved from: https://pressbooks.library.ryerson.ca/digcit/.

References

Bali, M., (2013). Critical citizenship for critical times. *Al Fanar Media*. Retrieved from: https://www.al-fanarmedia.org/2013/ 08/critical-citizenship-for-critical-times/

Bali, M. (2016). Critical digital citizenship: Promoting empathy and social justice online. *Connected Learning Alliance*. Retrieved from: https://clalliance.org/blog/critical-digital-citizenship-empathy-social-justice-online/

Brake, D. (2014). Are we all online content creators now? Web 2.0 and digital divides. *Journal of Computer-Mediated Communication, 19*, 591–609.

Buckingham, D. (2013). *Media education: Literacy, learning and contemporary culture*. Cambridge, UK: Polity Press.

D'Olimpio, L. (2018). *Media and moral education: A philosophy of critical engagement*. London, UK: Routledge. https://doi-org.ezproxy.canterbury.ac.nz/10.4324/9781315265452

Dahlstrom, E., & Bichsel, J. (2014). *ECAR study of undergraduate students and information technology*. Research report. Louisville, CO: ECAR. Retrieved from: http://www.educause.edu/ecar

Dewey, J. (1916). *Democracy and education*. New York, NY: Macmillan.

Dillian, K. (5 June, 2019). *Russian trolls who interfered in 2016 U.S. election also made ad money, report says*. NBC news. Retrieved from: https://www.nbcnews.com/politics/national-security/russian-trolls-who-interfered-2016-u-s-election-also-made-n1013811

Engesser, S., Ernst, N., Esser, F., & Büchel, F. (2017). Populism and social media: How politicians spread a fragmented ideology. *Information, Communication & Society, 20*(8), 1109–1126. doi:10.1080/1369118X.2016.1207697

Gerbaudo, P. (2018). Social media and populism: An elective affinity? *Media, Culture & Society, 40*(5), 745–753. doi:10.1177/0163443718772192

Global Digital Citizen Foundation. (n.d.). *Global digital citizenship quickstart guide.* Retrieved from: https://globaldigitalcitizen.org/resources

Hoechsmann, M., & Poyntz, S. R. (2012). *Media literacies: A critical introduction.* Chichester, UK: Wiley-Blackwell.

Koltay, T. (2011). The media and the literacies: Media literacy, information literacy, digital literacy. *Media, Culture & Society, 33*(2), 211–221.

Luke, A., Comber, B., & Grant, H. (2003). Critical literacies and cultural studies. In G. Bull & M. Anstey (Eds.), The literacy lexicon (2nd ed., pp. 15–36). Petaling Jaya, Malaysia: Prentice Hall.

Marchi, R. (2012). With Facebook, blogs, and fake news, teens reject journalistic "objectivity". *The Journal of Communication Inquiry, 36*(3), 246–262. doi:10.1177/0196859912458700

McDonald-Brown, C., Laxman, K., & Hope, J. (2016). An exploration of the contexts, challenges and competencies of pre-teenage children on the internet. *International Journal of Technology Enhanced Learning, 8*(1), 1.

McGillivray, D., McPherson, G., Jones, J., & McCandlish, A. (2015). Young people, digital media making and critical digital citizenship. *Leisure Studies, 35*(6), 724–738. doi:10.1080/02614367.2015.1062041

McIntyre, S. (2014). Reducing the digital literacy divide through disruptive innovation. *Higher Education Research and Development, 1*(July), 83–106.

McNaughton, S., & Gluckman, P. (2018). *A commentary on digital futures and education.* A report prepared for the Office of the Prime Minister. https://www.pmcsa.org.nz/wp-content/uploads/18-04-06-Digital-Futures-and-Education.pdf

Ministry of Education. (2014). *Digital technology safe and responsible use in schools: A companion to the guidelines for the surrender and retention of property and searches.* Retrieved from: https://www.education.govt.nz/assets/Documents/School/Managing-and-supporting-students/DigitalTechnologySafeAndResponsibleUseInSchs.pdf

Mintz, A. P. (2012). *Web of deceit: Misinformation and manipulation in the age of social media.* Medford, NJ: CyberAge Books.

Netsafe. (2018). *Digital fluency and digital citizenship.* Retrieved from: https://www.netsafe.org.nz/the-kit/netsafe-schools/digital-fluency-and-digital-citizenship/

Peterson, A. (2017). *Compassion and education: Cultivating compassionate children, schools and communities.* London, UK: Macmillan Palgrave.

Prensky, M. (2001). Digital natives, digital immigrants Part 1. *On the Horizon, 9*(5), 1–6.

Schradie, J. (2011). The digital production gap: The digital divide and Web 2.0 collide. *Poetics, 39*, 145–168.

Shao, C., Hui, P., Wang, L., Jiang, X., Flammini, A., Menczer, F., & Ciampaglia, G. L. (2018). Anatomy of an online misinformation network. *PloS One, 13*(4), e0196087. doi:10.1371/journal.pone.0196087

Shin, T. S., Hwang, H., Park, J., Teng, J. X. & Dang, T. (2019). Digital kids Asia-Pacific: insights into children's digital citizenship. Retrieved from https://unesdoc.unesco.org/ark:/48223/pf0000367985

UNESCO. (2015). *Global citizenship education: Topics and learning objectives.* Paris: Author. Retrieved from: https://unesdoc.unesco.org/ark:/48223/pf0000232993

Webster, A. (2016). *Preteens' concepts and development of privacy, and the relationship to decisions and actions undertaken in online social environments and with digital devices.* Unpublished master's thesis, University of Waikato, Hamilton, New Zealand.

Wintour, P. (10 January, 2018). Russian bid to influence Brexit vote detailed in new US Senate report. *The Guardian.* Retrieved from: https://www.theguardian.com/world/2018/jan/10/russian-influence-brexit-vote-detailed-us-senate-report

YoungMinds & Ecorys. (2016). *Resilience for the digital world; A positioning paper. United Kingdom.* Retrieved from: https://youngminds.org.uk/media/1491/resilience_for_the_digital_world_ym_positioning.pdf

Chapter 12
What's in a name? Finding ways to articulate leadership by teachers

Susan Lovett

Making sense of teacher leadership: Why it matters

As teachers begin to develop confidence in teaching, career questions of 'what next?' typically surface. Leadership work is one possibility. However, whether early career teachers aspire to leadership work, I argue, depends on conceptions of what it means to lead and engage in leadership activity. Such conceptions are often shaped by the kind of leadership an early career teacher has experienced over time. Those contemplating options for new motivations and challenges, will, I suggest, be reconciling what they have gleaned from their experiences and observations (both positive and negative) as they give consideration to their own decisions about engagement in leadership.

Making sense of conceptions of teacher leadership is the focus of this chapter, drawing upon research and scholarly writing to convey the ways in which this field of study has gained momentum and where it is currently moving. Work to enhance the appeal of leadership work is needed to ensure teachers want to become leaders. Illustrative examples drawn from participants in a New Zealand study, *Teachers of Promise*, show the need for more clarity regarding the scope of leadership influence, who counts as a leader, and the work understood as teacher leadership. An overview of scholarly literature surveying the field of teacher leadership from work undertaken in different countries provides evidence that the call for clarity in terminology about teacher leadership is of international concern. As an introduction a New Zealand study is used to highlight what teachers themselves say about what constitutes teacher leadership.

Evidence close to home: Teachers of Promise (TOP) study in Aotearoa New Zealand

Views about teacher leadership were sought as part of data gathering for a large New Zealand longitudinal study of 57 primary and secondary teachers. The teachers in the study were purposively selected from graduates of the country's initial teacher education programmes in 2003. They were described as teachers the profession ought not to lose. Participant selection as 'promising' prospects (hence the study's name, Teachers of Promise) was based on the endorsement they had received from both their initial teacher education provider and employer once appointed to a school. A fuller account of the study's design can be found in Cameron, Baker, and Lovett (2006) and Lovett (2007). The impetus for TOP was to find out the reasons for newly qualified teachers' decisions to stay in their schools, move schools, or leave teaching. Of particular interest were matters of job satisfaction, commitment, professional learning, and the development of expertise. Data from surveys and interviews were gathered on four occasions from 2005–11 to capture these teachers' personal experiences and movements within, across, and beyond schools. In 2016, five of these teachers participated in a further interview to explore the concepts 'teacher leader' and 'teacher leadership'. The specific focus on leadership was made because of a curiosity to see what had shaped their decisions about whether to lead or not and the scope of their leadership work.

The 2016 interviews began with a question probing the teachers' views about the existence of teacher leadership in practice. This question proved to be a difficult opener because the teachers were uncertain about the terminology. Their uncertainty brought into focus "the difficulty of having leadership terms which acknowledge the status or leader type as well as the work undertaken as leadership" (Lovett, 2018, p. 117). Put simply, this was about two opposing stances on leadership. While one could be undertaken within a formal position, the other was possible without being associated with a designated position. The scope of leadership work enacted by these five teachers reflected different motivations and aspirations. Despite their firm commitment to students and learning, their careers had unfolded in different ways. Two of the five (Jack and Robyn) had moved in an upward trajectory through the named positions of head of department and/or pastoral care (deaning) to reach the senior leadership team as assistant or associate principal. Jack realised that management units defined leadership work. He noted schools used management units to draw teachers into leadership work and that these were signals of leadership potential and experience. Robyn's initial leadership work recognised her curriculum expertise in her appointment to a head of department position. This was followed by roles focusing on assessment, accountability, and compliance as she moved closer to the senior leadership team. She did, however, acknowledge that leadership could occur outside formal positions but, at the same time, did not know what to call informal leadership.

Two others interviewed, Steven and Ruby, held formal leadership positions as heads of department yet were not looking towards a principalship or membership of a senior leadership team. Steven had dismissed an upward career trajectory despite having begun preparatory study with his enrolment in a postgraduate educational leadership programme. He gave job intensification as a reason why he had decided not to pursue his earlier aspiration of moving upwards in the hierarchy. Ruby contrasted her role as head of department with her other role in the position of specialist classroom teacher. Her preference was for the latter. Being a specialist classroom teacher meant she could lead and learn at the same time. Her leadership came from working alongside colleagues to address matters of classroom learning. It was not coloured by concerns for accountability and compliance and reporting to the senior leaders in the school. Rather, she was able to develop learner-to-learner relationships with her colleagues through their mutual interest in students' learning and sharing puzzles of practice.

Interestingly, Ruby expressed some disquiet about being acknowledged as a leader. For her, being called a 'leader' was associated with having superior status over colleagues. This was not how she wished to be seen. Instead, she was attracted to the combination of being a teacher, a learner, and a leader. This she explained in terms of the benefits possible when she moved beyond her own classroom to influence and support colleagues which often necessitated new learning for her as she considered how to help her colleagues. This learning, tied to leadership work, provided fresh challenges and stimulation for Ruby. What is interesting from her account of her leadership experience, both as head of department and specialist classroom teacher, is that it was accommodated through the appointments to two named, formal positions.

The remaining teacher, Rose, was a classroom teacher. She did not consider herself to be a teacher leader at all. Her strength was her most recent experience teaching in a bilingual unit where she described herself as an advocate but not a leader. Again, the absence of a formal title serves to reinforce the dominance of leadership as position rather than leadership as activity or the work done in the flow of everyday practice with colleagues.

Seven key messages emerged from my additional interviews with these five teachers who all struggled in different ways to articulate what teacher leadership actually meant. These matters point to difficulties in the terminology used, and how leadership by teachers is supported and valued in schools as an individual or collective pursuit. A fuller account of the seven matters is reported in Lovett (2018). In essence, these matters are:

1. the continuing perception that leadership occurs through a role taken in a named position
2. reluctance amongst some teachers to become leaders
3. teacher leadership is seen to involve personal risks, and requires courage and supportive colleagues
4. teachers' classroom leadership can be invisible
5. the moral obligation to enhance students' learning attracts classroom teachers into leadership work without necessarily knowing they are leading their colleagues (this type of leadership is collective rather than individual activity)
6. teacher leaders can provide clear evidence of their impact on students' and colleagues' work
7. teacher leaders see their work as remaining connected to classrooms.

I now move from my brief overview of five teachers' career pathways, aspirations, and experiences of leadership and their attempts at articulating the scope of teacher leadership work to highlight how the scholarly literature from three other countries regards the concept of teacher leadership.

Conceptualising teacher leadership: An international search for clarity in terminology

Entitling a book in the nineties as *Awakening the Sleeping Giant* suggested that two decades ago the concept of teacher leadership was not sufficiently recognised and understood (Katzenmeyer & Moller, 1996). Even today, this is in part due to the looseness of the term 'teacher leadership', a term Fairman and Mackenzie (2015) suggest might even be counterproductive. As an umbrella term, according to Neumerski (2013), teacher leadership captures both formal and informal leadership by teachers, but the combination gives more recognition to leadership within a named position held by an individual than to a broader organisational quality to which there may be many contributors. Ogawa and Bossert (1995) suggest when leadership is viewed as an organisational quality, it can occur anywhere regardless of an individual's status. The notion of anyone being capable of leadership work is inviting and inclusive but, at the same time, contributes to the difficulty in specifying the scope of that work, especially when it may not be associated with a designated leadership position. Informal leadership is harder to recognise because teachers may share their expertise at different times without necessarily seeing themselves as leaders. Silva, Gimbert, and Nolan (2000) relate this quality to the ways teachers come together to explore what works for students and their learning without the trappings of work labelled as leadership and confined to people with particular titles.

An alternative to formal leadership or leadership as position is to think of leadership as collective work to which many can contribute depending on their expertise and inclination. This view is more about the work to be done in achieving the moral purpose of schooling—namely improving students' learning and achievement—than the status of a leader as an individual. It enables a distinction between the terms 'leader' and 'leadership' to be made, which I find helpful. Thus, the connection can be made between leadership actions for the improvement of teaching outside designated positions emphasising how being a leader need not mean increasing the distance from classroom teaching. Cherkowski and Bradley-Levine (2018) refer to the concept of teacher leadership becoming "inextricably merged with continuous improvement of teaching and learning, and with more active participation sought by and for teachers in shaping, through their leadership, the learning culture of the school" (p. 1).

While the terms 'formal' and 'informal' leadership have been used to acknowledge the scope of leadership possible by teachers, this has not necessarily enhanced the understanding of what teacher leadership is about. Simpson's (2016) work to devise a three-part typology for leadership based on the earlier work of Dewey and Bentley (1949) goes some way towards explaining the different conceptions of leadership and recent thinking. One conception is to view leadership as 'self-action' recognising what an individual does in the capacity of the positional leader. This, as discussed earlier, is the firmly entrenched view surfacing again showing leadership in positional terms. A second conception is to think in terms of leadership as a set of practices where 'inter-actions' matter. This is typically when leadership is distributed so as to harness collective capacities and through which dialogue occurs between leaders and followers. The notion of leadership being 'distributed' nevertheless signals that leadership is contingent on what another leader allows to occur. A third and further conception of leadership in the flow of practice recognises the need for power *with* others, not *over* others. Here leadership is not hemmed in by formal hierarchies. It is instead emergent, spontaneous, unanticipated, and amongst peers, or to use the terminology explored so far in this chapter, progressing notions of informal and non-positional leadership expressed through the activities arising in practice as colleagues come together to solve issues of practice.

The literature to this point has underscored matters that, when taken together, lead to a contested or confused view of teacher leadership. From my reading, a first point to note is that leadership work is not dependent on having a designated position, title, or role. However, this broadening of what counts as leadership work contributes to the difficulty in identifying what constitutes teacher leadership. The same uncertainty applies to a second point which views leadership as collective rather than individual work. This means it gets harder to see who is engaged in leadership work when there are multiple players who cannot be identified according to named positions for their contributions. Similarly, if it is work (moral purpose) to improve students' learning and understanding that underpins leadership activity, then this also applies to teachers who have a continuous improvement mindset which sustains their interest and commitment to their actions as teachers. Likewise, if teacher leadership occurs through collegial conversations about students' learning, it can occur anywhere. This learning conversation flexibility is another factor that contributes to a lack of clarity. That such conversations may be intentional and deliberate or chance opportunities also adds to the uncertainty of being able to identify teacher leadership when it occurs. The matter of opportunity for leadership work is a further difficulty because, even when opportunities are distributed, the distribution occurs because others permit it. Leadership efforts that are generated by teachers without such permission tend to go unnoticed and even the teachers themselves do not seem to recognise their efforts as leadership work. That many teachers do not see this type of influence as leadership, and others only recognise leadership from the vantage point of a formal position, suggests there is still work to do to ensure conceptions of leadership encompass formal and informal work.

In my search for clarity regarding the term 'teacher leadership', my analysis and research preferences have led me to a view that teacher leadership is not about the separation of leadership work from teaching, or of talented teachers having to choose between classroom teaching and moving away from it to become a leader; rather, I favour an alternative which opens opportunities for teachers to confer, support, and share their expertise close to their work in classrooms. This type of leadership is centred on classroom teaching. It is why I am attracted to Frost's (2014) view in the United Kingdom that teacher leadership is a collective pursuit because the views, experiences, and insights of colleagues deepen understandings in ways that would not be possible if a teacher continued to draw on his or her own individual knowledge and insights.

The closeness of the connection between learning and leadership is a key feature of Frost's (2014) work. Leadership emanates from the need to continue learning and seeing colleagues as a source of influence. Frost claims leadership is an expression of teacher professionality and therefore is a natural part of being a teacher and being connected to others in the profession. Like me, Frost concentrates on the potential of viewing leadership as collective work with multiple players who can draw upon and influence each other's expertise regardless of status.

Hill (2014, p. 74) also explains how teacher leadership can be a dimension of all teachers' professionality, saying "it recognises the potential of all teachers to exercise leadership as part of their role as a teacher". Her view aligns teachers' desire to make a difference to students and their learning with the recognition that interacting and working alongside colleagues is the way to gain deeper understandings of what works and why. In this way, leadership comes from the curiosity to answer questions of practice seeing colleagues as a source of support for learning, where each contributes to the others' learning and what it means to lead and learn is intertwined.

Frost (2014, p. 3) draws attention to visibility and recognition for leadership work by posing the question, "does the word 'informal' suggest that teachers exercise leadership but without the benefit of the legitimacy or authority that might stem from holding a designated position?" This question warrants more attention. In answering, he suggests that the discussion of how to talk about teacher leadership comes back to "role-taking rather than leadership practice being a dimension of a teacher's professional identity" (Frost, 2014, p. 3). Recognition and legitimacy keep surfacing in debates about teacher leadership and are matters to which I return later in the chapter.

Looking to Australian research, the view that teachers can be leaders is also apparent. Andrews and Crowther (2006) attribute school revitalisation to the work of many contributors including teachers as leaders. School improvement—referred to as revitalisation—they explain, is about collaborative action involving whole school strategies. They, like Frost, refer to professionalism, but do so with a new kind of professionalism expressed as 'parallel leadership' in order to recognise the relationship between teacher leaders and administrator leaders. This is an indication that teacher leaders differ from administrator leaders, those referred to earlier as leaders with named titles, status, and designated positions in the hierarchy.

Three characteristics underpin the Australians' concept of this parallel leadership: mutualism, sense of shared purpose, and allowance for individual expression. The choice of the word 'parallel' preceding 'leadership' signifies the importance of work needed by both teacher leaders and principals for school revitalisation. This is recognising that leadership is present throughout a school's layers and tiers and is not just the preserve of those with named positions. Andrews' and Crowther's conception of leadership for school improvement once again picks up a collective thread around the moral purpose of schooling, recognising the need for multiple not individual players. The link to professionalism is enabling here because it signifies the work to be done by professionals supporting one another as leaders and learners, points already made by Frost (2014) and Hill (2014).

In Canada, Hargreaves and O'Connor (2018) have gone further with the term 'collaborative professionalism'. I suggest this is perhaps an indication that the word 'leadership' may no longer be helpful because of its perennially dominant focus on named positions, status, and the actions of an individual. Moreover, just as leadership was omitted, so, too, is the word 'teacher'. Personally, I am attracted to the notion of 'collaborative professionalism' because it captures the collective intent, and the ongoing learning that I associate with acting as a professional. I do, however, see a need to acknowledge the professional base of teaching for this kind of leadership work to be recognised in education.

The previous section has established some of the complexity in discussions surrounding the concept of teacher leadership. Despite the presence of contested views, I hold to some key points that I consider offer a concrete basis for a more defensible account of what constitutes teacher leadership. This is why I feel confident to place my mark in the scholarly literature on notions of collective rather than individual work, the connection between leadership and learning, and why I make the distinction between leadership as work to be undertaken versus leadership linked only with the person attributed a formal title, position, or responsibility. It is these three aspects that I consider fundamental to any clarification of the terminology associated with teacher leadership. In recent times, substantial work germane to the clarification I seek has been undertaken in significant reviews, to which I now turn my attention. Again, these reviews are wrestling with some of the uncertainties that are self-evident in the discussion thus far.

Major literature reviews on teacher leadership

Two major literature reviews have been undertaken on the concept of teacher leadership and what it looks like in practice. These reviews have been seminal, referenced by others researching in the field of teacher leadership. The first, undertaken by York-Barr and Duke (2004), tracked 20 years of research on teacher leadership. The outcome of that review indicated the construct of teacher leadership lacked conceptual and operational clarity. A subsequent review by Wenner and Campbell (2017) considered definitions of teacher leadership, the preparation of teacher leaders, their impact, and factors facilitating or inhibiting teacher leaders' work. The findings revealed there was no consensus around what teacher leadership meant. An analysis of the scope of teacher leadership research did, however, highlight several perspectives. These included instructional leadership by principals, coaches, and teachers (Neumerski, 2013), recognition by policy makers and educational organisations of teacher leadership as an important component of school reform, and reports on teacher leadership initiatives and professional standards for teachers with accompanying evaluation instruments assessing interpersonal skills, collaboration, and relationships with staff. Pertinent to the focus of this chapter exploring explanations of teacher leadership and what the term means, are five themes extracted from the depictions of teacher leadership in research findings summarised by Wenner and Campbell (2017, p. 146). These were:

1. Teacher leadership goes beyond classroom walls.
2. Teacher leaders should support professional learning in their schools (lead professional learning communities, lead formal professional development or assist colleagues).
3. Teacher leaders should be involved in policy and/or decision making at some level.
4. The ultimate goal of teacher leadership is improving student learning and success.
5. Teacher leaders working toward improvement and change for the whole school organisation.

What these points have in common is their implicit fidelity to the moral purpose of schooling, specifically the improvement of students' learning. These points are about the work to be done to achieve this purpose, namely the actions of teachers when acting as professionals wanting to do their best. These points are not concerned with a teacher leader in a particular position. Instead, they highlight leadership which is observable in activities to further students' learning and achievement. It is this natural expression of a teacher's professionality, the growth of confidence, and professional learning that occurs through the continuous asking of questions about practice by, with, and through others, which I consider captures the essence of the concept of teacher leadership. Moving on from these seminal reviews of teacher leadership, I now turn to focus on the United States to highlight continuing and more recent attempts to gain conceptual agreement of the term 'teacher leadership'.

Attempts to reconcile conceptual tensions surrounding teacher leadership in the United States

Continuing evidence of debates about what counts as teacher leadership is reported in a special issue of the *International Journal of Teacher Leadership* (*9*(1), 2018). This issue includes an account of the work done to establish two separate but complementary organisations for teacher leadership researchers. One operates within the auspices of the American Educational Research Association (AERA). This internationally recognised association attracts thousands of participants to their annual conference. The other is a Teacher Leadership Congress which attracts some of the same members.

Research fields are grouped according to Special Interest Group classifications inside broader divisions in AERA. Division K (Teaching and Teacher Education) is the division housing a newly developed section on teacher leadership entitled "Teacher leadership: Leading within and beyond the classroom (teachers as leaders, policy makers, community activists and decision-makers)". The AERA 2017 website[1] description of this new section states:

> This section invites investigations of teachers who demonstrate leadership, expert knowledge, and advocacy both from within the classroom and/or school settings, as well as beyond individual or local school contexts. This could include examinations into the definition and conceptualization of teacher leadership, the impact of teacher leadership on practice/curriculum/policy, innovative programs and models that support the identification and development of teacher leaders, case studies of teachers who lead, teacher research, etc.

Work undertaken (2014–18) on the evolution of the Teacher Leadership Congress has been carefully documented by Berg, Carver, and Mangin (2018). Protocols for the Congress demonstrate how the conceptualisation of teacher leadership has been interrogated through a process of facilitated dialogue. Each Congress has a particular theme, examples of which are: 2014, "What is teacher leadership?"; 2015, "Connecting and collaborating?"; 2016, "Agreeing to disagree"; 2017, "Examining the state of the literature"; 2018, "Unpacking contextual contrasts and commonalities". A journal article by Berg and Zoellick (2019) offers a further framework for defining dimensions of teacher leadership, incorporating: source of *legitimacy*; *support* to accomplish the work; *objective* of teachers' influence; and *method* of influence.

Although presented separately, these dimensions are interrelated, raising further questions. After briefly describing the dimensions and listing their related questions taken from Berg and Zoellick (2019, pp. 7–13), I offer my responses to add to this field of study and practice.

Legitimacy

There are many perspectives regarding how a teacher is acknowledged as a legitimate person to engage in teacher leadership work.

---

1 https://web.archive.org/web/20171018024839/http://www.aera.net/Division-K/Who-We-Are

Question: Can a person self-declare as a teacher leader?

My answer: Yes, but this will depend on the teacher's conception of what leadership work is and on the views of colleagues. If teachers acknowledge the ways they influence others which helps them in their practice, then this is an example of teacher leadership outside a named position. Acknowledgement by others provides the sense of legitimacy that all self-nomination requires.

Question: Can a teacher become a teacher leader by circumstance?

My answer: Yes. This is certainly possible when teachers respond to colleagues' needs for support, modelling, and coaching. They can be approached by colleagues regardless of whether they are recognised and labelled with a designated leadership title or position. They may initiate support themselves.

Question: Is active agency on the part of the teacher required?

My answer: Yes. The teacher will be responding because of a strong sense of commitment to the shared moral purpose of helping students and their learning. Helping other colleagues in their work with students is part of this collective commitment to students' learning at the workplace and in the wider profession.

Question: Can you be a teacher leader and not know it?

My answer: Yes. Teachers may influence colleagues without attributing such behaviours to leadership. They will be conversing about practice because such talk is a natural occurrence. It is what acting professionally means, moving beyond self to connect with others in the pursuit of a shared moral purpose.

Question: Whose endorsement is necessary to be regarded as a teacher leader?

My answer: This will vary depending on circumstances and teacher leaders themselves. Some people have more of a need for acknowledgement than others. Those with strong internal motivation will engage in leadership work regardless of recognition, though by its very nature, recognition underscores self-efficacy.

Berg and Zoellick (2019) have commented, "whatever its source, legitimacy was always a precondition of leadership" (p. 7). Their comment suggests that the impetus to reach out to others is why leadership actions occur. Again, we see the pulse of moral purpose linking individuals' actions in the workplace.

Support

Where supports for teacher leadership work originate has been another matter for discussion. While there has been agreement about the need for support for teacher leadership, no discernible agreement surrounds how it happens in practice. It is noted that support encompasses external and internal sources, as well as being direct and indirect.

Question: What external supports are available and who provides them?

My answer: Some supports need to be available if teachers are to lead in the flow of practice and begin sharing expertise with colleagues. A workplace that prioritises the conditions enabling the continual learning of its staff is deliberate about structuring the physical layout and timetabling to isolate the time for teachers to work together. Support may include explicit coaching around professional learning conversational skills, scheduled release time to observe colleagues, shared planning and assessment time, resources to support curriculum changes, and individual coaching about how to develop learner-to-learner relationships with colleagues.

Question: Can the provision of support legitimise teachers' roles as leaders?

My answer: Support is a visible way of acknowledging the importance of teacher leadership actions. It is a way to deepen expertise and send a message that colleagues can be a source of support for each other. This is a form of public validation recognising that those closest to classrooms can enhance colleagues' learning and improve teaching in the workplace.

Question: Are teacher leaders those who break ranks to address problems of practice without waiting for support or permission?

My answer: Yes. Teacher leaders do not need others to determine whether or not they will support their colleagues. They will be intrinsically motivated to reach out to colleagues because of the reciprocity of learning from each other, giving and receiving insights that enhance one's own and others' practice.

Berg and Zoellick (2019) argue "the source and nature of the support teachers draw upon in their leadership activities" (p. 8) will enhance the study and practices of teacher leadership. In other words, teacher leadership can flourish when workplace conditions are conducive to informal learning opportunities.

Objective

'Moral purpose' has been a consistent term used in the leadership literature to convey the objective or purpose of an educator's work. This is about the work educators (teachers) do to make a difference to students' learning. A matter to be reconciled is: *At what point does teachers' collegial influence become recognised as teacher leadership?* Following on from this question are sub-questions that explore the reasons for those interactions with colleagues.

Question: Does a teacher leader have to be someone in an instructional coach, mentor, or professional learning leader role?

My answer: No, although it is possible for a leadership position holder to cast aside hierarchical status to be one of a collective in the pursuit of improvements in practice. In this sense, the teacher leader is one of the pack, rather than someone with power over or superior knowledge to offer to others.

Question: Can a teacher leader be someone who has an impact on the cultural conditions of the workplace? For example, promoting a culture of trust and respect, reflective practice, collaborative ways of working.

My answer: Yes. A teacher leader can be modelling how to ensure the workplace is able to fulfil its moral purpose. This is consistent with the notion that the shared moral purpose is the pulse for the workplace, namely the actions needed to support students and their learning through the supports teachers give one another. Mutuality is a key concern for teacher leaders who show respect for their colleagues as co-learners. Furthermore, because teacher leaders are also searching for answers to the puzzles of practice, they are learners as well as leaders and others see them as approachable and credible.

Question: Can a teacher leader be someone who attends to the structural conditions that help teaching and learning? For example, decisions about curriculum, staffing, and timetabling.

My answer: Yes, teacher leaders have useful insights to offer decision making about organisational matters which will improve student and teacher outcomes. This could well mean that they can contribute suggestions to improve structural conditions that keep the continual improvement mindset to the fore as needs are identified, and opportunities and strategies considered.

Question: Can a teacher leader be someone who has a policy or advocacy role?

My answer: Yes, a teacher leader will act according to the strength of their moral purpose. It is this that drives their work.

What is noticeable from these sub-questions is that there is a wide array of possible activities, all making a contribution to the lives and life chances of students through learning.

Method of influence

How teachers influence colleagues is closely tied with methods that may be direct and/or indirect. Questions that help to realise the intent of this influence include:

Question: What counts as direct and intentional influence?

My answer: Teacher leaders who are responsive to context will recognise opportunities where they can usefully share their influence in pursuit of organisational and collegial learning. They will do this because they have a genuine desire to support their colleagues. They will be learning themselves as they work out how to help others.

Question: What counts as indirect and intentional influence?

My answer: Teacher leaders can lead through the efforts of other people too. An example is when groups of teachers secure the services of other agencies to help them work with student projects. Here the actual work is undertaken by the other agencies but is possible through the intentional influence of the teacher leaders who instigate the request for additional support.

Question: Is modelling reflective practice and collaboration teacher leadership?

My answer: Yes, because this is demonstrating a learning intent in order to help others see how to ask questions of their practice. The modelling is intended to demonstrate the process of sense making which an individual could later emulate on their own. The benefits of working with colleagues are realised as ways to improve practice and are how teacher leaders influence colleagues.

Question: How high up the hierarchy can a teacher go and still be a teacher leader?

My answer: This is an interesting question because, in my mind, teacher leadership operates more often than not beyond hierarchy and sometimes despite it. It is not about 'power over' as a position in a hierarchy suggests. Instead, it emphasises 'power with' and learner-to-learner relationships where superiority and status are not important. It operates within a flat structure rather than being leadership progressing up increasingly senior rungs/positions on an organisational ladder. Talking about hierarchy, however, necessitates recognition of positional leadership and notions of status. In teacher leadership, such matters are not the reason for or validation of leadership. Peer-to-peer interactions and transactions are valued because it is these that sustain and motivate teachers to continue their work serving students as learners. This is collective work rather than action concerned with individual status.

Berg and Zoellick (2019) suggest it is helpful to specify how influence is played out because this helps us to understand what teacher leadership is. Together, the four dimensions discussed above help us to understand what teacher leadership looks like in different workplace contexts allowing comparisons to be made. Berg and Zoellick (2019) argue that these dimensions may be a way to reduce the ambiguity and "enable research on teacher leadership to accumulate in productive ways and lead to much-needed theory building in this field" (p. 13). I now draw my reading of teacher leadership research and scholarly literature to a close revealing my current thinking about how to talk about and define teacher leadership.

Conclusion

In my own work, I have defined teacher leadership as interconnected activity recognising that it is embedded in collaborative learning cultures (Lovett, 2018). Like others (Collinson, 2012), I continue to recognise the impetus for teacher leadership work as being the activity teachers engage in to improve student learning and achievement, the primary purpose or objective of schooling (Berg & Zoellick, 2019). This is about accepting a learning orientation to leading and teaching, which I fully acknowledge blurs the two terms. I resist mention of roles in my definition because I consider this favours leadership from a formal positional base marginalising other ways of leading in the flow of practice and as professional interaction. I treat leadership as collective rather than individual work. I believe this acknowledges that expertise is generated from multiple sources and can be shared if workplaces operate on principles of trust, respect, inclusion, and support. I view the spaces available for leadership as being possible through the personal agency of teachers themselves (Frost, 2006) and others who legitimate their expertise and support their efforts by paying attention to how workplaces can be conducive learning environments. I also note how teacher leaders draw upon research findings in their work with other teachers to make meaning from practice and encourage teachers to do the same. Their proactive learning stance is an expression of professionality and illustrates how learning is generated from leadership work requiring a new skill set to work with colleagues attending to processes, relationships, and feelings associated with reflection, dialogue, and the gathering of evidence to feed into future actions.

I have wrestled with the words 'teacher' and 'leadership' in the combination term 'teacher leadership'. I have acknowledged and adopted an alternative conception of leadership as work or activity rather than as position. However, when the word 'teacher' precedes leadership, I still feel this tends to privilege position over activity, reinforcing a taken-for-granted orthodoxy. I have considered alternatives to naming teachers as leaders with terms emphasising professionality and professionalism. While these capture the same learning orientation, they do not make the notion of leadership as activity visible enough for my liking. This is why I have stalled on moving away from the term 'teacher leadership' altogether. I have seen the need to acknowledge leadership and its connection to and for learning as the essential work focus and at the same time recognise the actors, the teachers who lead, with the words 'teacher leaders'. The term 'teacher leadership' is therefore my preference at the moment, albeit a term that is still, more often than not, overshadowed by the acceptance of leadership as coincidental with specific positions and roles.

Recommended reading

Berg, J. H., & Zoellick, B. (2019). Teacher leadership: Toward a new conceptual framework. *Journal of Professional Capital and Community, 4*(1), 2–14.

Wenner, J. A., & Campbell, T. (2017). The theoretical and empirical basis of teacher leadership: A review of the literature. *Review of Educational Research, 87*(1), 134–171.

References

Andrews, D., & Crowther, F. (2006). Teachers as leaders in a knowledge society: Encouraging signs of a new professionalism. *Journal of School Leadership, 16*(5), 534–549.

Berg, J. H., Carver, C. L., & Mangin, M. M. (2018). Building a research community, developing a coherent field of study. *International Journal of Teacher Leadership, 9*(1), 9–32.

Berg, J. H., & Zoellick, B. (2019). Teacher leadership: Toward a new conceptual framework. *Journal of Professional Capital and Community, 4*(1), 2–14.

Cameron, M., Baker, R., & Lovett, S. (2006). *Teachers of promise. Getting started in teaching. Phase one overview.* Wellington: New Zealand Council for Educational Research.

Cherkowski, S., & Bradley-Levine, J. (2018). Editorial: Surveying the field of teacher leadership: Looking back. *International Journal of Teacher Leadership, 9*(1), 1–8.

Collinson, V. (2012). Leading by learning, learning by leading. *Professional Development in Education, 38*(2), 247–266. doi:10.1080/19415257.2012.657866

Dewey, J., & Bentley, A. (1949). *Knowing and the known.* Boston, MA: Beacon Press.

Fairman, J. C., & Mackenzie, S. V. (2015). How teacher leaders influence others and understand their leadership. *International Journal of Leadership in Education, 18*(1), 61–87. doi:10.1080/13603124.2014.904002

Frost, D. (2006). The concept of "agency" in leadership for learning. *Leading and Managing, 12*(2), 19–28.

Frost, D. (2014, September). *Non-positional teacher leadership: A perpetual motion miracle.* Paper presented in the symposium "Changing teacher professionality through support for teacher leadership in Europe and beyond" at the European Council for Educational Research (ECER) Conference, Porto.

Hargreaves, A., & O'Connor, M. T. (2018). *Collaborative professionalism. When teaching together means learning for all.* Thousand Oaks, CA: Corwin Press.

Hill, V. (2014). The HertsCam TLDW programme. In D. Frost (Ed.), *Transforming education through teacher leadership* (pp. 73–83). Cambridge, UK: University of Cambridge.

Katzenmeyer, M., & Moller, G. (1996). *Awakening the sleeping giant: Helping teachers develop as leaders.* Thousand Oaks, CA: Corwin Press.

Lovett, S. (2007). "Teachers of Promise": Is teaching their first career choice? *New Zealand Annual Review of Education, 16,* 117–126.

Lovett, S. (2018). *Advocacy for teacher leadership. Opportunity, preparation, support and pathways.* Cham, Switzerland: Springer.

Neumerski, C. M. (2013). Rethinking instructional leadership, a review: What do we know about principal, teacher and coach instructional leadership, and where should we go from here? *Educational Administration Quarterly, 49*(2), 310–347.

Ogawa, R. T., & Bossert, S. T. (1995). Leadership as an organizational quality. *Educational Administration Quarterly, 31*(2), 224–243.

Silva, D., Gimbert, B., & Nolan, J. (2000). Sliding the doors: Locking and unlocking possibilities for teacher leadership. *Teachers College Record, 102,* 779–804.

Simpson, B. (2016). Where's the agency in leadership-as-practice? In J. A. Raelin (Ed.), *Leadership-as-practice: Theory and application* (pp. 159–177). New York, NY: Routledge.

Wenner, J. A., & Campbell, T. (2017). The theoretical and empirical basis of teacher leadership: A review of the literature. *Review of Educational Research, 87*(1), 134–171. doi:10.3102/0034654316653478

York-Barr, A. J., & Duke, K. (2004). What do we know about teacher leadership? Findings from two decades of scholarship. *Review of Educational Research, 74*(3), 255–316. doi:10.3102/00346543074003255

Chapter 13
The complex epistemological terrain of teacher education

Mistilina Sato

Introduction

In a recent conversation I had with a student teacher, she said: "I learned more during my professional practice placement than I have in the courses at the university." I suspect that many teacher educators have heard this kind of sentiment from their student teachers. A 2017 report from the Education Review Office (ERO) in New Zealand summarised how newly graduated teachers perceive their preparation and confidence to teach. The report drew on data from semi-structured interviews with leaders in 227 early learning services and schools and 588 newly graduated teachers, and a survey completed by 70 teachers across 36 services. The good news from this report was that, generally, the beginning teachers reported that they felt confident in their preparation to begin their teaching career. Teachers reported that their field-based experiences were an important part of helping them build confidence and preparing them as teachers, and they thought that having a variety of field placements helped them develop their practice.

Of course, there was variability in the participant reports. The newly graduated teachers reported feeling more confident in content and pedagogical knowledge and less confident in processes such as using assessment data to identify student progress and for planning for instruction. The teachers who felt less prepared or confident reported that they knew the theory, but not how to implement it in practice, particularly in areas such as planning, formative use of assessment, and being responsive to diverse languages, cultures, and identities among their students. Additionally, school and centre leaders reported that they saw differences in beginning teachers' practices depending on the initial teacher education (ITE) provider from which they graduated, which led them to have more confidence in some programmes over others based on how well prepared they thought the newly graduated teachers were.

One of the key recommendations from this report for ITE providers is to "deliberately integrate theory and practice" (Education Review Office, 2017, p. 6). The opening summary of the report explains:

> ERO's findings point to a need for better integration of theory and practice both preservice and for beginning teachers. Both leaders and NGTs [Newly Graduated Teachers] told us the balance and alignment between theories learnt and the application of these in practice needed to be strengthened. Balancing theory and practice is about getting it right so NGTs enter their first teaching position with confidence to teach. Our findings reinforce the need for review and strengthening of programmes of teacher education, through the work of the Education Council and government agencies. (p. 5)

There are three major assumptions in this recommendation. First, that theories are meant to be 'applied' to practice. The idea of 'application' of theory is much too vague to help us understand what a beginning teacher actually does with the theories they learn in ITE. This chapter will explore how theories can be used to understand practice, to predict student behaviour, to guide the design of instruction and learning experiences, and to support a teacher in developing questions that they can ask about the education system and their own practice.

Second, there is an assumption that a desired end-state for programme design is one of balance between theory and practice. As will be explored later, if teacher education is a complex system, we should expect some disequilibrium within complex systems. Tensions are the places of emergent learning. When we seek balance and harmony as our end-state, we set ourselves up for the inevitable critique of not reaching an ideal of agreement and accord. Learning is anything but this. Learning is hard, full of tension, transgressive, and full of discord. This chapter will explore how ITE programme design can draw on multiple theoretical, epistemological, or philosophical perspectives, holding them in tension with each other by making them explicit; it will also explore how using an eclectic approach to theory may better serve learning rather than seeking alignment and balance.

Finally, the assumption that strengthening teacher education is an activity to be engaged by the Teaching Council and government agencies suggests that the people doing the work of teacher education—the teacher educators, the teachers, and the preservice teachers—are not agents of their own learning. We will leave that argument for another time, but it is important to recognise how the actors within the system are being positioned in government reports such as this one.

How do we understand the underlying conceptions of our teacher education curriculum when we are simultaneously listening to our graduates' retrospective analysis, the calls from policy makers who are seeking a well-prepared workforce, and our own field of research and development that draws on theoretical perspectives primarily from the social sciences? A core argument of this chapter is that a pluralistic approach to knowledges should be embraced in teacher education. We should not be arguing about whether or not psychological theories of learning have value, whether behaviourism is good or bad, or whether a teacher should have a role of social justice advocate or not. All of these stances are valid and needed in order to be a responsive and planful teacher. In adopting such a pluralistic approach, we run the risk of over-burdening the curriculum with too much stuff and in creating a hodge-podge of ideas that sit in isolation of one another. My argument will be that the idea of conceptual coherence within a programme is too limiting, and likely unachievable given the distinct epistemological roots of various aspects of learning to be a teacher. Rather, we should be considering the narratives, pedagogies, and representations of practice that illustrate to our student teachers how the eclectic sets of knowledges that they learn in teacher education can address the complexity they encounter when actually supporting the learning of a diverse range of students.

I think it is important to note here that I will not be addressing conceptions of teaching in this chapter. For example, in New Zealand the conception of teaching as inquiry (Education Review Office, 2012; Sinnema & Aitken, 2016) and teaching as adaptive expertise (Timperley, 2013) have been well-established in national reports and teacher support materials. Examining the underlying assumptions of how these concepts frame the work and learning of teachers is important, but outside of the scope of this paper. Both, however, may find their strongest links to positivist and postpositivist and pragmatic epistemologies while drawing on concepts from social constructionism. In the next section, I review five underlying epistemic frames of knowledge and how they relate to teacher education curriculum and programming.

Epistemological terrain of teacher education

It is sometimes difficult to make distinctions between naming a school of thought an epistemology or a philosophy. My apologies at the outset to my philosophy colleagues who hold tighter definitions than those that will be presented here. In teacher education programme design, curriculum, and pedagogy (henceforth referred to only as teacher education), we typically draw upon a wide range of ideas and practices, all of which have roots and histories in terms of their epistemic assumptions. My effort here is to describe some of these assumptions about the nature of knowledge production (epistemological assumptions), the foundational beliefs we have about where knowledge resides (philosophical assumptions), and our understandings about the way ideas work to explain phenomena (theoretical assumptions). My intention in providing these descriptions is to later make the case that we need all of these approaches (and those yet to be developed) in order to see fully the complexity of learning to teach—and that integrating these epistemological assumptions with practice may not be a sound approach to teacher education programme design.

Social constructionism

First, we will explore a social constructionist frame of knowledge production and theory. Interactions of people, lived experience, and historical and cultural situatedness are typically core aspects of the epistemological assumptions of social constructionism (Segre, 2016). Put simply, understanding the world is viewed as a subjective and constructed process. One of the assumptions within this epistemology is that meanings are interpreted by individuals and groups, making them contingent on social aspects of the lived world. Part of the social nature of this meaning-making is to acknowledge and value that people have come from their individual lived biography as well as the collective history of the people with whom they identify. We do not begin in the world without a history.

In more recent developments of this general approach to understanding the world, the social nature of interpreting the world through a human-centred lens is being accompanied by a recognition that the physical and material world is also an actor in the process of meaning-making. This new materialism philosophy views the social actors—humans and their histories—as only one element of interpretation rather than the central or only agentic force in the world as it exists (Fox & Alldred, 2018). For teacher education, an ontological assumption within social constructionism is that we can describe teaching in ways that reflect the real world of teaching. The job of the student teacher is to learn to see themselves within the practices of teaching, to take on the role and identity of teacher, and to assimilate into the culture of practice that exists within the school or early childhood centre.

Many of the social science theories that sit within a social constructionist epistemology from philosophy, sociology, anthropology, history, social psychology, and cultural studies are present in teacher education. Within these forms of knowledge, we value the human experience of teaching as well as the material nature of the tools and spaces that shape teaching. We can explore the interactions among people, within organisations, across ideas, and through the histories and cultures of people who are intersecting and colliding in spaces such as classrooms, early childhood centres, schools, and communities. These fields offer several conceptual tools to student teachers that assist them in pulling back the veil of teaching and revealing what lies within. We can teach beginning teachers how to analyse and see teaching through sets of interconnected concepts that have been gleaned from research data and assembled by education researchers. For example, Ladson-Billings (1994) gave us a three-part framework for understanding culturally relevant pedagogy when striving to meet the needs of minoritised students; Macfarlane (2004) gave us the Educultural Wheel which provides a set of five interwoven concepts that support bicultural classroom practices in New Zealand; and Bronfenbrenner (1994) offered us an ecological model of child development that portrays the nested features of the educational system in which teachers work. Frameworks such as these do not show beginning teachers how to practise and they do not guarantee that teachers will be successful in practice if they know these theories. Rather, they provide beginning teachers with the conceptual tools for the design thinking they need to engage in preparing to teach, and ways to interpret the complex interactions they witness and engage in as a teacher.

Positivism and postpositivism

Second, if we use a positivist and postpositivist assumption about knowledge for teacher education, we turn to questions of what kinds of specific teaching practices predict success for students. Positivist and postpositivist epistemologies spawn research and theory built on assumptions of causation and have an end goal of developing theories that can be broadly applied across multiple instances of a phenomenon. In order to do this, the phenomenon needs to be reduced to its constituent parts in such a way that allows those parts to be tightly described with agreed-upon definitions, have the capacity to be measured so that comparisons can be made across instances, and be generalisable across a population of instances (i.e., people, moments in time, or occurrences of the phenomenon).

For teacher education, teaching preservice teachers about psychological theories of learning, theories of development, and protocols for specific instructional routines are rooted in this epistemology. These theories and routines are meant to help teachers predict student behaviour and learning needs in order to be able to plan learning experiences that would be deemed appropriate for a particular age group, reading level, or capability of abstract thinking. Teachers in today's schools are working with classroom populations of students where having knowledge of theories of learning, reading development schemes, and mathematical competence benchmarks provide guiding principles that help predict what to expect out of the chaos of the individual lives that are collected in a single classroom or early childhood centre. These theories offer teachers: patterns and trajectories for learning at the level of group; starting points and best guesses at potential end-points in organising the groups in classroom-level activities; ways to narrow the scope of potential materials; and ways to nurture a nascent learning environment to support the collection of individuals inhabiting that space.

Positivist and postpositivist epistemological starting points can also help explain a desire for external measures of students' outcomes as indicators of learning, progress, or achievement that help beginning teachers understand the roots of many organisational and policy expectations. The assumption is that school is a treatment or intervention that should show some effect on the dependent variable—the students (in the language of experimentation with independent and dependent variables). This causative relationship seems like common sense—if we send our children to school, we should see an impact on them, with the desired impact being evidence of learning or academic achievement. It is important to recognise that we make choices about what to measure and what not to measure in this scenario. Through the positivist and postpositivist lens, we tend to focus on the universal and comparable elements that can be distilled, rather than focusing on the experiential aspects of going to school—the daily routine, the social conditions, the relational qualities, and the sense of wellbeing and belonging felt by the people who populate the school and its community.

Poststructuralism

A third epistemological underpinning for teacher education is poststructuralist thought, which arose in the mid-20th century as a response to structuralist thought that suggested human culture, thought, and language can be understood through its constituent elements and their underlying structural relationships. In today's educational practices, poststructuralism presses us to critique grand narratives and universal ideas in light of lived narratives; to consider the human condition to be partial, multiple, constructed, and malleable across time and space; and to question enlightenment approaches to knowledge construction that rest on experimentation and causality (Hodgson & Standish, 2009). In sum, "Rather than introduce critique as a means of clearing the way for truer descriptions of human affairs, it problematised the idea that a single authoritative description of human activities was possible or even desirable" (Rosiek & Gleason, 2017, p. 34).

Poststructuralist thought allows us to question the motives and purpose of schooling by drawing on critical theories, a core set of ideas within this epistemological frame. Critical theories provide explanations of the nature of power within relationships, institutions, and taken-for-granted norms of language and social interaction. Critical theory also provides a platform for critique that can expose injustices and potentially forge a path toward transformative actions that support a more just orientation to our work in education and the broader society. In teacher education, a poststructuralist epistemology, along with critical theory, allow us to examine with student teachers how schooling practices and societal trends can disadvantage some groups compared to others.

With teachers, we find that exploring a sense of identity (Beauchamp & Thomas, 2009) is a valuable aspect of learning to become a teacher, in addition to learning about social theory and instructional practices. A poststructuralist lens on learning about identity (Britzman, 1994) provides student teachers with the freedom to eschew labels that they have lived with, to construct a sense of self that is less limited than the social narratives they have adopted through their own schooling and life experience, and to explore the multiple ways in which their identity can be shaped. Mayo's interpretation of Foucault's notions of self is helpful here:

> Beyond critical reflection on what we have been taught or what we have experienced, Foucault encourages us to try to think thought differently, to ask ourselves not only how discourse has shielded us from our desires but

also how it has instilled those desires as what we presume ourselves to be. The temptation is to fall into the pleasures of our self-disclosures as a form of knowing and constituting more fully a subject tied to the pleasures of knowing, but not reformulating what it means to make one's life a project. (Mayo, 2000, pp. 110–111)

Today's shift toward modern learning environments in New Zealand, to personalised learning (Bolstad, Gilbert, McDowall, Bull, & Hipkins, 2012), and deeper learning (Darling-Hammond & Oakes, 2019) might be interpreted as a poststructuralist response that re-imagines what schools and learning can be when we remove the linguistic and conceptual structures of lessons, teachers, students, objectives, outcomes, curriculum, and even what it means to learn. Rather than working toward reforming old systems through incremental improvement and abiding by the traditions and grand narrative of the 'real' school experience, these efforts hint at transformative approaches to education that allow us to create new narratives about what it means to have school as a social institution that allows people to make their life the project of learning.

Indigenous knowledges

The fourth epistemological knowledge frame to explore is indigenous knowledges. Indigenous epistemologies speak to the lived experiences and histories of first nations, native people to the land, recognising and sustaining indigenous languages, cultural knowledge, and intellectual histories. The term indigenous recognises the stories, concerns, and struggles of globally colonised communities (Smith, 2012) and the recognition of indigenous knowledges becomes a project of decolonisation. Battiste (2000) reminds us that indigenous ways of knowing are not simply the opposite of Western knowledge. Rather, indigenous epistemologies show us the restrictions that colonial-centred knowledge structures have placed on ways of knowing the world. Indigenous knowledges can serve as a disruption to colonial practices and Western knowledges (Brayboy, 2006; Suina, 2017) and create a space for "cognitive justice" (Smith, 2012, p. 214) for native peoples.

In New Zealand, living out the principles of Te Tiriti o Waitangi is a bicultural commitment for teacher education programmes and is inscribed in the standards of the teaching profession as: "Demonstrate commitment to tangata whenuatanga and Te Tiriti o Waitangi partnership in Aotearoa New Zealand" (Education Council, 2017). This commitment should be reflected in the way that te ao Māori (the world view of Māori) and mātauranga Māori (knowledge and understanding or wisdom of Māori people) is represented in the teacher education curriculum and learning experiences. The ultimate goal of the educational commitment to Māori knowledge and ways of being in the world is to create educational spaces where Māori cultural identities are not only recognised and valued, but are also epistemologically and cognitively valid and legitimate (Bishop & Glynn, 1999).

Pragmatism
The fifth and final epistemological approach we will explore is pragmatism as a school of philosophical thought that centres on the human experience in the everyday world along with the moral and ethical convictions that both guide our choices in action as well as manifest in the actions we choose. In pragmatic thought, the nature of truth lies within what works; that is, what decisions, approaches, or knowledges allow us to move through a particular situation, problem, or dilemma. Pragmatism has roots in Aristotelian thought and the framing of forms of knowledge as technical (techne), philosophical (episteme), and practical (phronesis). In framing knowledges this way, Aristotle was making a point that there are multiple forms of knowledge and, importantly, that knowledge in practice and action is a form of knowledge gained through the wisdom of experience (Sato, Kern, McDonald, & Rogers, 2010). This epistemological stance suggests that practice is theoretical in that it contains its own form of knowing, that sense-making is guided by wisdom in conjunction with the desire to make moral choices. Some scholars view this as an onto-epistemological approach to understand the links between theory and practice (Rosiek & Gleason, 2017). Yet pragmatist philosophers from the 19th and 20th century do not ideologically ascribe to a set of unifying principles about the nature and structure of the world. And in some corners of this philosophy, questions of ontology are considered not worth consideration because they do not allow us to functionally move through the world (Rorty, 1982).

Teacher education is intentionally designed to allow preservice teachers to gain experience in real practice during professional practice placements. These opportunities to learn can be framed in a variety of ways. Pragmatist philosopher John Dewey suggested two distinct approaches (1904/1965): the apprenticeship model and the laboratory model. In the apprenticeship model, student teachers work alongside a practising teacher and learn to imitate what they do. The focus is on learning what is needed to be successful in the short term through mimicking the master. The laboratory model of learning in practice, on the other hand, focuses the preservice teacher on the setting for learning, the processes of learning, and situations or interactions of learning. The student teacher would be asked to carefully observe what is happening, to analyse it, dissect it, understand the processes in practice, and to query how those processes were created. In Dewey's perspective, the laboratory model of learning would help the novice teacher to develop the observational and questioning skills needed for a lifetime of learning in practice. In sum, apprentices learn the *what* of teaching and laboratory observers learn the *how* and *why* of teaching.

When student teachers report that they have learnt more in their professional practice placements than in their university courses, a key factor underpinning this perception may be that the kind of knowledge learnt during the professional practice placement is practical in nature and is viewed as useful in the short-term. There may not actually have been more knowledge gained, but there may be a lack of recognition of the different types of knowledges that underpin the other teacher education programme learning experiences. The knowledges that will feed the lifelong learner as teacher are viewed as less immediate, therefore, less important to master when one's success tomorrow is in question. I suggest that, rather than viewing all of these forms of knowledge as theory versus practice—as the practice of teacher education is typically framed—we should hold all of these forms of knowledge, including practical knowledge from a pragmatist epistemology, as representing the complexity of the knowledge landscape in teacher education. I will explore this further through the lens of complexity theory in the next section.

Knowledge complexity in teacher education

One approach to seeing teacher education in ways that acknowledge the whole of the enterprise is through complexity theory (Cochran-Smith, Ell, Ludlow, Grudnoff, & Aitken, 2014). One of the key aspects of complexity theory is to move our thinking away from linear, causative, and reductionist approaches to understanding complex problems and systems. Instead of imagining chain reactions and logical lines of causation through levers of change and drivers of behaviour (Bryk, 2015), complexity theory sees phenomena through metaphors of ecologies, multidimensional systems, nested feedback loops, and dynamic interactions. Complexity theorists accept chaos and disequilibrium as a given and expect people within the system to self-organise, learn, and change (Byrne, 1998; Morrison, 2008). The emergent nature of a complex system should not be discounted as random. There are boundaries, limitations, and form within the system that support some degree of predictability, although the question of predictability is one of the criticisms of the use of complexity theory for social systems that we desire to control (Davis & Sumara, 2006).

To understand teacher education through complexity theory, we would map out the multiple levels of the entire enterprise in order to understand the various interactions, forces, influences, and nested relationships. Cochran-Smith et al. (2014) describe this system to include:

> teacher education's individual participants (e.g., teacher candidates, school-based cooperating teachers, and course instructors), who are themselves complex systems, particularly university-based or alternate route teacher education programmes and pathways as systems; state or national teacher preparation, accreditation, and certification systems; national and international networks of actors and agencies engaged in the professional preparation of teachers and/or in research about teacher preparation; and the overall global enterprise of recruiting, selecting, preparing, supporting, and evaluating teachers in order to achieve economic, enculturation, and social goals. (p. 7)

This mapping focuses on the variety of actors within the teacher education system(s). I propose that teacher education can also be recognised as a complex set of knowledges that are simultaneously distinct and overlapping, foregrounded, and backgrounded, within teaching situations, and useful for both short-term practice and long-term professional learning. I frame these five stances as epistemologies not to claim that they represent a philosophical perspective on how knowledge is created in teacher education (as we would discuss with an eye toward research problem framing), but to represent a way of thinking, describing, understanding, and designing teacher education. My main intention here is to illustrate that a view toward teacher education as a complex epistemological enterprise provides a different lens on teacher education curriculum and programme design when trying to make sense of policy recommendations that do not view teacher education as epistemologically complex.

Revisiting the relationship between theory and practice in current policy

Partially in response to the results of the newly graduated teacher study (Education Review Office, 2017), along with other national issues, such as a long-standing decline in teacher education applicants and a teacher shortage in certain fields of study, the New Zealand Teaching Council has developed a new set of programme approval requirements that were approved in 2019 and go into full effect in 2022. Some of the core shifts that are coming into the programme accountability framework include adopting the teaching profession's *Our Code, Our Standards* (Education Council, 2017) framework for ITE, focusing programme design on assessment of preservice teacher performance through the implementation of a new assessment framework, and expecting ITE programmes to develop and sustain authentic partnerships with schools and early childhood centres. Underlying these shifts is the message and mandate to strengthen the integration of theory of practice. For example, the rationale for ITE partnerships is framed as: "Authentic partnerships ensure that ITE programmes are well integrated, to avoid theory and practice being enacted separately by different institutions" (p. 11).

The Teaching Council's programme approval requirements explicitly state that, "The programme must integrate theory and practice in an effective and coherent way" (p. 15). The requirements go on to describe the evidence to support meeting this requirement:

> The Council will want to see in provider documentation a diagram setting out the way in which theory and practice have been integrated with a focus on graduates meeting the Standards (in a supported environment). The approval panel will be looking to particularly test:
> - whether theory and practice have been integrated in a coherent way;
> - how the design, structure, delivery and assessments of the programme enable student teachers to build up sufficient theory and professional experience through the programme to be able to demonstrate that they meet the Standards (in a supported environment); and
> - how theory and practice for employment-based programmes will be integrated to ensure that learners receive high-quality teaching while the student teacher is learning teaching practices. (p. 15)

The key phrases in this requirement are "integrate theory and practice" and "effective and coherent way" as discussed below.

Theory and practice integration

Let us first explore what it means to integrate. Standard definitions of integrate suggest putting two or more elements together in such a way that they are combined, harmonious, inter-related, functioning co-operatively, or hold a set of common assumptions or norms. Integrate does not evoke images of putting things together in a way that they remain separate but equal, or that the things we put together may be dramatically different from one another once they are integrated, or that the elements to be integrated could possibly be incommensurable with one another. Integrate also does not suggest that, in order to hold all of the various parts together after integration, we might have to make compromises across the various elements in order to have them co-exist.

Fundamentally, the epistemological approaches discussed in this chapter, however, are distinct views of knowledge construction and existence to be appreciated for how they differ from one another. Positivist and postpositivist approaches that understand the world through generalised approaches of what works in comparison to pragmatists' views that seek what works based on the local circumstances that are laden with value and purposes (Sato, 2005) are fundamentally different theoretical (epistemological) views of the world and how knowledge is created and mobilised. The ontological assumptions of poststructuralism that views the existence of the world as constructed through human thought lies in contrast to the social constructivist view that we are merely trying to construct our lives in a world that already exists. Learning to see and appreciate these differences would not be an exercise of integration. Rather, it may better be described as an exercise in seeing the complexity of teacher education. Within this complexity, we would not only name the participants, the policy landscape, the practice landscape, the career pathways, and the structural elements that are named in the Cochran-Smith et al. (2014, p. 7) quote above, we would also recognise the complexity of the knowledge (epistemological) landscape that comprises teacher education. Sometimes, teachers need a generalisable theory of development or culture to make sense of the trends they see in a group of students. Sometimes, teachers need to interpret the local context like an anthropologist in order to see the implicit culture of a classroom or community. Sometimes, teachers need actions and routines that keep the day running smoothly and safely or they need to make decisions that will benefit the majority of students in a given moment. And sometimes teachers need to ask tough questions about the fair and just nature of the educational system and advocate for change.

These forms of knowledge need to be held simultaneously as distinct windows onto teaching, learning, schooling, and educational processes. The policy is misleading by calling for the integration of theory and practice, both in terms of expecting integration and naming theory and practice as singular and distinct entities. To acknowledge these multiplicities, we should be discussing theories and practices. And rather than imagining teacher education programme design as a smooth integration of multiple theories with multiple practices, we can call on complexity theory to help us name disequilibrium as a normal feature of emergent opportunities for learning, growth, change, decisions, shift, or choice. When disequilibrium occurs—those senses of discomfort, uncertainty, volatility, imbalance, and even conflict within a teacher education programme—amongst ideas or between theories and practices, we should recognise these moments not as a failure of teacher education to integrate theory and practice. These are moments of dialogue and sense-making across the epistemological landscape of knowledges for teaching. It is then the job of teacher educators to provide those sense-making opportunities that help preservice teachers to better see and understand the complex terrain of teaching. Through complexity theory, preservice teachers can actively develop an understanding that pedagogy can be contingent and that learning can be a co-evolution process with teaching (Fels, 2004) as compared to, or in addition to, expecting that pedagogy is a linear process of teacher intervention with students that then produces learning as we might understand it through a positivist/postpositivist perspective.

Theory and practice coherence

Finally, the requirements expect that the integration of theory and practice is done in a coherent way and that this coherence can be represented in a diagram as evidence for programme approval. Two dominant views of coherence in teacher education are structural coherence and conceptual coherence (Feiman-Nemser, 1990; Hammerness, 2006). Structural coherence would lead us to examine the sequencing and alignment within and across courses and learning experiences. Conceptual coherence would lead us to examine epistemological assumptions of the concepts within the curriculum and learning experiences (Kessels, Koster, Lagerwerf, Wubbels, & Korthagen, 2001; Tom, 1997). We tend to hold an assumption that coherence is an innate good in programme design because coherence will steer learning toward agreed-upon concepts or goals. We might also be implicitly working toward coherence as a way to limit contradictions and competition among concepts and ideas. In other words, coherence can serve as a way to mitigate against dissonance and conflict while supporting learning processes that are conceptually integrated and sequenced to be reinforcing over time. Again, we are left to ponder how we can simultaneously value the diverse epistemological terrain of teacher education while also meeting expectations that implicitly seek to even out differences.

A key assumption about requiring coherence (especially coherence that can be depicted in a diagram) is that we can actually arrive at coherence in learning as a static end-state—that is, that we see coherence as a noun, a place to go. Conceiving of programme coherence as a desired end-state of programme design gives external agencies an assurance of quality—programme designers know where they are leading students—and it provides students with some predictability about what is coming next—students know where their learning is going. We must then ask about the implicit assumptions about learning when we so clearly know the end-goal and that programmes have been woven tightly together to ensure that the pathway to that goal is clearly laid out for the learner.

If we guide learning as a process of reaching a predetermined end-goal, our underlying assumptions about the way the world is ordered and knowable may harken back to the positivist/postpositivist epistemological assumptions with the difference being that, instead of knowledge production, we are aiming toward knowledge learning. Behavioural models of learning and apprenticeship learning might align here in that we ask preservice teachers to mimic practices that we already know 'work' based on empirical evidence that can be generalised to their practice. We ask them to practise particular skills, to demonstrate competency with particular routines, or to organise instruction in a particular way based on prior research that illustrated the probability of success with learners when those practices were used. Some aspects of learning to be a teacher can align nicely with this conception of knowledge for teaching we need to support in teacher education. But not all knowledge for teaching can be learnt or taught in this manner.

Other knowledges, from other epistemological stances, are also valuable to learn as a teacher. What if we want preservice teachers to learn how to engage in a community of practice (Wenger, 1998) as a way to learn how to teach? This model of learning would have roots much more strongly from the social constructionist epistemological stance. The construct of 'community' is established and it is the role of the members of the community to construct the interactions that allow the community to learn and work together. The outcomes of learning are much less well-defined in this case if the community is to actually define its joint work. Programme coherence, then, might be considered as becoming a member of a community of practice. Entering a community of practice is a process of observing local practices, learning how to use the intellectual tools within the community, and navigating the social relationships that make up the community, as well as reshaping one's own identity within the community. In order for beginning teachers to find a sense of unity within the community, we would pay close programmatic attention to the community processes—defining the relevant communities within the school, locating the centre and periphery of the community practice, naming the local tools and reified ideas employed in the successful work of the community, understanding the social relationships including conflict, progressive and regressive activities, and marking the moments when beginning teacher identity is being shaped by and having influence on the community activities.

Coherence within a social-constructivist frame might also be considered as opportunities for making sense of the messiness of real-world engagement. Programmes are often designed in a rarified space where the ends of learning can be predetermined, while real-world teaching is messy and sometimes chaotic and the learning is what happens through the experience of a given circumstance. What if messiness, tension, conflict, uncertainty, and dilemmas were part of the curriculum of teacher education and coherence was viewed as intentional processes for confronting, coping, dealing with, managing, and negotiating this messiness? If this were the case, then coherence would be taken up in curriculum and learning activities that brought discontinuity to the surface—dilemma-based cases, critical examination of curriculum, video analysis of lessons gone awry, scenario-based learning activities, real-world observation with intentional theoretical frames for interpretation, community and classroom ethnographies. These curricular and learning activities would allow the student teachers to work through the messiness by 'thinking like a teacher', examine situations through multiple perspectives, and work toward understanding their own stances on issues where no one right answer is obvious. This sense-making coherence would honour artefacts from situated practice (Ball & Cohen, 1999; Putnam & Borko, 2000), create opportunities for addressing the multiple and sometimes diverging concepts that are mobilised in practice, and help beginning teachers develop a 'research attitude' that supports them in interpreting recurring dilemmas of practice (Davis & Sumara, 2006) through the lens of complexity. I'm not sure how to create a diagram of that kind of learning.

Concluding remarks

This discussion has traced how reports from newly graduated teachers led the New Zealand Education Review Office to recommend stronger integration of theory and practice in ITE and how the New Zealand Teaching Council has partially framed its new ITE programme approval requirements to carry that recommendation forward. The idea of theory and practice integration has been problematised based on a discussion of the complex epistemological terrain of teacher education and holding theory and practice as dichotomous entities has been identified as one of the core issues of the new policy to problematise. Additionally, expectations of coherent relationships between theory and practice seem to favour some epistemological stances on what counts as knowledge and how to represent the learning of particular kinds of knowledges.

When policy makers assume that a complex system can be dissected into its constituent parts in order to fix, strengthen, or reform the system, we typically see recommendations that have an underlying linear and causative architecture. For example, the opening statement of the ERO report reads:

> In this evaluation, ERO met with newly graduated teachers (NGTs) and leaders in early learning services and schools to find out how confident and prepared NGTs were as a result of their ITE programme. (Education Review Office, 2017, p. 4)

The suggestion here is one of a linear and causative relationship between ITE programme participation and the degree of confidence that a beginning teacher has to practise teaching. Further, this suggests that the ITE programme is the sole causative agent—not the beginning teachers' prior experience in working with or caring for children, not the subject matter knowledge they gained prior to entering ITE, or the alignment of the teaching assignment they acquired when they were hired as a teacher to what they were prepared to teach, and not the degree of support and mentoring they have access to as a beginning teacher. Causation, linearity, and simplified systems are some of the epistemological assumptions that this chapter has attempted to unpack by examining a variety of ways that knowledge is constructed, warranted, and mobilised within teacher education.

Portraying theory and practice as dichotomous and their relationship as one of applying theory to practice or needing to integrate the two is part of the fallacy in our thinking when we are really working within complex systems. The practice of teaching is theoretical in and of its own right (Sato & Rogers,

2010). Even when teaching is described as practice-based we must remember that practice itself is imbued with decision rules (values), patterned behavior (wisdom), and purpose (what drives a phenomenon) much like theory from the sciences and social sciences—or, as an epistemology, practice comprises pragmatic forms of knowledge (phronesis). Finding ways within the education of teachers to value, make explicit, and represent the diverse array of ideas, theories, and epistemologies could better serve the complex epistemological terrain of teacher education and better support the design of teaching and learning, how preservice teachers understand and enact their identities, and the emergent learning of our students.

Recommendations for further reading

Clandinin, D. J., & Husu, J. (2017) *The SAGE handbook of research on teacher education*. London, UK: Sage.

Ministry of Education. (2011). *Tataiako: Cultural competencies for teachers of Māori learners*. Wellington: Author. Retrieved from: https://teachingcouncil.nz/required/Tataiako.pdf

Ministry of Education. (2018). *Tapasa: Cultural competencies framework for teachers of Pacific learners* Wellington: Author. https://pasifika.tki.org.nz/Tapasa

References

Ball, D. & Cohen, D. (1999). Developing practice, developing practitioners: Toward a practice-based theory of professional education. In L. Darling-Hammond & G. Sykes (Eds.), *Teaching as the learning profession: Handbook of policy and practice* (pp. 3–32). San Francisco, CA: Jossey-Bass Publishers.

Battiste, M. A. (2000). *Reclaiming indigenous voice and vision*. Vancouver, BC: University of British Columbia Press.

Beauchamp, C., & Thomas, L. (2009). Understanding teacher identity: An overview of issues in the literature and implications for teacher education. *Cambridge Journal of Education, 39*(2), 175–189. doi:10.1080/03057640902902252

Bishop, R., & Glynn, T. (1999) *Culture counts: Changing power relations in education*. Auckland: Dunmore Press.

Bolstad, R., Gilbert, J., McDowall, S., Bull, A., & Hipkins, R. (2012). *Supporting future-oriented learning and teaching: A New Zealand perspective*. Wellington: New Zealand Council for Educational Research.

Brayboy, B. M. J. (2006). Toward a tribal critical race theory in education. *The Urban Review, 37*(5), 425–446. doi:org/10.1007/s11256-005-0018-y

Britzman, D. P. (1994). Is there a problem with knowing thyself? Toward a poststructuralist view of teacher identity. In T. Shanahan (Ed.), *Teachers thinking, teachers knowing: Reflections on literacy and language education* (pp. 53–75). Urbana, IL: National Council of Teachers of English.

Bronfenbrenner, U. (1994). Ecological models of human development. *Readings On The Development of Children, 2*(1), 37–43.

Bryk, A. (2015). *Learning to improve: How America's schools can get better at getting better.* Cambridge, MA: Harvard Education Press.

Byrne, D. (1998). *Complexity theory and the social sciences.* New York, NY: Routledge.

Cochran-Smith, M., Ell, F., Ludlow, L., Grudnoff, L., & Aitken, G. (2014). The challenge and promise of complexity theory for teacher education research. *Teachers College Record, 116,* 1–38.

Darling-Hammond, L., & Oakes, J. (2019). *Preparing teachers for deeper learning.* Cambridge, MA: Harvard Education Press.

Davis, B., & Sumara, D. (2006). *Complexity and education: Inquiries in learning, teaching, and research.* New York, NY: Routledge.

Dewey, J. (1904/1965). The relation of theory to practice in education. In M. Borrowman (Ed.), *Teacher education in America: A documentary history* (pp. 140–171). New York, NY: Teachers College Press.

Education Council New Zealand. (2017). *Our code, our standards: Code of professional responsibility and standards for the teaching profession.* Wellington: Author.

Education Review Office. (2012). *Teaching as inquiry: Responding to learners.* Wellington: Author.

Education Review Office. (2017). *Newly graduated teachers: Preparation and confidence to teach.* Wellington: Author.

Feiman-Nemser, S. (1990). Teacher preparation: Structural and conceptual analysis. In W. R. Houston, M. Haberman, & J. Sikula (Eds.), *Handbook of research on teacher education* (pp. 212–233). New York, NY: Macmillan.

Fels, L. (2004). Complexity, teacher education and the restless jury: Pedagogical moments of performance. *Complicity: An International Journal of Complexity and Education, 1*(1), 73–98.

Fox, N. J., & Alldred, P. (2018). New materialism. In P. A. Atkinson, S. Delamont, M. A. Hardy, & M. Williams (Eds.). *The SAGE encyclopedia of research methods.* London, UK: Sage.

Hammerness, K. (2006). From coherence in theory to coherence in practice. *Teachers College Record, 108*(7), 1241–1265.

Hodgson, N., & Standish, P. (2009). Uses and misuses of poststructuralism in educational research. *International Journal of Research & Method in Education, 32*(3), 309–326. doi:10.1080/17437270903259865

Kessels, J., Koster, B., Lagerwerf, B., Wubbels, T., & Korthagen, F. A. J. (2001). *Linking practice and theory: The pedagogy of realistic teacher education.* Mahwah, NJ: Erlbaum.

Ladson-Billings, G. (1994). *The dreamkeepers: Successful teachers of African American children.* San Francisco, CA: Jossey-Bass.

Macfarlane, A. (2004). *Kia hiwa ra! Listen to culture—Māori students' plea to educators.* Wellington: NZCER Press.

Mayo, C. (2000). The uses of Foucault. *Educational Theory, 50*(1), 103–116.

Morrison, K. (2008). Educational philosophy and the challenge of complexity theory. In M. Mason (Ed.), *Complexity theory and the philosophy of education* (pp. 16–31). Chichester, UK: Wiley Blackwell.

Putnam, R. T. & Borko, H. (2000). What do new views of knowledge and thinking have to say about research on teacher learning? *Educational Researcher, 29*(1), 4–15.

Rorty, R. (1982). *The consequences of pragmatism*. Brighton, UK: Harvester Press.

Rosiek, J., & Gleason, T., (2017). Philosophy in research on teacher education: An onto-ethical turn. In D. J. Clandinin & J. Husu (Eds.), *The SAGE handbook of research on teacher education* (pp. 29–48). London, UK: Sage.

Sato, M. (2005). Practical leadership: Conceptualizing the everyday leadership work of teachers. *The New Educator*, *1*(1), 55–71.

Sato, M., Kern, A. L., McDonald, E., & Rogers, C. (2010). On the rough ground: Instantiations of the practical across the teacher professional continuum. *Teacher Education & Practice*, *23*(1), 66–87.

Sato, M., & Rogers, C. (2010). Case methods in teacher education. In P. Peterson, E. Baker, & B. McGaw (Eds.), *International encyclopedia of education* (3rd ed., vol. 7, pp. 592–597). Oxford, UK: Elsevier.

Segre, S. (2016, March). Social constructionism as a sociological approach. *Human Studies*, *39*(1), 93–99.

Sinnema, C., & Aitken, G. (2016). Teaching as inquiry. In D. Fraser & M. Hill (Eds.), *The professional practice of teaching in New Zealand* (5th ed., pp. 79–97). Albany, New Zealand: Cengage Learning.

Smith, L. T. (2012). *Decolonizing methodologies: Research and indigenous peoples* (2nd ed.). London, UK: ZED Books.

Suina, M. (2017). Research is a pebble in my shoe: Considerations for research from a Pueblo Indian standpoint. In E. S. Huaman & B. M. J. Brayboy (Eds.), *Indigenous innovations in higher education: Local knowledge and critical research* (pp. 83–100). Rotterdam, The Netherlands: Sense Publishers.

Teaching Council of Aotearoa New Zealand. (2019). *ITE programme approval, monitoring and review requirements*. Wellington: Author.

Tom, A. R. (1997). *Redesigning teacher education*. Albany, NY: State University of New York Press.

Timperley, H. (2013). *Learning to practice: A paper for discussion*. Wellington: Ministry of Education.

Wenger, E. (1998). *Communities of practice: Learning, meaning, and identity*. Cambridge, UK: Cambridge University Press.

Chapter 14
The changing spaces of education in Aotearoa New Zealand

Letitia Fickel, Julie Mackey, and Jo Fletcher

Introduction

New understandings about the nature of learning, widespread integration of learning technologies, and a change in the physical configuration of learning environments are challenging conventional conceptions of education internationally, and in New Zealand schools. The most visible of these changes is the design of new school buildings to accommodate two or more teachers and multiple groups of children in large, flexible learning spaces. In a simplistic view, these architectural changes are positioned as educational enablers in the mission to equip 21st century learners with the knowledge, skills, and attributes needed to live and work in a rapidly changing world. The rhetoric behind such 'innovative learning environments' often reflects an assumption that changes in the built space will result in changes in pedagogy and improved outcomes for learners. This chapter will test that assumption with particular reference to the bicultural context of Aotearoa, and question the relationships between physical environment, pedagogy, and learner outcomes in order to highlight the dynamic and critical role of teachers working in innovative learning environments.

We begin the chapter by briefly exploring the international research on the changing nature of education and the rationale for reconfiguring physical learning spaces. We then reflect on the relationship of the built learning environment to assumptions about teaching and learning before moving to consider how the kinds of culturally responsive pedagogies demanded in bicultural contexts can be integrated within innovative learning environments. We close the chapter by reviewing current research from Aotearoa New Zealand on challenges and opportunities within innovative learning environments.

The changing nature of education

In today's world, the purpose of education is multifaceted and often contested. Perspectives on the purpose of education range from a commitment to producing measurable learning outcomes around specified curriculum content—thereby increasing collective and individual intellectual and social development—to more holistic perspectives including acculturation, socialisation, and cultural reproduction (see, for example, Bruner, 1996; Egan, 2008; Lamm, 1976). Whatever perspective is taken, education is generally accepted to be vital in preparing learners to function and contribute in the context of a globalised world where technological innovation continues to accelerate, changing how people live, learn, and work. Today's learners need the skills and attributes to understand their place in and their contribution to a global society; the resourcefulness and creativity to tackle 'wicked' problems (Rittel & Webber, 1973) in ways that address social justice and equity; the interpersonal skills to connect, communicate, collaborate, and contribute to knowledge-building activities in teams; and the adaptability, flexibility, and resilience to respond to the unknown. *The New Zealand Curriculum* (Ministry of Education, 2007)—along with contemporary literature (see, for example, Bolstad & Gilbert, 2012; Fullan & Langworthy, 2014)—encapsulates these elements in the role of what is referred to as 'future-focused education'; that is, education to develop citizens who are socially aware lifelong learners able to function in local and global contexts engaging with complex, inter-related issues of sustainability, globalisation, citizenship, and enterprise (Ministry of Education, 2007).

This view of education contrasts with earlier conceptions of education that emerged from 1800s Great Britain where the working class were educated in order for them to be more compliant and able citizens to meet the growing needs of the industrial workforce. At the same time, the colonisation of countries such as Australia, Canada, and Aotearoa New Zealand saw the introduction of education policies aligned with the British system, but with little acknowledgement of the local context or Indigenous peoples and their ways of learning. The model of industrial-age education valued knowledge transmission in a standardised system designed to sort learners on their ability to reproduce knowledge (Gilbert, 2005). It served a time when most school leavers would enter a career for life, and favoured the dominant culture, resulting in detrimental long-term impacts on educational and social outcomes for Indigenous people. For example, in Aotearoa New Zealand, the ongoing historical trauma from colonisation in the 19th century has meant many Māori experience circumstances that negatively impact wellbeing, sustenance, nutrition, and educational outcomes (Chamberlain, 2008, 2014; Martin, 2017; Ministry of Education, 2003, 2004, 2009a, 2009b, 2013).

This transmission model of education is no longer appropriate for the 21st century, when knowledge is now understood as fluid and developed through human interaction, and where the learner's role is to create and deploy knowledge in ever-changing contexts to solve complex problems (Bolstad & Gilbert, 2012; Carvalho & Yeoman, 2018; Fullan & Langworthy, 2014; Gilbert, 2005). Today's future-focused education is grounded in current understandings of socio-constructivist learning generated through multidisciplinary research weaving together research in cognition, emotion, motivation, and learning and development (Dumont, Istance, & Benavides, 2010). Drawing on sociocultural theories of learning from theorists such as Vygotsky (1978) and Bruner (1966), recent research affirms that learning and knowledge is actively constructed by the learner through social negotiation with others. Moreover, learning takes prior knowledge into account and is sensitive to the context in which it occurs. This means that in today's future-focused learning environment, the teacher's challenge is to design deep learning activities (Fullan & Langworthy, 2014) that enable students to build knowledge through collaborative activity in real-world contexts (Bolstad & Gilbert, 2012; McDowall, 2013). Ideally, these activities will be purposeful, meaningful, and bring benefits to the student and their community (Bolstad & Gilbert, 2012).

This shift from an industrial, transmission model of education to a student-centred, knowledge-building model informs the current transformation of school buildings from individual classrooms to large, flexible learning spaces catering for multiple teachers and groups of children. Architectural designs are changing to accommodate and reflect the evolving purposes of education and understanding about learning. Of particular note is the influential OECD

Innovative Learning Environments Project that maintains "learning environments should: make learning and engagement central; view learning as social and often best done collaboratively; be highly attuned to learners' emotions; reflect individual differences; be demanding for all while avoiding overload; use broad assessments and feedback; and promote horizontal connectedness" (OECD, 2017, p. 11). The OECD use of the term 'innovative learning environment' is *not* referring to the physical space alone, but includes the whole ecosystem of organised learning, including the activity and outcomes of learning, and the leadership design decisions that optimise learning for its participants (OECD, 2017, p. 16). Schools in New Zealand, and internationally (for example, Finland, Australia, Portugal), are considering the implications of this use and are investing in flexible learning spaces to support new ways of teaching and learning (Daniels, Tse, Stables, & Cox, 2019).

Reflections on school design: Past and present

Winston Churchill (1943) has famously been quoted as noting that, "We shape our buildings; and afterwards our buildings shape us." This notion of the interplay of the built infrastructure and human activity is evident across all aspects of society, and has been ever present in education, from the early days of one-room schoolhouses, to egg-crate design of single cell classrooms (Lortie, 1975), to today's reconfiguration of learning spaces. However, educators rarely stop to reflect on how the political mechanisms and consequent requirements of education systems and their built environments can shape what, where, when, and how learning takes place. How do our schools reflect our assumptions about what is learning, how it takes place, where it takes place, and what the role of the teacher and the student is in the learning process? Reflecting on historic changes to building design in the past 70 years can illuminate the changing views of learning and teaching across these decades, and provide insights for understanding the recent changes to school design that are being conceptualised.

The modern era of schooling in Western countries such as Great Britain arose during the Industrial Revolution as a means of education for the masses. School designs reflected the goal of preparing workers for factories and other emerging economic activity, and themselves were a reflection of the factory model. Thus, individual single cell classrooms were aligned along a single corridor, supervised by individual teachers, where students moved through the school from grade to grade, much as items in production moved through a factory. This arrangement reflected a view of learning as linear and additive.

The design was set up so that teachers could be interchangeable, as required by the system, and the educational focus was on basic knowledge pertinent to being a 'good worker'. Moreover, the traditional design of schools reflected not only factory designs, but the design of offices and prisons as well, with a focus on rules, surveillance, and control (Dovey & Fisher, 2014; Edwards & Clarke, 2002). In this era, education was very much differentiated based on social position and perceived social and economic futures of the learners. Alongside such schools aimed at the 'working class', there existed public and private schools that served to educate the elite classes along more classical views of preparation for leadership in society, government, and the church.

In Great Britain in the years after World War Two, there emerged a revised view of childhood that fostered a view of learning through active engagement and exploration (Cooper, 1981). Moreover, education was recast to serve the goal of social cohesion and cultivate a democratic society that was more inclusive of all members. As a consequence, the vision of what children should be doing in school underwent change. This gave rise to the era of the open plan school building design from the 1960s to 1980s. Many school buildings shifted from the single cell classroom toward designs that would allow children to move into different areas to seek suitable spaces for learning, rather than be contained at their allotted chair and desk by their teacher. This was a radical change from classrooms arranged to facilitate teacher directed learning (Cooper, 1981), to a design focused on fostering greater student autonomy to lead their own learning via exploration and active engagement. The architectural change to school buildings and the accompanying teaching philosophies emanated not only in Great Britain, but also in the US, and made an impact on school designs in Aotearoa New Zealand (Cameron & Robinson, 1986; Cooper, 1981; Horwitz, 1979).

By 1974, in Aotearoa New Zealand, there were 150 teachers in 52 open plan units. Ten years later in 1984, the number had increased more than ten-fold to 1,650 teachers in 550 open plan units. Approximately 10% of the primary school population were in an open plan unit or variable space (Cameron & Robinson, 1986). In these flexible open plan schools, there was an expectation of better communication between the students and their teachers, and amongst the students to foster social inclusion among students of diverse class, race, ethnicity, and learning needs. The focus on autonomy and active learning was further seen to foster the skills that underpin democratic society. However, over time and in the face of growing dissatisfaction of teachers and parents regarding concerns over classroom management and general efficacy for learning outcomes, there was a move back to single cell, single teacher classrooms. In retrospect, it was recognised that long-term professional development in collaborative teaching was needed for in-service and pre-service teachers to effectively make a pedagogical change in teaching practice that would realise the benefits of more collaborative spaces (Cameron & Robinson, 1986). Moreover, on reflection, there was a resounding silence regarding a bicultural approach and engagement with Māori pedagogies that may have offered more encompassing and responsive approaches for the range of learners.

Secondary school design also reflects a set of assumptions about the nature of knowledge, how it is developed and measured, and how teaching and learning should take place. Overwhelmingly, secondary schools have been designed for teaching that facilitates measured achievement in learning and the awarding of qualifications, rather than reflecting the wider purposes of education. In many countries, including Aotearoa New Zealand, the dominance of national assessment regimes provides a central controlling feature that shapes teaching and learning. The secondary school years are driven by nationally set time frames, subjects, and content knowledge, plus what is assessed and how this is implemented whether through national examinations or assessment systems such as the National Certificate of Educational Achievement (NCEA). Content-focused, teacher-centred, transmission pedagogies with traditional approaches to learning are the prevailing practices within these learning contexts. To cater for this view of teaching and learning, the majority of secondary schools in Aotearoa New Zealand and Great Britain have had a building design that manifests a number of traditional single teacher classrooms organised around departmental or year groups (Clegg & Williams, 2019).

However, as noted, internationally there is now a new era of school design emerging, including in Aotearoa New Zealand, Australia, Germany, and Great Britain, again influenced by a particular view of learning and a particular argument about the needs of young people for the future (Byers, Mahat, Liu, Knock, & Imms, 2018; Ministry of Education, 2015; OECD, 2013; Tse, Learoyd-Smith, Stables, & Daniels, 2015). This new type of school building design has larger, more flexible spaces with smaller break-out spaces surrounding a central hub. Across all these national contexts there is a focus on ensuring these spaces are highly technologically enabled to support blended learning opportunities and designed to be adaptably reconfigured into areas for individuals and small or large groups (Ministry of Education, 2015; Shank, 2005).

These spaces feature a diversity of furniture to support the flexible grouping of students. Within these new learning spaces, there can be two to six teachers with 40 to 150 or more students. Therefore, criteria for their design include visual transparency for monitoring student activity, along with good use of natural light, quality acoustics, good ventilation, and controllability of heating. These new designs reflect more recent understandings from cognitive science of learning: that it is social and often best done collaboratively; they support learners to develop adaptive expertise; that is, the ability to apply knowledge and skills flexibly and creatively as life-long learners (OECD, 2017). The role of the teachers in such environments is no longer to impart knowledge. Rather, it is to facilitate students through problem posing and problem solving so they can become self-regulated, independent learners. Thus, these views of learning and of learning spaces place new expectations on teachers to work collaboratively with colleagues in designing rich learning opportunities that incorporate a range of pedagogical approaches to scaffold student engagement with curriculum content and skills.

Schools are not the only educational settings that have been undergoing changes in design that reflect emerging views of learning. Early childhood centres have adopted building structures to incorporate larger flexible design which often flows out onto an outdoor area, continuing to expand on the ideas from child-centred progressive movement of the early 20th century. As a consequence, early childhood teachers have, for many years, worked alongside their colleagues to teach collaboratively. The *Te Whāriki* curriculum document (Ministry of Education, 2017) for the early years of learning reflects the holistic way that young children grow and develop: "Every aspect of the context—physical surroundings, emotional state, relationships with others and immediate needs—will affect what children learn from any particular experience" (p. 19). Arguably, the early childhood sector has been leading the way and provides a robust exemplar of effective practices in collaborative teaching for the recent move in primary and secondary schooling to larger, flexible learning spaces.

Culturally responsive and inclusive innovative learning environments

Daniels (2010) has suggested that institutional structures—such as the design of school buildings, the structure of the curriculum, and how and what is assessed—are cultural-historical artefacts. As such, their institutional structures and the working assumptions that underpin those structures most often emerge from the views and perspectives of the historically dominant social group. In turn, these institutional structures shape teaching and learning outcomes, often doing so in ways that maintain the status quo of the dominant culture (Anyon, 1997; Oakes, 2005). As detailed in other chapters of this collection, in Aotearoa New Zealand, Māori learners continue to experience educational disadvantage. As Penetito (2015) and Macfarlane (2010) have stressed, the inequality in schooling outcomes for Māori provokes reflection on whether Māori students are failing the New Zealand education system or whether the New Zealand education system is failing Māori students. Extensive research shows that an education system that acknowledges and embeds the culture and language of ethnic minority students has significant impact on enhancing these students' education outcomes (see, for example, Au, 2002; Bishop, Berryman, Tiakiwai, & Richardson, 2003; Ladson-Billings, 2014; Macfarlane, Macfarlane, Graham, & Clarke, 2017). Such a culturally responsive approach supports an inclusive pedagogy where all students are recognised as having valuable knowledge and capabilities (Guerin & Morton, 2017) that enliven the learning context for everyone.

When considering school design and positive learning environments for our students who have been least well-served thus far, in particular Māori, due care and consultation should be taking place to establish culturally and linguistically appropriate learning environments (Berryman, 2013; Macfarlane & Macfarlane, 2015). Spaces and relationships are socially and culturally constructed. In Aotearoa New Zealand, the heart of Māori culture is centred on the marae (place/buildings where formal greeting and discussions take place) of iwi (tribe). The vital essence of each marae is steeped in Māori art, carvings, and a deeply embedded sense of whakapapa (genealogy, lineage, descent) and customs. As Macfarlane (2015) has described, the sociocultural reality converges the boundaries between 'social constructs' such as rituals, feedback, relationships, pedagogy, and care with the 'cultural constructs' of identity (whakapapa), beliefs, feelings, language, and thoughts. Whose culture and how this is represented and enacted by teachers and school leaders are critical. The physical space where learning takes place, or the online space where learners may be interacting and learning with one another, should reflect the language and cultural identity of learners, as well as foster a sense of interdependence and inclusion of all. Within Aotearoa New Zealand, the legal, ethical, and moral weight of the two texts, Te Tiriti o Waitangi and the Treaty of Waitangi, should guide practice. The Treaty's main emphasis is to provide partnership, participation, and protection of Māori culture between Māori and non-Māori communities. The provision of school and early childhood centre buildings that explicitly reflect this bicultural partnership should be foundational.

However, in the move towards innovative learning environments within the context of education in Aotearoa New Zealand, what appears to be neglected within building criteria has been any explicit discourse about the connection between culture and the types of physical spaces that should be created for a bicultural nation (Everatt, Fletcher, & Fickel, 2018; Fletcher, Mackey, & Fickel, 2017). Considering the wealth of research regarding the benefits of culturally responsive teaching, and the ongoing evidence of the underachievement of Māori students and Pacific students, it seems clear that this discourse should be more explicit within government documents relating to the increasing introduction of innovative learning environments. Despite this general lack of bicultural emphasis, some school leaders are engaging with local iwi to understand the cultural and historical significance of their local context and that this knowledge informed, and was reflected in the design of, buildings, landscaping, internal organisation, and naming conventions.

Research insights from Aotearoa New Zealand: Challenges and opportunities

Innovative learning environments have been advocated as a mechanism to positively impact on student outcomes in schooling (Ministry of Education, 2015). Yet, in a systematic review of research on innovative learning environments and the impact on improving student learning, which included one study where space was isolated as a variable, there was little evidence of innovative learning environments in Australasia improving student learning outcomes (Byers, Imms, & Hartnell-Young, 2014; Byers et al., 2018). There is a noticeable need for more research to understand the impact of learning spaces on student learning in general, and the cultural impact of learning spaces for Indigenous learners in particular.

Whatever the aesthetics of the built environment, a substantial level of intricacy occurs when teachers are in a collaborative teaching space and need to spend time together to plan, evaluate, share information, review logistics, and decide upon teaching strategies and next steps of learning (Johnson, 2003; University of Kansas, 2014). This can impact upon teacher workload, stress levels, and the positivity within a learning environment. There are distinct benefits to be realised when teachers work closely together developing their collaborative expertise to improve student learning outcomes (Hattie, 2015). This was evidenced in our research when teachers spoke of the value of working alongside others, particularly working with team leaders, in co-teaching situations. Teachers recognised the potential to learn from each other to improve the learning environment and the increased capacity of the co-teaching team to cater for differentiated learning to meet diverse student needs (Mackey, O'Reilly, Jansen, & Fletcher, 2017). However, successful co-teaching that builds on the strengths of the team involves interdependency and complementarity and requires teachers to overcome interpersonal and professional differences in their quest to work together (Pratt, 2014). We found that school leadership is absolutely critical to the transition to collaborative teaching and that a lack of 'buy in' by teachers can seriously hamper the development of effective collaborative teaching practices. Our research findings (Everatt et al., 2018; Mackey et al., 2017) endorsed the critical role of professional development to justify and enable co-teaching pedagogy, build collaboration and interpersonal skills for teachers to work together effectively, and support the transition into flexible learning spaces.

Although a principal may be tasked with changing the approach to learning, this needs to be strongly supported by long-term effective professional learning development as well as the formation of informal learning mechanisms and a commitment to inquiry within the innovative learning environment. For teacher practice to change, numerous opportunities to trial other approaches to teaching are required in a safe and supportive environment. Co-teaching involves a culture of professionalism, support, and accountability in concert with thorough processes to strengthen teacher knowledge, understandings, and development (Troen & Boles, 2012). A sensitive balance between teacher autonomy and collective ownership in collaborative learning environments necessitates a sound theoretical framework with shared agreement about outcomes for students. Such shared agreement enhances decision making on explicit teaching to meet individual learners' needs that guides co-joint teacher decisions to improve student learning (Timperley, Wilson, Barrar, & Fung, 2007). In order to change the status quo, appropriate professional learning opportunities to develop teachers' shared understanding and support social learning conditions are needed to optimise the shared resources and expertise of the teaching team (Lynch, Madden, & Doe, 2015).

That the domains where students learn can include—as well as combine—physical and virtual sites, has challenged traditional assumptions about student learning. Edwards and Miller (2007) explain how, in education, learning has often been 'centred' as occurring within particular institutional sites, yet in discourses around the 'decentring' of learning, there is a wide range of contexts where learning can take place. For example, online and face-to-face flexible opportunities, where students are able to actively engage in learning and develop self-regulated learning to fit their individual needs, are advocated as being an intrinsic part of the innovative learning environments. However, in a national survey, many teachers and principals in Aotearoa New Zealand challenged assumptions that online and self-regulated learning can only occur in innovative learning environments (Everatt & Fletcher, 2019; Everatt et al., 2018). Respondents stressed that the strengths of the teacher, and the relationships with colleagues, are key to what pedagogical approaches to learning are implemented, rather than the type of building they occur within. The principal of a school serving a multicultural and lower socioeconomic community explained the importance of relationships for staff and students, noting the power of teacher collaboration and the benefits of students being exposed to different perspectives of the curriculum.

As noted previously, managing change for teachers to effectively work in innovative learning environments is underpinned by well-planned, and sustained, professional learning development (Alerator & Deed, 2013; Mackey, O'Reilly, Jansen, & Fletcher, 2018; Villa, Thousand, & Nevin, 2013). However, our research on innovative learning environments has found that the delivery of such professional development at the national level appears to have been lacking and, when it has happened, was often led by the principal taking the initiative with varying degrees of success. It is apparent to us that, while school leaders recognise that every context is unique depending on the people involved, wider demographics, and school characteristics, there are fundamental aspects that would benefit from a systemic approach. We would argue that, with appropriate investment in professional development and learning, Aotearoa New Zealand could be leading the way in developing co-teaching strategies that maximise the opportunities afforded by the combination of flexible learning spaces, collaborative pedagogies, and culturally responsive approaches.

Conclusion

Future-focused learning, and repositioning and rethinking the roles of the teacher, the learner, and their whānau, has been an ongoing process within Aotearoa New Zealand education sectors. For the early childhood sector, the concept of building spaces that are large and flexible, where multiple teachers work collaboratively together, has been evident in many centres and underpinned by their curriculum document. However, for primary—and even more particularly for secondary schooling—this has opened up the need for a radical change to the ways teachers, students, and whānau think about learning in innovative learning environments in a bicultural society. Aotearoa New Zealand is unique in the strong thrust for a deeply embedded bicultural society. In order to make this change, the education system has been tasked with incorporating bicultural practices within teaching and learning for our upcoming generations. As discussed in this chapter, Westernised contexts are frequently normalised, which marginalises our Indigenous learners. We advocate that further consideration and accountable implementation is needed when considering the architectural types of building structures in schooling. Careful consultation with local iwi on ways to enhance school building designs so that they strongly reflect the bicultural nature of Aotearoa New Zealand is critical, to ensure that the essence of the Treaty of Waitangi/Te Tiriti o Waitangi is evident. Furthermore, sustained and effective professional development needs to be resourced to ensure effective changes to teaching collaboratively in innovative learning environments.

Recommendations for further reading

Tse, H. M., Daniels, H., Stables, A., & Cox, S. (2019). *Designing buildings for the future of schooling: Contemporary visions for education*. Oxford, UK: Routledge.

References

Alerator, S., & Deed, C. (2013). Teacher adaption to open learning spaces. *Issues in Educational Research, 23*(3), 315–330.

Anyon, J. (1997). *Ghetto schooling: A political economy of urban education*. New York, NY: Teachers College Press.

Au, K. (2002). Multicultural factors and the effect of the instruction of students of diverse backgrounds. In A. E. Farstrup & S. J. Samuels (Eds.), *What research has to say about reading* (pp. 392–414). Newark, DE: International Reading Association.

Berryman, M. (2013). Leaders' use of classroom evidence to understand, evaluate and reform schooling for Indigenous students. In M. Lai & S. Kushner (Eds.), *A developmental and negotiated approach to school self-evaluation* (pp. 147–161). Bingley, UK: Emerald Group.

Bishop, R., Berryman, M., Tiakiwai, S., & Richardson, C. (2003). *Te Kōtahitanga: The experiences of year 9 and 10 Māori students in mainstream classrooms*. Wellington: Ministry of Education.

Bolstad, R., & Gilbert, J. (2012). *Supporting future-oriented learning and teaching—A New Zealand perspective*. Wellington: New Zealand Council for Educational Research. Retrieved from: https://www.educationcounts.govt.nz/__data/assets/pdf_file/0003/109317/994_Future-oriented-07062012.pdf

Bruner, J. (1966). *Towards a theory of instruction*. Cambridge, MA: Harvard University Press.

Bruner, J. (1996). *The culture of education*. Cambridge, MA: Harvard University Press.

Byers, T., Imms, W., & Hartnell-Young, E. (2014). Making the case for spaces on teaching and learning. *Curriculum and Teaching, 29*(1), 5–19. doi.org/10.7459/ct/29.1.02

Byers, T., Mahat, M., Liu, K., Knock, A., & Imms, W. (2018). *A systematic review of the effects of learning environments on student learning outcomes*. Melbourne, VIC: The University of Melbourne. Retrieved from: http://www.iletc.com.au/wp-content/uploads/2018/07/TR4_Web.pdf

Cameron, P., & Robinson, G. (1986). Ten years of open plan. *set: Research Information for Teachers, 1*(2), 2–19.

Carvalho, L., & Yeoman, P. (2018). Framing learning entanglement in innovative learning spaces: Connecting theory, design, and practice. *British Educational Research Journal, 44*(6), 1120–1137.

Chamberlain, M. (2008). *PIRLS 2005/2006 in New Zealand: An overview of national findings from the second cycle of the Progress in International Reading Literacy Study (PIRLS)*. Wellington: Ministry of Education.

Chamberlain, M. (2014). *PIRLS 2010/11 in New Zealand: An overview of findings from the third cycle of the Progress in International Reading Literacy Study (PIRLS)* (revised ed.). Wellington: Ministry of Education.

Churchill, W. (1943). Prime Minister speech in the House of Commons, British Parliament, 18 October 1943. *HC Deb 28 October 1943 vol 393 cc403-73*.

Clegg, P., & Williams, J. (2019). Schools as an enabler for progressive teaching. In H. M. Tse, H. Daniels, A. Stables, & S. Cox (Eds.), *Designing buildings for the future of schooling: Contemporary visions for education* (pp. 67–86). Oxford, UK: Routledge.

Cooper, I. (1981). The politics of education and architectural design: The instructive example of British primary education. *British Educational Research Journal, 7*(2), 125–136.

Daniels, H. (2010). Implicit or invisible mediation in the development of interagency work. In H. Daniels, A. Edwards, T. Engestrom, T. Gallagher, & S. Ludvigsen (Eds.), *Activity theory in practice: Promoting learning across boundaries and agencies* (pp. 105–125). London, UK: Routledge.

Daniels, H., Tse, H. M., Stables, A., & Cox, S. (2019). School design matters. In H. M. Tse, H. Daniels, A. Stables, & S. Cox (Eds.), *Designing buildings for the future of schooling: Contemporary vision for education* (pp. 41–66). Oxford, UK: Routledge.

Dovey, K., & Fisher, L. (2014). Designing for adaptation: The school as socio-spacial assemblage. *The Journal of Architecture, 19*(1), 43–63. doi:10.1080/13602365.2014.882376

Dumont, H., Istance, D., & Benavides, F. (Eds.). (2010). *The nature of learning: Using research to inspire practice. Educational Research and Innovation*. Paris: OECD Publishing. doi:10.1787/9789264086487-en

Edwards, R., & Clarke, J. (2002). Flexible learning, spaciality and identity. *Studies in Continuing Education, 24*(2), 153–165. doi:10.1080/0158037022000020965

Edwards, R., & Miller, K. (2007). Putting the context into learning. *Pedagogy, Culture and Society, 15*(3), 263–274.

Egan, K. (2008). *The future of education: Reimagining our schools from the ground floor up.* London, UK: Yale University Press.

Everatt, J., & Fletcher, J. (2019). Children with learning difficulties and the move to innovative learning environments. *Australian Journal of Learning Difficulties: Special issue on reading and writing difficulties, 6*(1), 49–73.

Everatt, J., Fletcher, J., & Fickel, L. (2018). School leaders' perceptions on reading, writing and mathematics in innovative learning environments. *Education 3–13, 47*(8), 906–919. doi:10.10 80/03004279.2018.1538256

Fletcher, J., Mackey, J., & Fickel, L. (2017). A New Zealand case study: What is happening to lead changes to effective co-teaching in flexible learning spaces? *Journal of Educational Leadership, Policy and Practice (JELPP) Special edition: Leading innovative learning environments, 32*(1), 66–79.

Fullan, M., & Langworthy, M. (2014). *A rich seam: How new pedagogies find deep learning.* London, UK: Pearson.

Gilbert, J. (2005). *Catching the knowledge wave: The knowledge society and the future of education.* Wellington: NZCER Press.

Guerin, A. P., & Morton, M. (2017). Sociocultural perspectives on curriculum, pedagogy and assessment to support inclusive education. In G. Noblit (Ed.), *Oxford research encyclopedia of education.* New York, NY: Oxford University Press.

Hattie, J. (2015). *What works best in education: The politics of collaborative expertise.* London, UK: Pearson.

Horwitz, R. A. (1979). Psychological effects of the 'open plan classroom'. *Review of Educational Research, 49*(1), 71–85.

Johnson, B. (2003). Teacher collaboration: Good for some, not so good for others. *Educational Studies, 29*(4), 337–350.

Ladson-Billings, G. (2014). Culturally relevant pedagogy 2.0: a.k.a. the remix. *Harvard Educational Review, 84*(1), 74–84. doi:10.17763/haer.84.1.p2rj131485484751

Lamm, Z. (1976). *Conflicting theories of instruction: Conceptual dimensions.* Berkely, CA: McCutchan.

Lortie, D. C. (1975). *Schoolteacher: A sociological inquiry.* New York, NY: John Wiley.

Lynch, D., Madden, J., & Doe, T. (2015). *Creating the outstanding school.* London, UK: Oxford Global Press.

Macfarlane, A. (2010). Motivating Māori students in literacy learning: Listening to culture. In J. Fletcher, F. Parkhill, & G. Gillon (Eds.), *Motivating literacy learners in today's world* (pp. 89–98). Wellington: NZCER Press.

Macfarlane, A. (2015). Sociocultural foundations. In A. Macfarlane, S. Macfarlane, & M. Webber (Eds.), *Sociocultural realities: Exploring new horizons* (pp. 19–35). Christchurch: Canterbury University Press.

Macfarlane, A., & Macfarlane, S. (2015). Education, psychology and culture: Towards synergetic practices. *Knowledge Cultures Journal, 3*(2), 66–81.

Macfarlane, A., Macfarlane, S., Graham, J., & Clarke, T. H. (2017). Social and emotional learning and indigenous ideologies in Aotearoa New Zealand: A biaxial blend. In E. Frydenberg (Ed.), *Social and emotional learning in Australia and the Asia–Pacific* (pp. 273—289). Singapore: Springer.

Mackey, J., O'Reilly, N., Jansen, C., & Fletcher, J. (2017). What do teachers and leaders have to say about co-teaching in flexible learning spaces? *Journal of Educational Leadership, Policy and Practice, 32*(1), 93–106.

Mackey, J., O'Reilly, N., Jansen, C., & Fletcher, J. (2018). Leading change to co-teaching in primary schools: A 'Down Under' experience. *Education Review, 70*(4), 465–485.

Martin, R. (2017). *Te whakarauora reo nō tuawhakarere—Giving our children what we missed out on: Māori language revitalisation for Māori/English bilingualism*. Unpublished doctoral thesis, University of Canterbury, Christchurch. Retrieved from: https://pdfs.semanticscholar.org/1152/a2dd29de1bd259a5ecbe95ee41a821eea0df.pdf

McDowall, S. (2013). Using ICT to develop knowledge-building communities in subject English and the arts. *set: Research Information for Teachers, 1, 29-36.*

Ministry of Education. (2003). *Raising the achievement of Pasifika students: Literacy leadership*. Wellington: Learning Media.

Ministry of Education. (2004). *Focus on Pasifika achievement in reading literacy*. Retrieved from: https://www.educationcounts.govt.nz/publications/pasifika/2119

Ministry of Education. (2007). *The New Zealand curriculum*. Wellington: Learning Media.

Ministry of Education. (2009a). *Ka hikitia: Managing for success Māori education strategy*. Wellington: Author.

Ministry of Education. (2009b). *Te piko o te māhuri, terā te tupu o te rākau, Language and literacy in marae-based programmes: Literacy, language and numeracy research*. Wellington: Author.

Ministry of Education. (2013). *Pasifika education plan 2013–2017*. Wellington: Author.

Ministry of Education. (2015). *Designing schools in New Zealand. Requirements and guidelines*. Wellington: Author. Retrieved from: http://www.education.govt.nz/assets/Documents/Primary-Secondary/Property/Design/Design-guidance/DSNZ-version-1-0-20151014.pdf

Ministry of Education. (2017). *Te whāriki: He whāriki mātauranga mō ngā mokopuna o Aotearoa: Early childhood curriculum*. Wellington: Author.

Oakes, J. (2005). *Keeping track: How schools structure inequality*. New Haven, CT: Yale University Press.

OECD. (2013). *Innovative learning environments*. Educational Research and Innovation. Paris: OECD Publishing. doi:10.1787/9789264203488-en

OECD. (2017). *The OECD handbook for innovative learning environments*. Educational Research and Innovation. Paris: OECD Publishing. doi:9789264277274-en

Penetito, W. (2015). Choosing to be both provincial and cosmopolitan: Straddling two worlds. In A. Macfarlane, S. Macfarlane, & M. Webber (Eds.), *Sociocultural realities: Exploring new horizons* (pp. 36–51). Christchurch: Canterbury University Press.

Pratt, S. (2014). Achieving symbiosis: Working through challenges found in co-teaching to achieve effective co-teaching relationships. *Teaching and Teacher Education, 41,* 1–12.

Rittel, H., & Webber, M. (1973). Dilemmas in a general theory of planning. *Policy Sciences, 4*(2), 155–169. doi:10.1007/bf01405730

Shank, M. J. (2005). Common space, common time, common work. *Educational Leadership, 62*(8), 16–19.

Timperley, H., Wilson, A., Barrar, H., & Fung, I. (2007). *Teacher professional learning and development*. Wellington: Ministry of Education.

Troen, V., & Boles, K. (2012). *The power of teacher teams*. Thousand Oaks, CA: Corwin.

Tse, H. M., Learoyd-Smith, S., Stables, A., & Daniels, H. (2015). Continuity and conflict in school design: A case study from Building Schools for the Future. *Intelligent Buildings International, 7*(2–3), 64–82. doi:10.1080/17508975.2014.927349

University of Kansas. (2014). *Keys to successful co-teaching*. Retrieved from: http://www.specialconnections.ku.edu/?q=collaboration/cooperative_teaching

Villa, R. A., Thousand, J. S., & Nevin, A. I. (2013). *A guide to co-teaching: New lessons and strategies to facilitate student learning*. Thousand Oaks, CA: Corwin.

Vygotsky, L. S. (1978). *Mind in society: The development of higher psychological processes*. Cambridge, MA: Harvard University Press.

Index

accountability 37, 127
    children's own accountability for mistakes 99
    shared accountability 79–80
    teachers 116, 218, 245
achievement 68, 69, 70, 71, 73, 75, 90, 102
    see also underachievement
    and culturally relevant pedagogy 13
    data analysis 143, 144, 235, 239
    Kāhui Ako | Communities of Learning 79, 82
    and learning spaces 123
    link to student engagement 133, 134, 135, 138, 139, 144
    in meritocracy 48
    PISA (Programme for International Students Assessment) 113, 127
    reporting 127
    and secondary school design 259
    standards 100
activism
    digital activism 205, 209
    Māori 57–61
adaptive learning 144, 236, 260
adolescent learners 99–103
agency 73, 89, 94, 101, 115, 116, 117, 140, 145, 227, 232
Ahmed, Farid 179
ako (reciprocal teaching and learning) 18, 21, 79, 144, 212
American Educational Research Association (AERA) 225–31
anger 179, 180, 181, 184–85, 187, 188, 189
    riri 185, 186

anxiety 64, 102, 179, 181, 184, 186, 187, 188, 190
apprenticeship model of learning 242–43
Ardern, Jacinda 47, 62, 152, 179, 180, 185
Aristotle 3, 25, 73, 161, 181, 242
aroha 179–80, 185, 195
Artificial Intelligence (AI) 144–45
assessment
    and curriculum relationship 114, 126–28
    data 143, 144, 235, 239
    secondary schools 259
attachment 90–92, 97
attention deficit hyperactivity disorder 96
Australasian Survey of Student Engagement 142
Australia, New Zealand's colonial comparisons 54–55
authoritarianism 35
autonomy 18, 32, 36, 94, 97, 121, 124, 125, 258, 263
Awhinatia dimension of Hikairo Schema 16, 17

balance of power principle of Hikairo Schema 18
Beeby, Clarence 5
behavioural engagement 139, 144, 145
Bernstein, Basil 72
Best Evidence Synthesis (BES) project 156
biculturalism 6, 7, 63, 118, 146, 238, 241–42, 259, 261–62, 265
"big data" 143
blended learning 134, 136, 145, 146, 259

Bourdieu, Pierre 73–74, 75
Brash, Don 61
bullying 98, 99, 102, 140–41
    cyberbullying 140–41
burnout 188, 191–92

calming down 93, 98
Canterbury College 166–67
    see also University of Canterbury
capitalism 31, 37, 71
    see also cultural capital; economic capital; social capital
Carr, Rod 168
challenging behaviour 93
child rearing 32
Children's Commissioner 62
Christchurch
    earthquakes, 2010–2011 168–70, 179, 189–95 (*see also* Student Volunteer Army (SVA), Christchurch)
    mosque attacks, 15 March 2019 47–48, 151–52, 179–80, 203
citizenship 176–77, 255
    see also digital democratic citizenship
    democratic 204–05
    global 208, 209–10
class conflict 71–72
classrooms *see* school learning spaces
Clayton, Patti 171
co-construction of learning contexts 18, 19, 93, 94
cognitive engagement 138, 139, 141, 145
cognitive strategies 96, 190–91
collaboration 69–70, 78, 79, 80, 81
    digital media 207, 209, 212
    Hikairo Schema 16–17, 18, 19
    learning networks 121, 122–23, 137, 143–44
    and school learning spaces 140, 255, 256, 257, 262–63, 264–65

teacher leadership 223–24, 229, 230, 231
collaborative professionalism 223–24
collective consciousness 70
colonialism 51, 61, 241, 255–56
    see also decolonisation
    colonial schools 53
    colonisation impacts on Māori 48, 49–51, 54–55, 57–58, 59, 61–62, 182, 193, 195, 256
    New Zealand history in schools 61–62
    settler colonialism 49–51
communication channels 205
Communities of Learning *see* Kāhui Ako | Communities of Learning
communities of philosophical inquiry 162–63
community engagement 167, 170–76, 177–78
Community of Inquiry pedagogy 136, 137, 212
community of practice 248–49
compassion 207, 208, 211, 212
    see also empathy
competencies
    for 21st century learners 121, 125
    key competencies of adolescents (13–18 years) 100–03
    key competencies of children (5–6 to 12 years) 96–99
    key competencies of young children (2.5 years to school entry) 90–94
    NZC key competencies 99–100, 119–20, 122
complexity theory 243–44, 247
computational thinking 211
conflict theory 72, 81
connections 17, 75–76, 80, 81, 82, 145, 255
    Māori 193–94
coping strategies 96, 100
critical education 37–39

critical perspectivism 204, 206, 207, 213
critical theory 240
critical thinking 202, 211, 212
cultural capital 74–75
cultural competence 9, 13, 22
    tools and resources 9–10, 13 (*see also* Hikairo Schema)
cultural, ethnic and racial diversity 12–13, 21, 22, 151–52, 153, 156, 157, 159, 238
    in context of globalised world 75
    in emotions 185
    and service learning 172, 173, 174
cultural invasion 53–54
cultural lag 18
culturally responsive learning environments 260–62
culturally-based evidence and practice 14–15, 21–22
curriculum
    and diversity 152, 155
    Hangarau Matihiko 211
    New Zealand colonial history 57, 61–62, 113
    New Zealand Curriculum (NZC) 94–95, 99–100, 114, 118–20, 122, 124–25, 152, 177, 255
    New Zealand history 62, 113
    Te Marautanga o Aotearoa (TMoA) 95, 114, 118–19
    Te Whāriki (Ministry of Education) 15, 89, 93, 94, 114, 152, 192, 260
    technology 211
curriculum studies 112–13, 128–29
    assessment relationship 126–28
    contemporary and emerging issues 117–18
    curriculum developments 115
    curriculum discourses 115–16
    knowledge and curriculum 118–20
    Māori-medium curricula 118–19
    Pasifika perspectives 119
    teachers' curriculum role 116, 117, 120, 124–25, 128
    tight–loose curriculum reform 123–26
    twenty-first century learning and future-focused curriculum 121–23
    types of curriculum 114–15
cyberbullying 140–41

Darling-Hammond, Linda 11
Darwin, Charles 181–82
data and data management systems 81–82, 143, 235
Dearden, Robert 29, 30
decolonisation 59–60, 63–64
    see also colonialism
deep learning 121, 241, 256
deficit theorising 62, 140
Delpit, Lisa 11
Department of Education 57, 60
    see also Ministry of Education
Descartes, René 181
developmental systems theory 90
Dewey, John 7, 10–11, 25, 28–29, 204, 221, 242–43
difference *see* diversity
digital democratic citizenship 201, 204–05, 207–11
    activism 205, 209
    global 209
digital media literacy 204, 205, 206, 207–11, 213
    online content creation 203, 206, 207, 208–09
    role of schooling and education 211–12
"digital natives" 203
digital technology 121–22, 123, 134, 138, 140, 143, 145–46
    see also flexible and distance learning; media literacy; online modes of education

availability 208
risks and negative influences 140–41, 203, 204, 210–11
skills and capabilities 208, 211
disability/ability diversity 152, 153, 156
disasters
  emotional responses 189–90
  responses 176–77 (*see also* Student Volunteer Army (SVA), Christchurch)
disengagement of students 135–36, 140
distance learning *see* flexible and distance learning
diversity 151–53, 156–57, 163, 258, 263
  see also cultural, ethnic and racial diversity; inclusive education; norms
  acknowledging differences 32–33, 158–59, 160–61
  dialogue across differences 33
  difference positioned as deficit 153–55, 159–60
  experience of teachers 74–75
  holistic approach 159–63
  polarising effect of media algorithms 204
  and teacher education 12–13, 235
Durie, M. 21
Durkheim, Émile 70–71

early childhood education (ECE)
  design of centres 260
  Hikairo Schema 15
  key competencies of young children (2.5 years to school entry) 90–94
  Kōhanga reo 60, 89
  preparation for school 89–90
  Te Whāriki (Ministry of Education) 15, 89, 93, 94, 114, 152, 192, 260
  understanding learners 89–94
earthquakes, Canterbury, 2010–2011 168–70, 179, 189–95

see also Student Volunteer Army (SVA), Christchurch
economic capital 74, 75
"educated person"
  attributes of women 32
  distinguishing features 30, 31–33
education
  see also early childhood education (ECE); higher education; inclusive education; Māori education; policies and practices in education; primary schools and education; psychology of education; secondary schools and education; sociology of education
  changing nature 255–57
  colonial schools 53
  democratic rights 2, 5, 72
  feminist research 5–6
  fundamental questions 26
  future-oriented 121–23, 255, 256
  interdisciplinary nature of 3–5
  interdisciplinary study 3–4
  learning, the moral purpose 225, 227, 229, 231, 255
  meaning 29–31
  place in society 5
  politics of 31, 37, 116, 126–27
Education Council 236, 245
education outside the classroom (EOTC) 114
Education Review Office 156, 234, 235, 244, 250
Education Work Programme 82
educational theory 10–12, 21
educators' roles 6–7
  see also principals; teachers and teaching
Educultural Wheel 238
Eisner, E. 11
e-learning *see* digital technology; online modes of education
Emotion Facial Action Coding system 182

emotional competence 93, 94, 96, 97–98, 99
emotional engagement 138, 139, 141, 145
emotional intelligence 180, 184, 187, 188, 190
emotional labour 187–88, 190
emotional regulation 184, 188–89, 190, 191, 192
emotions
　in education 32, 186–89, 195, 256
　historical trauma 193–95
　impact of disaster 189–92, 193
　Māori perspectives on origin 182–83
　Māori theories 185–86, 195
　Western perspectives on origin 180–82
　Western theories 184–85, 195
empathy 32, 160, 161, 180, 207, 212
　see also compassion
engagement of students 133–36, 146, 175, 260
　case study 145–46
　as conceptualised in Aotearoa 138–39
　in flexible and distance learning 136–46
　key issues and developments 143–45
　organisational approaches 139–43
Engels, Friedrich 71–72
English language 53
Epicurean philosophy 181
epigenetics 90
epistemic exploitation 59
epistemology (study of knowledge) 33, 34, 38
equity 11, 17, 22, 31, 69, 77–78, 82, 112, 115, 138, 139, 144, 157, 158, 162, 255
　see also biculturalism; colonialism; decolonisation; diversity; Treaty of Waitangi / Te Tiriti o Waitangi; underachievement

Equity Unbound courses 212
ethics 33, 38–39, 145, 204, 205, 206, 207, 242
ethnic diversity *see* cultural, ethnic and racial diversity
evidence-based practice 13–14, 79, 81–82
executive functioning 96, 98–99, 101
expectations 76, 79

failure, toleration of 99
feminism 5
　critique of Peters' 'educated man' notion 31–32
　feminist postmodernism 77
　Māori women 59
　theory and pedagogy research 5–6
flexible and distance learning 133–34
　see also digital technology; online modes of education
　cultural sensitivity 143–44, 146
　student engagement 136–46
flow theory 137–38
Foucault, Michel 240–41
Freire, Paulo 33–36, 53, 54, 77
Freud, Sigmund 181, 182
friendships 93, 96, 98, 102
functionalist theories 71
future-oriented education 121–23, 255, 256

Gay, Geneva 11
gender and sexuality diversity 152, 153, 157
Global Digital Citizen Foundation 209–10
globalisation 75, 78, 121, 255
　citizenship 208, 209–10
Goleman, Daniel 180

habitus 73–74
Hangarau Matihiko 211
hidden curriculum 114–15

higher education
  see also University of Canterbury;
    University of Otago
  critical citizenship 212
  neoliberal policy ideas 37
  student engagement 134, 139,
    141–44, 145–46
  universities as critic and conscience
    of society 37–38
Hikairo Schema 13, 14–15, 22
  core principles 17–18, 20
  dimensions 15–17
  poutama (five stages of
    competency) 20
  ways to use 19–20
Hirst, Paul 29, 30
historical amnesia 61
history, New Zealand, in schools 61–62
Hobson's Pledge 61
hopo 185–86
Huataki dimension of Hikairo
  Schema 16
Human Rights Act 1993 152
humanisation 34
Hurricane Katrina, New Orleans 171,
  173, 177

identity and self 101–02, 103, 162,
  240–41
ideologies 19
  curriculum 116–17, 128–29
Ihi dimension of Hikairo Schema 16
Ihumātao occupation 64
Ilustre, Vincent 171, 173
inclusive education 72, 143, 151, 152,
  155–59, 162, 163, 258
  inclusive learning
    environments 260–62
independence 94, 96
Indigenous peoples 14, 49, 51, 255
  knowledges 241
indoctrination 30–31

inequity see equity
information
  ease of access 202, 204–05, 208
  misinformation and fake
    information 203, 204, 205, 207
  role in supporting power
    structures 208
information channels 76, 82
Initial Teacher Education (ITE) see
  teacher education
inner speech 93
innovative learning environments see
  school learning spaces
institutional racism 52–53, 57, 62–63
interactive media 203, 206, 209
intergenerational closure 76
*International Journal of Teacher
  Leadership* 9(1), 2018 225–26
internet 203, 204, 205, 208, 209
  safety 140–41, 203, 204, 210–11
Investing in Educational Success
  policy 79
Ira Manaaki dimension of Hikairo
  Schema 16, 17

James, William 181, 182
Johnson, Sam 168–69, 176

Ka Hikitia (Ministry of Education) 15
Kāhui Ako | Communities of
  Learning 78, 79–82, 140–41
Kant, Immanuel 2
knowledge
  as a commodity 37
  complexity in teacher
    education 243–44, 246–47, 250–51
  and curriculum 118–20
  epistemology (study of
    knowledge) 33, 34
  future-oriented education 122, 256
  Indigenous peoples 241
  innate 27–28

Māori (mātauranga) 22, 118–19, 182–83, 195, 241–42
  multiple forms 242, 250
  Pacific people 119
  socially constructed 28, 237–38
knowledge building pedagogy 140
knowledge societies 121, 122
Kōhanga Reo 60, 89
Kotahitanga dimension of Hikairo Schema 16–17

laboratory model of learning 243
Ladson-Billings, Gloria 11
language skills 91, 93–94, 98
Lazarus's theory of emotion 184–85
leadership
  see also teacher leadership
  as collective work 220, 221, 222, 223–24
  expertise 80–81
  parallel leadership 223
  Simpson's three-part typology 221
learning
  apprenticeship and laboratory models 242–43
  collaborative networks 122–23
  connection to leadership 222, 224, 225, 227, 228, 229, 230, 231, 232
  connection to teacher leadership 222, 224, 225, 227, 228, 229, 230, 231, 232
  deep learning 121, 241, 256
  life-long learning 29, 260
  moral purpose of schooling 225, 227, 229, 231, 255
  personalised learning 121, 122, 123, 140, 241
  philosophical thought about 26–29
  prerequisites 28
  sociocultural theory 256
  understanding learners in adolescence 99–103
  understanding learners in early childhood education 89–94
  understanding learners in middle childhood 94–99, 100
learning spaces *see* school learning spaces
limbic system 100–01
literacy 34, 36, 113, 126, 127
  see also digital media literacy
Locke, John 25, 28
London School 30, 31

Māori
  see also Hikairo Schema; te reo Māori; Treaty of Waitangi / Te Tiriti o Watangi; Waitangi Tribunal
  assimilation and integration policies 51–54, 56–57, 58, 60, 182
  colonisation impacts 48, 49–51, 54–55, 57–58, 59, 61–62, 64, 182, 193, 195, 256
  comparisons with indigenous Australians 54–55
  creation stories of te timatanga o te ao 183, 192
  in criminal justice system 48
  emotions 182–83, 185–86, 193–95
  housing 56
  integrity of knowledge 22
  Ka Hikitia national strategy 15
  land 49–50, 55, 64
  leaders 12
  less affected by stress after Christchurch earthquakes 190, 192, 194
  mātauranga (knowledge and understanding) 22, 118–19, 182–83, 195, 241–42
  popularised image 58
  radicalism 57–61
  separatist label 61
  sovereignty 49–51, 53

student engagement in flexible and distance learning 146
te ao Māori 182, 242
tikanga Māori 80, 89, 144, 182, 185, 193
urbanisation 56, 57
worldview 19, 20, 89, 119, 144, 186, 195

Māori education
colonial schooling 53–54
educational contributors 12
engagement with whānau 143–44
kaupapa Māori values 60–61, 143, 144, 212, 259
Māori-medium schools 95, 118–19
Pākehā education in state schools 56–57
racial biases 62–63
school design and learning environments 261–62, 265
teachers 188
underachievement 48, 60, 62, 79, 256, 261, 262

Māori Perspective Advisory Committee 52

Marjory Stoneman Douglas High School, Florida 175–76

market model 36–37

Martin, Jane Roland 31–32

Marx, Karl 71–72

Marxist perspective on education 31, 71–72

media
see also interactive media; social media
multimodal texts 205
negative impacts 202–03, 204
quality 202, 204, 207
and society 201–06

media literacy 201, 202–03
see also digital media literacy
definition 205–06

memory 28, 93, 98, 100, 189
meritocracy 48, 57, 61, 72
metacognition 102–03
methods 33, 36
Microsoft, "promote digital civility" programme 211
middle class 74–75
Ministry of Education 62, 79–80, 82, 138–39, 141, 152–53, 156, 210
see also Department of Education
moods 184
moral formation 29
mosque attacks, Christchurch, 15 March 2019 47–48, 151–52, 179–80, 203
motivation 14, 94, 100, 133, 140, 146, 184, 186, 227, 256
multiculturalism 119

National Administration Guidelines 152
National Certificate of Educational Achievement (NCEA) 100, 102, 114, 127–28, 259
National Education Goals 152
National Survey of Student Engagement (NeSSE) (United States and Canada) 141–42, 175
neoliberalism 36–37, 72, 78, 81
Netsafe 141, 210
New Zealand Bill of Rights 1990 152
New Zealand Curriculum (NZC) 94–95, 99–100, 114, 118–20, 122, 124–25, 152, 177, 255
New Zealand History Teachers' Association 62
New Zealand identity 51–52, 64
New Zealand Qualifications Authority (NZQA) 100
New Zealand School Trustees Association 62
New Zealand Teaching Council 245, 250
New Zealand Wars 50, 55–56, 57, 113

Ngata, Apirana 11–12, 53
norms 12, 48, 76, 117, 153, 154, 156, 158, 159, 163, 174, 180
   see also diversity
numeracy 127
NZCER
   Me and My School engagement survey 141
   Wellbeing@School toolkit 140–41, 156

obligations 76, 79
observational learning (OBL) 137
OECD 121, 134, 256–57
online modes of education 133, 134, 136, 137, 138–39, 145–46, 264
   see also flexible and distance learning
   monitoring student activities 142–43
   socio-emotional risks 140–41
ontology (study of existence or being) 33
open plan spaces 123, 258–59
Ōrākau, 50th anniversary of battle 55–56
Oranga dimension of Hikairo Schema 16, 17, 19
Our Code, Our Standards framework (Education Council) 245
outside curriculum 115

Pacific people
   knowledge 119
   racist experiences of students 62
   underachievement of students 262
parents, online learning 143–44
Paris, D. 11
partnerships 79, 82, 115
peer relationships 73, 76, 91, 92, 97, 99, 101, 102, 135, 138, 141, 187, 231
Pemberton, Jason 176
Pere, Rose 12, 21
Perry, Lane 171–72, 173, 175

personal mobile devices (PMDs) 143
personalised learning 121, 122, 123, 140, 241
Peters, R. S. 29–30, 31–33
"Philosophy for Children" (P4C) practices 162, 212
philosophy of education 25–26, 36–39
PISA (Programme for International Students Assessment) 113, 127
planning 14
Plato 3, 6, 25, 27–28
play 90, 92, 93–94
policies and practices in education 33, 36–39
   see also Kāhui Ako | Communities of Learning
   biculturalism 63
   curriculum 113, 114, 115, 116, 121, 122, 123–26, 128–29, 152
   decolonising education 63–64
   diversity 152–53
   global education policy communities 78
   inclusive education 152, 155–59
   integration of theory and practice in teacher education 234, 244–49, 250
   priorities for subjects, learning areas and knowledge domains 126
   "spatial turn" 122–23, 126
   "work of connections" 75
politics of education 31, 37, 116, 126–27
populism 203
positivism and postpositivism 238–39, 246
postmodernism 32–33, 76–78
poststructuralism 32–33, 240–41, 246
power
   balance of power principle of Hikairo Schema 18
   curriculum and power relations 116, 120

of language 157
and leadership 221, 229, 231
postmodern attention to power relations 77
power-sharing 22
social power inequalities 155
pragmatism 242–43, 251
primary schools and education 94–99, 126, 127, 177, 190, 210, 258–59, 265
principals 218, 223, 263, 264
career pathways for "outstanding" principals 81
psychology of education 88–89, 103–04
adolescents 99–103
early childhood education 89–94
middle childhood 94–99, 100

race relations myth, New Zealand 56, 58, 59
racism
euphemisms for 62
institutional racism 52–53, 57, 62–63
low consciousness of Pākehā 58
racial amnesia 61
South Africa 58
radio 202, 205, 206
Rangatiratanga dimension of Hikairo Schema 16, 17
rationality 30, 32
reason, central to education process 30, 32, 120
relationships 94
see also attachment; friendships
responsive reciprocal relationships 93
social relationships 94
relevance principle of Hikairo Schema 17–18
religious and belief diversity 152, 153, 157

resilience 100, 255
riri (anger) 185, 186
risk-taking behaviours 100–01, 102
Roa, Tom 185–86
Rua Kēnana 50, 51, 64
Ryerson University digital citizenship toolkit 211

scaffolding 22
Hikairo Schema principle 18
Scheffler, Israel 29, 30
Schmid's concept of an art of living 161, 162, 163
school learning spaces 254–55, 256–57, 264–65
culturally responsive and inclusive innovative environments 260–62
Innovative Learning Environments Project (OECD) 256–57
research insights 262–64
"spatial turn" in educational policy 122–23, 126
schools
see also primary schools and education; secondary schools and education
Māori-medium schools 95
past and present design 257–60
relocation and closure following Christchurch earthquakes 190, 191
revitalisation 223
and society 71, 72, 74, 75, 78, 83, 158
state and state-integrated schools 94
secondary schools and education 99–103, 126, 127–28, 190, 210–11, 259, 265
self and identity 101–02, 103, 162
self-esteem 102, 194
self-regulation 91, 94, 96–97, 98, 99, 101, 103, 136, 141, 260, 264

Serve for New Zealand (SFNZ) campaign 177
service learning 169, 171–72, 173, 174, 175, 177–78
sexuality and gender diversity 152, 153, 157
Sheppard, Kate 54
social capital 74, 75–76, 79, 80
social classes 71–72, 73–75
social constructivism 122, 158, 159, 160, 185, 237–38, 246, 249, 256
Social Emotional Learning (SEL) 187
social justice 13, 112, 120, 157, 162, 202, 212, 236, 240, 255
social media 140, 145, 203, 206, 207
   misinformation 203, 204
   social and ethical challenges 204, 211
social problem solving 93
social realism 70
social skills 93, 97, 211
socialisation 157–58, 162, 255
socioeconomic diversity 152, 153, 157
sociology of education 68–69, 82–83
   see also Kāhui Ako | Communities of Learning
   collaborations 69–70
   conflict and social change 71–73
   education for social cohesion 70–71
   forms of capital 73–76
Socrates 3, 6, 28
Springbok rugby tour, 1981 58
Stoic philosophy 181
student engagement see engagement of students
Student Experience Survey (Australian Department of Education and Training) 142
Student Volunteer Army (SVA), Christchurch 169–70, 171, 172, 173–74, 175–76, 177, 178
student wellbeing 100, 102, 134, 140–41, 187, 190
subjectivities 33
SVA Service Award 177–78

Taha Māori 60
Takaparawhā (Bastion Point) occupation 58
Te Kete Ipurangi 153
te kite me te rongo (to see and to feel) 186
Te Kura 139, 143–44
Te Marautanga o Aotearoa (TMoA) 95, 114, 118–19
te reo Māori 53, 57, 89, 95, 119, 182, 185, 186, 193–94
Te Whāriki (Ministry of Education) 15, 89, 93, 94, 114, 152, 192, 260
teacher education 234–37, 250–51
   culturally congruent tools and resources 10, 13, 15
   and diversity 12–13, 235
   epistemological terrain 237–43
   evidence-based practice 13–14
   integration of theory and practice 235–36, 242, 243, 244–49, 250
   knowledge complexity 243–44, 246–47, 250–51
   practice placements 234, 242–43
   programme coherence 247–48, 250
teacher leadership 216–19, 231–32
   as collective work 220, 221, 222, 223–24, 231, 232
   connection to learning 222, 224, 225, 227, 228, 229, 230, 231, 232
   formal and informal work 217–18, 220–22, 223, 224, 227, 231–32
   international concepts 220–24
   legitimacy 223, 226–27, 232
   major literature reviews 224–25
   method of influence 230–31
   objective 229–30
   opportunities 221–22

recognition 223, 224, 228
support 228
United States concepts 225–31
Teacher Leadership Congress, United States 226
teachers and teaching
   accountability 116, 218, 245
   and assessment 127–28
   career pathways for "good" teachers 81
   collaboration 123, 140
   curriculum role 116, 117, 120, 124–25, 128
   and diversity 74–75, 159
   early childhood education 91–92
   emotions 187–89, 190–92
   first responders after Christchurch earthquakes 190–92
   in flexible and distance education 140, 143
   Freirean perspective 34–36
   indoctrination 30–31
   instructional support 92, 93, 228
   intentions 31
   interventionist process 35
   and learning spaces 123, 254, 257–59, 260, 262–63, 264–65
   management of peer aggression 99
   Māori teachers 99
   reactions, effect on children 99
   social-emotional support 92, 93
   and student engagement 134, 135, 136
   teaching as inquiry, and as adaptive expertise 236–37
Teachers of Promise (TOP) study 217–19
television 202, 205, 206
tertiary education *see* higher education
theory of mind (ToM) 92–93
thinking 29
third way 14
Thorndike, Edward 10, 11, 21
thought, and emotion 180, 181, 184
Tight but Loose framework 123–26
tikanga Māori 80, 89, 144, 182, 185, 193
Tomorrow's Schools 78
transmission model of education 255–56
Treaty of Waitangi / Te Tiriti o Waitangi 7, 156, 195
   commitments and opportunities 80, 146, 241–42, 261–62, 265
   discrepancies between te reo and English versions 49
   "legal nullity" 51
   "one people" 54, 60
   principles 10
   rights of Māori 50–51, 118, 265
   study of 57
   te reo Māori 182–83
trustworthiness of social environment 76, 79
Tulane University 171, 173
Tyler, Ralph 10, 11, 21

underachievement 48, 60, 62, 79, 113, 154, 256, 261, 262
understanding self and others 92–93
United Women's Convention, 1979 59
University of Canterbury 166–68
   CHCH101: Rebuilding Christchurch 173–75, 176, 177, 178
   College of Education, Health and Human Development distance learning case study 145–46
   community engagement 170–76, 178
   Community Engagement Hub 172, 175–76
   Ilam campus 167–68
   Learning Evaluation and Academic Development (LEAD) 142
   student involvement in cleanup after earthquakes of 2010–2011 168–70
University of Otago, Quality Advancement Unit 142

Virtual Learning Network 143–44
vocationalism 80
Volunteer Army Foundation 175
volunteering 172, 173, 174, 175, 177
    see also Student Volunteer Army (SVA), Christchurch

Waitangi Tribunal 49
    "grievance industry" views 61
washback 127
Washington, Illinois, tornado 2013 176
Web 2.0 204
Weber, Max 72
wellbeing
    and compassion 207
    Māori approach 89, 194–95
    role of emotions 181, 182, 189
    student wellbeing 70, 82, 100, 102, 134, 140–41, 187, 190
Wellbeing@School toolkit 140–41, 156

Weston, Jessica 176
whakamā (shame or embarrassment) 186
Whare Tapa Whā model of health and wellbeing 194–95
white supremacy 47–48, 63, 64, 151–52
Wi Parata v The Bishop of Wellington 50–51
Wikipedia authors 209
women, qualities brought to educational process 32
World Wide Web 203, 204
worldviews
    and class relationships 31
    differences 32–33
    global 208
    Māori 19, 20, 89, 119, 144, 186, 195

zone of proximal development 97